DATE DUE

MORE PRAISE FOR
MAU MAU

"Superbly documented ... Edgerton, as always, writes beautifully, and his characters come so vividly to life that we can feel with them the painful human cost that is embodied in the modern socio-economic world order."

"A remarkable achievement. Much has been written about the Mau Mau, but no one has ever presented such a comprehensive, sensitive, and balanced account of the movement and its impact. Edgerton's book is destined to become the standard by which all other works on the subject are judged."

"A welcome corrective to the romanticized *Out of Africa* view of Kenya ... Populist and patriotic, the Mau Mau, in Edgerton's view, have been poorly served, though he concedes some of the allegations of brutality and failures of leadership. A thoughtful book on an important African country."

"Edgerton sweeps away the myths of the unilateral butchery of the black warriors, detailing the atrocities perpetrated by the British troops. This narrative benefits from Edgerton's wider portrayal of Kenya's multinational society and the black citizens' clamor for jobs and land reform."

"The Kikuyu rebellion against British settlers in Kenya in 1952–56 is skillfully described and analyzed."

MAU MAU

Also by Robert B. Edgerton

LIKE LIONS THEY FOUGHT:
THE ZULU WAR AND THE LAST BLACK EMPIRE
IN SOUTH AFRICA

MAU MAU

AN AFRICAN CRUCIBLE

ROBERT B. EDGERTON

BALLANTINE BOOKS ► NEW YORK

CONTENTS

PREFACE

Mau Mau, the first great African liberation movement, precipitated what was probably the gravest crisis in the history of Britain's African colonies. The Mau Mau rebellion began in late 1952, leading the government of Kenya to declare a State of Emergency. The rebellion was eventually crushed with heavy loss of life but, until the end of 1954, it appeared to many in the British Government that the Mau Mau rebels were winning. The rebellion was largely confined to one African "tribe," the Kikuyu, and the Mau Mau rebels were poorly armed with no outside source of weapons or financial support. Still, it took 21,000 paramilitary police, many thousands of armed "loyalist" Africans, plus the equivalent of a full division of British troops, supported by the Royal Air Force with Vampire jets and heavy bombers, more than 4 years to neutralize the Mau Mau military threat, and the State of Emergency was not officially ended until 1960.

Mau Mau not only made headline news in Britain and the Commonwealth countries, it fascinated the world press with its mystery and menace. American newspapers gave prominent coverage to the rebellion, and magazines like *Time*, *Newsweek*, and *Life* contributed frequent photographic essays. Interest was also great throughout Western Europe and the Soviet bloc countries, as well as in newly independent countries such as Egypt and India. The colonial government of Kenya steadfastly refused to admit that the people they called "Mau Mau" were fighting for land and freedom. Instead, they succeeded in convincing the world press that Mau Mau was a "crime wave," not a military rebellion, and that the Mau Mau rebels were bestial "gangsters" who, crazed by unspeakable, primitive ceremonies involving cannibalism, the drinking of menstrual blood, and sexual orgies, indiscriminately terrorized white settlers, especially women and children. In fact, some Mau Mau attacks were brutal by any standard, and Kenya Government news releases, photographs, and newsreels provided the world with ghastly depictions of the mutilated victims—hamstrung cattle, burned children, decapitated men, and disembowelled women. Novelist Robert Ruark reinforced this official version in his best-selling novel, *Something of Value*. The book, which caricatured white heroism and black savagery, was so widely read that it was reprinted every year from 1955 through 1980 in both the United States and Britain. In 1957, *Something of Value* was made into a motion picture starring Rock Hudson as a white settler, and Sidney Poitier as his childhood Kikuyu friend who became a Mau Mau "terrorist." In a somber prologue to the movie, Prime Minister Winston Churchill warned viewers that the problems that had led to Mau Mau were not unique to Kenya. As if to fulfill Churchill's prophecy, black churches in America collected money to support the Mau Mau rebels, and some black Americans wondered if they too would have to fight to achieve their civil rights.

Ever since Kenya was opened to British colonization shortly after the turn of the century, the colonists referred to it as a "white man's country." In 1952, Kenya's more than 40,000 whites were determined that they would never relinquish control over "their" beautiful and prosperous country. The white settlers' prosperity was not shared by Kenya's Africans, most of whom remained desperately poor. White Kenyans economically exploited over 5 million Africans in Kenya, and imposed a color bar more extreme than the one that existed in the American South. Africans were allowed no voice in Kenya's government.

Supported by hundreds of thousands of Kikuyu in the Kikuyu home-
lands, and by other Africans throughout Kenya, perhaps as many as
30,000 young men and women took up arms in forested, mountainous
areas to the north of Kenya's principal city, Nairobi, and the movement
grew. Despite British military intervention, Mau Mau forces won some
surprising victories, but they were so severely limited by shortages of
arms and ammunition that they could not sustain a battle for long, and
by 1955—not quite three years after the start of the fighting—some Mau
Mau units were reduced to the use of bows and arrows. Cut off from
food supplies and other sources of support, the Mau Mau were bombed,
shelled, stalked, and ambushed in the forests until they were finally over-
come. British battalions, aided by African soldiers and police, were known
to have killed over 11,000 rebels, more than 1,000 of whom were hanged
as criminals.

The whites and their African allies not only killed thousands of Mau
Mau, they often surpassed them in ruthlessness. Mau Mau captives and
suspects were tortured and many were killed "trying to escape." More
than 80,000 who survived were sent to concentration camps where they
were subjected to continuing brutality so terrible that many died. The
treatment of helpless men, women, and children in these camps was an
infamous episode in the history of British colonialism. The courage and
devotion of thousands of Mau Mau men and women under the terrible
conditions of their detention was extraordinary. Many endured years of
privation and pain without renouncing Mau Mau or accepting the legitimacy of the Kenya Government.

But not until 1959, when the killings of 11 men at a remote detention
camp were revealed, was the brutality of the system finally exposed. The
Kenya Government's attempt to cover up these murders failed and many
in the British Government were outraged. These killings made Mau Mau
resistance known to the world, and British Prime Minister Harold Macmillan concluded that he would have to grant Kenya its independence
to avoid another blood bath. The deaths of 11 men in 1959 had accomplished what the earlier deaths of 11,000 men and women had not.

Jomo Kenyatta, the Kikuyu nationalist leader, had been arrested as the
"evil genius" behind Mau Mau on the day that the State of Emergency
had been declared. In 1961, the British Government accepted African
demands that Kenyatta be allowed to return to politics, and in 1963 he
became the first Prime Minister, and later that same year the first President, of newly-independent Kenya. But the men and women of Mau
Mau were not rewarded with land, or even medals, and they were not

given positions in Kenyatta's government. Instead, wealthy Africans who had been loyal to the colonial government retained their land, bought other land vacated by whites, and dominated Kenya's business world. Known as "Black Europeans," they moved into large, walled estates in formerly all-white neighborhoods of Nairobi, where guards, dogs, and barbed wire continued to defend their wealth against poor Africans like those who fought for Mau Mau and died in concentration camps. In their wake came newly wealthy African entrepreneurs and European investors. President Kenyatta and his relatives became so rich and imperious that they were known as the "Royal Family."

Kenya today is a bastion of prosperity and privilege, the passions of Mau Mau nearly gone as the scramble for a better life involves increasing numbers of Kenya's more than 20 million people. For many of these millions, Mau Mau is a dark period of Kenya's history that is best forgotten; but others insist that it must never pass from memory, that its lessons are important not only for Kenya but for people everywhere. Mau Mau was an epic of sacrifice, cruelty, and courage. This struggle between black Africans and white minority rule was the first to take place in modern Africa, but it was followed by others, some of which continue to this day. Why and how the Mau Mau fought, and why the whites of Kenya and Britain reacted as they did, is a story that should be remembered not just in Kenya or in Africa—it is a lesson for us all.

ACKNOWLEDGMENTS

My interest in Mau Mau began in 1961 when I first visited Kenya as a participant in a large research project in cultural ecology led by anthropologist Walter Goldschmidt. The project took me to Tanganyika and Uganda as well as to various parts of Kenya, and everywhere that I travelled I met settlers, white government officials, former detention camp guards, and policemen who told me about their experiences during Mau Mau. Many Africans told me about Mau Mau as well, especially men and women of the Akamba people with whom I did research. Early in 1962, I quite literally bumped into three armed members of Mau Mau (or perhaps the recently formed Land and Freedom Army) while walking in the Lari forest near Limuru. I gave them cigarettes and they told me, in Swahili, that I should leave Kenya. I did not leave Kenya, but I did leave the Lari forest without delay.

It is impossible to thank all the people who helped me during the long, if intermittent history of my interest in Mau Mau. Among the first was the late Donald L. Barnett, whom I had known when we were both graduate students at the University of California, Los Angeles, and who was in Kenya during my first visit. I only saw him a few times in Kenya, however. Later, in Los Angeles, I did discuss Mau Mau with him several times, and on subsequent trips to Kenya my interest in Mau Mau deepened.

Many Kenyans, black as well as white, have requested anonymity. Kenyans who deserve my special thanks include the late Simeon Kioko, Bildad Kaggia, Paul Ngei, the Honorable Fred Kubai, the Honorable Taita Towett, Margaret Kenyatta, Sir Michael Blundell, George Dennis, H. D. Montgomery, Jack Bissel, Arnold Hopf, and Mary Wambui. I am also indebted to the staff at the Kenya National Archives in Nairobi, the Bodleian Library of the University of Oxford, and the Public Record Office in London. Lyddia Degarrod helped me locate photographs, Rachel Blachly drew maps with her usual skill, and Lupe Montano, Thelma Woods, and especially Esther Rose heroically revised the manuscript more times than I, or they, care to remember. Both Hilarie Kelly and Aly Kipkorir Rana helped in so many ways that I cannot thank them enough, and the editorial judgment of Jorja Prover was simply invaluable. I also want to thank my editor at The Free Press, Adam Bellow, for his encouragement and his keen editorial eye.

To avoid confusion, I have written "tribal" names as they were commonly written in the 1950s, not as they are used now. Hence, I have written "Kikuyu" rather than "Gikuyu," which is often preferred today, Luo rather than Jaluo, Kamba rather than Akamba or Wakamba, and Luhya rather than Abaluhya. Also, when I am referring to the period when Mau Mau took place, I refer to Kenya's ethnic groups as "tribes" because that was common usage at the time by Africans as well as whites, and tribal affiliation was all-important. One's ethnic affiliation is still important in Kenya, but African scholars justifiably object to the term tribe because it connotes primitivity. When I refer to ethnicity in the present day I have avoided the use of tribe.

MAU MAU

"THERE WILL BE A
GENERAL RISING"

THE COLONIZATION
OF KENYA

The colonial regime the Mau Mau rebels challenged came into being as a result of a grand imperial achievement—the construction of a railroad. Sometime before the turn of the century, a famous Kikuyu prophet warned that white strangers would come out of the sea, bringing with them a great iron snake that would belch fire as it travelled from the coast far beyond the lands of the Kikuyu to the west.[1] His prophecy was fulfilled when a railroad was built stretching 580 miles inland from Kenya's Indian Ocean coast to Lake Victoria. It was called the Uganda Railway because its purpose was to link Uganda—"the pearl of Africa," according to John Speke, the British explorer who "discovered" it—with the seaport city of Mombasa and the outside world. This remarkable engineering accomplishment cost the lives of 2,493 Indian laborers (many

of them lost to man-eating lions), and an expenditure of more than
£5,000,000.

The Uganda Railway was built as part of the imperial scramble for
spheres of influence in Africa. Britain had a long-standing interest in
Zanzibar, off the East African coast, as a naval station and as a possible
jumping-off point to the interior of East Africa. To Britain's growing
distress, Germany had a similar interest. In a move to avoid this kind of
conflict, the European powers met in 1885 in Berlin to carve up much
of Africa among themselves. It was agreed that the British "sphere of
influence" would include Kenya, while Germany would take Tanganyika
(now Tanzania) to the south. By the terms of the Berlin Conference, no
imperial power could retain its sphere of interest unless it established
what was called "effective occupation." This could mean European settlement, military presence, or governmental administration, but all of
these options meant expense, and the British Government was greatly
concerned with avoiding any cost to the Exchequer. As happened so
often in Britain's imperial history, a cost-free solution became available
with the formation of a chartered company. Modeled after the Hudson's
Bay Company and the British East India Company, the Imperial British
East Africa Company, or IBEA as it was commonly known, duly received
its royal charter. Founded by Sir William Mackinnon, a Scot who had
dreams of building a railroad to the interior of East Africa, the IBEA
had its own flag, postage stamps, capital city, army, and money—but very
little of the latter. The company set up small forts and trading outposts
in some parts of Kenya, but these were not a commercial success. In
Tanganyika, a German trading company was more prosperous, partly
because it planted tobacco successfully, but primarily because it was led
by one of the most energetic imperialists of all time, a man named Carl
Peters.

Peters, who wrote a Ph.D. thesis on metaphysics, was frail. With a
droopy mustache and pince-nez, he was a caricature of an unworldly
academic, but his appearance was deceptive. Peters was brutal to the
point of sadism, and ruthless in his pursuit of German dominion. According to the Berlin Conference, Uganda was clearly within the British
sphere, but knowing that occupation was the key to possession, Peters
decided to "occupy" Uganda for Germany, and set off to steal Uganda
before the British could defend it. But the IBEA got wind of the German
expedition, and quickly organized its own expedition, led by no less an
adventurer than the American journalist, Henry Stanley, who had
"found" Doctor Livingstone. This time Stanley was less successful. In

1890, after incredible adventures, theatrical diplomacy, and utter ruth-lessness—Peters shot down many Maasai who opposed him, and hanged his African mistress when he discovered that she had been unfaithful to him with another African—Peters had control of Uganda. However, by then Germany faced crises with France and Russia, so in return for pledges of British support and Heligoland in the North Sea, Germany ceded both Uganda and Zanzibar to Britain. The IBEA now had a clear field in Uganda, but to exploit its newest market, Mackinnon decided to push his dream of a railroad. Unfortunately, he did not have nearly enough money to build one. Spurred by the fact that the indomitable Peters had begun his own railroad from the coast of Tanganyika to the interior (and perhaps planned to extend it, the IBEA feared, ultimately to Uganda), Mackinnon turned to the British Government.

In 1895, when a new Tory government under Lord Salisbury took office, various proponents of the railroad, led by Mackinnon, argued, albeit somewhat vaguely, that it would help to destroy slavery, spread Christianity and civilization, and facilitate the shipping of ivory to the Coast. Furthermore, other European powers were building railroads in Africa, so of course Britain could not be left behind. Most compelling for the British was a nightmarish fear that some enemy power—France, Germany, Belgium, and Italy were all suspected—would seize Uganda and dam the headwaters of the Nile.[2] Such a dam, the nightmare had it, would so desiccate Egypt that Britain would have to withdraw its forces and lose control of the Suez Canal with it, and thereby control of India as well. Those who were tormented by this bizarre vision did not explain how a foreign power could be expected to carry enough engineering equipment and building material to Uganda to prevent Lake Victoria from spilling its excess water into the White Nile, or how these same villains would dam the Nile's other tributaries as well. When the British in Uganda finally built a dam at the source of the Nile in 1954, it re-quired a good deal more engineering skill than was available in the 1890s; it also took six years of construction and cost £22,000,000. Nevertheless, fears of furtive foreign dam-builders spurred the British Government to think of the railway as a necessary means of quickly transporting troops to Uganda. Parliament voted the funds for the Uganda Railway, which quickly became known as the "lunatic express" because the public—along with some in government—still had great difficulty understanding what purpose the railroad was going to serve.

The British Government did not ask what the African residents of Kenya might think about the plan to construct a railroad through their

homeland. It was an entirely predictable oversight. The British Government, like the other European Powers, saw no reason to consult with
"natives" in their "spheres of influence" regarding their plans. An occasional voice was raised in opposition, like that of Sir William Harcourt,
formerly a professor of international law, who declared that "Every act
of force you commit against a native within a sphere of influence is an
unlawful assault; every acre of land you take is robbery; every native you
kill is a murder."[3] But Harcourt and others who spoke in protest were
ignored. The railroad would be built.

The track was laid along the same route that huge Arab slave caravans
had followed as they marched from Mombasa to the interior during the
nineteenth century. Although the slavers sometimes paid tribute to the
warlike Maasai, the firepower of their thousand or so rifles was sufficient
to overcome African resistance when necessary. The IBEA lacked the
numbers of the earlier Arab slavers, and, when they established small
trading stations and forts in advance of the construction crews, their
reception from African peoples was seldom friendly. In Kikuyu territory,
the first explorers and traders encountered a mixed reaction: sometimes
open hostility, at other times a generous welcome. But because many
Europeans believed that their safety was best assured by displays of force
that included shooting a few Africans for effect, even the Kikuyu who at
first welcomed them soon withdrew their hospitality. By 1890, the Kikuyu
were implacably hostile to Europeans, particularly to agents of the IBEA
who had established one of their forts at a place called Dagoretti in
Kikuyu territory.

The scattered IBEA forts like the one at Dagoretti were protected by
ill-trained African soldiers led by young and inexperienced British officers who were, for the most part, not regular army officers. Whatever
inclination the Kikuyu may initially have had to welcome the white for-
eigners disappeared when the IBEA's African troops, who were very often staggering drunk, stole Kikuyu crops or raped Kikuyu women, killing
some who resisted.[4] When the Kikuyu fought back, the British officers
organized punitive expeditions that went on "nigger hunts," as they were
known to white Kenyans. In 1893, an officer of the IBEA named Francis
Hall (after whom the town of Fort Hall was later named) mounted two
so-called punitive expeditions that killed about 90 Kikuyu. The following
year, Hall's troops killed a similar number. Hall was so incensed by continuing Kikuyu resistance that he wrote to his father, a British colonel,
that "There is only one way of improving the Wakikuyu [and] that is
wipe them out; I should be only too delighted to do so, but we have to

depend on them for food supplies."[5] However, beginning in 1894 and lasting until 1899, nature made it unnecessary for Hall to "improve" the Kikuyu. Plagues of locusts, prolonged drought, cattle disease, and small-pox decimated the southern region of Kikuyu territory closest to the route the railroad would follow. Contemporary European observers es-timated that at least 50 percent and perhaps as much as 95 percent of the population in the Kikuyu district of Kiambu died. It was this disaster that created what appeared to be empty land when the first European settlers arrived in 1902.

Even the most starry-eyed empire builders admitted that "uncivilized" African populations of Kenya and Uganda were not likely to become paying customers of the railroad in the foreseeable future. But if enough white settlers could be induced to live in Kenya, they would have to use the railroad because there would be no other way for them to obtain goods from overseas or to ship their farm produce to world markets. The British colonial administration urged settlers to come to Kenya; and first by the hundreds, then by the thousands, settlers responded to prom-ises of virtually free land, plentiful and cheap labor, and large profits. Most of them settled in Kenya's fertile and well-watered central high-lands, often displacing African peoples as they did so. The agricultural tribe most affected by the loss of farming land was the Kikuyu.[6] In order for the white settlers to clear their land and produce their crops they needed African labor. Again the tribe that was most affected was the Kikuyu.

To protect the settlers, Britain sent better-trained African soldiers un-der the command of experienced British Army officers. One of the of-ficers who played a central part in pacifying the Kikuyu was a young Harrow-educated Captain named Richard Meinertzhagen. Despite his German name, Meinertzhagen came from a wealthy upper-middle-class British family, and he was more than ready to pacify the enemies of Britain's Imperial progress. The arrival of white farmers who appropri-ated temporarily-vacant Kikuyu land did nothing to ease tensions. The Kikuyu continued to attack, and the British regularly sent out military expeditions, typically killing 10 or 20 Kikuyu before returning to the relative safety of their forts.

In early September, 1902, Kikuyu rage against the white settlers reached a peak. A white settler was pegged to the ground, his mouth wedged open with a stick; then an entire village—men, women, and even children—urinated into his mouth until he drowned. They also cut off his genitals, disemboweled him, and defecated on his body. The British reacted quickly, surrounding the village with troops during the night. The officer in command, Richard Meinertzhagen, ordered that everyone in the village except children be killed. In the first light, the execution order was carried out with gusto. There were no children in the village (they had been taken to the forest for safety) but everyone else, including old women, was shot or bayoneted to death. Meinertzhagen, who took an active role in the slaughter, was surprised at how easily a bayonet entered the human body.[7] Those who were appalled by the savagery of Mau Mau killings or the white response to them should be reminded of this encounter 50 years earlier.

The Kikuyu fought so bravely against British rifles and machine guns in ensuing battles that Meinertzhagen was greatly impressed by their courage.[8] The Kikuyu warriors who fought against Meinertzhagen's soldiers looked very different from the men in ragged European clothes who later fought in Mau Mau. These warriors carried six-foot-long spears with three-foot-long blades, two- to three-foot-long swords, known as *simis*, in leather scabbards, as well as bows and poisoned arrows. Most warriors were naked except for a string of beads or a narrow beaded apron that they wore around their waists well above their naked genitals. Their bodies, glistening with butter fat and painted with white clay and red ochre, were ornamented with copper rings on their arms, wrists, and ankles. Their hair, too, was colored red and ornamented. Some men wore a colobus monkey-skin or ostrich plume headdress and fur anklets, and in cold weather warriors might drape a skin cape over one shoulder. In battle they crouched behind toughened cowhide shields that stood much taller than the Kikuyu men themselves, who at that time averaged around 5'4" or 5'5" in height. The Kikuyu did not have the renown as warriors that their neighbors the celebrated Maasai did, but when the Maasai invaded their lands, the Kikuyu usually won, and they sometimes carried out successful raids into Maasai territory, stealing cattle and women.[9]

Fighting between the British and the Kikuyu continued throughout 1903, and in the following year, the people of a Kikuyu district where a new British fort had been built—complete with a moat—rose in open defiance of the British. The British sent three large columns of troops against the defiant Kikuyu "to put them in the right frame of mind," as Meinertzhagen wrote. Meinertzhagen's column alone killed 796 Kikuyu, burned innumerable homesteads, and confiscated 782 cattle and 2,150 sheep and goats. The almost embarrassed official British report put the Kikuyu death toll at 400, but Meinertzhagen estimated that a conservative guess at the numbers killed by all three columns would be 1,500.[10] By the end of 1904, organized Kikuyu resistance had ended. The futility of attacking machine guns with arrows had been acknowledged by Kikuyu elders and warriors alike. Still, the Kikuyu had tested their bravery against British firepower for 15 years. The rifles and machine guns of Meinertzhagen's men devastated Kikuyu resistance but he was so impressed by their rebellious spirit that in 1902 he predicted that when the Kikuyu became educated, and were led by "political agitators" instead of "medicine men," there would be a "general rising."[11]

The Maasai, whose military prowess was thought by most Europeans to be almost unsurpassed among African peoples, chose not to test themselves against British guns at all. Instead they fought with the British against the Kikuyu and were handsomely compensated for doing so. To be sure, the Kikuyu were not the only people in Kenya to take up arms against the British. For example, in 1904 and 1905 the Gusii near Lake Victoria and the Nandi to the north both had to be crushed by overwhelming military force, and in 1914 the Giriama near the coast fought until they too suffered heavily.[12] There were occasional minor uprisings all through the years preceding Mau Mau, but no tribe fought the British for as long a period as the Kikuyu did, and probably none suffered as many deaths as a result.

Although the white settlers who fought so savagely against the Mau Mau would have trouble believing it, during the years that British firepower was conquering the Kikuyu it was by no means certain that white Britons would settle Kenya. In 1902, when the Secretary of State for the Colonies, Joseph Chamberlain, returned to England after a visit to Kenya, he offered a large portion of the country to European Zionists as a national homeland. The Zionist Congress sent a commission to Kenya to examine the land they had been offered. One of the guides chosen to lead them to their proposed promised land was Ewart "Grogs" Grogan, who like other early British settlers, was opposed to Jewish settlement. The Jews, led by a former British Army Major, were anything but fainthearted, but the rigors of a Grogan-guided tour tested their enthusiasm for Kenya. One night their camp was almost trampled by elephants; the next night it was lions that prowled among the tents, and the night after that the Commission was surrounded by spear-wielding Maasai who kept them awake all night with threats of mayhem. Nevertheless, the Commission completed its survey before asking to be taken back to Nairobi; the British offer of a Zionist state in Kenya was subsequently rejected. Grogan later denied that he had intentionally camped on a path used by elephants, or in an area frequented by lions, or that he had arranged for a Maasai war party, but the gleeful British settlers did not believe him.[13]

Hard-drinking and fast-shooting adventurers from many European countries came to Kenya, but settlers did not rush to Kenya. Only a handful had taken up land in central Kenya before the railroad was completed in 1902, and there were many officials of the IBEA and the British Foreign Office who were convinced that the climate was unsuitable for whites. They believed that Indians instead of British colonists should be encouraged to settle in Kenya. And in fact, at this time, there were many more Indians in Kenya than whites. Roughly 7,000 of the 32,000 or so Indians who worked on the Uganda Railroad elected to stay, and by 1900 most of Nairobi resembled an Indian bazaar. Indians so dominated trade that the rupee was used as Kenya's currency (until 1921, when it was replaced by the shilling), the Indian Penal Code was adopted almost intact, and Indian police guarded every government station.

The idea that Kenya could become "India's America" died in February 1901 with the arrival of Sir Charles Eliot, the brilliant and scholarly new Commissioner of the East African Protectorate, as Kenya was then known.[14] Eliot fell in love with the central highlands and proclaimed that Kenya was a white man's country, just like Canada, New Zealand, Australia, and South Africa. Thanks to Eliot, Indians in Kenya found themselves unable to buy land, and further Indian immigration was discouraged. At the same time that Eliot was blocking Indian settlement, he was offering inducements to white settlers. Most of those who accepted were South Africans of British origin. They were a rough-and-ready lot who arrived with fixed ideas about white supremacy. (Many writers continue to portray Kenya as a colony settled solely by English aristocrats, but in fact South Africans—including the even more racist Africaans-speaking Boers, who chose to settle far to the northwest of Nairobi and to stay out of politics—outnumbered settlers from England until 1912.)[15]

With the Indians' aspirations squashed, Eliot turned his attention to the native Africans. Soon after Captain Meinertzhagen arrived in Kenya in 1902 with the 3rd Battalion of the King's African Rifles, Eliot invited him to dinner in Nairobi. Meinertzhagen thought that Eliot was a "very able man," but he was "amazed" by Eliot's vision of Kenya as a colony dominated by thousands of Europeans. Meinertzhagen was horrified to learn that Eliot intended ". . . to confine the natives to reserves and use them as cheap labor on farms."[16] When the newly arrived captain brashly said that Africa belonged to the Africans, Eliot would have none of it.

Later, in a dispatch to British Foreign Secretary Lord Lansdowne, Eliot was candid, to say the least:

> No doubt on platforms and in reports we declare we have no intention of depriving natives of their lands, but this has never prevented us from taking whatever land we want.... Your Lordship has opened this Protectorate to white ... colonization, and I think it is well that, in confidential correspondence at least, we should face the undoubted issue—viz., that white mates black in a very few moves.... There can be no doubt that the Maasai and many other tribes must go under. It is a prospect which I view with equanimity and a clear conscience.[17]

Although the dispatch was marked "secret and confidential" it was leaked to the press. There was much criticism of Eliot in Britain and he eventually resigned, but most of the settlers he had recruited to Kenya were in complete sympathy with his views.

Many of these settlers came in response to newspaper advertisements like this:

> Settle in Kenya, Britain's youngest and most attractive colony. Low prices at present for fertile areas. No richer soil in the British Empire. Kenya Colony makes a practical appeal to the intending settler with some capital. Its valuable crops give high yields, due to the high fertility of the soil, adequate rainfall and abundant sunshine. Secure the advantage of native labor to supplement your own effort.[18]

They came to make their fortunes, not to extend the benefits of British civilization to Africans. Africans were to be used for labor. Even that ultimate imperialist, Winston Churchill, who visited Kenya in 1906, was concerned about the welfare of Kenya's African population if they were not protected by the "impartial" administration of the Crown, and were instead "abandoned to the fierce self-interest of a small white population."[19] The Crown reiterated its intention to protect Kenya's African population, and some of its officials opposed the settlers. Nevertheless, the first settlers were determined to see Kenya become a "white man's country," and British government officials in Kenya initially did little to restrain the interests of the white immigrants.

Some settlers sailed north to Kenya from South Africa, but others made the long journey from Britain, after a scorching voyage through the Suez Canal, then south along the East African coast; those who came from England were enthralled by the sight of Mombasa's white sand beaches and its lush green landscape dotted by the red tiled roofs of its white-washed European houses. Once ashore among the tall coconut palms and purple bougainvillaea, they found Mombasa voluptuously exotic. Arab dhows rocked at anchor in Mombasa's Kilindini Harbor, men in long white nightshirt-like gowns screamed at near-naked black boys who scampered about yelling insults in return, while black-veiled women sat in the shade of mango trees, and there was music from melodious Arab flutes. The fresh sea air wafted over odors of rotting fish, coffee drying in the sun, and the cloying sweetness of jasmine.

Mombasa was definitely not England, but there were reassuring signs of British dominion, from deferential Indian customs officers who sat sweating in an oven-like tin-roofed customs shed, to rickshaws pulled by waiting Africans. It was also reassuring to find dark-skinned men ready to serve them. Once their baggage had been picked up by Africans—it would never do for white people to be seen touching their own luggage—the newly-arrived settlers climbed aboard the coaches of the Uganda Railway. The rail-bed was remarkably well-kept, and although the rolling stock came from India, and was less than elegant by European standards, the trip "up-country" was smooth. As the train passed through the lush vegetation of the coastal zone, passengers gaped at the bright colors of the birds and butterflies with five-inch wing spans, and they could not fail to notice that plantations growing rubber, sisal, and cotton were already well-established. Farther upcountry, every mile along the route was marked by an iron signpost, and every 30 miles there was a train station complete with water tank, telegraph office, and, what the British immigrants often liked best, well-tended flower beds.

Soon the country changed to near-desert and then to better-watered plains, studded with ant-hills and scraggly green thornbushes. This was tse-tse-fly country—large flies that bit with the sting of bees and infected humans and animals alike with sleeping sickness—but fortunately for the passengers the flies left them alone. Throughout the journey, nothing was more memorable than the red dust of Africa that covered the passengers. Food was not served on the train, so when it stopped in the evening at a way-station called Voi, everyone sought the comfort of its restaurant. The service by white-coated and gloved Goan waiters was indeed splendid but the food was dreadful, and the mosquitos were irrepressible. After dinner, passengers were served a large snifter of brandy which was thought to repel mosquitos. To make matters worse, there were no bathing facilities, so passengers reboarded the train for another day's journey toward Nairobi still covered with red dust. The next day was spent passing through higher-elevation plains marked by flat-topped olive-green thorn trees and "upside-down" trees—baobabs whose trunks spread wider than their branches—where all the African animals seemingly assembled to entertain the new arrivals. Against a background of flat-topped thorn trees, there were lions, elephants, and rhinos, ostriches and giraffes, zebras and wildebeests, warthogs and wild dogs, and all manner of antelopes and gazelles including frolicsome dik-diks no bigger than rabbits. Some of the settlers felt inspired to shoot a few of these unsuspecting animals, and the train obligingly stopped so that they could blaze away to their hearts' content.[20] Sometimes the train was forced to stop when millions of wildebeests migrated across the tracks like a dark lava flow inexorably moving toward few pastures. There was no shooting then; the passengers watched in awe.

At the 327-mile post the train arrived in Nairobi. In 1906 it was a squalid but bustling maintenance center for the railroad, built on a swampy plain where the Maasai used to graze their herds. In addition to government offices, railway depots, repair sheds, barracks for the King's African Rifles, a few retail shops, numerous bars, and whorehouses, Nairobi already counted about 600 whites, more than 3,000 Indians, and close to 11,000 Africans. It was as unlovely a place as one could find in Kenya's highlands, but it was here that new arrivals had to begin their stay in Kenya by applying to government officials for grants of land.

Once their land claims had been properly filed, the new arrivals set out in ox-drawn wagons that carried everything from plows and bags of seeds to tin bathtubs, sewing machines, hand-wound gramophones, fine china, and that ultimate necessity, toilet seats. As they moved toward their new homes they were often impressed by the distant ranges of hills and mountains that after a rain stood out so clearly in their blue or black outlines that it seemed possible to touch them. The Kikuyu called such times a "clear darkness." As their wagons moved slowly along rough tracks, yellow-throated francolin ran alongside them; the settlers passed by woods filled with storks and nightingales, and near streams and lakes where the newcomers marveled at brilliant blue kingfishers. After the long rains ended in July, the wild flowers grew in bewildering profusion. When the settlers finally reached their farm lands after bouncing over roadless miles that soon became known as "MMBA," meaning "miles and miles of bloody Africa," most of them set up house in the same kind of mud and thatch huts that the Kikuyu lived in, the one difference being that the Europeans crammed expensive furniture into their modest quarters. They did not seem surprised to find small Indian stores, the ubiquitous *dukas*, there ahead of them. Although the whites bought necessities from Indian shopkeepers, and hired Indians (the only skilled artisans in Kenya) to build stone houses for them, they refused to have any social contact with "coolies," as they called Indians.

Unlike the settlers who came from South Africa, the earliest British settlers were probably the most wealthy and aristocratic immigrants ever to leave Britain. In 1903, 103 settlers arrived; 300 came in 1904, 599 in 1904, and 1,861 in 1905.[21] So many of them were aristocrats that the Norfolk Hotel, where they congregated when they visited Nairobi, quickly became known as the "House of Lords." Enough of them were old Etonians that one, Lord Cranworth, declared Etonians (and other public-school boys) perfect for Kenya because the goal of a public school education was not to prepare a boy to work, but to oversee the work of others.[22] As Lord Delamere, the acknowledged leader of these first settlers, made plain, their goal was to recreate the Virginia plantocracy in which white gentlemen of breeding and leisure oversaw vast plantations worked by black men. Sir Charles Eliot's plan for Kenya was to attract more men of breeding and wealth like Lord Delamere. The healthy and fertile highlands were reserved for men like these. Indians would not be allowed to own land in the highlands and poor whites were discouraged from coming to Kenya at all. And as one English gentleman told Winston Churchill when Churchill visited Kenya, "It would destroy the respect of the native for the white man, if he saw what miserable people we have got at home."[23] These gentlemen-settlers also thought it dangerous to let Africans see white men actually *working*.

The lands these men of wealth acquired were enormous. Lord Delamere received title to 100,000 acres in 1903, and to 60,000 more later. Eventually he owned 176,768 acres.[24] Others did nearly as well. Even someone of very limited means, such as aviatrix and writer Beryl Markham's father, who initially worked for Lord Delamere on his vast "Equator Ranch," was soon able to earn enough money to buy a 1,000-acre farm of his own.[25] The initial grants of land were so large that there was only room in the highlands for a few thousand farms.[26] The leases were originally for 99 years, but, when the settlers complained, the government extended the leases to 999 years.[27]

As the settlers began to establish their new estates and sort out their possessions, they became concerned about their health. Lord Cranworth joked that two of the major "diseases" to be concerned about in Kenya were "lion bites" and "whiskey,"[28] but most settlers were convinced that the high altitude was so dangerous that only long vacations at sea level, preferably in England, could prevent nervous debility, known as "Kenya nerves." In addition, almost all of the newcomers to Africa were terrified of the sun's rays. It was widely believed, by Churchill among others, that the "actinic" rays of the sun would cause loss of memory, irritability, nervous exhaustion, loss of energy and initiative, violent temper tantrums, high blood pressure, insomnia, female disorders (delicately left unspecified), and sterility.[29] All Europeans were cautioned to wear hats—ideally made of two layers of felt—not only when they were in the sun, but indoors as well, because roofs were not considered sufficient to deflect the deadly actinic rays. In addition, the body should be protected by many layers of sun-repellent clothing (scarlet undergarments were prescribed for women), and houses were to be kept as dark as possible, which accounts for the practice of building large and elegant stone houses with very small windows. Even Captain Frederick Lugard, the conqueror of Uganda, whose courage often crossed the line into rashness, was in mortal fear of the sun. He insisted that if it were necessary to remove one's hat even for a moment, it should be done under the shade of a tree.[30]

The altitude and sun notwithstanding, the climate in the highlands proved to be remarkably healthy, and the settlers slowly began to notice that some of the least affluent among them who could not afford African labor managed to work all day in the sun without any ill effects. Even so, fear of the sun persisted well into the 1930s, although somehow this anxiety did not prevent the settlers, women as well as men, from hunting and riding their horses in the sun for hours at a time.[31] Polo matches were popular and so was wearing "pink" (as red hunting jackets were known) and riding to hounds, although a jackal had to be substituted for a fox. A race course was built near Nairobi and "race week," held four times a year, became the high-point of the social season.

The most pressing domestic problem for the new settlers was hiring servants. Even a very modest household required a cook, kitchen "boy," two or three "houseboys," a similar number of gardeners called *shamba* (garden) boys, a laundry boy, and an *ayah* (baby sitter). Wealthier families might hire 20 or 30 such "boys." Except for *ayahs*, servants were invariably men, some of whom had no duties except caring for a beloved dog, or watering a special flower garden. The best families also competed to hire elegant, imperious Somalis to serve as major-domos. Lord Delamere had Hassan; explorer and hunter Denys Finch-Hatton had Bilea; and author Karen Blixen had Farah, who followed her about with a cashmere shawl and loaded rifle. (A rich American named Billy Sewell may have topped them all by importing Chinese servants.) They also competed to see who could have the most smartly uniformed "rickshaw boys" to pull them about when they visited Nairobi. Most settlers addressed their household servants in a form of KiSwahili, a complex language as it was spoken by the Swahili themselves, but a form of baby-talk running largely to shouted imperative verbs and simple nouns as the settlers used it. It was called "Kitchen Swahili" or "Ki-Settler" (pronounced "Ki-settlah").[32]

In addition to household servants, the settlers had to obtain farm laborers. Except for a few impecunious whites, many of them Boers who actually worked their own fields, the settlers' fields were cleared, tilled, planted, and harvested by Africans, just as they also saw to the daily needs of the cattle, horses, and other livestock. Many settlers were dismayed to discover that their dreams of prosperity based on an endless supply of cheap labor were not coming true because most Africans had little desire to work for wages, and those who did seldom displayed the sort of work ethic the British had hoped for. The father of the Kenyan writer Elspeth Huxley tried to recruit Kikuyu laborers by playing "the Bluebells of Scotland" on his hand-cranked gramophone; he was puzzled when no one marched to his tune.[33]

Huxley should have tried offering higher wages because many laborers soon learned to appreciate the white man's money. As early as 1907, Kikuyu laborers walked more than 300 miles to Mombasa, where wages were twice those offered in the highlands.[34] But white farmers were not interested in paying higher wages. Lord Delamere explained to the government that Africans should be forced into the labor market by cutting the amount of land available to them so that wage work would become their only means of survival.[35] When the government was slow to take action, other settlers threatened to use force to obtain labor. Alarmed, the government responded by ordering chiefs to deliver a quota of laborers to desired localities. Even so, there were too few volunteers, so, in the spirit of slavery, the chiefs were allowed to use force. Enough men were killed that the British Government, alarmed by reports of wholesale butchery in King Leopold's Belgian Congo, had to intervene to prevent more slaughter.[36] Instead of strongarm methods, a hut tax was imposed on Africans in the belief that it would force them to accept wage work in order to pay their taxes, and steps were also taken to deny Africans alternative means of making money. For example, they were prohibited from growing the most profitable cash crops such as coffee and sisal, and in the highlands even maize was made a white monopoly.[37] These measures were effective, and thousands of Africans, many of them Kikuyu, became laborers for the white settlers. To control the men who were being removed from their tribal areas and forced to work on distant European farms, every African who was away from his tribal reserve was required to carry a pass that bore his name, tribe, fingerprints, past employer's recommendations, and his present employer's signature. This pass, called a *kipande*, was worn around the neck in a little metal container, the size of a small cigarette packet. It jingled like a bell as a person walked. The Kikuyu called it *mbugi* (goat's bell), and detested it as a mark of their servility.

The settlers' lives of sport and profit were interrupted by the outbreak of war in 1914. British hopes of an early victory over the Germans in Tanganyika were quickly shattered, and thousands of British troops fought in Kenya and Tanganyika for four years before the Germans, led by their resourceful general, Paul von Lettow-Vorbeck, were forced to acknowledge defeat.[38] Throughout the war, the British pressed Africans into military service as porters in their Pioneer Carrier Corps. In all, 165,000 Africans served, most of them conscripted by force, and more than 42,000 died. In 1918, when the war ended, an influenza epidemic struck Kenya with appalling results. It was estimated that 120,000 Kikuyu died. The anthropologist Louis Leakey recalled that, as a boy, he ran from one Kikuyu homestead to another to announce happily that World War I had ended. Most Kikuyu were too ill to care. One man responded this way: "What does it matter that the war is over now? When my son comes home he will find his mother and wife and we too, dead."[39]

As the Kikuyu and other Kenyans tried to recover from their losses, Kenya Government officials developed a scheme to attract demobilized British officers as settlers. They came in large numbers. Among them were 69 who were listed in Burke's *Peerage*. One who bought land was Lord Kitchener, Britain's famous field marshal.[40] To provide farms for these so-called soldier settlers, more land had to be made available. By 1920, 5.5 million acres of African land had been confiscated for European use. Africans who had served in the war got nothing but a few shillings as a gratuity, and some who had their land taken from them in the bargain were understandably bitter.[41]

Whites who had served as soldiers were given free land or allowed to buy it at a nominal price. More than 120 square miles of this land was confiscated from the Kikuyu (the total Kikuyu Territory was 1,640 square miles).[42] As time passed, and birth rates rose, more and more Africans, particularly Kikuyu, found themselves with no land of their own. These men had no choice but to become wage laborers for the settlers. Others who already recognized the value of education sought out wage work in order to pay school fees for their sons. In 1919, 16,000 Africans, mostly Kikuyu, lived and worked on the land of white settlers in the Rift Valley near Nakuru and Naivasha. The total white population of the area was only 215 people, including women and children.[43] In the ensuing years, more and more Kikuyu servants and farm laborers would go to work for the settlers.

Not all of the white settlers lived on farms in the highlands. Some settled on the coast, and others set up businesses in Nairobi. But to African eyes, all were "Europeans," members of Kenya's ruling white minority. Few of these Europeans were attracted to intellectual pursuits. Guns, horses, sex, and strong drink were the stuff of life. Books, music, and art were seldom in evidence in settlers' homes. White Kenya was a muscular, manly society, and women often matched the men not only in hunting and riding, but in the conspicuous display of sexuality as well. A well-known couplet summed up the white Kenyan's reputation in Britain: "Kenya born and Kenya bred, strong in the arms, empty in the head."[44] Alcohol was never far from a man's lips, or a woman's for that matter. Champagne was drunk instead of water, and a guest was offered a pink gin, or something stronger, even if he arrived at daybreak. In small towns like Eldoret or Kitale, weekends at whites-only clubs like the "Rat Pit" were bacchanalian to say the least. Drinking began early on Saturday (after Africans had been turned out by the police to sweep the streets), and the inevitable Saturday night dance at the Kitale or Pioneer Hotels usually ended in a series of amorous escapades and drunken brawls.

It was little different in Nairobi, except that more affluent settlers could congregate at the elegant Muthaiga Club, known as the Moulin Rouge of Africa. It was a pink stucco mansion with a golf course, tennis courts and stables; guests who spent the night in its huge rooms typically went to bed very late and often with someone else's spouse. Elsewhere in Nairobi it was traditional for men to dance on tables, and for horse-men to ride into the "Lord Delamere" bar at the Norfolk Hotel (and sometimes shoot at the mirror or the ceiling), to have fist fights with friends as well as enemies, and, as the shank of the night came on, to make a pilgrimage to the "Japanese Legation," an inelegant but large building that housed high-spirited and increasingly wealthy Japanese prostitutes. How these enterprising women found their way to Nairobi is not recorded, although some reports had it that they came from Zanzibar. Equally mysterious is how some of the settler ladies came to choose their costumes. Some of them dressed exactly like "cowgirls" in turn-of-the-century Dodge City or Tucson, except that they were given to wearing gold-rimmed monocles and smoking cigarettes in long, ivory holders.[45]

One part of the highlands came to be known as "Happy Valley" in recognition of a life-style that was nothing if not sybaritic. The prevailing joke in Britain was, "Are you married or are you from Kenya?" It was not an empty jibe. In at least one Happy Valley house, weekend guests were required to switch partners, frequently more than once before the weekend was over. In another house, the lovely hostess insisted on bathing and dressing in full view of her dinner guests while she carried on a lively if rather narcissistic conversation. The aristocratic settlers of Happy Valley were not at all reluctant to use narcotics as well as alcohol, and both cocaine and morphine were commonplace, so much so, in fact, that when all the guests including the Prince of Wales (later, King Edward VII) were casually offered morphine at dinner, one settler who was more clear-headed than the others hustled the heir to the Crown away before he could be corrupted in this too-public way. Sexual hijinks were so common that it often seemed that everyone slept with everyone else; then, after a period of repose, did so again. The situation persisted through the years. Occasionally, however, someone took umbrage. During World War II, one of the most notorious womanizers in all of Kenya was shot dead, presumably by the husband of the woman whom he was openly romancing, although no one was ever convicted of the murder. The event was notable principally because the victim, Lord Errol, was of such high social rank that he was the first subject of the Queen in Scotland, after the Royal family.[46]

Even quite ordinary settlers were astonishingly full of themselves. They believed they were a master race—a "superior people," and they never doubted that they were entitled to prosper in Kenya. If the government showed signs of opposing them, as happened now and then when regulations were introduced that protected the interests of Kenya's African population against exploitive labor laws or practices, the settlers proposed the violent overthrow of the colonial government. They never actually seized power, but they often planned to do so, and several times came very close to taking action. In addition to challenging the legitimacy of the Government of Kenya, they demanded that the government subsidize their increasingly inefficient and unprofitable farms by passing favorable land and labor laws, allowing low-interest loans and freight rates, and protecting them against African competition.[47] All the while, they warned the government about the evils of socialism.[48]

The government that the settlers so often challenged was a typical colonial administration. Beneath the governor were secretaries of departments of law and order, finance, development, agriculture, African affairs, education, labor, commerce and industry, health, and local government. Some of these secretaries also served as members of Kenya's Legislative Council, where they were joined by elected members of the white settler community. Each of Kenya's six provinces had a commissioner who directed the activities of other administrative officers, who in turn governed districts within each province. There also were substantial numbers of officers who worked in each of the Colony's five technical departments—agriculture, education, medical services, veterinary services, and labor. Most Africans lived in "reserves" set aside by the government for the exclusive use of each tribe. Each reserve was governed by a panoply of government-appointed chiefs, tribal courts, and tribal police. Behind all of this was the distant presence of the Colonial Office in London.

The settlers were never reluctant to express their "ferocious self-interest." For example, they made it perfectly plain that Indians (known as "Asians" after the partition of India in 1947) would never occupy land in the highlands, would never be allowed to share power or interact as equals with the Europeans, and moreover would never be permitted to forget their origins as "coolies" who, as representatives of India's lowest castes, came to Kenya to work on the Uganda Railway. As most of the settlers saw it, all that the Indians contributed to Kenya's Africans was "disease, crime, alcoholism, and venereal disease."[49] Settler attitudes were disingenuous at best. Many Indians who immigrated to Kenya after the railroad had been built were not of low-caste origins at all. Indeed, many were fair-skinned Sikhs and Muslims from the north of India. Nevertheless, the settlers scorned the Indians, but they feared them too, for if the Indians allied themselves with the Africans, settler power could be threatened. Due largely to African dislike for Indian traders, who had a monopoly on retail trade and often treated their African customers badly, the British were not threatened by an Indian-African alliance, but they could not prevent the growth of Indian affluence. By 1952, there were three times as many Indians as Europeans in Kenya, and as a population they were wealthier than the Europeans; still, their political power was slight.[50]

The settlers did their best to ignore the Indian community, but they could hardly ignore the Africans who worked for them as servants and farm laborers. On some farms, African servants and laborers were treated with kindness and compassion, their children fussed over, their ills treated, and certain aspects of their humanity respected. This was to be expected from upper-class Britons who were used to caring for their servants and tenants. It was also what the Virginia plantation model called for—good, kind, but firm masters. In a number of instances, Africans who worked under these circumstances developed affection and loyalty for the whites. In return, the British liked to believe that their servants and laborers were happy and faithful. Karen Blixen did much to romanticize this faithful servant ideal in *Out of Africa*, but she also felt that she shared a covenant with Africans, an idea that other settlers thought ridiculous, if not downright dangerous.

There was another side to the white masters, a far less compassionate one. At the settlers' urging, the compliant colonial administration imposed taxes, insisted on the kipande pass law, restricted educational opportunities for Africans, and denied them means of self-support, all as devices for compelling them to work as field hands for low wages. The standard monthly wage for a man who worked every day of the month, including Sundays, was 14 shillings. A shilling was then worth about 14 United States cents. In 1952, when the Mau Mau rebellion erupted, Michael Blundell, a relatively moderate man who was the political leader of the settlers, paid his farm laborers 12 shillings a month; the contract also called for women and children to work as might be required.[51] At that time, a cheap shirt bought in an African market cost 4 shillings, and the annual poll tax was 20 shillings. With wages like these a laborer could only stay alive by cultivating the single acre that he was lent as a tenant farmer. Regulations required the "squatters," as the British called their tenant laborers, to sell the produce from their plot of land to their employers at a fixed price. For example, an employer would pay his "squatter" 14 or 15 shillings for a bag of maize. Thanks to government subsidies, the employer could then sell that same bag for 32 shillings.[52] Moreover, while it was the Europeans who benefitted most from government services, until 1930 it was African taxes that paid the bulk of the expense. In addition, the Europeans paid no direct income tax until 1936.[53]

Africans bitterly resented this economic exploitation just as they detested their treatment as inferior beings. Charity Wacuima, an educated Kikuyu woman who as a child worked with her parents as a laborer on a settler's coffee plantation, remembered that ". . . I rapidly grew to dislike these white men who made people work like slaves and paid them half a shilling a day for it, who sometimes struck the grown men as if they were children and who indeed always treated us as if, mentally and emotionally, we were permanently children."[54] Most white settlers believed that Africans rarely exceeded the mental development of a 12-year-old and thus had to be treated as naughty and irresponsible children. As recently as 1954, two years after the Mau Mau rebellion broke out, a settler wrote that "the uneducated African is a child in many respects. He is forgetful and irresponsible, careless and idle, ungrateful and often quite stupid."[55] Elspeth Huxley, probably white Kenya's most honored and widely read writer, was also willing to believe that Africans were less intelligent than Europeans. She approvingly cited unspecified doctors to the effect that African brains have "a shorter growing period" and may possess "less well-formed, less cunningly arranged cells than brains of Europeans. . . . In other words, that there is a fundamental disparity between the capabilities of his brain and our's."[56]

Many settlers did not confine themselves to comments about the intellectual inferiority of Africans. Many forced their laborers to work through heavy rainstorms and thought nothing of interrupting the prayers of their Muslim workers with orders to go to work. When an African laborer offended his master, he was liable to be punched, cuffed, or kicked because almost all whites believed that they should never demean themselves by arguing with an African. More serious offenders were caned or flogged with a *kiboko*, a hippo-hide whip. Some were flogged to death.[57] Communication was limited to however much Swahili a settler knew, because a European should not speak English to an African (it was believed to give them a sense of self-importance), and few settlers could speak Kikuyu or any other African language. Africans were also required to salute any European they encountered, and address all men and even little boys as "bwana" (Sir) and all women, including girls, as "memsahib" (Madam). They were also forbidden to wear shoes. Many house servants were given derisive nick-names in English like "stupid" or "damn-fool," and Africans were commonly referred to as "monkeys." Africans had nicknames for their employers, too, but these were based on personality, not the presumption of stupidity.

Settlers not only believed that Africans had the minds of children, they were convinced that they did not feel pain as Europeans did, were able to will themselves to die whenever they wished (both Elspeth Huxley and Karen Blixen subscribed to this view), and had altogether different nutritional requirements than white people.[58] For example, it was widely argued that a bowl of maize-meal porridge was all that an African needed for good health.[59] As a result, many settler employers gave each of their laborers a pound and a half of *posho* (maize meal) per day, a ration that was thought quite adequate.[60] Many settlers, particularly women, never quite overcame their fear of Africans' blackness, or their supposed resemblance to apes.[61] In 1913, a British Colonial officer, Captain Chauncey Stigand, wrote that "for the proper understanding of the savage African, one must not look on him as a human being, but as a rather superior kind of animal."[62]

For many whites, this "proper understanding" never changed. For example, when Labour M.P.s Fenner Brockway and Leslie Hale visited Kenya shortly after the outbreak of Mau Mau violence, they met with a group of white settlers to urge, as they routinely did, the acceptance of racial equality as a step towards peace. The settlers' spokesperson, a middle-aged woman, insisted that there could be no possibility of equality because "Every African is dishonest, a liar, and lazy. Their language has no words for love, gratitude, loyalty." Stunned, Hale asked the woman if she were serious. She said that she was, and the other settlers agreed. When Brockway and Hale got back to their car, they asked their Kikuyu driver the words for love, gratitude and loyalty. Puzzled, the man replied, *"wendo, ngatho, wathikeri."*[63] Even well after the Mau Mau revolt had ended, it was still not considered impolite when discussing Africans' inability to do something to a European's satisfaction, for a settler to say soberly, "Well, they haven't been out of the trees long enough, don't you see!" Other whites would nod approvingly.[64]

The Maasai and Somali were partially exempt from the stereotype applied to other Africans, probably due to their light skin color, Caucasian facial features, and free nomadic life-style that many Europeans admired and romanticized; but Kenya's largest tribe, the Kikuyu, were not. Like most other Africans they were generally considered lazy, cruel, cowardly, unfaithful, ungrateful, and dishonest. They had a reputation for thievery, for lying, and for poisoning their enemies. They were also said to be unusually disputatious.[65] Almost all Europeans agreed that there were some positive things about the Kikuyu as well—they were unusually enterprising, eager for education, and intelligent. Most Europeans apparently saw no contradiction in this view of the Kikuyu as both lazy and enterprising. It was common for the whites to acknowledge Kikuyu initiative, energy, and business acumen by referring to them with anti-semitic scorn as the "Jews" of Kenya.[66]

World War II brought far-reaching changes to Kenya. First, nearly 100,000 of Kenya's Africans voluntarily joined the British Army. Almost all of these men saw service outside of Kenya, and what they experienced kindled their hopes for a better life after the war. What they found when they returned left them painfully disillusioned. For Kenya's whites, how-ever, the war was nothing less than a bonanza. The depression years of the 1930s had hit Kenya hard. Most settlers were in debt to banks and many were near bankruptcy, so when Britain chose to station thousands of troops there and to assign Kenya a major role in supplying food for the war effort, they seized their chance to recover. By the end of the war, most of Kenya's white settlers had paid off their debts and were happily prosperous. The post-war years promised more of the same. Italian sol-diers who had been interned in Kenya during World War II, and had helped to build its roads and public buildings, now wanted to stay. Be-ginning in 1951, 1,000 Italians each year were admitted to Kenya. Some would die as victims of Mau Mau attacks.

Kenya's post-war atmosphere was greatly affected by the arrival of large numbers of demobilized British officers, many of them officers of the Indian Army who left India at the time of its partition in 1947. After World War II, these men and other middle-class officers settled in Kenya, hoping to share in the good life that clearly would not be available in post-war Britain. The lands offered to them were hardly as grand as those given to Lord Delamere and the other early settlers, but they averaged 700 acres. These new settlers worked hard, quickly turned a profit, and began to live like country gentlemen. As one historian has put it, al-though they "clearly lacked the gentleman's principles," they were "quick to grasp his privileges."[67]

The impact of these men and their families in Kenya disturbed Mi-chael Blundell, who had been a Kenyan since 1925 when he arrived at the age of 18 after leaving public school. Blundell was reelected to Ken-ya's Legislative Council (better known as "Legco") without opposition in 1952, and was chosen to be the "leader" of the Europeans in Kenya's governing body. As Blundell acknowledged, it was obvious from his lack of opposition that his views were acceptable to most members of the European community. At this stage of his political career, Blundell was far from being an advocate of equality for Africans, but the British set-tlers who arrived in Kenya after World War II alarmed him because, as he described them, they were inflexible, reactionary, racist, and brought

to Kenya an "almost fascist concept of organization and massed emo-
tion." They were determined to see that Kenya would forever be a bastion of white supremacy.[68]

In 1952, Kenya was "white man's country," as its original settlers like
Lord Delamere had insisted it should be. Larger than France and only a
little smaller than Texas, Kenya was one of the most majestic and capti-
vating places on earth. Its white settlers loved it with a fanatic intensity;
visitors rhapsodized about it; and virtually every writer who saw Kenya
tried to capture something of its beauty, drama, and excitement. Some
wrote about its brilliant flowers, birds, and butterflies; some about its
snow-capped mountains, lush green highlands, and trout fishing; others
about its endless skies, its racing clouds, its vast vistas, and the wonder
of the lion-colored plains of the Great Rift Valley. Still others wrote about
its peoples, usually the Maasai or other more or less naked spear-wielding,
cattle-herding nomads. But most wrote about its animals that roamed
freely on vast plains that had names like Tsavo, Amboseli, and Mara.

But there was another Kenya, one that was not rhapsodized about by
visitors. More than half of "white man's country" was rarely seen by
whites and almost never celebrated in print. Except for a narrow coastal
strip, most of the eastern half of Kenya was low-lying semi-desert that
attracted few animals and fewer people. The northern third of Kenya
was even hotter and drier, and it too was sparsely populated. There was
too little rainfall to allow agriculture except along the banks of permanent rivers like the Athi or Tana. The people who lived in this huge, dry,
tse-tse-fly-infested area were nomads who herded their cattle, goats, don-
keys, and camels and sometimes fought with one another. The best known
of these people were the Somali, Boran, Rendille, Samburu, Turkana,
Pokot (also known as Suk), and Karamojong. Much of this vast northern
part of Kenya—known as the Northern Frontier District—was off-limits
to visitors because of the dangers of inter-tribal warfare.

Much of Kenya south of the railroad was also sparsely populated, but
this area was visited by tourists because it was the land of the photogenic
Maasai and the game parks. The western highlands, peopled by the
Nandi, Elgeyo, Tugen, and other smaller tribes, were off the tourist track,
as were the lush green lands of western Kenya adjoining Lake Victoria,
which were the homeland of more than 2 million people such as the
Kipsigis, Gusii, Luo, and Luhya. There were vast tea estates near Kericho,
but most of these were owned by large London companies, not by settlers. The town of Kakamega enjoyed such tremendous annual rainfall
that it was one of the greenest places in Kenya, as the lush fairways and

polished greens of its famous golf course attested. Gold had been discovered there in 1930 and it had briefly been a boomtown, but by 1952
it was a colonial backwater where only a few settlers managed to hang
on. Much of the land near Lake Victoria was marshy, but hillier areas
contained rich agricultural land. Relatively little of this region had been
appropriated by Europeans, because most of it lay at an altitude of only
about 4,000 feet, was much hotter and more humid than the much higher
central highlands, and was considered unhealthy. For most white Kenyans, like most tourists, Kenya in the post-war years meant Nairobi, the
cool central highlands, the game parks, and the white sand beaches of
the coast. Tourists never saw either the squatters on European farms or
the dismal African slums in Nairobi.

At least 3,000 Europeans lived on the coast, most of them near the
port city of Mombasa. Some owned or managed large plantations, but
others were businessmen or retirees who lived in sparkling white villas
with red-tiled roofs that overlooked the Indian Ocean and caught the
prevailing sea breezes. During holidays, thousands of Europeans either
took the train or drove down the only road from Nairobi to Mombasa
in order to spend a week or two at a beach hotel or rented house. Except
for a few miles near the two cities, the road was unpaved and corrugated,
one of the world's longest and most dangerous washboards. During dry
seasons, passengers arrived covered with red dust; during rainy seasons,
parts of the road would be washed out, and travelers could arrive days
late. At any time of the year, the drive was dangerous. Motorists, many
of whom drove at alarming speeds, had to be wary of huge trucks and
oil tankers that tried to stay on top of the high-crowned road; and there
were many fatal accidents when cars struck a zebra or some other large
animal. Mombasa's deep-water port was Kenya's access to the world, and
the Muslim population of the coastal area had a long, prominent, and
fascinating history. But for most Europeans in Kenya the coast was simply the place for a pleasant holiday. For Kenya's white settlers, "real" life
took place in Nairobi and the nearby highlands, and it was there that
the movement called Mau Mau developed.

Government officers, white missionaries (many of them Americans),
and a few doctors were scattered throughout Kenya, and a handful of
white farmers had settled in places like Taita and Machakos to the south-
east of Nairobi, as well as in towns such as Kisumu, Kericho, and Kakamega near Lake Victoria. But the great majority of white settlers lived in
the central highlands, which fall into three distinct areas. First, to the
north of Nairobi, a high mountainous region extended like an inverted

triangle. On the eastern side were towns like Thika, Fort Hall, Nyeri, and Nanyuki at the foot of massive Mt. Kenya; on the north were Thomson's Falls and Rumuruti. This entire area was the Kikuyu homeland, but there were many European farms near the towns; and closer to Nairobi, much of the land was occupied by Europeans (93 of the 120 square miles taken from the Kikuyu by Europeans were in the most southerly Kikuyu district of Kiambu, just north of Nairobi). This highland area was bordered on the west by the Aberdare Mountain Range which, like the forests around Mt. Kenya, would become a refuge for Mau Mau rebels.

A second area was the Great Rift Valley, where the air was so clear that, after a rain, stars could be seen at noon. Two to three thousand feet straight down a precipice from the Aberdares on the east, and the near-vertical Mau escarpment to the west, the 30- to 40-mile-wide Rift Valley cut a deep trench between the central and western highlands. A single road serpentined its way down the eastern face of the almost vertical escarpment, before it crossed the Rift Valley to Nakuru, Kenya's third-largest city. Originally occupied by the Maasai and their herds, the Rift Valley had been carved into huge wheat farms and cattle ranches by the earliest white settlers. Lord Delamere's Rift Valley ranch was so large that 1,000 miles of barbed wire were needed to enclose it. In 1952, there were probably 100,000 African laborers in the Rift Valley, most of whom were Kikuyu. Another vast highland area extended north and northwest from Nakuru. At elevations ranging from 6,500 to 9,000 feet, green patches of farmlands had been cut out of the forest. The town of Kitale, at the extreme north of the area, near 14,000-foot Mt. Elgon, was known as the "place of Colonels" because so many retired British officers settled nearby, and many likened the area to the Cotswolds in the west of England. Boers had settled near Mt. Elgon too, most of them in the Uasin Gishu plateau near the large town of Eldoret.

Although some Europeans lived in highland towns where they owned hotels or businesses, most were farmers who lived on widely scattered farms connected by dirt roads that became impassable during heavy rains. Even the main roads through the highlands were unpaved, and during the two rainy seasons only 4-wheel-drive vehicles could be expected to reach their destination without considerable difficulty. By 1952, the days when most settlers were wealthy aristocrats who did no work around their estates were largely over. Although some settlers still hired British managers to run their farms while they lived in Nairobi, and a few—like Lord Francis Scott, who had close friendships with members of the Royal Family—continued to be diffident about overseeing their lands, most of the settlers, and all of those who came to Kenya after World War II, took an active part in running their farms and ranches.[69]

Heavy farm labor was almost always done by Africans, but there were enough chores around a farm to keep the Europeans busy. Up early, they dealt with the usual and unusual run of events on their farms where they grew cereals, coffee, and pyrethrum, and raised cattle and sheep; there was always something that needed seeing to. But they also went riding, or hunting, and sometimes had visitors. At the end of the day, after bathing, some settlers dressed formally for dinner, but others changed into their pajamas before being served their meal by servants. After din-ner, they chatted, listened to the BBC, or read. Weekends were usually lively. Even small towns had a hotel and a social club as well, where settlers congregated for dinner and dancing, games and gossip, drinking and flirting. They often staged amateur theatrical productions, ex-changed the latest air mail versions of London newspapers, played cards or darts, and complained about the government. Many women had learned to manage their family farms while their husbands were away during World War II, and some continued to do so after the war, but many women used their leisure time to have flings with other women's husbands.[70] British officers who served in Kenya during Mau Mau were delighted to find so many women with lusty appetites, but they some-times remarked that socializing with the settlers was difficult because they could not tell who was married to whom.[71]

Nairobi was the hub of the highlands. It was Kenya's capital and its largest city, with an estimated 150,000 inhabitants in 1952; it was also the center of Kenya's commerce and industry. Almost all of the 33,000 tour-ists who visited Kenya in 1952 passed through Nairobi, where they stayed in hotels, outfitted themselves for safaris, and bought souvenirs. For tour-ists, Nairobi was a stopping-off place on the way to see or shoot animals, but for the white farmers, it was the place to shop for any major pur-chase, and it was the center of Kenya's social life. Nairobi had movie theaters, nightclubs, restaurants, and clubs that drew many farmers for a long weekend of fun. Nairobi was not a place for concerts, libraries, or art galleries, but late in 1952 Ralph Richardson opened the Kenya Na-tional Theatre across from the Norfolk Hotel. It soon attracted perform-ing artists from around the world. During "race week," thousands of highland settlers converged on Nairobi to bet at the horse races and spend the nights in bawdy epics of drinking, dancing, fighting, and sex-uality. Now a biannual event, race week continued to be the highlight of Kenya's social season.

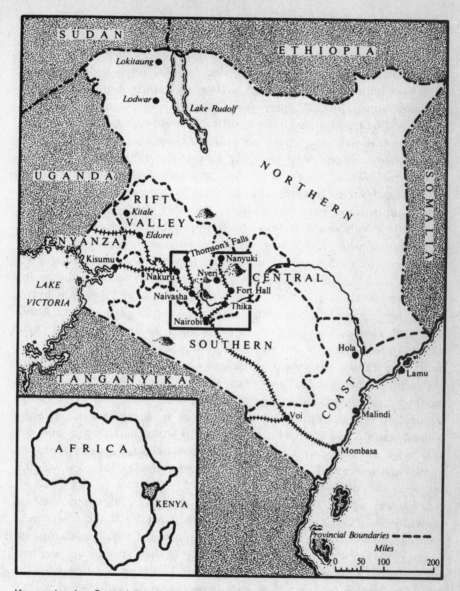

Kenya showing Central Area most affected by Mau Mau

For close to 15,000 Europeans, Nairobi was home. Surrounded by white plumeria, scarlet flame trees, purple bougainvillaea, and brilliant blue jacarandas that left their blossoms on the ground like blue snow, they lived in spacious two- and three-storied houses, some with swimming pools and tennis courts, on large well-kept grounds in exclusive white neighborhoods. The city center was modern, but increasingly congested. Traffic was heavy and parking was difficult, and one's car might be broken into while shopping (there were almost twice as many thefts in 1952 as there had been in 1951). There were beggars on the streets, too, some of them pitifully deformed by leprosy, who offended passing Europeans by holding out their fingerless hands in supplication. African shoe-shine "boys" importuned passersby to have their shoes shined, and other Africans often bothered Europeans by stopping them to ask for a job.

Still, downtown Nairobi was not too unpleasant, and the pace of life in the suburbs was leisurely. The day began when a servant brought tea to one's bedside. Many businessmen and their wives took two hours for lunch, frequently at the Norfolk or New Stanley Hotel's elegant buffet where they consumed formidable amounts of cold pigeon, beef, lamb, ham, fish, cheese, fruit, and salads of all sorts, followed by a hot curry washed down with beer and wine. There was also an array of a dozen or so desserts. Lunch was served by African waiters who changed from their European clothes into "kanzus" (long white cotton gowns) and put fezzes on their heads. Although these men ordinarily wore shoes, they were required to serve barefooted. They were very attentive waiters, but when a guest wanted something he or she would snap their fingers and call out, "boy!" All guests were white. No Africans or Indians were permitted to stay at the Norfolk, or at other leading hotels like the New Stanley, nor were they allowed to eat there.

For many whites, high tea at 4:30 was a daily ritual, often followed soon after by a visit to one of Nairobi's exclusive social clubs, where most men exercised strenuously and most women socialized. The Europeans began drinking whiskey or gin around 6:30 or 7:00 and dinner was usually served at 7:30 or 8:00, followed by more drinking and cigars for the men. On weekends there were houseguests, riding, golf, polo, cricket, tennis, badminton, croquet, and other sports in which women were often as active as men. There was likely to be more drinking than usual on weekends, and on Saturday nights there would be dances at various nightclubs that often went on until dawn.[72]

It is unlikely that any European resident of Nairobi lived without at least one servant; most white families employed several. The majority of

Nairobi's white population was middle-class. In Britain they could not have afforded a single servant, but in Nairobi an ordinary white family would hire a woman to look after their small children, and also hire men to cook, wash dishes, do the laundry, clean the house, tend the garden, wash the car, and perform other tasks that needed doing, like going to the market, picking up mail at the post office, or delivering something to a friend. Because of the alarming post-war increase in burglaries, most homeowners barred the ground-floor windows of their houses, and they also hired a man or two to guard their houses at night, which they did by patrolling with heavy wooden clubs. They also bought watch dogs, and their "Beware of Dog" signs were printed in Swahili, not English; the dogs were trained to attack black men, not whites.[73] Many people also hired an African to sleep inside their car at night to prevent anyone from breaking into it.

Crime was a nuisance to the whites, but the availability of servants at minimal cost was a godsend. An experienced full-time servant could be hired for $5.00 a month; an accomplished cook might earn $10.00. Less-skilled servants were available at a cost of no more than a few dollars a month. If a servant did not perform up to expectations, there were always others clamoring for a job. In fact, hundreds of men walked from one European house to the next each day hoping to find work.

Although it was a rare European who found sufficient fault with his or her servants to do without them altogether, most of the whites in Nairobi and in the highlands complained about their servants incessantly. It seems that things were always being broken, orders forgotten, water left running, rules of hygiene ignored, and small amounts of tea, sugar, and flour misappropriated. The Europeans were fond of saying, and only partly in jest, that while it was true that their servants were paid very little, they earned far more than they were worth. It rarely occurred to them to say "please" or "thank you" to their servants, or to try to understand the problems these people faced in their lives. Instead, they amused one another with stories about the incompetence or perversity of their servants, often adding homilies such as, "there is no such thing as an honest Kikuyu." Visitors to Kenya observed that as racist as Kenya's white men were, white women were far worse, a distinction that was well-known to Africans.[74] There were some relatively liberal and tolerant whites in Kenya, but it was not just a few extremist settlers who expressed racist views.[75] Kenya's Governor, Sir Philip Mitchell, wrote that the Europeans who had been elected to Kenya's Legislative Council, its highest legislative body, were "obstinately full of racial bitterness."[76]

The whites often boasted that they "knew the Africans," but the only Africans they had contact with were servants, laborers, or shop clerks. They would probably have been startled to learn that about 95 percent of the Africans in Kenya had no contact with Europeans except for an occasional government official or missionary. Kenya's Europeans did not see, and did not care to see, below the surface of African life. They would cluck their tongues disapprovingly as Kikuyu women struggled along the roads burdened by loads of wood that could weigh over 100 lbs while Kikuyu men walked alongside with their hands free, but they did not attempt to understand what Kikuyu men or women actually thought or felt, even when they lived in thatched-roof huts on the so-called "labor lines" of their own farms. What Africans thought or felt about anything was simply irrelevant to most white settlers.

In 1950, the District Commissioner of Nakuru District, one of the seed beds of Mau Mau, noted in his annual report that a "Hitherto unknown secret society called Mau Mau" had come to light and that white settlers in the district had begun to express concern. The District Commissioner wrote that "... if the farming community wishes to assure its own continued security, it is essential that all, and not merely a few, individual farmers should show a sympathetic interest in their employees and their individual problems." He went on to say that too many farmers were inclined to "bully and subdue" rather than "lead" their African employees, and he concluded that the emergence of Mau Mau as a society dedicated "to the expulsion of all Europeans" was due "principally to an entire lack of understanding and appreciation of the African and his mental processes by the majority of employers."[77]

The settlers saw no reason to understand Africans because they believed absolutely that before the coming of the white men, Kenya had been nothing more than a "howling wilderness" of superstition and death.[78] They were proud to have raised the benighted Africans out of their barbarism by the gifts of Christianity, education, public health, and peace, and they were furious that the Africans were not "grateful."[79] Most of all they prided themselves for establishing *Pax Britannica*; "The Superior People had stamped out internecine warfare," as one writer put it.[80] In reality, Kenya had never been as warlike a place as Europe; except for the violence of Arab slave raiders, who were responding in part to the demands of the European and American markets, Kenya's warfare usually had consisted of episodic cattle raids with little loss of life. Large-scale battles that left hundreds dead did occur but they were not common. In return for suppressing this relatively benign pattern of warfare, the British involved Kenya's Africans in two World Wars.

The "superior" civilization the whites brought to Kenya did not include racial integration. A visitor to Kenya in the early 1950s was quickly introduced to its color bar. In Nairobi airport, there were bathrooms marked "European Gentlemen," "European Ladies," and others marked "Asian Gentlemen," and "Asian Ladies." There was no bathroom at all for Africans. After surveying all of Africa, James Cameron, a journalist, wrote that Kenya had established a color bar "of singular crudity and arrogance."[81] An example of what Cameron meant was provided by a European woman who said that she didn't mind employing Africans, or even shaking hands with them, "but pray with them I will not." Some congregations would not even allow Africans into their churches for separate Swahilli-language services.[82] As for African policemen, most white Kenyans either ignored them or treated them with open contempt. Trains, hotels, and restaurants were segregated, and African children were not allowed to attend school with white children. It is hardly surprising that white children acted as if they did not believe it was possible to be rude to an African, and most adults were no more polite.[83]

And so whites continued to talk about the price of coffee (their main export), about cricket matches, about trout fishing, and the evils of labor unions. While they talked, the Africans they did not choose to see were organizing a rebellion that came to be known as Mau Mau. Two months after Mau Mau led the government to declare a State of Emergency, former governor Sir Philip Mitchell, who had recently retired, wrote that the greatest danger for Kenya lay not in Mau Mau but in Kenya's "colour bar, prejudice and rudeness."[84] He was probably right, but his warning came far too late.

Governor Mitchell was a short, fat man whose almost total lack of social graces led many settlers to sniff about his middle-class origins. But even after developing a serious heart condition in 1949, Mitchell had a mission—he was determined to transform Kenya into a multi-racial state. Although the police along with many district officers and settlers provided him with regular expressions of their concern about Kikuyu political agitation and what they believed was a secret society called Mau Mau, he simply would not listen to anyone who warned him that Kenya was about to explode into racial war. When Mitchell retired on June 21, 1952, he was praised by many, including Kenya's leading newspaper, the *East African Standard*, for his accomplishments. On his return to Britain, although he criticized its color bar, he continued to insist that all was well with Kenya's emergent multi-racial harmony. As late as October 19, only one day before the State of Emergency was declared, he insisted that Kenya had never been more peaceful.[85]

In 1902, Richard Meinertzhagen had predicted that when the Kikuyu became educated and were led by "political agitators" instead of "medicine men," there would be a "general rising." Two years later, he wrote that he was sorry to leave the Kikuyu, whom he had come to like, adding that they were the most intelligent of the tribes he had met. Meinertzhagen also understood what Europeans who settled in Kenya later did not grasp. He wrote that the Kikuyu were "cheerful, honest, and truthful" with Europeans who treated them fairly, but when European administrators treated them like "bloody niggers" they became "unscrupulous, dishonest, and treacherous." Meinertzhagen also warned against the policy of forcing Africans to work as cheap labor, predicting "much trouble" if European settlers encroached on Kikuyu land.[86] He clearly foresaw that Kenya's Africans would eventually demand their independence and, alone among his contemporaries, he believed they would achieve their goal.

In 1949, then a retired Colonel, Meinertzhagen returned to Kenya. He met with a Kikuyu chief whom he had known almost half a century before. The old chief warned Meinertzhagen that there was likely to be a violent rebellion led by a "secret society" that he called "Maw Maw."[87] Meinertzhagen wrote to Governor Mitchell expressing his concern. He received no reply.

2

"SOMETHING CALLED
MAW MAW"

THE EVOLUTION
OF A
REBELLION

The movement that came to be known as Mau Mau grew out of the actual conditions of African life that the white Kenyans chose not to see. The whites in Nairobi lived in sublime ignorance of the lives of the more than 100,000 Africans who crowded into the shabby slums that were known as "African Locations." Most of these Africans were Kikuyu who came to Nairobi because they owned no land in the Kikuyu Reserve, where as many as 1,000 people struggled to survive within each single square mile. Nairobi offered the hope of jobs, but there were too few of those and too many competitors. There was also too little housing. In filthy, fly-ridden Pumwani Location, a center for Kikuyu settlement and political activity, only someone with a job could afford a bed of his own. Most beds were used in shifts, and many people slept on the floor—ten, twelve, or more in a small mud-walled shack with a tin roof. Perhaps

20,000 slept outdoors wherever they could find partial shelter from Nairobi's cold nights.[1] Many women lived by illegally brewing maize or millet beer for sale, or by working as prostitutes; men lived by their wits and on the earnings of their women. But everywhere in "African" Nairobi, life was dominated by a search for food and for a place to sleep.

To make matters worse, economic inflation had a devastating effect on these poor Africans. Between 1939 and 1953, for example, while wages rose only slightly, the price of maize meal rose between 600 and 800 percent, and the prices of many other necessities also rose alarmingly.[2] By 1952, even men who had a job could rarely afford more than one meal a day.[3] Yet, with the major exception of Thomas G. Askwith, the Municipal African Affairs Officer for Nairobi, no one in Kenya's Government recognized the seriousness of African homelessness and poverty.

Meanwhile these Africans were continually reminded of their destitute condition by the conspicuous affluence of most Europeans and many of Nairobi's Indians, who usually dressed well, if not elegantly by European standards, lived in large houses, and drove fine cars. African men typically wore a pair of tattered European trousers, a badly frayed shirt, a ragged woolen sweater, a threadbare suit coat, and a floppy felt hat. At night and on cold days many wore khaki overcoats captured from the Italian army in World War II, or ragged topcoats that would have been rejected by any Goodwill Center in the United States. Although most men wore shoes, they usually lacked laces, and few men could afford socks. Some wore rubber sandals made from old tires. Women, who were almost always barefooted, wore dresses made of cheap cotton or a kind of calico known as "Amerikani," usually covered by a sweater or a man's suit coat. Most women covered their heads with a cotton cloth, but some, particularly older women, shaved their heads and left them bare. Many of these African men and women could not afford a change of clothing.

For the most part, white Kenyans and Indians treated Africans they met in Nairobi like "bloody niggers"; even the more polite term, "native," was quite rightly taken as an insult by many Africans. Rudeness was expected from Indians and Europeans alike, but whether it came from a large blue-turbaned Sikh whose black beard was secured by a matching blue hair net, or from a small white child eating an ice cream cone, its predictability did nothing to lessen the resentment that grew as jobless and homeless people gathered to share their grievances. Young men whose fathers could not afford to pay their school fees had reason to be angry when they saw that good jobs required a European education. Those who were fortunate enough to be able to go to school, and later found a job, had to accept the fact that by government policy an Indian in the same position would be paid more than they were. The more educated among them were humiliated by discriminatory laws, such as those that made it illegal for any African to own firearms or to drink "hard" liquor such as whiskey or gin. As late as 1952, Jomo Kenyatta was embarrassed at a public gathering when he had to hide his whiskey for fear that Europeans would report him to the police.[4]

The rebellious mood of these angry Africans was also fueled by what they saw was an outrageously unequal standard of justice. African policemen, almost always recruited from tribes other than the Kikuyu, routinely stopped and abused the Kikuyu in Nairobi. If the accused man or woman did not quickly offer a bribe, he or she was often beaten. If they were charged with a criminal offense, Africans were not privileged to have a jury trial. Unlike Europeans who did have this right, Africans were tried by a magistrate advised by tribal elders representing the accused's tribe. Where the Kikuyu were concerned, these elders represented the interests of wealthy and pro-British Kikuyu, not those of the young, landless men who were typically charged with crimes. Africans in Nairobi also took note of the ways in which Europeans accused of crimes against Africans were treated before the bar of justice. For example, as late as June 6, 1952, when a young European named Richard Gerrick was charged in Nairobi with assaulting an African by beating him on the head with a revolver, he was found guilty and fined £5 (about $14). On a second charge, that of possessing a firearm without a license, he was also convicted. The fine for that offense was £20.[5] This disparity in punishment was typical and did not go unnoticed by Africans.

Angry, with no hope of finding employment, and harassed by the police, many young Kikuyu organized themselves into street gangs. Armed with knives and pangas—the African equivalent of machetes—they terrorized Nairobi's slums by robbing and extorting money from non-Kikuyu Africans and Asians. The most powerful of these gangs, the Forty Group, controlled most of the prostitutes who served Asian men, and also controlled the illegal trade in European beer. So named because most of its members were circumcised in 1940, the Forty Group was more than a criminal organization. It had connections with other Kikuyu political organizations, and it had plans to make Kenya independent. The Kenya Police Special Branch (charged with intelligence) learned through an informant who had infiltrated the Forty Group that its members had decided, in October 1947, that all Europeans had to be driven out of Kenya.[6] Some members of the group took an oath to obey orders and to kill if necessary. One member of the Forty Group was a 32-year-old half-Kikuyu named Fred Kubai, who would soon play a leading role in the development of Mau Mau.

Kikuyu farm laborers in the "white highlands" felt very much as their fellows in Nairobi did. These laborers worked almost every day for very low wages and a small ration of maize meal. Some of them noted grimly that many dogs owned by Europeans ate better food than the owners' African servants did.[7] Women with babies on their backs joined men in the daily grind of agricultural work, sometimes in drenching rain, sometimes under a hot sun. It was seldom a comfortable life or a secure one. The laborers, who were usually referred to as "squatters," lived in constant fear that they would be fired, because a man could be fired for any reason including a few days' illness. Many had been fired in the 1930s as a result of the worldwide depression, and later the advent of farm machinery displaced many others. To make matters worse for these Kikuyu, most of whom owned no land of their own, the law required that any laborer who was fired had to move his family and all his belongings away from his employer's land within a few days. Unless a man was lucky enough to find another job immediately, he could not remain in the highlands because it was illegal to stay even for a single night with friends or relatives who worked on another estate. If a man who lost his job chose to break the law by wandering through the highlands looking for work, he and his family members risked abuse, humiliation, and arrest. The only alternative was to return to the Kikuyu Reserve with the hope that already hardpressed relatives would offer support.[8]

Africans had once been able to joke that when Europeans came to Kenya, they had Bibles and the Africans had land, but now the Europeans had the land and Africans had the Bibles. Now, faced with constant reminders of their helplessness as squatters in the highlands, they became embittered, their faces barely masking their fear and hostility.[9] Most squatters signed a contract, usually for three years, committing themselves to work 270 days per year for an employer in return for about 8–10 shillings per month and the right to cultivate a small plot of land (usually an acre) and pasture a few sheep or goats (but no cattle). Some white settlers would not even allow goats because they destroyed pasturage and damaged trees; that goats were essential for all Kikuyu religious rituals was irrelevant. When the white farmers evicted these people, their contracts offered no protection.[10] Some landless people who did not return to the Kikuyu Reserve often sought employment in Rift Valley towns such as Nakuru or Naivasha, where they lived in squalor.[11]

In earlier times, Africans who worked as rickshaw "boys" in Nairobi had amused themselves by making up jingles like this:

> Great and wise and wonderful is the European.
> He came into our land with his wisdom and his might.
> He made wars to cease.
> He causes our fields to bring forth plenty
> And our flocks to increase.
> He gives us great riches, and then—
> He takes them all away again in taxes.
> Great and wise and wonderful is the European.[12]

Now, instead of bitter jingles, discontented Kikuyu men and women made up songs and slogans about land and freedom. And some of them, like the men of the Forty Group in Nairobi, began to make plans that called for more than singing. They planned to drive the whites out of Kenya.

Although the Kikuyu Reserve was ringed by white farms and administered by white officials, the white Kenyans living there had little understanding of the tensions that were driving more than one million Kikuyu toward armed rebellion. In 1952, the District Commissioner at Nyeri, the most militant of the Kikuyu districts, wrote, "I do not think one settler in a hundred had set foot in the Reserve. They had gone through to Nairobi on the main road and had fished in the Chania and Gura rivers, but I do not think there was one who knew what life and agriculture in the Reserve really meant."[13]

What white Kenyans saw as they drove past the Kikuyu Reserve was Kikuyu women, usually with a child tied on their backs, bent forward at the waist, their legs perfectly straight as they tilled the red ochrous soil that was just like the soil on the whites' own farms. They also saw African boys dressed only in a filthy shirt herding sheep and goats, just as they did for their white employers. White Kenyans would have breathed in the same clear, cool air that the Kikuyu did, tinged by the aromatic smoke from hundreds of cedar log fires, and they may have noticed forested ridges, crystal streams in the valleys, green pastures dotted with white clover and solitary fig trees, thought sacred by the Kikuyu. They probably saw Kikuyu men sitting, talking, drinking tea and walking to and fro, seemingly aimless and untroubled. To the white Kenyans, the countryside was as tranquil as it was beautiful. Sometimes they clucked their tongues at the sight of big-bellied children, their hair yellowed by kwashiorkor, their noses perpetually running, flies gathered on their inflamed eyes. They were inclined to blame such sights on African ignorance and neglect, not poverty. They probably would have been astonished to learn that 90 percent of the Kikuyu recruits for the British Army in World War II had to be rejected because of malnutrition, primarily due to a lack of animal protein in their diets.[14] They saw what they wished to see and they did not notice that beneath its apparent tranquility the Kikuyu Reserve was a tormented place.

Much of the torment was a result of the British decision to create powerful chiefs, a practice that created deep divisions in Kikuyu society. When the men of the IBEA first contacted the Kikuyu, not all Kikuyu fought against them. Some willingly served them as porters, guides, interpreters, or bodyguards, and others supplied provisions. It was these men, many of them rogues, all of them eager for power and wealth, whom the British first appointed as chiefs. In traditional Kikuyu culture there was no position of authority like that of a "chief," although some men came to exercise power through the force of their personality or their accomplishments. Instead of chiefs, the Kikuyu were governed—or more accurately, guided—by a council of elders. Nevertheless, many among the British newcomers assumed that every African society must have chiefs, more or less as European societies did. A few realized that even if the Kikuyu did not recognize chiefs, they nevertheless could not be ruled effectively without the help of men who had the authority to speak for and control them. And so "chiefs" were appointed and charged with the responsibility for maintaining order, collecting taxes, recruiting labor, and dealing with minor offenses. As we have seen these chiefs were not men of prestige or standing in Kikuyu society, nor were they elders—most were simply opportunists who were eager and able to enforce British rule. One of the men the British appointed soon after they arrived was a landless hunter without property of his own named Kinyanjui. He soon became one of the wealthiest and most powerful of Kikuyu chiefs.[15]

The chiefs' power derived from the armed might of the British, who authorized them to govern by force if need be. Their wealth came from their ruthlessness. Accompanied by an armed entourage of "tribal police," these early British-appointed chiefs extorted money from virtually everyone in their district, appropriating livestock, demanding plots of land, and ordering attractive women to sleep with them. Those who protested were killed.[16] Although chiefs tempered their use of violence over time, even during the period of Mau Mau and into the post-independence era a location chief could cane someone who did not remove his hat and bow at the sight of him, and could arrest someone who inadvertently coughed while he was addressing a meeting.[17]

In time, the flagrant use of force was replaced by more subtle, but no less enriching forms of abuse, such as taking bribes for actions involving court cases, land disputes, forced labor, or taxation. Most chiefs were remarkably successful in enriching themselves. By 1912, Kinyanjui had acquired land, many cattle, and over 100 wives; by the 1920s, many chiefs, including Kinyanjui, lived in large British-style stone houses, had many tenant farmers to work their large farms, and, more remarkable still, owned expensive automobiles.[18] Some white settlers could not live as well. As time passed, many of these early chiefs and their families consolidated their wealth. Although by 1952 there was a growing number of newly-prosperous farmer-traders, most of the richest Kikuyu were chiefs and their families. Some built up coteries of devoted followers by sharing some of their wealth, but most did not; and by 1952, the wealth and power of the chiefs had left the poor Kikuyu over whom they ruled deeply resentful.

Other factors also fueled Kikuyu hostility. In the late 1940s the colonial administration became aware of what it perceived as an agricultural crisis in the Kikuyu reserves, brought about by soil erosion, overstocking, continuous cultivation, and other practices that British agricultural officers believed were counter-productive. Without consulting the Kikuyu themselves, the government decided that the solution lay in specifying which crops could be grown, and in terracing the land to prevent further erosion. Chiefs were ordered to compel Kikuyu women to dig terraces. Despite bitter protests, Kikuyu women were forced to dig three mornings every week, along with planting grass seeds and doing additional work on the chiefs' own land. The work was very hard and the reasons for it were misunderstood. Terracing was not a part of traditional Kikuyu agriculture. Kikuyu farmers saw the solution to declining agricultural yields to be more land, not terraces and not restrictions on the kind of crops they could grow. Moreover, there was widespread suspicion that the land was being terraced to make it ready for European occupation. The terracing program was continued through 1952, with the result that ordinary Kikuyu farmers became seriously discontented.[19] The terracing program still further widened the gap between the chiefs and the people, and, once again, most white settlers were unconcerned about a crisis that was bringing more and more Kikuyu into sympathy with the Mau Mau movement.

Another deep rift in Kikuyu society was created by missionaries from the African Inland Mission (AIM), who first opened their doors to con- verts in Kikuyuland in 1903.[20] Initially, many Kikuyu sought out the mis- sionaries in search of Western education or personal advantage; later they hoped that the missionaries would protect them against the tyranny of the chiefs. Soon a division emerged between the Christian converts and other Kikuyu, often including members of their own families, who continued to maintain traditional religious beliefs and practices.

An even more serious rift took place in 1929, when AIM and its Afri- can converts attempted to prohibit the traditional Kikuyu practice of circumcising girls prior to marriage. For reasons that remain obscure, the church did not object to the Kikuyu practice of circumcising teen-aged boys, but it regarded the circumcision of adolescent girls as barbaric. The Kikuyu, like many other African societies, made female circumcision a prerequisite for marriage and for full participation in the traditional world of women. From time to time, groups of girls were circumcised in a traditional ceremony which included the surgical removal of the tip of each girl's clitoris and some portions of her labia minora. The operation, which was performed without anesthetic by old women whose knives would never be mistaken for surgeons' scalpels, was terribly painful, yet most girls bore it bravely and few suffered serious infection or injury as a result.[21] Circumcised women did not lose their ability to enjoy sexual relations, nor was their child-bearing capacity diminished.[22] Nevertheless, the practice offended Christian sensibilities.

Many Kikuyu members of the AIM left the church in protest against its anti-circumcision policy; they were known as *aregi*, while those who supported the policy were known as *kirore*. The two groups hurled insults at one another and there was violence. The aregi formed a new Christian church with its own schools, which later became known as Kikuyu In- dependent Schools, while the kirore remained within the AIM. Antago- nism between the two groups grew worse over the ensuing years and when the Mau Mau rebellion broke out, the aregi largely joined its ranks, while the kirore remained loyal to the British government and fought against the Mau Mau.[23]

Very few Europeans suspected that the battle lines for Mau Mau had already been drawn within Kikuyu society by the division between the families of wealthy Christian chiefs and the poor aregi. Furthermore, before 1950, few recognized the signs of serious discontent among the Kikuyu. Those who did notice signs of trouble were ignored or regarded as alarmists.[24] When the District Commissioner at Fort Hall ended 1947 with a report to the Director of Intelligence and Security that he had heard a rumor from two sources that the Kikuyu would attempt to right their wrongs by killing all the Europeans, his warning was not heeded.[25] Over the next five years settlers were joined by administrative officials and police officers in reporting clear signs of Kikuyu unrest as well as growing indications of Mau Mau activity. Previously secret files of the Kenya and the British Governments contain detailed intelligence reports that should have been sufficient to alarm any reasonably astute officials. That they did not must partly reflect Governor Mitchell's reluctance to accept any evidence that his "multi-racial" policies were failing, as well as the widespread ignorance about the Kikuyu on the part of Mitchell's secretariat.[26] Also, the Kenya Government, along with many white settlers, simply could not believe that the Kikuyu were capable of mounting an armed revolt.

The white settlers had long dismissed the Kikuyu as "cowards," citing what they believed to be their traditional distaste for warfare. Many in government agreed. On July 5, 1951, the Director of Intelligence and Security wrote to the government's member for law and order that one reason why it was unlikely that the Kikuyu would rebel against the government was their "natural cowardice."[27] It would be easier to understand this arrogant dismissal of the Kikuyu as people of no courage if there had not been a long history of Kikuyu protest against British rule and social injustice. That the Kikuyu had fought against British guns from 1890 to 1904 was forgotten.

In dismissing them as cowards, the government was also ignoring a long history of political protest by Kikuyu activists. The first militant protest by the Kikuyu against the British Government of Kenya took place thirty years before the Mau Mau rebellion. It was organized by a 24-year-old government employee named Harry Thuku. The group he led, called the Young Kikuyu Association, protested several government policies, including compulsory hut taxes and labor laws, and especially the kipande identity card system. Thuku, who had once been abused by a drunken European for having the effrontery to dress better than he did,[28] pointed out that any European employee could prevent an African from finding work simply by writing "lazy" or "cheeky" in a man's kipande.[29] He planned to dramatize opposition to the kipande system by enlisting Africans all over Kenya in a concerted movement to throw away the metal kipande containers they were required to wear around their necks. In a speech made early in 1922, Thuku openly accused the Kenya Government of stealing Kikuyu land, and he urged the Kikuyu not to work for the Europeans any longer. He also accused the missionaries of preaching the word of the devil, and added that he hoped all the whites would leave Kenya. In addition to his words of confrontation, Thuku urged all Africans to throw away their kipandes on the lawn of Government House in Nairobi, the seat of the colonial administration.[30] A few days later Thuku was arrested.

Jomo Kenyatta, the man who would be accused of masterminding Mau Mau, joined the crowd of Africans gathered outside the Nairobi central police station where Thuku was held.[31] A line of 150 nervous African policemen with fixed bayonets on their rifles surrounded the jail. At first, the crowd was peaceful, but eventually a number of Kikuyu prostitutes, led by one Mary Nyanjira, began to taunt the policemen. She approached to within a few feet of the police line, and raising her dress above her head, insulted the manhood of the policemen while urging the crowd to rush the jail and release Thuku. Without warning, the police opened fire, killing Nyanjira and many others. Some white Kenyans who were drinking on the veranda of the Norfolk Hotel, which was located across the street from the police station, also began firing into the panicky, fleeing crowd. The next day, the *East African Standard* reported that 25 people had been killed and 27 wounded, but African eyewitnesses estimated the death toll at from 150 to 250.[32] As time passed, accounts sympathetic to the government attempted to dismiss the tragedy by reporting that "some Kikuyu were shot,"[33] that there was "some loss of life," or that "a number" were killed.[34] When the official Kenya Government "Corfield Report" about the causes of Mau Mau was published in 1960, it declared confidently that only 3 Africans had been killed.[35] The testimony of an African who said that he had counted 56 bodies in a morgue was dismissed.[36] As for Harry Thuku, he was exiled for a period of 9 years in what is now Somalia. He was never put on trial.

During Thuku's exile, his organization was replaced in 1925 by the Kikuyu Central Association (KCA). Although the issues remained the same, it was obvious that protests would have to be made more circumspectly. It was also obvious soon enough that unlike Thuku's organization, this one would appeal only to the Kikuyu. Three years after the birth of the KCA, Jomo Kenyatta became its general secretary. Kenyatta had first come to the notice of whites in 1909, when he presented himself at a Scottish mission station, the kind that favored cold baths and vigorous "physical jerks." He was a naked herd boy who appeared to be 11 or 12 years old; his name then was Kamau Ngengi. He made little progress with English or his other studies, and although he remained at the mission five years, he received no special attention. He was baptized as K. N. Johnstone. Later, while working as a water meter reader in Nairobi, the young man began to wear a beaded Maasai belt called *akinyata* and he soon began telling everyone that his name was "Kenyatta."[37]

After years of living by his wits in Nairobi, where he admitted to indulging in an over-fondness for women and strong drink, Kenyatta became a full-time employee of the KCA, apparently because he knew some English and was resourceful. He was the first African in Kenya to own a motor bike, which he rode everywhere. His reputation as a young man of promise grew.[38] In 1929, KCA's leader, James Beauttah, recommended that Kenyatta be sent to London in the hope that he could make contacts that would further the cause of Kenya's Africans. Beauttah chose not to go to England himself because he did not want to leave his family.[39] Kenyatta felt differently. Leaving his wife and two small children behind, he sailed for England.

Now calling himself Johnstone Kenyatta, he arrived in London with very little money and barely passable English. The idea that one man, a scarcely educated Kikuyu alone in London, could make a difference for Kenya's future was preposterous; but Kenyatta's magnetic presence, his great, resonant voice, his riveting eyes and his masterful sense of showmanship quickly made him friends and supporters in left-wing circles. During Kenyatta's early days in England he was known as a frivolous dandy who affected flamboyant costumes, brandished a walking stick, waved his large red-stone ring like Merlin the magician, and seduced British women whenever he could. He also took advantage of several people who befriended him.

Kenyatta made a trip to the Soviet Union that same year, followed by another in 1932–33. Little is known about his activities, but it is clear that the Soviets attempted to indoctrinate him as a revolutionary and a future leader of African liberation.[40] On his return trip to England he travelled through Germany, where he attended one of Hitler's earliest mass meetings. What Kenyatta thought of Hitler is not clear, but he may have absorbed some of Hitler's skills in controlling a large crowd. When he returned to London he became somewhat, if not entirely, more serious, and his close association with two West Indian radical intellectuals, George Padmore and C. L. R. James, did much to increase his political sophistication.[41]

Slowly, his message was being heard. Much of it was the same as Harry Thuku's had been, but Kenyatta remained abreast of events in Kenya, and raised new issues. In 1936, for example, he wrote an article in the *New Statesman* complaining that the Kenya Government had alienated African farm land around Kakamega to accommodate Europeans who were hoping to find gold.[42] He soon became convinced that only "detribalized" Africans could break the grip of colonial rule, because only they could move beyond the constraints of tribal tradition. He personally embodied that idea with his Savile Row suits, his flair for European wit, and his growing knowledge of revolutionary politics. Most important, he was a natural leader. He commanded attention with his showmanship, his imposing figure, and his increasing mastery of English. By the mid-1930s, his command of the language had become as remarkable as his voice, although he had a marked accent that would remain with him all his life.

Kenyatta's vision of himself as the man who would free Kenya was no less remarkable, considering that he was deeply in debt, without income—except for rare contributions from the KCA—and without the apparent ability to improve his own bleak fortunes, much less liberate his homeland. Yet thanks to a fortuitous introduction to a famous anthropologist at the University of London, Bronislaw Malinowski, he was able to study in a university setting (his classmates included Louis Leakey and Elspeth Huxley), and he learned a good deal about anthropology. Sir Raymond Firth, another distinguished anthropologist who knew Kenyatta at the University of London, praised his academic work.[43] With Malinowski's encouragement, he wrote a book, *Facing Mt. Kenya*, that provides a still useful if idealized description of the Kikuyu. Kenyatta's photograph appeared on the cover of the book; he was cloaked in a hyrax and blue monkey fur robe borrowed from a fellow Kikuyu, the soon-to-be influential, American-educated Peter Mbiu Koinange. In the photograph, Kenyatta pensively fingered the tip of a spear.[44] The book sold only 517 copies in its first printing (it is still available in paperback editions) but it created a stir, partly because Kenyatta vigorously defended female circumcision, and partly because Malinowski gave the book his endorsement. The book was rejected by white Kenyans as Kikuyu propaganda, but it was not that at all. It was a description of Kikuyu culture, and it gave Kenyatta an intellectual and social stature that he had hitherto lacked.

Because he had decided that the leader of a movement for liberation from colonial oppression should not have a "colonial" name like Johnstone, his name on the book appeared as Jomo Kenyatta. With the help of Peter Mbiu Koinange, whose political sophistication acquired while earning a Master's degree from Columbia University came in handy, Kenyatta invented the name, "Jomo." It sounded revolutionary to him, and it was similar to the Kikuyu word for the sound made when a sword was pulled out of its scabbard.[45] After urgings from the KCA, Kenyatta agreed to return to Kenya but while he was preparing to do so, World War II broke out and he was forced to remain in England, where he stayed throughout the war. He spent most of this time in the village of Storrington in Sussex, 40 miles outside London. Before Kenyatta originally left for England, he had taken an oath of loyalty to the KCA that included a pledge not to marry a white woman. Nevertheless, he married a 32-year-old governess named Edna Clark and fathered a child.

Despite his past visits to Moscow, his close association with the former Communist George Padmore, and the belief of British intelligence that he had joined the Communist Party, Kenyatta was paid to lecture to British soldiers, including Africans serving in the army, about Africa. It is intriguing to imagine what he told them. Now about 50 years old or so, Kenyatta was short and stocky, but he cut such an imposing figure that the villagers of Storrington called him "Jumbo," a nickname he disliked. Nevertheless, if any of his contemporaries in England thought that he would become the first African head of state of Kenya, they neglected to record their convictions at the time.[46]

During the 1930s, while Kenyatta was in England, the KCA emerged as the main voice of African protest in Kenya. Land was still the key issue, but jobs and unionization were important too, as was eliminating social injustice. Throughout this period, the leaders of KCA did everything they could to keep Kenyatta's name alive as Kenya's hope for the future, but with the outbreak of war in 1940, the KCA was banned as a threat to security, its small Swahili-language newspaper was shut down, and several of its officers arrested. During the war years, land continued to be the central question for Kenya, but Kenya's white community had been asked by the British Government to supply food for the war effort, and they insisted that their patriotic duty made any compromise about land unthinkable. The record profits they were making were not mentioned.

For many young Kikuyu, the early years of World War II were a time of intense excitement and revolutionary fervor. Boys from 10 to 16 dressed as traditional Kikuyu warriors, their heads adorned with long feathers, their ankles bound with rattles made from tin cans filled with

stones. Brandishing wooden swords, they danced as warriors of old, singing defiant songs that swore them to fight against any enemies, especially
the military forces of the British Empire. Young men in their twenties
also sang defiantly, but their songs were less exuberant, prophesying
many deaths despite great bravery, and they mournfully deplored the
poverty that gripped the Kikuyu people.[47] Many of these young men
nursed juvenile dreams of martial glory, but others bitterly resented white
dominance and gave thought to political resistance. Despite their doubts,
as hard-pressed British forces fell back from Axis attacks in 1940 and
1941, this mood of rebellion changed and tens of thousands of Kikuyu
men answered the call to defend the British Empire. Almost 100,000
young men who might otherwise have continued their protests for more
land would soon be overseas serving in the British Army.

In 1944, while Kenyatta marked time in England, the leaders of the
Kikuyu Central Association were released from detention. Along with
older militant leaders like James Beauttah, younger men began to set
plans for continuing their protests against the government. They agreed
to use strikes, demonstrations, and even political terror in their campaign for land and for an end to social injustice, but their preparations
led to little of significance. What mattered most for the protest movement took place on the morning of September 24, 1946, at Mombasa:
Jomo Kenyatta returned to Kenya.

With characteristic showmanship, Kenyatta was the first person off the
ship. He walked down the gangplank alone. Kenyatta had left his English
wife, pregnant with their second child, behind. He abandoned her so
abruptly that his friends in England thought him brutal. There were no
plans for the couple to be reunited.[48] Like his former name, Johnstone,
an English wife would be a liability in the struggle for independence.
Besides, his pledge to the KCA not to marry a white woman might have
been remembered. He was met in Mombasa by a KCA-organized depu-
tation of Kikuyu including his first wife, Grace Wahu, his son, now 25,
and his daughter, now 18.[49] Easily recognizing him by his distinctive Van
Dyke beard, the dock workers thronged to Kenyatta, leaving the white
passengers to fend for themselves. Kenyatta took the train to Nairobi,
where an enormous crowd was waiting to carry him on their shoulders
out of the station. As he was driven through Nairobi toward his home in
Kiambu, crowds of Africans enthusiastically sang, trilled, and cheered.
Their leader had returned.

Peter Mbiu Koinange had arranged for Kenyatta's old KCA friends to welcome him in Kiambu. James Beauttah was amazed and pleased that Kenyatta remembered the names of everyone he met even though he had not seen any of these men for 15 years.[50] Likewise, no one who met Kenyatta would forget him. Carrying an elephant-headed ebony walking stick, usually dressed in a leather or tweed jacket and flannel pants, with his beard and trademark beaded belt, he would never be mistaken for anyone else in Kenya. But it was Kenyatta's eyes that people most re- membered. His gaze intimidated people; many white Kenyans felt ema- nations of evil from his eyes, perhaps because they were hooded and almost as red as the huge carnelian signet ring he always wore on the little finger of his left hand.[51] It was as large as a napkin ring. For most Kikuyu he was the "*mzee*," the elder, the promised one who would lead them to freedom and procure the return of their land.

Kenyatta had enormous popularity in Kenya, but many of the tradi- tional tribal leaders of the Kikuyu—including the British-appointed Christian chiefs, strongly supported the government. Fortunately for Kenyatta, Peter Koinange's father had succeeded Kinyanjui as senior chief in 1929. For years, the elder Koinange had supported government policies, but now he was embittered. The old chief and Kenyatta quickly forged an alliance which Koinange sealed by giving Kenyatta one of his daughters as his third wife. Kenyatta was installed at the nearby Kenya Teacher's College where he served as the school's president. He planted a shield and two crossed spears on his lawn, filled his large personal library with books by Nietzsche, Schopenhauer, H. G. Wells, and Gals- worthy, among others,[52] and on his walls he hung photographs of Lenin, Paul Robeson, and Jawaharlal Nehru—enough to horrify any white Ken- yan.[53] Somehow, despite the critical shortage of land in Kiambu, he ac- quired a 300-acre farm.[54] Kiambu was an ideal base for Kenyatta. Located just north of Nairobi, it was the district that held the richest, best edu- cated, and most politically astute Kikuyu.

Kenyatta believed that freedom for Kenya's Africans could not be achieved by the Kikuyu alone; it would have to come as the result of a national movement. Accordingly, he organized a new political body, the Kenya African Union, known as KAU (pronounced "cow") to replace the tribally-based Kikuyu Central Association. With the help of Chief Ko- inange and the traditional, conservative politicians of Kiambu, KAU quickly enrolled 150,000 members. KAU's executive committee met every Thursday night at Chief Koinange's comfortable, European-style house, called Banana Hill, and they soon became known as the Kiambu "Parliament." Like the KCA before it, the organizers of KAU needed a means of assuring the loyalty of its members and creating a sense of unity and purpose. They chose a traditional Kikuyu device, an oath.

The Kikuyu, like many other East African societies, employed a variety of oaths in traditional life. Oaths might be required to prove one's innocence in legal cases, to pledge one's loyalty before going to war, or to show devotion during religious ceremonies. Even educated young men who no longer "believed" in such oaths were often eager to take them to prove that they had not impregnated a particular young woman. Just as swearing on a Bible had great significance for many Europeans, these oaths were surrounded by powerful sacred symbols that most Kikuyu believed had the power to kill if the oaths were violated. As early as 1925, leaders of the KCA used an oath to insure its members' loyalty, but this oath was not traditional; indeed, it used a Bible as one of its central symbols.[55] In contrast, the KAU oath would return to Kikuyu traditions. Kenyatta was among the first to take KAU's simple oath of obedience:

> If you ever argue when called,
> If you ever disobey your leader,
> If called upon in the night and you fail to come
> May this oath kill you.

As this oath spread and KAU attempted to extend its influence throughout Kenya, white Kenya was becoming increasingly resistant to African pressure. The influx of officer settlers to Kenya after World War II that brought large numbers of frankly racist families to Kenya had been reinforced by the still more highly conservative body of officers and their families who left India in 1947, when the British granted independence. Their accounts of the terrible violence that spread through India at the time of its partition alarmed many settlers, and the new Indian Government's open support of African liberation movements increased tensions between white Kenyans and Africans.[56] Kenyatta's display of a photograph of Nehru was as inflammatory as his photograph of Lenin.

To implement its plan of settling the ex-soldiers in the highlands, the Kenya Government chose Major Ferdinand W. Cavendish-Bentinck, heir to the Dukedom of Portland. "C.B.," as he was known, was an extreme conservative who was trusted by the settlers to represent their interests. Kikuyu leaders were greatly alarmed by this appointment, as they were by the discovery that the government was preparing a plan that would ensure white political control of Kenya for decades to come. Although this "Kenya Plan," as it was known, was not officially released until 1949, leaks about its proposals for continued white supremacy spread widely among the Kikuyu in 1948, and particularly angered the young radicals in Nairobi who made plans to oppose it.

During 1947 and most of 1948, KAU was publically opposed to militancy. Instead, it presented the same issues that the KCA had in the 1930s and it offered the same largely peaceful solutions. An exception took place in 1947, when Kikuyu workers went out on strike against the Uplands Bacon factory outside of Nairobi, near a place named Lari that would soon become infamous. When the strikers showed signs of becoming violent, the police opened fire, killing three and wounding six others.[57] When another strike loomed, T. G. Askwith, who believed in Kenyatta as a political moderate, asked him to speak against it. Kenyatta agreed. Speaking forcefully and brandishing his elephant-head walking stick, he warned the crowd that "if anyone should talk of striking, I will knock his block off." The strike was averted.

Askwith later wondered why the Kenya Government never tried to work with Kenyatta. In fact the liberal Chief Native Commissioner, P. Wyn Harris, did propose that Kenyatta be brought into the government, but Governor Mitchell rejected the idea, and quickly got rid of Harris by having him promoted to Governor of Gambia. Askwith, himself a public-school boy, attributed the government's refusal to cooperate with Kenyatta to the "public school attitude" that led British administrators not to consult with Africans (just as headmasters did not consult with their boys) but instead to decide what was best for them.[58] That authoritarian attitude clearly existed, but in Kenyatta's case there were other reasons why the government did not choose to consult with him.

Although Kenyatta was struggling to avoid violence, the Kenya Government was convinced the KAU was a dangerous organization, and that Kenyatta as its leader and public spokesman was a menace to Kenya's security. Agents of the Special Branch of the Criminal Investigation Division put him under surveillance, and informants were paid to collect information. As warnings about Mau Mau spread, British administrators, who were impressed and sometimes intimidated by Kenyatta's hypnotic personality and his magnetism, could not imagine that anyone other than he was in charge of the movement. In reality, Special Branch was looking in the wrong place. Control over events had already slipped away from Kenyatta, as he tried to tell disbelieving government officials.[59] Unable to control the young men in Nairobi and the Rift Valley, who had lost all patience with KAU's moderate approaches, and accused by the

Kiambu elders of misappropriating KAU money, Kenyatta lost confidence in his ability to guide political events toward independence. He began drinking heavily, usually downing a bottle of whiskey every day.[60] Dictatorial and moody, he was depressed by his inability to control the young militants; further, he missed the kind of intellectual stimulation he had come to enjoy in London, and he could not bear his obligatory round of attendance at tribal ceremonies.[61] As Kenyatta despaired, Mau Mau and the future of Kenya was being shaped by militant younger men in Nairobi.

Most of the men who organized Mau Mau had served in the British Army during World War II. Their wartime experiences had taught them that the British were only human. They learned that white soldiers were afraid, cried in battle, collapsed with fatigue, and smelled when they sweated. They were emboldened by their new-found sense of equality with white men, but they were disillusioned when they returned to Kenya filled with hope for jobs, land, and the destruction of the color bar, only to find that Kenya was still "white man's country." Many tried to establish themselves as small traders, but few had enough capital to survive the uncertain market, the high government license fees, transportation costs, and the competition of established Asian businessmen. Kikuyu traders who attempted to set up shop in non-Kikuyu areas of Kenya also encountered tribal jealousy and were sometimes reported to the police for allegedly illegal activities.[62] Most failed in business and joined other out-of-work men in the reserves or Nairobi.

A testament to the despair felt by those returning soldiers was expressed by uneducated Kikuyu dock workers in Mombasa a few months after a general strike had shut down the port:

> The European wants the African to be poor.... The European comes and takes everything belonging to them and then asks for brotherhood.... The lion and the goat cannot lie down together. Why is government ... not good to the Africans?[63]

In 1948, the most burning issue was still the unavailability of agricultural land. As the rising Kikuyu birthrate made the land shortage increasingly acute, the Kikuyu looked more and more to the "white highlands" for relief. They could readily see how crowded people were in the reserves and how vast stretches of land in the highlands remained undeveloped.[64] In fact, 3,000 European families owned more arable land in the highlands than was available to the more than one million Kikuyu in their reserves. Many landless men were ready to use violence to free Kenya from what they called "white settler" rule. They were joined by some older men like James Beauttah, who was a decade older than Kenyatta but much more militant, and Makhan Singh, an Indian Communist labor organizer whom the Kenya Government inexplicably allowed to return to Kenya in 1947 after several years of exile in India.[65] Most of the young men in Nairobi had already become disillusioned by what they saw as the timid, conservative leadership of KAU, and had turned to the more radical trade unions in search of a means to improve their fortunes and eventually to free Kenya.

One of the leaders among these radicalized men was Bildad Kaggia. Born the son of a poor tenant farmer, Kaggia did very well in elementary school and was one of a very limited number of Africans who qualified to enter high school. To Kaggia's distress, his father could not afford the school fees so he had to forego high school and go to work as a clerk. During World War II, he served with the British Army in the Middle East where he was influenced by black American soldiers, who were better educated and more politically sophisticated than he was. Later, when he was transferred to Britain, he was shocked to see white men actually doing physical labor as stevedores. He was also amazed by the friendly reception given him by English dock workers and ordinary British working-class families. One family, the Evanses, virtually made him a member of their household. Mrs. Evans was astonished to learn from Kaggia that Englishwomen in Kenya did not do their own cooking and she simply could not understand why a white family in Kenya would need eight servants. Daily contact with white people convinced Kaggia that with education and opportunity, Africans could become the equals of Europeans. Before the war, he had been a devout Christian but now he turned against Christianity and the mission schools, convinced that church teachings had created a sense of inferiority among Africans. In 1948 he was 37 years old, a short, stocky man with metal-rimmed glasses, a receding hairline, and a full beard. Kaggia was one of the men who would launch Mau Mau.[66]

A second and even more influential leader of the Mau Mau was Fred Kubai. Born in Mombasa of a Kikuyu father and Giriama (a coastal people) mother, Kubai had only a primary school education, but he had a quick mind and soon found employment as a telegraphist. As early as 1939, he had publically demanded independence for Kenya.[67] During World War II he remained in Nairobi where he assumed an increasingly important role in the growing trade union movement. A burly man, who unlike Kaggia had never been a Christian, Kubai became a leader in the Forty Group as well as in several trade unions. In 1949 he became the President of the East African Trades Union Congress. A year earlier he had become a member of the ruling central committee of the Mau Mau. Kubai has said that Mau Mau was his "brain-child," and he surely had as much to do with its organizational development as anyone. From 1947 until his arrest in 1952, he was in charge of administering the Mau Mau oath in Nairobi, and of executing anyone who violated it. He was perhaps the most militant of the Mau Mau leaders, and the one most feared within Mau Mau inner circles. In 1948 he was 33 years old.

Late in 1948, the Kiambu "Parliament," along with Kenyatta, agreed that although KAU had been successful in "oathing" large numbers of rural Kikuyu, they had not done well at all with Nairobi's more militant urban population. Kenyatta turned to Kubai, Kaggia, and a few others for help. He did so reluctantly, fearing that he could not control what he referred to as "their dark and uneducated minds."[68] Peter Mbiu Koinange was sent to ask Nairobi's two most powerful union leaders, John Mungai and Fred Kubai, to join the "movement," little imagining that Kubai was already well ahead of KAU in planning for independence. They readily agreed to help, and to take the oath themselves on three conditions: that recruitment no longer be restricted to those who could afford to pay the required fee of 62/50 shillings, that the oath be given to any trustworthy Kikuyu, not just those approved by "Parliament," and that the oath be made more militant. "Parliament" agreed to these conditions, and Mungai and Kubai brought eight of their most trusted colleagues, including Bildad Kaggia, to Banana Hill to take the oath. These ten men, known as the "action group," created Mau Mau.

Kubai carefully recruited 24 trusted union leaders, and a substantial number of carefully selected "criminals," as he called them, who were given the assignment of stealing weapons and ammunition. Mungai enlisted the taxi drivers from his own union, and these men would play a crucial role in the movement by providing secure and dependable transportation for the Mau Mau. Also, more than 400 Nairobi prostitutes were given the oath and ordered to collect information and ammunition. Many began to accept only bullets in payment for their services; depending on the client, the price could range from a single bullet to as many as ten.

The men of the action group took a new and stronger oath, and so did many of those they recruited. This oath originated among some 12,000 Kikuyu squatters who were dispossessed by the government from a prosperous farming area in the Rift Valley known as Olenguruone.

When these people were evicted from the Rift Valley and forced to re-turn to the Kikuyu Reserve where they owned no land, their sense of outrage helped the oath to spread. The oath was more demanding and the ceremony that accompanied it had greater power.[69]

> If you ever disagree with your nation or sell it, may you die of
>   this oath.
> If a member of this Society ever calls on you in the night and you
>   refuse to open your hut to him, may you die of this oath.
> If you ever sell a Kikuyu woman to a foreigner, may you die
>   of this oath.
> If you ever leave a member of this Society in trouble,
>   may you die of this oath.
> If you ever report a member of this Society to the Government,
>   may you die of this oath.

The ceremony, which was patterned after traditional male initiation cer-emonies,[70] involved slaughtering a male goat, of one solid color if pos-sible, collecting its blood in a gourd bowl, and cutting out its chest area. The goat was then skinned and the skin cut into one long thin piece, which was tied together to form a large ring. The oath administrator, who often wore a long white gown, smeared himself with clay or red soil. The persons taking the oath each put on a large necklace of woven grass, and the administrator put the goat skin ring around them. The entrance to the ceremonial area was a traditional Kikuyu arch made of rushes, flanked by stalks of sugar cane and arrowroot. In front of the arch was a trough filled with various kinds of Kikuyu food mixed together with soil and goat's blood. Those to be oathed were cut seven times, (seven was an ominous, an evil number for the Kikuyu), and their blood was mixed with that of the goat in the bowl. (Later on, after the arrest of some of the oathers, the practice of cutting stopped, because the result-ing scars were conclusive evidence of oath taking.) After the oath admin-istrator had encircled the initiates with the skin ring, he asked each one "What are You?" The proper answer was "I am a Kikuyu." As each ini-tiate answered, the administrator made a cross on his forehead with a stick dipped in blood from the bowl, saying that he had been marked on his forehead as a sign of unity with other Kikuyu who would fight for their country's freedom. The oath administrator also said that the cross was a sign of Gikuyu and Mumbi, the mythical parents of the Ki-kuyu people. Finally, initiates had to bite meat from the chest, heart, and lungs of the goat—all of which had first been dipped in the bowl of blood—seven times, and then walk through the arch. They were then taken to a nearby hut for a lecture about the oath and the "movement."

Oathing spread rapidly during 1949 and into 1950. The elders of the Kiambu "Parliament" and the young militants from Nairobi jockeyed for control of KAU while reports of mass oathing, theft, and cattle maiming became so frequent that the government arrested several oath administrators and banned the secret organization they knew only as Mau Mau. The government also closed more than 300 of the Kikuyu Independent Schools, which were accused of indoctrinating their students with nationalist ideology. Over 60,000 students were affected. The government still had little idea what Mau Mau was or might become, and, with a very few exceptions, officials continued to dismiss it as an atavistic religious cult like those developed in previous years by some Christian religious sects. They were particularly offended by the oath ceremonies, which they usually dismissed as "mumbo jumbo," or as "sexual orgies."[71] But in fact the Mau Mau rebellion was almost entirely secular and political. Except for its oaths, the movement's religious trappings were insignificant.

The long-expected political confrontation between KAU's "Parliament" and the urban radicals of the action group came early in 1950, when Fred Kubai's East African Trades Union Congress initiated a highly visible campaign against the British Government's proposal to grant a Royal Charter to the City of Nairobi. It was rumored that the charter would bring several surrounding districts under Nairobi's European-controlled city government, and that Nairobi would be declared a "whites only" city. In protest, Kubai's men planned two assassinations. First, there was an abortive attempt to kill Tom Mbotela, a pro-government, moderate, non-Kikuyu leader of KAU.[72] Next, Nairobi City Councillor Muchohi Gikonyo was attacked. Both attempts failed, partly because the gunmen were drunk.[73] Soon thereafter, Kubai and Makhan Singh publicly demanded independence for East Africa. When, predictably enough, they were arrested, other officers of the trade unions—and members of Mau Mau—ordered a general strike that lasted 18 days and erupted into violence before being put down by police and soldiers using armored cars and—for the first time in Kenya—tear gas.[74] The strike vividly symbolized the contrast between the restraint of the KAU moderates and the more violent tactics of the "action group." By early 1951, the young Nairobi militants had firm control over the movement to free Kenya, and violence was central to their plans.

While Kenyatta and the other leaders of KAU were still attempting to build a nationwide coalition out of Kenya's many tribal peoples, the young men in Nairobi were consolidating a militant movement that was almost exclusively Kikuyu. It was not surprising that a movement led by Kikuyu, and unified by a Kikuyu oath, would have its greatest appeal for fellow Kikuyu, but the leaders of Mau Mau nevertheless attempted to bring men and women from other Kenya peoples into the movement. Some people from the Luo, Luhya, Kamba, and Maasai joined, as did larger numbers from the closely related Embu and Meru peoples, but recruitment went very slowly. The Kikuyu were unpopular with many of Kenya's other Africans. Kikuyu traders had alienated people in many parts of Kenya with their aggressiveness and arrogance. Moreover, African migrants to Nairobi were often treated badly by Kikuyu landlords who owned most of the housing available to Africans, and by Kikuyu street gangs that intimidated and tyrannized newcomers.[75] Many of Kenya's Africans yearned for independence but they were leery about trusting the Kikuyu to lead them.

Although the older, more conservative leaders of KAU who made up the Kiambu "Parliament" had lost control over their country's independence movement, they did not yet know it, and the young leaders of Mau Mau took great pains to make certain they did not find out. KAU had to remain visibly vibrant as a symbol of a national "movement," and, perhaps even more importantly, as a recognized organization that could be used as a platform for pursuing the foreign support that the leaders of Mau Mau hoped would be forthcoming. Kenyatta would have to remain as the symbolic head of KAU, but he could not be made aware of the action group's plans because he was followed everywhere by the Special Branch and, just as importantly, because he would not have approved of the plans for the use of violence. And so, in a splendid irony, Kenyatta— the supposed mastermind of Mau Mau—was never privy to details of the planning that led to Mau Mau. Bildad Kaggia said that Kenyatta "knew nothing" about the organization of Mau Mau, and Fred Kubai agreed.[76] Yet Kenya's white population never doubted that Kenyatta was the evil genius behind the movement, its "puppet-master," as his one-time fellow student, Elspeth Huxley, put it.[77]

Kenyatta not only remained as the acknowledged leader of KAU, he was sent all over Kenya to enlist widespread support for national liberation. Accompanied by Fred Kubai, and others, he had remarkable success. The Mombasa branch of KAU was brought back to life, and in Western Kenya tremendous crowds of Luo and Luhya came to hear his speeches. In all, Kenyatta made more than 100 speeches across the country, and people flocked to hear him and to join the KAU. Many of these crowds became unruly, and on July 26, 1952, the 25,000 people he attracted to a rally at Nyeri were so truculent that even Kenyatta had difficulty calming them. The police, who were badly shaken by the explosive atmosphere, restricted all future KAU meetings to Nairobi, where they felt better able to exercise crowd control.

The government now put tremendous pressure on Kenyatta to denounce Mau Mau. The clear message was that if he did not, he would be arrested. The government gave him a challenge he could not side-step when in August 1952, they arranged for him to speak to a large crowd in Kiambu where, unlike Nyeri, which was known for its militancy, the people were thought to be cool on Mau Mau. Kenyatta denounced Mau Mau so convincingly that the leaders of the movement called him to meet with them in Nairobi. They warned him to temper his criticism and they were not gentle about it; the young leaders of Mau Mau were ready to kill Kenyatta if he continued to criticize the movement.[78] This confrontation was Kenyatta's first meeting with what had become Mau Mau's "Central Committee," and he was stunned to see that Kubai, Kaggia, and other young men whose "dark and uneducated minds" he feared were now giving orders to him.

The leaders of the movement for land and freedom did not call their organization "Mau Mau." They referred to their rebellion as "the movement," "Muhimu" (Swahili for important), "muingi" (the community), "our government," the "African government," the "Gikuyu and Mumbi society," "land and freedom," "the KCA," and various other names. Eliud Mutonyi, Chairman of the Central Committee, said that the movement's name was "The Freedom Struggle Association."[79] But this name did not catch on. Eventually, the name "Land and Freedom Army" became most common. Nevertheless, the words "Mau Mau" had been heard as early as 1947, and by 1949 they were so common that oath administrators had to warn initiates that the organization they had just vowed to die for was *not* called Mau Mau.

There is still no agreement about the origin of the name "Mau Mau" or its meaning. Not even former members of the Central Committee can agree. One common explanation is that when the Kenya Police broke into an oathing ceremony in Naivasha, the administrator yelled, "Mau Mau," which was a form of Kikuyu pig-latin (known to all Kikuyu children) that transposed the words, "*uma uma*," meaning, "out out." After that, according to this version, the police and Kikuyu alike began to refer to the movement as Mau Mau. Another explanation came from a Mau Mau military leader known as General China who reported that the name originated when the Kenya Police interrogated a Maasai who had recently taken the oath. The man reportedly said that he had taken part in "Mumau," mispronouncing *muma*, the Kikuyu word for oath. The police report misspelled it "Maumau."[80] This version is plausible, but a third equally plausible explanation is that a fiercely pro-government Christian preacher from the Rift Valley, named Parmenas Kiritu, referred to the movement as "mau mau," using a children's anagram that meant "a childish thing."[81] It has also been suggested that "Mau Mau" meant greedy eating in the Kikuyu language. But it is more likely that this explanation was invented well after the fact, as were the many versions of what the double "m's" might be made to stand for in support of the "movement."

What matters most for understanding this period in Kenya's history is that the whites in Kenya, and the British Government that supported them, knew the movement as Mau Mau. They did so partly because they believed that what they feared as a primitive "secret society" had actually been given this mysterious name, but also because some leaders among them did not want the movement to be seen by the world community as a rational political organization fighting for land and freedom. Thus, when Sir Oliver Lyttleton, Secretary of State for the colonies, visited Kenya shortly after the government had declared a State of Emergency, members of the Christian Council of Kenya, led by Bishop Beecher, told him categorically that the cause of Mau Mau was economic. Yet, a few days later, Lyttleton informed the press that "Mau Mau is not the child of economic conditions."[82] He said that Mau Mau instead was a primitive, irrational attack against the forces of law and order.

The Mau Mau movement was directed by what they usually called "Muhimu," or the Central Committee. The Central Committee consisted of 12 men, including Kubai and Kaggia, with Eliud Mutonyi as its chairman. When the police began to make arrests at oathing ceremonies, the Central Committee created another group, known as the "30 Committee," to direct oathing and to shield the true directorate from government detection. Under the direction of Fred Kubai, the 30 men on this committee were responsible for coordinating the activities of local leaders in the tribal reserves and townships.[83] In addition, the leaders of Mau Mau were advised by what they called the KAU Study Circle, a kind of brain trust composed of four or five KAU members and an equal number of outsiders who were sympathetic to KAU's stated goals. These men prepared background research on policy matters that the Central Committee might need to address in Kenya, as well as international concerns, especially ways of attracting foreign support.

Curious as it may seem in retrospect, the leaders of Mau Mau allowed three non-Africans to serve on the Study Circle. One, Pio de Gama Pinto, was a Goan. Two were Europeans: Peter Wright, a former professor of history at Cawnpore, India, who served as a Lieutenant-Colonel in the British Intelligence Corps during World War II, and John P. B. Miller, a former Royal Navy Lieutenant Commander, then a resident of Kenya. The Study Circle originally met in the Nairobi offices of the Indian National Congress, and later, as police surveillance tightened, in private homes. Even so their activities were uncovered. In July 1952, Commander Miller was appointed Provincial Education Officer for the Coast and moved from Nairobi to Mombasa. The government then restricted Miller to the Coast; he would have no further contact with KAU. Gama Pinto was detained without charge, and, in November, Stephen Wright's living quarters were searched. It was reported that "incriminating" documents were found, and Wright was expelled from Kenya without a hearing. Wright, who was the principal of an Indian high school in Nairobi, protested that he had always deplored subversion or violence, had only been working toward inter-racial cooperation, and was "certainly not a Communist." Despite Wright's complaints to the British Government, the deportation order stood.

These were heady times. Like revolutionaries throughout history, the leaders of Mau Mau lived with intense excitement, a growing sense of power, and constant fear of detection and arrest. Members of the Central Committee took taxis to Kiambu to meet with leaders of "Parliament," gathered in late-night sessions at Kiburi House in Nairobi, and when police attention was drawn to that location, the leaders of Mau Mau conducted business in houses in Nairobi's largely Kikuyu slum of Pumwani. The movement's leaders had little time for their families; they faced too many problems. For one thing, they had to solidify their intelligence network by convincing well-placed Kikuyu clerks in government employment to provide information of government intentions. Some of these educated young men aided Mau Mau willingly, but others had to be bribed or seduced by the young women of the movement. Eventually, this campaign was so successful that the Central Committee had access to most government plans; Mau Mau clerks at Government House removed secret files at night, returning them before morning.

The acquisition of guns and ammunition was a more difficult problem.

Kenya's white government had long ago passed laws that made it virtually impossible for Africans to own guns. It was even very difficult to
steal weapons because most whites locked their weapons in "gun safes"
when they were not in use. A few illicit dealers would sell handguns but
only at high cost and risk.[84] Stanley Mathenge, who would later become
a prominent Mau Mau military leader, was chosen by the Central Committee to lead an operation to steal guns directly from the police.
Mathenge's men would follow a lone policeman, waiting for an opportunity to steal his pistol or rifle. If need be the policeman was killed and his
body dismembered and buried in remote places. Because no bodies were
ever found, police officials were led to believe that the missing men, who
were often illiterate new recruits from Kenya's distant Northern Frontier, had simply gone home. It was not until Mathenge's men made the
mistake of leaving a portion of a policeman's body (his booted foot, and
blue puttee-wrapped lower leg) where it could be found, that the police
were alerted, and began to patrol in pairs.[85] Although the shortage of
guns and ammunition was the most glaring weakness of Mau Mau, without the help of a foreign government there was little that the movement
could do to obtain weapons in greater numbers; so large numbers of black-
smiths were hired to produce rifles and pistols. Many of these homemade
weapons were ingeniously put together, but few of them proved to be reliable combat weapons.

While efforts to obtain arms continued, more and more people—Meru,
Embu, and Kamba as well as Kikuyu—were inducted into the movement
by force. The initiation of a young Kikuyu clerk named Ngugi Kabiro in
February of 1950 was typical. One night in his Kiambu village, a man
approached Kabiro and some other young men, asking them to help him
with some work he was doing in a nearby hut. The unsuspecting initiates
were led to an abandoned house. When they entered, the dim light was
extinguished and Mau Mau guards shoved the frightened youths into the
pitch black room. After a few moments, hurricane lamps were lighted
and Kabiro saw an arch made of banana leaves that was tall enough for
a man to walk through. Looking back at the door, he saw that it was
guarded by men brandishing Kikuyu swords. The initiates were told to
remove their shoes and anything foreign, especially metal objects including watches and coins. The oath administrator spoke:

> We want you young men to join us in the struggle for freedom and
> the return of our lands. That is why we have brought you here to
> swear an oath binding you with us in this struggle. Mind you, this

is no joking matter. Any who refuse to take this oath will be killed
and buried right here in this hut.[86]

One man who protested that he had never heard of such an oath was
struck hard in the face and quickly acquiesced. Each initiate had a ring
of twisted goat skin placed around his neck and was given a ball of soil
to be held against his stomach, symbolizing his willingness to do anything
to regain the lost Kikuyu land. The oath itself was no different from the
one described earlier, but the ceremony was more impressive. As armed
men looked on, each initiate took seven sips of a vile-tasting mixture of
blood, soil and the fecal matter from a goat's intestines, and seven bites
from a goat's thorax. They also pricked the eyeballs of the dead goat
seven times, and performed other acts seven times. The oath administrator then poured cold water over the initiates' feet and made a cross on
their foreheads with the bloody mixture they had just drunk. For the
Kikuyu, seven was an evil and unlucky number typically used in witchcraft, and its power to harm was reinforced by the last act of the ceremony. Several men grasped the goat skin ring around each initiates' neck
and began to count. When they reached seven, they all pulled, and as
the ring broke, they intoned, "May you be destroyed like this ring if you
violate any of these vows."[87]
When Joseph Kiboi Muriithi was forced to take the oath early in 1952,
the ceremony was more shocking (among other things, an initiate had to
place his penis in the vagina of a goat) and the oath had become more
demanding. Now, in addition to pledging to obey all orders and never
to betray the movement, which some oath administrators now openly
referred to as "Mau Mau," these words were sworn to:

> I swear that I will fight for the African soil that the white man has
> stolen from us. I swear that I will always try to trick a white man
> and any imperialist into accompanying me, strangle him, take his
> gun and any valuables he may be carrying. I swear that I will offer
> all available help and further the cause of Mau Mau. I swear that I
> will kill, if necessary, anybody opposed to this organization.[88]

This was the "warrior" or "*batuni*" oath (after the English word pla-
toon). Muriithi and the young men who were initiated with him were
thrilled to become members of the Mau Mau, but not everyone who was
forced to take the oath reacted positively. When some Kikuyu, especially

older Christians, were forced to make this increasingly murderous pledge, many refused. Some were killed, while others, including old women, were badly beaten or strangled to unconsciousness. Some of these Christians, who did not believe in the oath's power in any event, went directly to the police as soon as the ceremony was over. By the middle of 1952, the Mau Mau warrior oath with its promises to kill white men was well known to the police. As knowledge of this oath spread among white Kenyans and the British Government, they reacted with predictable horror. Secretary of State Lyttleton wrote that,

> The Mau Mau oath is the most bestial, filthy, nauseating incantation which perverted minds can ever have brewed. I am not unduly squeamish, but when I first read it I was so revolted that it got between me and my appetite.... I can recall no instance when I have felt the forces of evil to be so near and so strong.[89]

Although by this time perhaps 90 percent of all Kikuyu adults, women as well as men, had sworn to one or another version of the Mau Mau oath, the rebellion was plagued by disunity. Mau Mau courts were set up to try persons accused of betraying the movement, and what the Central Committee referred to as "strong men" carried out death sentences. Betrayal was feared at every level of the rebellion, and rightly so; because according to Kaggia a member of the Central Committee had already become a police informer.[90] He was found out, tried in a taxicab, and executed. Although members of the Central Committee were not yet arrested, their identities were now known to the police. It is possible that other highly placed persons in the movement also became police informers without being discovered.

Betrayal was only one symptom of disunity. The rebellion's greatest weakness was the failure of the Central Committee to achieve control over its rapidly growing ranks. A good many of the new recruits took action on their own, bringing unwanted police scrutiny into areas of the Kikuyu Reserve where guns or ammunition were being hidden. Most of these men and women were simply over-eager, but some of them were criminals who used Mau Mau as a license to pursue their own goals. More serious in the long run was the near autonomy of several entire areas or districts. Kiambu still remained under the control of "Parliament," not of the Central Committee, and most of the recruits from among the squatters in the Rift Valley gave their allegiance to "Parliament" as well. Although the Central Committee had substantial control over the Nyeri and Fort Hall districts, they did not control all of Nairobi. The Nairobi slum of Karobangi, for example, was largely independent.[91]

Some Kikuyu rejected Mau Mau. Many of those who opposed it were better-educated people who did not believe that its rag-tag warriors could defeat the forces of the British Empire. Most of the uneducated adherents of Mau Mau thought that they would only have to defeat the white settlers; they had no conception of the forces that Britain could bring to bear against them. Many educated Kikuyu also did not want to risk their jobs, their elite status, or their relationship with the government, for which many of them worked. They were also offended by the Mau Mau oath, which many found "primitive" and degrading for Western-educated people and Christians. The Mau Mau referred to these white shirt and tie-wearing Kikuyu as "tie-ties." The term came to mean traitor.

Mau Mau leaders failed to convert most of the wealthy Christians among the Kikuyu, whose families continued to support the Christian missions and the government and to speak out against Mau Mau. On August 22, 1952, Kikuyu elders and ministers from both Catholic and Protestant churches met in Kiambu to announce that "God has a plan for Kenya" and charged that Mau Mau "thwarts God's wishes." They adopted the following six-point resolution:

1. We will fight this secret and violent organization to the end; we see the way to achieve this is by all men and women of good will cooperating to work together for their just rights.
2. As true Christians and members of God's family we will have nothing to do with, nor cooperate with Mau Mau because its teachings are contrary to Christian teachings and our customs.
3. We are against it because it is against the Government which maintains the law and order of the country and thus our safety and happiness.
4. We oppose Mau Mau because it is retarding the progress of Africans and also demoralizing them. It is also retarding the general progress of the country.
5. We will exclude its followers from our churches and also expel their children from our schools, lest they infect the others.
6. We do not fear Mau Mau at all. If the Government does not succeed in stamping out the organization we are prepared to fight the Mau Mau adherents, even if it is with *pangas*.[92]

Two days later the schism in Kikuyu society was dramatized at a huge public meeting in Kiambu. Organized by the government to give Kenyatta and other African leaders the "opportunity" to denounce Mau Mau, the government bussed in thousands of Kikuyu to the sports ground at Kiambu township. The police were ready with motion picture cameras and sound recording equipment so that Kenyatta's promised repudiation of Mau Mau could be broadcast across Kenya. As 30,000 people listened, Kenyatta was introduced by senior Chief Waruhiu who had recently been awarded an M.B.E. by Queen Elizabeth. The dignified chief, who had long stood for British law and order and the glories of Christianity, was dressed impeccably as always in a Western suit, tie, and hat. He climbed on a table waving a tuft of elephant grass in the air: "Kikuyuland is like this grass, blowing one way and another in the breeze of Mau Mau. We have come here to denounce this movement; it has spoiled our country and we do not want it." Kenyatta, as usual flamboyantly dressed, theatrically brandished his ebony walking stick, as he continued the denunciation. Among other things, he said: "Mau Mau has spoiled the country. Let Mau Mau perish forever," and, "all people should search for Mau Mau and kill it." It was this speech that led the Central Committee to warn Kenyatta to tone down his criticism.

When Kenyatta sat down, Harry Thuku, Eliud Mathu, and others continued the denunciations. Chief Njoro, another stalwart conservative, said the Mau Mau would "put us back 50 years."[93] Finally 84-year-old Chief Koinange rose. He singled out a white man in the audience and began to speak. "I can remember when the first European came to Kenya. I worked alongside your father and you are my son. In the First World War you asked our young men to go to fight with the British against the Germans and many were killed. In the Second World War you came again and asked us to fight against the Germans and the Italians and our young people were again ready to go. Now there are Italians and Germans in Kenya and they can live and own land in the highlands from which we are banned, because they are white and we are black. What are we to think? I have known this country for eighty-four years. I have worked on it. I have never been able to find a piece of white land."[94]

Koinange's stinging rebuke was not lost on the British, nor was it forgiven; but the headline the next day in Nairobi's newspaper, the *East African Standard*, ignored Koinange. It read, "Kikuyus Decry Mau Mau." Most Kikuyu felt as old Koinange did, but KAU was doing its best to avoid provoking the British. More than 400 Kikuyu were already in jail for administering the Mau Mau oath, and hundreds more were awaiting trial. The leaders of Mau Mau desperately needed to cover their tracks, too, but they could not halt the spread of violence. On September 26, *Reuters* reported that Mau Mau raiders had killed 100 sheep and 84 cattle, and burned down a power station on European farmlands near Mount Kenya. In the Legislative Council, a European member declared that to date, the Mau Mau had murdered 23 Africans, including 2 women and 3 children. He added that there had been another 12 attempts at murder, 12 assaults, 24 acts of arson, and the desecration of 2 churches. Even though all these acts may not have been committed by members of Mau Mau, many whites believed they had been, and they clamored for government action. But others remained remarkably indifferent, even though October brought news of attacks against white settlers. On October 3, Mrs. A. M. Wright, who lived near Thika, only 10 miles from Nairobi, was stabbed to death near her home. Two days later, there was another attack against a white settler couple, who despite being shot at and stabbed, managed to fight off their assailants. The police attributed both crimes to the Mau Mau.

Earlier in 1952, while Kenyatta, Fred Kubai, and another KAU leader, the diminutive Jesse Kariuki, were driving to a KAU meeting, Kenyatta asked Kubai how long he thought it would be before Kenyans would be ready to take over their country. Kubai, the Mau Mau leader, said three years. Kariuki said 20 years. Kenyatta came closest with an estimate of 10.[95] Yet, if the rebels had been even a little less rash, Kubai might have been nearer the mark. It is ironic that the Kikuyu, whom the British so confidently dismissed as "natural cowards," may have lost all chance for victory by being too reckless. But instead of a well-armed and organized rebellion striking white Kenya, the Kenya Government would soon declare war on Mau Mau, disrupting the movement's plans and leaving them pitifully unprepared to stand against the military forces of the British Empire. Later, Fred Kubai said, "We needed another year."[96] They needed at least that much time.

3
"A STATE OF EMERGENCY"

FOUR YEARS
OF WAR

At 4:00 in the afternoon of October 9, 1952, Senior Chief Waruhiu left Nairobi where he had spent the day presiding over a Native court. Dressed in a European suit as usual, the 62-year-old Kikuyu chief joined two friends in his immaculate Hudson sedan, and his driver headed out of Nairobi toward the chief's house some 15 miles away. Waruhiu was a steadfast supporter of the colonial government, a devout Christian, and among all the senior Kikuyu chiefs, no one had spoken out against Mau Mau as harshly as he had. Waruhiu's life had been threatened several times before, and now, as his car wound up a narrow road in a light rain, past glistening banana trees and tea plantations not far from the elegant European-only Muthaiga club, he complained to his companions about the reluctance of the recently-arrived governor, Sir Evelyn Baring, to take strong action against the Mau Mau. As Waruhiu's car turned a corner on the hilly road, it was waved to a stop by three men wearing police uniforms. One of the men approached the Hudson and asked if Senior Chief Waruhiu was in the car. As soon as Waruhiu identified himself, the uniformed man shot him in the mouth, then three more times in the body. Before leaving, the "policeman" shot out a tire on the Hudson, but the driver and the other passengers were not harmed.[1] Soon, many Kikuyu were celebrating Waruhiu's death. The chorus of one of their triumphant songs went like this:

> I will never sell out the country,
> Or love money more than my country.
> Waruhiu sold out his country for money,
> But he died and left the money.[2]

It was not terribly catchy in English, but this song, like many others, played an important role in celebrating the accomplishments of the Mau Mau.[3] Chief Koinange, now an opponent of Waruhiu and the government, was arrested for the crime, but there was not enough evidence against the old man to allow a conviction.

Governor Baring saw Jomo Kenyatta for the first time at Chief Waruhiu's funeral. Like many others, he felt what he described as the demonic force of the man he had been told led Mau Mau. Ever since Baring's arrival in Kenya on September 30, when he replaced Sir Philip Mitchell, agitated members of the white community had pressed him to take action, assuring him that the entire Kikuyu "tribe" had regressed to their "savage" past. Baring's arrival in Kenya as Mitchell's replacement had been delayed for several months by an injury suffered in England. In the interim, Acting Governor Sir Henry Potter, a courtly if lackluster administrator, had refused to respond to settler pressure for immediate action against the Mau Mau, but once Baring arrived Potter warned him about the movement with the fervor of a man long frustrated. Baring listened to Potter and others, all of whom warned him that Mau Mau was evil, irrational, and dangerous. No one told him that Mau Mau might be a nationalistic movement with legitimate social and economic grievances. When he wore his full regalia, topped by a high-crowned white helmet with its ostrich plumes, the tall, strikingly handsome Baring personified a regal colonial ruler. Yet despite his long experience with colonial administration—he was the son of Lord Cromer, the first British ruler of Egypt, who was so imperious that he was known as "over-Baring," and he'd earlier served in South Africa as well as Southern Rhodesia—Baring was reluctant at first to take strong action.

One of those who urged Baring to do so was Dr. Louis Leakey, who would later become famous for his discoveries of fossil skeletal remains of early man in Olduvai Gorge. The son of a missionary, Leakey had been raised among the Kikuyu, and spoke their language almost as well as he did English. He believed that the Mau Mau movement was a wholly evil perversion of everything that was good in Kikuyu life. The murder of his good friend and fellow Christian, Chief Waruhiu, convinced him that the government would have to act. He also believed that although the Mau Mau rebels would bring violence to Kenya, the movement would die out quickly.[4] Encouraged by an ear-shattering expression of white Kenyan opinion, Baring was convinced, and late in the evening of October 9, 1952, he cabled the Colonial Office in London for permission to declare a State of Emergency. After five days of deliberation, the Colonial Office agreed, and the new governor began to organize what was called "Operation Jock Scott."

"Jock Scott" was set for midnight, October 20, when 187 men thought to be the leaders of Mau Mau would be arrested in their homes. Three battalions of the K.A.R.—the King's African Rifles—were alerted to move from Uganda, Tanganyika, and Mauritius to Kenya where they would join the three K.A.R. battalions already stationed there. Together, the six British-led battalions of African soldiers numbered nearly 6,000 men. The Kenya Police Reserve, made up of white settlers, was put on notice of active duty, and so were some 400 white Kenyans who served in the Kenya Regiment. Under normal conditions the young men of this regiment were trained as officers who would serve with other British units during wartime, but now they would fight together against the Mau Mau. They wore a bull's-head badge on their berets, which led the rebels, who hated and feared men of this unit, derisively to call them "Kenya N'gombe" (it meant Kenya cow, not bull). Several British battalions were also alerted for possible shipment to Kenya, and one, the 1st Battalion, Lancashire Fusiliers, stationed in Egypt, was ordered to move out on the 20th. A State of Emergency would be declared on October 21.

Word of the planned arrest of the men who were thought to be the leaders of Mau Mau leaked out. The leak was not surprising. Most government clerks were Kikuyu, and Mau Mau sympathizers were everywhere—including in Government House, now surrounded by police guards, where Baring attempted to control events. Furthermore, Operation Jock Scott was organized by the Kenya Police, and some African policemen's sympathies lay with the Mau Mau. The KCA burned its records,[5] but although the men who learned of their impending arrest gave some thought to fleeing Kenya, in the end none of them did. Between midnight on October 20 and early the following morning, all 187 men were arrested, among them Eliud Mathu, the first African to serve in Kenya's Legislative Council, and Jomo Kenyatta, who was in bed at home when no fewer than 20 police arrived after midnight. When they awakened him, he was said to have asked what took them so long. In addition to arresting Kenyatta, the police confiscated one and one-half tons of documents.[6]

The operation was conducted with farcical melodrama. As each suspect was brought in handcuffed, the white police officers cheered loudly, convinced that they were smashing Mau Mau by arresting men like Fred Kubai, Bildad Kaggia, and Jomo Kenyatta. "Jock Scott" did disrupt the senior leadership, but it left the control of the rebellion in the hands of younger men who would prove to be even more violent than the men of the Central Committee.

At 7:30 P.M. on October 20, the first contingent of Lancashire Fusiliers landed at Nairobi's Eastleigh airfield in 12 long-range Royal Air Force transport planes that had taken off from Egypt that morning. As they climbed down from the R.A.F. planes, each of the weary soldiers was rewarded with a large bottle of Kenya-brewed Tusker beer. For the Fusiliers, the war was off to a promising beginning. Early the next morning, shivering in the unaccustomed cold of a Nairobi morning, the Fusiliers were loaded onto trucks. With fixed bayonets, their black berets sporting bright primrose yellow hackles, they were slowly driven around Nairobi to "show the flag," as the British put it. Because the sight of white soldiers had been a rarity since the end of World War II, the government thought that Nairobi's African population would be cowed and whites would be reassured.

As the soldiers passed that bastion of white supremacy, the bougainvillaea-draped Norfolk Hotel, they were cheered, and elsewhere on the streets of Nairobi Europeans sometimes gave them a thumbs-up sign; but African on-lookers merely stared impassively or ignored the troops altogether. If Africans were intimidated by the sight of white soldiers they gave no sign of it. The presence of the British troops also failed to intimidate the rebels, who that afternoon ambushed another senior Kikuyu chief named Nderi. Chief Nderi, accompanied by several armed men, was on his way to break up what he thought was a Mau Mau meeting when he and his men were surprised and killed by rebels led by Stanley Mathenge. Later that day, Governor Baring broadcast the news that a State of Emergency had been declared. Chief Nderi's badly muti-lated body was not found until the next day.

Despite Chief Nderi's death and the growing military build-up, there was no great sense of emergency in Kenya. For some months districts close to the Kikuyu reserve had reported isolated instances of oathing ceremonies, arson, theft, the mutilation of settler-owned cattle, and the murder of Kikuyu loyalists; still, the life of the Colony had not yet been seriously affected.[7] Many settlers were convinced that Mau Mau was a serious danger and demanded that the government take stronger mea-sures to deal with it. But others in the government down-played the threat, and in reality although there were 14 percent more crimes against property in 1952 than 1951, crimes against persons in 1952 *fell* by an even larger percentage.[8] Business was conducted as usual in Nairobi, and although the settlers on their outlying farms worried about Mau Mau, they continued to rely on their Kikuyu servants and laborers to manage their crops, livestock, and household, and to care for their children.

When a British cruiser named *H.M.S. Kenya* steamed into Mombasa's Kilindini Harbor a few days after the Emergency was declared, even the most vociferously anti-Mau Mau white settlers made disrespectful jokes about the Royal Navy's plans to aim the cruiser's big guns against the Mau Mau who were located more than 300 miles inland. When the *Ken-ya*'s sailors and marines, accompanied by their band, marched through Mombasa, the spectators enjoyed the parade, but it was difficult for the people of Mombasa to connect the military's presence in that peaceful city with the troubles so far away in the highlands to the west. Many of Kenya's whites reassured themselves that all was well by recalling the royal visit of Princess Elizabeth and Prince Philip earlier in the year. Despite warnings, she had stayed at the Sagana Lodge (soon to be known as the Treetops Hotel) near Nyeri in the center of Mau Mau militancy, and there had been no trouble. The British Colonial Office's annual report for 1952 in Kenya smugly began with these words: "Of all the events of the year, the most memorable is the visit to the Colony of Her Majesty the Queen (then Her Royal Highness the Princess Elizabeth) and His Royal Highness the Duke of Edinburgh."[9]

Although the colonial office report did not mention it, on October 28 Kenya's post-Emergency complacency had been shattered by a sensa-tional murder. Fifty-year-old Eric Bowker, a veteran of both World Wars, lived alone on a small isolated farm. Unlike most settlers, he did not keep a gun in his home. His Kikuyu headman said that he was good to his employees, but during the evening of the 28th, several of these men entered his house, killed two teen-aged African servants and chopped Bowker to death while he was taking a bath. All three bodies had been terribly mutilated by repeated blows with *pangas*.

White Kenyans were horrified by the brutal murder, but the deaths of African protestors continued to go almost unnoticed. For example, when shortly after Bowker's death a crowd of unarmed Kikuyu men and women near Fort Hall menacingly approached a police patrol and ignored an order to disperse, a white police officer ordered his men to fire into the crowd. The Kikuyu dragged away scores of wounded people, leaving 25 dead bodies behind them.[10] There was no inquiry and M. S. O'Rorke, the Commissioner of Police, took no action against the officer who said that he ordered his men to fire in self-defense. For the police, as for most white Kenyans, Bowker's death was much more significant than the death of 25 Kikuyu.

Instead of concerning himself about the dead Africans, the Commissioner of Police hurriedly sent security instructions to every European household. Everyone was urged to have a loaded weapon at hand at all times. Windows were to be barred; no one was to leave the house at night unless protected by another person armed with a gun; the exterior of the house was to be illuminated at night; water, flares, and fire extinguishers were to be kept ready. All Kikuyu staff were to be ordered out of the house at dusk and if a servant returned for any reason, he was to be covered by a gun at every moment.[11] Although at first most of the settlers laughed at the police commissioner's instructions, it would not be long before they took them very seriously. Soon a pistol would seem as commonplace beside a soup plate as a spoon, and cars would look natural with their doors removed for rapid escape.

Early in 1952 the Mau Mau Central Committee formed what they called the Kikuyu War Council, and the campaign to steal or buy weapons was intensified. The weapons were sent to the forest, where small groups of men assembled under the overall leadership of Stanley Mathenge, the man who later led the attack against Chief Nderi.[12] As soon as the Emergency was declared, new men took control of the War Council, while thousands of young men, accompanied by several hundred young women, left their homes for the forests of the Aberdares and Mt. Kenya. Most were unarmed except for pangas or Kikuyu swords, but Mathenge, General China and other Mau Mau leaders began to organize them into military units.

In response to the Mau Mau build-up in the mountain forests, the government designated various one-mile-wide areas around Mt. Kenya and the Aberdares as "prohibited," meaning that security forces could shoot anyone (by which they meant any African) in these areas on sight. In addition, censorship was enforced, regulations were imposed that allowed fines, confiscation of property, forced labor, and enforced relocation of Kikuyu populations; passes were required for all Kikuyu, and the death penalty was extended to many crimes, including administering Mau Mau oaths and possession of a single bullet. It was immediately alleged by Africans that the police sometimes planted a bullet on suspects whom they feared they could not otherwise convict.[13]

Toward the end of November, white Kenya was shocked by two more killings. Like Bowker, retired Naval Commander Ian "Jock" Meiklejohn had fought in both World Wars and his ships had been torpedoed three times. He now lived quietly on a farm near Thomson's Falls to the north of the Kikuyu Reserve with his wife, a retired doctor. On the night of November 22, five men silently entered the Meiklejohn house and attacked both the commander and his wife with pangas, leaving them for dead. Dr. Meiklejohn, although terribly wounded, survived, but her husband died. Four days later, Tom Mbotela, a leading opponent of Mau Mau who had survived an earlier assassination attempt, was killed in Nairobi as he walked home after attending a town meeting. Although hundreds of Africans must have seen his body, no one reported his death until 8:00 A.M. the following morning when a European on his way to work found it. That night the nearby "Burma" market, where Africans sold their produce in hundreds of ramshackle stalls, was burned to the ground. The fire was allowed to burn unchecked, and African witnesses insisted that it had been set by police who were infuriated by the failure of Africans to report Mbotela's death.[14]

There were no more attacks against Europeans for the remainder of 1952. However, a week before Christmas, Mau Mau leaders from all parts of the forest met and agreed on a coordinated attack intended to kill loyalist Christian Kikuyu while they attended church services on Christmas Eve. Fearful of white reaction, the War Council in Nairobi cancelled the plan at the last moment, although one unit was not notified; it killed eleven loyalists.[15] Kenya's whites were unaware of this plan and Christmas passed uneventfully for them. So did New Year's Eve. Despite the Emergency, many settlers left their farms to attend parties in Nairobi, and although formally-dressed women carried guns, and there may have been even more drinking and dancing on tables than usual, 1952 was seen out peacefully enough. For many among the European colony, the liveliest topic of conversation was the arrival in Kenya of Grace Kelly and Ava Gardner to act in the film "Mogambo" directed by John Ford. On New Year's Day, 1953, however, two more European farmers were killed, and over the next two weeks 35 Africans, most of them loyalists, were also killed. Then, on January 24, white Kenyans were shaken as they had never been before by the murder of the Ruck family.

Roger Ruck, his wife Esme, a doctor, and their six-year-old son, Michael, lived on a farm not far from Eric Bowker's. Aided by some family servants, several Mau Mau raiders lured Ruck out of the house and killed him with pangas. When his wife rushed to her husband's aid she was killed too. The Mau Mau rebels then entered the house where they stole a shotgun and some ammunition while one of them played the piano with bloody fingers. When Michael called out from his bedroom, apparently frightened by the noise, he too was killed with a panga. The sight of his small body, hacked terribly, was enough to sicken the most hardened policeman. Newspapers reported the murders in gruesome detail and published photographs of Michael's room where his teddy bears and toy train lay scattered on the floor.[16] The man who confessed that he killed the child was one of the Rucks' Kikuyu servants, who only a few days before had carried the little boy home tenderly after he fell off his pony. This contradiction in behavior terrified the settlers; if Mau Mau could compel trusted servants to kill like this, then no one was safe. It is little wonder that white Kenyans were distraught. Something inexplicable and terrible was happening in Kenya.

For many whites, the Ruck family symbolized everything that was good and hopeful about Kenya. Roger Ruck was good looking, athletic, and sociable; Esme gave free medical treatment to African children from far and wide; and little Michael was an innocent child. The murders took place on the same weekend that the judge who was hearing the case against Jomo Kenyatta was deciding whether there was enough evidence to bring him to trial. Although there was not, in an atmosphere of white rage it was inevitable that the judge would decide to proceed with the trial.

The day after the killings, 1,500 enraged white Kenyans marched on Government House in Nairobi to demand that the government crush the Mau Mau. Governor Baring refused to recognize the settlers, but, a day later, Kenya's security forces were removed from police control and transferred to the British Army. Major-General W. R. N. "Loony" Hinde, a tankman who earned his nickname for his fearlessness while leading an armored brigade of the "Desert Rats" against Rommel's Afrika Corps, flew in from Cyrenaica to take command. Army General Headquarters in Cairo had instructed Hinde to "jolly them along," referring presumably to the settlers, not the Mau Mau. Hinde had little difficulty being jolly with the settlers; he had several friends among them, and he shared their views about Africans.[17]

Hinde was not a flamboyant commander able to generate excitement by his mere presence; he needed help to organize Kenya's Security Forces, as they were called, but he got very little. When he arrived in Nairobi, there was neither a devoted staff awaiting him, nor an excited city clamoring for great deeds. The settlers who had marched on Government House had dispersed to their farms, and the whites who lived in Nairobi itself were not only calm, they were seemingly frivolous, with no sense of urgency about anything except profit-making and party-going. Mau Mau violence had not yet spread to Nairobi. Still perplexed by the unexpected normalcy of Kenya's capital, General Hinde toured the white highlands where he was shocked by the words of virulent hatred that the white settlers hurled at the government. Nairobi was apparently oblivious to the Emergency, while settlers in the highlands were determined to take over the government and kill every Kikuyu in sight.[18]

Shaken by his brief tour of inspection, General Hinde returned to his modest headquarters to take stock. His police and army forces were spread out around the vast expanse of troubled areas north of Nairobi. Even though his intelligence service had been organized by Sir Percy Sillitoe, the director of Britain's MI-5, soon after the Emergency had been declared, it was still rudimentary. Hinde's best guess was that some 12,000 Mau Mau were encamped in the forested areas adjacent to the Kikuyu reserve (the actual number at this time was probably well over 15,000). These men were thought to have no more than 1,000 pistols, rifles, or automatic weapons stolen or purchased from profit-minded Indians and some Europeans in Nairobi, as well as an unknown number of homemade weapons—pangas, spears, swords, and bows and arrows. The rebels had very little ammunition, and were unable to manufacture bullets, grenades, or larger explosives. Some African soldiers of the King's African Rifles were willing to sell ammunition along with an occasional weapon, and so were a few British soldiers who had fallen for Kikuyu women; but the rebels needed thousands of weapons, not the handful they got from these clandestine traders. Despite wild accusations that the rebels were being supported by the Soviet Union, Egypt, Ethiopia, China, and India, in actual fact they had no foreign supporters to send them weapons, money, or military advisors. Except for encouraging radio broadcasts from Cairo and New Delhi, they were entirely on their own. Nevertheless, the British Colonial Office continued to investigate every suspected Communist influence,[19] and showed themselves acutely sensitive to world opinion, maintaining files marked "secret" of newspaper clippings from all over the world including obscure American newspapers such as the *Toledo Blade* and the *Salt Lake City Tribune*.[20]

The rebels chose to fight primarily in the forested areas near the Ki- kuyu reserve. To Hinde, the military solution early in 1953 was obvious— surround the forest and cut off their lines of supply. It was not quite that simple, however, as Hinde would learn. The forested areas that the Mau Mau had chosen as their bases and refuges covered almost 900 square miles. This enormous expanse of territory was not only covered by dense forests, it was mountainous and cut by thousands of ravines. Forcing the Mau Mau out of rugged retreats like these would be no simple undertak- ing. The western boundary of their forest refuge was the 70-mile-long Aberdare Mountain Range, thrusting up as high as 13,000 feet. For more than 40 miles, this range was flattened on top, forming an 11,000-foot- high moorland plateau of swamps, lakes, marshes, perpetual mist, and icy wind. Below the moorlands was a zone of 60-foot-tall bamboo, some as thick as a man's waist, with leaves that cut like razors. Below the bam- boo, at about 9,000 feet, a "black forest" of juniper and cedar stretched over hundreds of square miles of ridges and steep-sided ravines. Some 40 miles to the east, 17,000-foot-high Mt. Kenya, the home of the Kikuyu God, Ngai, stood above everything, its permanent ice cap glittering in the sun. The forests that surrounded it provided the Mau Mau with an- other relatively safe war zone.

Mostly consisting of tall cedar, but with some podocarpus, wild fig, olive, and sweet-smelling cape chestnut trees, the Aberdare and Mt. Kenya forests were so densely packed that virtually no light penetrated, giving the impression that the forest was in fact "black." In many places, the undergrowth was so thick that neither humans nor animals could pene- trate it. In perpetual twilight, the many sounds of the forest—monkeys that chattered, birds that made whistling and bonging sounds, insects that buzzed and whirred, elephants that trumpeted, furry rabbit-sized hyrax (the closest living relatives of the elephant) that screeched with elephant-sized voices—added to the sense of unreality. The forest was perpetually wet. No part of its floor was level ground, and there were few trails that allowed one to walk without being tormented by thorns or branches. There were a few open areas where animals gathered, and there were some lovely grassy glades here and there where flowers grew and bush buck leaped after a rain shower. The Mau Mau rebels found

European Settled Areas and African Reserve affected by Mau Mau in Central Kenya

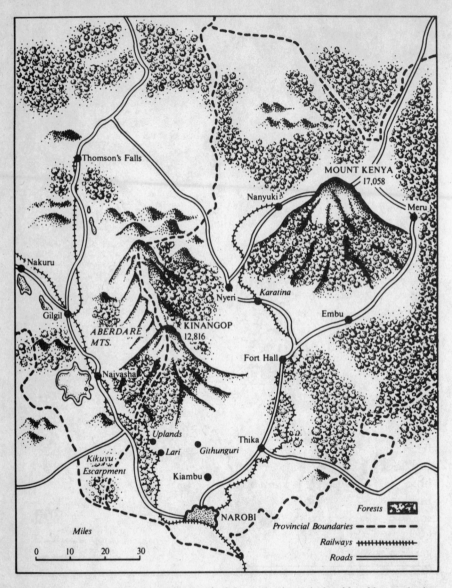

Forest and mountain terrain where most of the operations during Mau Mau took place

and appreciated places like this, but to most of the British who eventually had to fight there, the forest was nearly as unreal as life under water.

In order to cut these forested areas off from the Kikuyu farmlands that would have to feed the rebels, Hinde would have to man more than a 500-mile perimeter. While he waited for reinforcements from Britain, Hinde built up loyalist "Kikuyu Guard" forces (more commonly known as the "Home Guard"). But before he could establish an efficient Home Guard, the settlers forced the government into an ill-considered action that sent thousands of new recruits into the ranks of the Mau Mau.

Although many white settlers still refused to believe that their own Kikuyu servants were disloyal or dangerous, others wanted all Kikuyu removed from the highlands. In early 1953, more than 100,000 Kikuyu servants and laborers lived and worked on white farms in the highlands. Many of these people had lived outside the Kikuyu heartland reserves for many years, and few owned land in the reserves. Most were landless people who had been forced to become "squatters" on European farms in order to survive. Over the years, however, some became so prosperous that their white landlords were threatened by their competition in local markets, and by their growing numbers of livestock.[21] Many whites had wanted these rich squatters resettled for years. Now without warning they got what they hoped for—wholesale evacuation.

Governor Baring assured Kenyans in a radio address in February 1953 that his planned repatriation of Kikuyu squatters would not' leave the countryside overrun by destitute, homeless people; but in fact, the government rounded up these people at gun point. Literally dragged away from unfinished meals, thousands of frightened people were herded onto trucks to be shipped back to the Kikuyu Reserve. Their livestock, household possessions, even their clothing and personal effects were left behind. Many children were separated from their families as well. Even some of the most militantly anti-Mau Mau settlers were upset by the government's inhumane treatment of these Kikuyu,[22] most of whom soon gave active support to the Mau Mau. General Hinde regarded as madness this needlessly harsh action that created more hungry and embittered people. He had more than enough problems as it was.

Despite the negative effects from the squatter evacuation, General Hinde was cheered by the relative absence of Mau Mau attacks. By the end of February, 1953, four months after the Emergency was declared, the Mau Mau had killed 9 Europeans, 3 Indians, and 177 Kikuyu—serious enough for the families involved, but hardly the bloodbath feared by government officials. Caught unprepared by the Emergency, the rebels were still organizing their forces and arming themselves. Through February and most of March there was little action. But on March 26, that would change. What was soon to come was announced by a badge that was left on the chest of a dead Mau Mau soldier found by a British patrol early in 1953. The badge read "blood and fire."[23]

The small dusty town of Naivasha in the Rift Valley was best known for the flamingos that flocked to the nearby lake of the same name; but it was also a rail and administrative center, and a market town for the European farmers. Military forces were usually encamped there and it had a permanent contingent of Kenya Police. The Naivasha police station consisted of several well-built administrative buildings, a large jail, and a police barracks located several hundred yards from the station's armory. The main complex was surrounded by barbed wire, and an armed sentry stood guard in a watchtower. It seemed like one of the last places the Mau Mau would choose to attack. The police apparently felt secure because on the evening of March 26 no white officer was on duty, the barbed wire had several gaps in it, and all but five or six policemen were asleep in their quarters with their weapons locked securely in the armory three hundred yards away.

At 9:30 P.M., about 80 Mau Mau soldiers began a well-coordinated attack. After shooting the sentry in the watchtower, they burst through gaps in the barbed wire, overpowered the startled police who were on duty, killing one of them, and drove away the remaining sleepy and unarmed policemen. The rebels then broke into the armory, where they took 18 sub-machine guns, 29 rifles, and a truck-load of ammunition. Before they drove away, having suffered only one casualty, they released 173 prisoners, many of them Mau Mau, from an adjacent detention camp. They were gone before the four platoons of Lancashire Fusiliers stationed nearby in Naivasha could react. Commissioner O'Rorke and the Kenya Police were a long time living down their embarrassment, and the Mau Mau had gained new respect.[24] Even so, some settlers refused to believe that the Mau Mau were capable of such a well-coordinated attack. One settler wrote what many others said about the attack: "(it) was too brilliant a piece of work to have been devised by a primitive brain: it bore all the hall-marks of civilization." In fact, the raid was led by a prominent Mau Mau Commander, Major-General Mbaria Kaniu, whose men had only 3 rifles, 1 shotgun, and a pistol.[25]

Only half an hour later, at a place called Lari, Mau Mau was discredited in the eyes of white Kenya, much of the world, and most importantly, many Kikuyu. Lari was a farming area seven miles long and three miles wide located a few miles north of Nairobi, near the edge of the high Kikuyu escarpment looking down into the Rift Valley. The Kikuyu population of Lari was evenly divided between landowners who were followers of a government loyalist, Chief Luka, and landless people who lived as tenants on the owners' land. The hostility between these two groups was deep and long-standing. In 1940, 600 Kikuyu had been forced off their land in Kiambu to make way for European settlement. Many refused to leave their farms and as a result the government detained them for several years; but Chief Luka agreed to move, and became established on considerable acreage in the new area of Lari. As a result he became a symbol of collaboration with the government.[26]

Not surprisingly, Chief Luka's followers supported the government while the landless tenants who came to work on his land were sympathetic to the Mau Mau movement. Some Mau Mau supporters had planned to attack Chief Luka's loyalists for several weeks, but word of their plans leaked to the British. On March 18 a company of K.A.R. troops was sent to Lari to reinforce Chief Luka's well-armed 150-man Home Guard, but on the morning of March 26 the K.A.R. company was ordered away. That same night, at 10 o'clock, between 1,000 and 3,000 men who had been positioned all around the Lari area attacked selected widely-separated homesteads. Many loyalists, including Chief Luka and his eight wives, were burned to death in their houses; others were killed with pangas as they tried to escape, and still others were shot. Children were hacked to death along with their parents, and many of the victims were horribly mutilated. One woman who survived said that a Mau Mau raider slit her small son's throat and licked his blood before killing him (press accounts later changed "licked" to "drank"). When the loyalist Home Guard recovered from its first shock, and was joined by army and police reinforcements, the fighting spread and intensified over an area of nearly 40 square miles.

In the morning, 97 residents of Lari were found dead, with another 32 grievously wounded. Over 200 huts had been burned and more than 1,000 cattle maimed.[27] The government invited the press, including author Graham Greene, to witness the carnage, and distributed grisly photographs and newsreels of horribly burned and mutilated men, women, children, and animals. These press reports and photographs of the butchery at Lari quickly came to symbolize Mau Mau savagery. Government press releases did not mention the fact that perhaps as many as 400 additional people at Lari who were alleged to have been Mau Mau had also been killed and some of them had been mutilated too, presumably by vengeful Home Guards or security forces.[28] The government later admitted that most of the killing at Lari had been the work of squatters who had been expelled from the Rift Valley, and not by organized Mau Mau units. Mau Mau leaders also charged that some of the 97 Lari dead were poor tenants who were victims of Chief Luka's own loyalist Home Guard. There is probably some truth in this charge, but while it is likely that Mau Mau leaders did not order the attack, local people who were committed to the movement were responsible for beginning a terrible orgy of killing in which women and children were sometimes the victims.[29]

Much of the news about Mau Mau originated from government press office "handouts" made available almost every day. Some were relatively straightforward reports of action, but others, like those incorporated into the following government report on Lari, were decidedly lurid:

> Armed terrorists stole upon the clustered huts of Lari, in the Kenya Highlands, in the dead of night. The sleeping Kikuyu people awoke to find flames roaring above them, as the Mau Mau fired the tinder-dry thatched roofs.
>
> Escape was impossible to most for the doors had been securely fastened outside by fanatical Mau Mau attackers.
>
> Men, women and children, forcing their way out of the windows, were caught and butchered. Some perished terribly in the flames; others were chopped and mutilated by the knives of their enemies—their own fellow tribesmen.
>
> Dawn revealed the macabre scene left behind by the bestial wave of Mau Mau; the mangled corpses, human remains literally chopped in pieces all mingled with the smoking ashes of the burnt homesteads.
>
> The survivors, terror-stricken and helpless, told their pitiful stories to the police and government officials who rushed to Lari when the alarm was raised. They told of children being cut up with knives in the sight of their mothers; of others cut down as they tried to run to hide in the tall maize, by terrorists insatiable for blood.[30]

Stories in some newspapers such as the *East African Standard* and the *Times* of London, were relatively free from sensationalism, but others, especially British tabloids, invariably wrote about "innocent," "helpless," or "heroic" whites being "slaughtered" or "butchered" by "fanatical," "bestial," "satanic," "savage," "barbaric," "degraded" or "merciless" Mau Mau "gangsters" or "terrorists."

While Kenya Government press releases bombarded the world with news of Mau Mau atrocities, the government neglected to publicize what their own troops did near the Kayahwe River in the Aberdare Forest. Ninety-four newly recruited men of the redoubtable General Kago's Mau Mau command were captured by a K.A.R. unit, stripped of their clothing and possessions, and then, as white officers looked on, machine-gunned to death. Only two of them survived to describe the massacre.[31] Understandably, no photographs were distributed to the press.

After Lari it was much more difficult for Kikuyu to be ambivalent about Mau Mau. Although many of the members of the so-called loyalist Home Guard had taken the Mau Mau oath, and were of two minds about the conflict, the enmity between many of the loyalists and the Mau Mau began to harden into hatred. The government had thus far yielded to settler demands not to arm the Home Guards with rifles and shotguns, forcing them to fight with spears, pangas, and bows and arrows. Now it began to issue shotguns and rifles. Despite this decision, and the arrival of more British forces, the Mau Mau were in their ascendancy. Perhaps as many as 30,000 young men and women were assembled in military camps throughout the forest. Most still relied on their pangas or some sort of homemade gun, but increasing numbers had British Army rifles or Sten sub-machine guns, and a few had Bren (light machine) guns. Supplies of ammunition were still minimal but more ammunition was being captured or stolen every day. Supply lines to the Kikuyu Reserve and to Nairobi were open, and there was a steady flow to the forest of food, money, and information, often carried by young women for whom the Mau Mau at this stage of the conflict represented the *beau ideal* of warrior manhood. There were also many more young men who wished to come to the forest than could be armed.

Fear of the rebellion now spread from the isolated farms of the highlands to Nairobi, where some whites organized private armies. The men in one such para-military group, which they called "white home guards," were under these orders: "If you see any numbers of Africans assembling and get no quick, satisfactory reply to your first challenge, shoot immediately and to kill."[32] A rumor spread throughout the city that on April 8, the date when the court was due to give its verdict on the charges against Jomo Kenyatta, all Kikuyu servants had been ordered to kill the white children in their charge. Hundreds of white families were said to have taken their children to the coast to escape this threat. Fear spread overseas as well. After an Italian immigrant to Kenya had been killed in a Mau Mau attack, the Italian Government openly discussed sending a detachment of "volunteers" to Kenya to protect other Italians, declaring (to the embarrassment of the British Embassy in Rome) that Italians in Kenya were not being protected as well as Kenyans of British ancestry. The British were able to prevent an international incident and they sub-sequently classified information about the matter as "secret."[33]

Although the government persisted in describing the Mau Mau as "ter-rorists" or "gangsters" and their fighting units as "gangs," at this time in mid-1953 almost all the rebels in the forests were organized into large military units, some with more than 3,000 men. Led for the most part by men who had served in the British Army in World War II, the British military stamp was heavily imprinted on these units. They were called "Brigades" or "Armies" and their commanding officers were self-proclaimed "generals" or even "field marshals." Unlike the well-armed, tactically sophisticated guerrilla forces that much of the world later came to take for granted, the Mau Mau soldiers were poorly trained, badly armed, and sometimes ineptly led by men with no combat training or experience. Even so, at this early stage of the conflict, the Mau Mau soldiers were a deadly threat, especially to Home Guard posts.

Despite their undiminished desire to drive the whites out of Africa, it was increasingly clear that the most intense hatred of the poor, illiterate men who made up the Mau Mau fighting units was focused on the loy-alist Home Guards, who were a kind of landed gentry that had been made wealthy and privileged by colonial governmental patronage.[34] Many of the Mau Mau smarted under the ridicule of loyalist chiefs like Mu-hoyo, who told them that they could not govern Kenya because they were incapable of making something as simple as a needle.[35] Because of the Mau Mau movement, most of the poor, uneducated and non-Christian Kikuyu were in the forests fighting for "independence" against the wealthy, educated, and Christian loyalist Kikuyu who remained on their tribal land. At this point in the conflict, the Mau Mau were more than a match for the loyalists. In fact, the Mau Mau were so confident that on Coronation Day, June 7, 1953—a day meant to honor Queen Elizabeth—they crowned a young woman, Wagiri Njeroge, "Mau Mau Queen." She was later captured and sentenced to 10 years in prison for this offense.[36]

Mau Mau units seldom had enough weapons and ammunition to at-tack British Army positions, but in April of 1953 they began a series of raids against police and Kikuyu Home Guard posts. Usually attacking at night, they sometimes overwhelmed the loyalists, killing men, burning their huts and taking their ammunition, once by cutting the ropes that held up a drawbridge over an otherwise formidable moat. But some Home Guard posts were protected by barbed wire and defended by machine guns, grenades, and mortars. When Mau Mau units tried to over-come these defenses with their home-made rifles, Molotov cocktails, and a few British rifles and sub-machine guns, they were usually driven off, sometimes with heavy casualties. British troops often rushed to the rescue of the Home Guards and pursued the Mau Mau into the forest in running battles that sometimes lasted two or three days and occasionally involved hand-to-hand fighting as British troops with fixed bayonets faced Mau Mau warriors armed with pangas.[37]

There was no overall Mau Mau military command and, for the most part, their raids were uncoordinated, but early in 1953, Stanley Mathenge, who had planned the Naivasha raid, again devised a plan for co-ordinated strike. Mathenge tried to order Mau Mau units in Nairobi and in the reserves to join soldiers in the forest in a concerted attack against bridges, railways, and power and telephone lines, as well as European farms. Cattle were to be driven away or killed and crops burned. Fortunately for the Europeans, many Mau Mau units refused to acknowledge Mathenge's leadership, and relatively little damage was done by the scattered forces that did attack.[38] No such coordinated strike was attempted again, and most Mau Mau units returned to their pattern of isolated hit-and-run-attacks. In a spectacularly defiant gesture, one Mau Mau unit shot up and burned the Royal Sagana Lodge near Nyeri where Queen (then Princess) Elizabeth had stayed the year before. No one was hurt but the Lodge was destroyed.[39]

The conflict was not going well for General Hinde. He was aware of the need to concentrate his forces if he was to strike effectively, but his army units were hopelessly dispersed in small groups supporting the Kenya Police and the Home Guards. Compelled to patrol the seemingly endless perimeter around the Mau Mau forests, Hinde could not reasonably mount an offensive. He tried his best to mollify the increasingly anguished settlers and to improve relations among the army, police, and administrative officers; but conditions gradually worsened and in May, 1953, the decision was made to replace him with a more senior officer.

General Sir George Erskine had a fine record in World War II and extensive experience with intelligence operations in India and Egypt. He was also a close friend of Prime Minister Churchill. Erskine was given "full powers of command over all the Colonial, Auxiliary, Police, and Security Forces."[40] Hinde, and a newly arrived major general, G. D. G. Heyman, would serve as his deputies. As soon as he took command, "Bobbie" Erskine toured the troubled areas before writing an exultant "top secret" letter to his superior, Field Marshal Sir John Harding, saying that he felt tremendous goodwill from all communities in Kenya.[41] Incautiously, he promised Kenyans an early end to the rebellion. Erskine was a stout, rumpled sort of man who unfortunately lacked the "smart" military bearing that might have helped intimidate the settlers who were fond of General Hinde and resented his demotion. As it was, the brusque new general immediately clashed with the settlers.

Their representative on the Colony Emergency Committee (later called the War Council) was Michael Blundell, and through him the settlers quickly tried to control the new commander. Erskine ignored Blundell and took a profound dislike to the settlers, writing to his wife that, "I never want to see another Kenya man or woman...."[42] Erskine later wrote that while "the Africans" had confidence in the British Army and some Government Administrative Officers, "they hate the police and absolutely loathe the settlers. It is difficult to realize how much the settler is loathed and the settler does not realize it himself." But he also found fault with the government, saying that the cause of the Mau Mau was "... nothing except rotten administration.... in my opinion they want a new set of civil servants and some decent police."[43]

Erskine also had his difficulties with Governor Sir Evelyn Baring. Tall, patrician, and seemingly robust, Baring was in fact so frequently ill that important work was typically left unattended. Baring was a highly intelligent man who had received First Class Honors in Modern History at Oxford and was an authority on Swahili literature. Yet he was such a pitiful failure at speaking plainly to settler audiences that the settlers turned against him. Although pleased that Baring was an aristocrat (he later became First Baron Howick of Glendale), they found him aloof and thought him weak. They were also displeased to learn that he was a devout Roman Catholic who had turned a room of Government House into a chapel, where it was said that he spent an immoderate amount of time. Groups of settlers often called for Baring's removal, and on more than one occasion they almost had their way.[44] Ironically the only time white Kenyans would see Baring as an admirable man of action came shortly before his retirement in 1959, when despite a serious heart condition he unhesitatingly plunged into the Indian Ocean off Mombasa in an attempt to save two drowning Indian girls. He managed to save one of them but very nearly died himself.[45]

The settlers disgusted Erskine and Baring disappointed him. When it became obvious that he could not see eye-to-eye with Baring on Mau Mau and the governor was infuriatingly slow to reach any decision, Erskine had nowhere to turn but to the army. Erskine's army would have to deal with the Mau Mau on Erskine's terms. The general could afford to be independent, because thanks to Churchill he carried a letter in his glasses case authorizing him to proclaim martial law and take over the government at any time. Now and then, the general was inclined to intimidate his political opponents by snapping his glasses case open and shut.

Soon, despite his political problems, Erskine began to feel more confident that he had the forces necessary to defeat the Mau Mau. In addition to the greatly reinforced Kenya Police, the Home Guards, and the Kenya Regiment, Erskine had at his disposal an armored car squadron, a battery of artillery, six battalions of King's African Rifles, and three battalions of British troops—the 1st Battalion of the Lancashire Fusiliers, the 1st Battalion of the Devons (newly arrived from service in the jungle war in Malaya) and the 1st Battalion of the famous "Buffs," the third-oldest regiment in the British Army, but now mostly an assortment of inexperienced national servicemen, or "draftees" in American terms.

Unfortunately for Erskine, the British troops—including the Malaya-hardened Devons—were not prepared for forest warfare in Kenya. A few of the officers quickly adapted to conditions by forming six-man combat teams that learned to use stealth as a weapon (it is said that some of the soldiers who proved to be most adept at forest warfare were men of Gypsy ancestry),[46] but other officers seemingly cared more about hunting and fishing than improving their men's combat efficiency. Others went to absurd extremes to provide their men with what they conceived of as combat essentials. Officers of the Buffs, for example, had iron bedsteads carried to their forest camps on muleback so that their troops could sleep in comfort.[47] Despite, or more likely because of, their beds, the British troops were slow to adapt: the altitude fatigued them, they made every imaginable noise, shot at phantoms, and fell into pits dug by the Mau Mau. Worse, they accidentally shot one another, were panicked by elephants, rhinos, and buffaloes, and in sum did little harm to the rebels. It was not a proud time for these once-proud battalions.[48] Erskine wisely pulled his British troops out of the forests and replaced them with his K.A.R. battalions. The British forces would now patrol the periphery of the forests, ready to respond to rebel attacks, while African soldiers would do the fighting in the mountain forests.

Erskine also had available several units of the Royal Air Force, especially several flights of Harvard light bombers. The Harvard was an American-designed training plane which the British had used throughout World War II. It was chosen for service in Kenya because it was slow enough, with a top speed of only 205 miles per hour, to allow it to operate over the mountainous forests without overshooting its targets. These light aircraft, fitted with racks of 18-pound bombs, caused considerable panic and some casualties among the Mau Mau. Several of these planes crashed when caught in sudden mountain downdrafts, however, leading various Mau Mau groups to believe that they had shot them down.

Erskine also had under his command a squadron of nine 4-engined Lincoln heavy bombers that dropped 1,000-lb bombs on the forest. Although the army acknowledged that bombing and strafing by the R.A.F. did cause some Mau Mau casualties,[49] the R.A.F. lost credibility with the army, which was always skeptical about its claims, when it was revealed that it had charged the Kenya Government the full cost of modern bombs while actually dropping bombs that were obsolete.[50] The small Pipers and Cessnas of the Kenya Police Air Wing were unquestionably effective in spotting Mau Mau camps, and later these small observation planes were fitted to carry four 19-lb bombs apiece. How effective the bombing from these light planes was, was not clear at the time to General Erskine and his command, but subsequent interrogation of Mau Mau prisoners made it plain even to skeptics that the bombing and strafing forced the Mau Mau to move their camps and led to considerable demoralization. Before the Emergency ended, the R.A.F. dropped the amazing total of 50,000 tons of bombs on the forests and fired over 2 million rounds from machine guns during strafing runs. It is not known how many humans or animals were killed.

Although the British were spending millions of pounds to defeat the Mau Mau, Erskine continued to be plagued by administrative muddles. The British had used tracker-dogs with success in Malaya, and Erskine's command wanted dogs to be used in the forests. A retired army colonel in England offered his trained dogs to Erskine, but the Air Ministry in London refused to send the animals until it could be assured that kennel accommodations in Kenya "would be in accordance with the Ministry of Works specifications."[51]

Erskine wanted a military specialist in psychological warfare even more than he wanted bloodhounds, but, despite "Top Secret" requests to the War Office, nothing happened. Finally, the Kenya Government set up its own secret "propaganda working party" made up of civilians and including Dr. Leakey,[52] one of whose first recommendations horrified Erskine. Leakey wanted the Colonial Office to invite Ralph Bunche, the distinguished United Nations statesman and recipient of the Nobel Peace Prize in 1950, to Kenya to speak against Mau Mau, but the Colonial Office pointed out that according to its information, Dr. Bunche was "half-Kikuyu" and had been given the Kikuyu name of "Kariuki."[53] Erskine, who knew Bunche personally, eventually vetoed the visit.

The second half of 1953 was marked by a number of large-scale battles between the Mau Mau and the Home Guard, but the Mau Mau units were usually able to slip back into the forest before British troops could arrive. With the arrival of two additional British battalions in September, 1953 (the Royal Northumberland Fusiliers and the 1st Royal Inniskilling Fusiliers), and the replacement of the Lancashire Fusiliers with the Black Watch (which had just returned from heavy fighting in Korea), Erskine attempted offensive action of his own.

Erskine now had 10,000 British and K.A.R. troops, 21,000 police, and more than 20,000 Kikuyu Home Guardsmen, almost 3,000 of whom had been issued guns. His major operation was an attempt to surround Mau Mau forces south of Nyeri in November. Three separate battles, each lasting for a period of several days, inflicted heavy casualties on the Mau Mau. Much of the fighting was between unseen enemies, as the British blasted the forest with artillery and mortar shells and sprayed it with machine-gun fire. They were answered by rifle fire from Mau Mau hidden in the forest. But sometimes the two forces found themselves at close range in the forest, and British soldiers again fought with bayonets against pangas and swords.

By the end of 1953, the Mau Mau had lost 3,064 confirmed killed, 1,000 captured, and an unknown number of wounded. In addition, almost 100,000 Mau Mau supporters had been arrested and 64,000 of these had been brought to trial.[54] British losses had been light but on Christmas Eve, 1953, Major Archibald J. A. Wavell, the commander of a company in the Black Watch—and the only son of the famous World War II field marshal—was killed in a fight near Thika against the men of General Kago.[55] On the same day that Lord Wavell's death was reported, the Mau Mau struck for the first time in Tanganyika, killing a loyalist Kikuyu family (including two children), and critically wounding two other persons. Within 3 days the police rounded up 650 Mau Mau suspects whom they intended to return to Kenya.[56]

A month earlier, when Governor Baring visited London to discuss the Emergency with Foreign Secretary Oliver Lyttleton, the two men had agreed that the situation was serious. The British press also expressed concern about the continuing resistance of the Mau Mau. The *Times* reported that "the gangs are showing extraordinary resilience, in spite of the weight of the forces against them, which have now been supplemented by heavy bombers."[57] In reality, the situation was even worse than press reports suggested. The Mau Mau rebels were not just holding their own against the growing weight of the security forces; Baring told Lyttleton that the young Kikuyu "were more fanatic than ever." Moreover, he was concerned because in addition to the attack in Tanganyika, Mau Mau activity had been reported in Uganda as well as among several large tribes in Kenya.[58]

Nevertheless, despite graphic and sometimes exaggerated reports of Mau Mau violence in the world press, tourists continued to visit Kenya. As many as 26,437 tourists entered Kenya in 1953, compared to 33,000 in the relatively normal year of 1952.[59] And during the first week of January, 1954, while attacks against Europeans increased and large battles raged in the forests, 15 young American women arrived in Nairobi with a CBS camera crew to film an "all-girl" safari.[60] As the safari set out, a patrol from the King's African Rifles found the skeleton of a Mau Mau soldier lying nearby next to a loaded light-machine gun.[61]

Early in 1954, a British Parliamentary delegation returned from a tour of Kenya and reported that Mau Mau influence had "increased" since the Emergency began; in addition, it reported that police brutality was so widespread that public confidence was threatened. The report called for the government to make a "supreme effort" against the Mau Mau and asked it to make more rapid progress in "destroying the colour bar."[62] The Kenya Government responded by insisting that the security forces were doing their best to destroy the Mau Mau, and that the forces were not being defeated, a conclusion which many of the settlers, particularly retired army officers, vocally rejected. Erskine was not at all pleased by the settlers' criticism. In letters to his wife he wrote that Kenya was "a sunny place for shady people," and that he hated "the guts of them all. They are all middle-class sluts."[63] Hoping to quiet the settlers, Erskine responded to the Parliamentary delegation's call for a "supreme effort" by ordering a new registration of male Europeans between the ages of 18 and 45. The delegation had also noted that Mau Mau activity in Nairobi had become so widespread and brazen that the situation was "both grave and acute."[64] Erskine had to agree that the best way to defeat the enemy was not by mounting large-scale military operations against phantom Mau Mau bands in the forest, but by destroying their base of support in Nairobi.

Despite the arrest of many senior leaders at the start of the Emergency, Mau Mau operations were still being coordinated by the War Council in Nairobi and its sub-committees throughout the reserves and in some smaller towns. Mau Mau activists in Nairobi were stepping up their thefts of money and guns, and they became increasingly violent in their efforts to destroy loyalist opposition in the city. In October, 1953, they killed the prominent loyalist Chief Kimburi, and his inappropriately named headman Shadrach. They also forbade "European" practices such as smoking European cigarettes (although marijuana or African tobacco was acceptable), drinking European beer, wearing hats (a European custom that had been adopted by many Africans), and riding city buses. They established courts that tried and punished persons found guilty of violating these and other proscriptions, and they sometimes sentenced violators to death. As General Erskine later said, the Africans in Nairobi took Mau Mau orders very seriously, but they largely ignored the government, [65] and Mau Mau operations became so open that the Royal Inniskilling Fusiliers had to be sent to the city where they patrolled the streets with fixed bayonets.[66] Early in April, 1954, four-year-old Andrew Stephens, son of a R.A.F. Officer, was decapitated with a panga as he rode his tricycle outside his house in Nairobi while his parents were inside making breakfast.[67]

The situation in Nairobi was so extreme that Erskine decided on a massive sweep of the entire city that would clear it of Mau Mau supporters once and for all. His view of the operation is evident from the code name he gave it—"Anvil." Anvil required delicately balanced planning that would allow him to mass troops and police in Nairobi without leaving other areas vulnerable to attack. He had to build detention camps to hold arrested suspects, find men to guard these camps, and establish teams that could separate Mau Mau supporters from people the government thought innocent. Moreover, all of this had to be done without alerting the Mau Mau.

While Erskine's plans for Operation Anvil were being developed, his troops wounded and captured a 32-year-old Mau Mau leader who proved to be Waruhiu Itote, better known as "General China." China was in overall command of about 5,000 Mau Mau rebels in the Mt. Kenya area. Although he initially resisted interrogation skillfully carried out for 68 hours by Ian Henderson, a Kikuyu-speaking police officer, China eventually revealed some details of Mau Mau military organization, and the general location of forces. General China said nothing that seriously compromised Mau Mau fighting ability, but with a death sentence hanging over his head, and believing that warfare had taken Mau Mau as far as it could, he agreed to write letters to his officers asking them to meet with British delegates to discuss surrender terms. Oliver Lyttleton approved the plan, and General China, dressed in the uniform and blue steel helmet of a Kenya Policeman, was spirited from his safe house in

Nairobi to Nyeri, closer to the fighting. He wrote 26 letters to Mau Mau commanders urging them to surrender and pledging safe passage and amnesty from the British. The letters were placed in secret Mau Mau tree mail boxes in the forest that China identified.

Contact was made with Mau Mau leaders in the forest, and to the surprise of the suspicious British, many of the Mau Mau rebels seemed receptive. The proposed surrender talks appeared so promising that, with Baring's approval, a cease fire was agreed on, beginning March 30 and lasting through April 20, at which time General China's men and perhaps others as well were to meet a British delegation and discuss a mass surrender. Believing that the British amnesty offer was a sign of weakness and that a major concession might be forthcoming, at least 2,000 of General China's men, followed by perhaps another 1,000, were converging on the meeting place near the village of Gathuini when a smaller, independent force of Mau Mau led by General Gatamuki encountered the 7th Battalion, K.A.R., commanded by Brigadier John Reginald Orr. Orr's men promptly opened fire, killing 25 rebels and capturing 9 others including General Gatamuki, who protested that his men were coming in to surrender. Needless to say the other Mau Mau were convinced that the British had callously set a trap for them—a reasonable if erroneous conclusion—and the planned surrender was over. Most settlers were infuriated when they learned of the amnesty offer, and applauded Brigadier Orr who said, "I regard the action with nothing but satisfaction." The settlers' political leader, Michael Blundell, angrily said that everyone in the country would now believe that Governor Baring had taken the Mau Mau oath (Blundell later apologized). A more thoughtful settler was quoted as saying, "Perhaps Kenya died at Gathuini."[68]

To signal the resumption of hostilities, Erskine's Harvards dropped 6,000 lbs of bombs in a single day, and later the same day a flight of Vampire jet bombers arrived in Kenya. Erskine ordered that Operation Anvil begin two weeks later, on April 24. A ramshackle former military camp had been readied as a detention facility at Langata, adjoining the National Game Park, 5 miles outside Nairobi, and two other large camps had been built 250 miles away near the coast. The Mau Mau in Nairobi knew that an operation against them was being planned, but did not know exactly when it would take place and did not believe that it would be very effective. The 25,000 men needed for Anvil moved into position the night before, and when the residents of Nairobi awoke on the 24th, they found the city completely surrounded. Although most of the Mau Mau leaders had already left the city, the British had achieved enough surprise to trap everyone else.[69] While the troops maintained their cordon around Nairobi, police swept through one sector of the city after another. Every conceivable hiding place was checked and broken into if necessary. All Kikuyu along with related Embu and Meru tribesmen were screened on the spot, usually by the less-than-gentle Kenya Police and the Kenya regiment. Anyone who was in any way suspicious was sent to Langata, and then shipped by rail to one of the coastal camps.

Not everyone picked up in Nairobi was sent to a detention camp. More than 3,000 women and 6,000 children were sent to the reserves by bus, truck, or train. When the women were given cans of milk and meat and packages of biscuits, they threw them at the railway staff. When sandwiches were substituted, these too were thrown. Finally, the train was fitted with metal screens to prevent the "waste of food." Police officials may have been concerned about the waste, but they were obviously embarrassed when the women refused their food and then defiantly danced and sang Mau Mau songs. The British had thought that these women were sufficiently free of the taint of Mau Mau to be returned to their homes.

In the first 48 hours of Operation Anvil, 8,300 out of the 11,600 people screened were sent to Langata. When Anvil ended a month later, 24,000 Africans, almost all Kikuyu, had been sent to a detention camp.[70] Detainees were routinely beaten, often with rifle butts, and robbed of their valuables if they had any. If they had none, they were beaten some more. Families were separated without concern for the welfare of children. One of those who was roughed up by British troops was a young man named Tom Mboya, who would soon play a major part in Kenya's politics.[71] Anvil was brutal, as no one tried to deny, but it was effective. The operation was followed up by random sweeps of Nairobi in the ensuing months and the introduction of a forgery-proof passbook system. In order to qualify for a passbook an African had to be vouched for by a European employer, a government official or a prominent loyalist. The passbook was difficult to forge because it carried a stamped photograph of the bearer. Anyone found without a passbook was summarily arrested. Thanks to these measures, Mau Mau's control over Nairobi was broken and the effect on the men and women fighting in the forest would soon become devastating.

Erskine's next target was the lifeline of supply that stretched from the reserves into the forest. Operation Anvil had destroyed Mau Mau's urban base, but the nearly 2 million Kikuyu, Meru, and Embu in the reserves around the Mau Mau-occupied forest were still supplying badly needed food, weapons, and ammunition. Towns, and then Kikuyu locations, were swept as Nairobi had been. But Erskine intended to do more. His plan

was to dig a 50-mile-long ditch that would cut off the sympathetic population in the reserves from the forest. The ditch was monumental. In
most places it was 10 feet deep and 16 feet wide, filled with impenetrable
mazes of booby-trapped barbed wire and sharpened bamboo stakes, and
every half mile there was a police post that patrolled the barrier day and
night. This astonishing barrier was constructed by many thousands of
forced Kikuyu laborers who also built access roads for military patrols.
Every loyalist chief was empowered by the government to call up labor
for tasks such as these, and call it up they did, ruthlessly requiring everyone, including children and the very old, to work from 6:00 A.M. until
6:00 P.M. Sometimes women were forced out of bed at two o'clock in the
morning to begin work.[72] These conscript laborers, who were fed very
little, were also obliged to provide various services for loyalist families.
Anyone who resisted was beaten.[73]

In addition to digging the great barrier ditch, the decision was made—
this time with the enthusiastic support of Governor Baring—to forcibly
move the Kikuyu from their traditional pattern of widely scattered homesteads into "villages." The idea of gathering civilians into villages that
could easily be defended had been pioneered in Malaya. Now with the
strong support of Dr. Leakey and a favored government psychiatrist, Dr.
J. C. Carothers—who thought that the "villagization," as it was called,
would reduce the Kikuyu's individualism—Baring was eager to try it in
Kenya. Despite the protests of many settlers, who felt that the plan would
alienate the loyalists because the idea of living in villages was so foreign
to the traditional Kikuyu pattern of scattered settlement, Baring ordered
villagization to proceed. Many thousands of Kikuyu were forced to build
dwellings, access roads, barbed wire fences, watchtowers, cattle pens,
schools, dispensaries, and all the other necessary features of the "new
villages," as they were sometimes called. Kikuyu protests were waved
aside, and by the end of 1954, the astonishing number of one million
Kikuyu had been resettled from their scattered homes to 800 newly constructed and completely controllable villages.

The barbed-wire-enclosed villages could be easily defended against Mau
Mau attacks by a few armed guards, freeing security forces for action
elsewhere; but that was only one of the purposes the villages served. The
government also wanted to prevent sympathetic Kikuyu in the reserves
from making contact with Mau Mau rebels, and Governor Baring particularly wanted to punish areas that were thought to have supported Mau
Mau.[74] From nightfall to dawn, curfew regulations required everyone to
be inside their villages, and when women went to their fields during the

day, they were accompanied by armed escorts. Because the fields were unguarded at night, both the Mau Mau and the security forces helped themselves to the crops, and the villages soon experienced hunger. With the Kikuyu unaccustomed to close living conditions, diseases reached epidemic proportions and the malnourished young and very old began to die in large numbers. Despite government efforts, there were thousands of deaths, perhaps tens of thousands. As the suffering and loss of life continued, the government took advantage of the captive populations by installing radios in each village that bombarded the Kikuyu with messages comparing the depravity and defeat of the Mau Mau to the virtues of the government and the victories of its military forces.[75]

While these plans of General Erskine were being carried out in 1954, the fighting in the forest continued. Although most Mau Mau attacks were small-scale night raids, now and then a general chose to launch a large daytime attack. Early in 1954, General Ihura assembled more than 500 men to assault the well-defended District Police Headquarters complex at Kandara. He told his men that they would attack this difficult target in broad daylight to prove that the Mau Mau were willing to face the "imperialists" in the open. As his troop marched through the farmlands of the Kikuyu Reserve in a long military column led by a huge red flag, women gave them water and honored them by making the five ululating trills usually reserved to announce the birth of a baby boy. A large crowd of men and boys fell in behind the column hoping to join in the battle but these unarmed volunteers were ordered away. Like other soldiers, Mau Mau fighting men liked to sing, and many of their songs mentioned Jomo Kenyatta. One of these was sung to the tune of "Onward Christian Soldiers."

> Onward Mau Mau Soldiers,
> Marching as to war,
> Looking unto Jomo,
> Who has gone before,
> Jomo the Royal Master,
> Leads against the foe,
> Forward into battle,
> See his banners go.[76]

Even the most ardent government propagandists could not dismiss a force of over 500 men as a "gang," and most of the government personnel withdrew before the Mau Mau forces attacked. The police who remained tried to defend the partially fortified complex, but they were quickly shot down or grenaded. The Mau Mau cut the telegraph wires and carried away weapons, ammunition, boots, and other supplies. British troops were seen rushing toward the battle in armored personnel carriers, and the Mau Mau forces prepared to withdraw, but before they retreated they lowered the Union Jack and raised their own red flag. As the Mau Mau retired toward the forest, their rear guard was attacked by a mounted police patrol. Four of the mounted men—who had tied themselves to their saddles—were shot, and the Mau Mau watched their horses drag them away. Eleven Mau Mau were killed in the action, and probably twice that many policemen, including some whites.[77]

The next morning the retreating rebels found themselves cut off by K.A.R. and British army units that had been directed into position by spotter planes. After a hurried consultation with his subordinates, General Ihura ordered his men to break the British lines. Bugle calls mingled with tribal war cries as the warriors charged. Despite British superiority in automatic weapons, the Mau Mau were able to use cover well enough to break through one British line after another, six in all. In fighting that was often hand-to-hand, one 23-year-old British lieutenant with a K.A.R. battalion was reported to have killed eight Mau Mau with his bayonet.[78] The Mau Mau fought back with their swords, and they also fired their guns so continuously that the weapons became too hot to hold. There was no precise count of the casualties, but eyewitnesses saw large numbers of dead on both sides.[79]

Although Mau Mau casualties were always reported, large engagements like this received little publicity either in the local or international press; yet six or seven battles as large as this one occurred during 1954,[80] and a major Mau Mau success occurred in September when, with the help of a sympathetic guard, rebel raiders liberated Mau Mau prisoners held at Lukenya Prison, 22 miles outside of Nairobi. In a well-executed attack, the prison was broken into, guards who had been cruel to the prisoners were identified and killed (sometimes after having their eyes gouged out), and all the prisoners were released, most of them managing to avoid recapture.

During the first half of 1954, while large Mau Mau units battled security forces around the forest's edges, the government was alarmed by evidence that Mau Mau was spreading, especially to the 600,000 Kamba whose lands stretched south and east from the Kikuyu reserve. In May, Kenya's new police commissioner warned that the Kamba were drifting toward active Mau Mau involvement,[81] and in June the Blundell-led War Council's greatest fear was the threatened spread of Mau Mau.[82] After Operation Anvil cleared Nairobi of most Kikuyu residents, more than

20,000 Kamba moved to the city, becoming its majority African population. Many of these Kamba took Mau Mau oaths.

In the past, the Kamba had been enemies of the Kikuyu, but by 1952 they had come to share Kikuyu grievances against poverty, land shortage, population growth, and white racism. Several hundred young Kamba formed themselves into Mau Mau units, killing pro-government chiefs and headmen in the Kamba reserves, while others joined combat units in the Mt. Kenya forests. Still, the great majority of the Kamba population watched and waited to see how the rebellion would succeed. When government security forces had little visible success in defeating Mau Mau during 1953, the Kamba became more restless, and, by 1954, many thousands had taken the Mau Mau oath, and thousands more were openly on the verge of committing themselves to armed rebellion.

The prospect of the Kamba was particularly frightening to the government because Kamba soldiers and policemen formed the backbone of both the K.A.R. and the Kenya Police. If these men with their military training and their weapons had joined the rebels the result for white Kenya could have been disastrous. Many of these armed Kamba discussed joining Mau Mau, and some considered turning their weapons against their white officers; but concerned Kamba loyalists alerted the government and Baring wisely chose to respond not with threats but with benefits.

The government spent millions of pounds, including a large grant from the United States, to produce unprecedented prosperity for the Kamba reserves, but even so it was not until early 1955 that it was reasonably certain that the Kamba, and Kenya's other wavering tribes, would not take active part in the Mau Mau movement.[83] Later, when Jomo Kenyatta said that "we all fought for Uhuru," he was repeating a politically expedient slogan, not a fact. Still, in reality many more Kenyans gave their support to Mau Mau and its call for freedom than the government liked, or wanted the world to realize. Information relating to the spread of Mau Mau was classified, and although some of it leaked to the press, the magnitude of the threat was not known to the public.

Kenya's need for additional manpower to fight the Mau Mau was so acute that a compulsory call-up was issued to all "Asians" of military age, and the great majority complied,[84] although few saw actual combat. Meanwhile, settler hostility to Indians remained high. The white community was pleased when a Sikh artisan from the highlands town of Molo was sentenced to death for selling two revolver bullets to a Home Guardsman disguised as a Mau Mau rebel.[85]

Despite Operation Anvil and subsequent sweeps of Nairobi, Mau Mau raids in the city continued to take place. In July, the Mayor's house was attacked, and shortly afterwards a 60-year-old Polish woman who lived alone was shot and strangled to death.[86] Several other Europeans and Indians were wounded in Mau Mau attacks as well, and later in the year a prominent settler's stable was burned, killing two horses, one of them a champion steeplechase jumper belonging to Governor Baring.

Mau Mau attacks now took place anywhere in Kenya from Mombasa to Kisumu on Lake Victoria, but for white Kenyans in Nairobi life went on more or less as usual. Race meetings were held, restaurants were packed, weekend parties were gay, and business exceeded government expectations.[87] Late in 1954, Danny Kaye paid a well-publicized visit and was shown a Home Guard post. A lioness made news by spending four days in Nairobi—much of the time perched on the steps of the Nairobi Cathedral—before she was declared a menace and shot. There were widespread sightings of flying saucers (leading some citizens to speculate about their relationship to Mau Mau) and in November, George Baron, fresh from his role as the leading dancer in the London Production of "Guys and Dolls," was shown an exhibition of Kamba dancing. He declared that he intended to use the Kamba dance steps he had just seen in his upcoming part as Man Friday in "Robinson Crusoe."[88] And through everything, tourists arrived. The Mayor of Nairobi welcomed a "safari" of 15 persons from South America, and despite the rebellion, Kenya's economy took in more than £3.5 million from the tourist trade in 1954.

Later in the year, the continuing conflict produced a particularly gruesome episode. While Dr. Louis Leakey continued to advise the government, especially Governor Baring, on means of defeating the Mau Mau, his elderly cousin, Gray Arundel Leakey, and his wife were living quietly on their farm in Nyeri District. Leakey's son Nigel was the first Kenyan soldier to be awarded the Victoria Cross in World War II. Gray Leakey, who spoke fluent Kikuyu and was a ritual blood-brother of the tribe, was convinced that he would not be harmed and had in fact once before talked Mau Mau raiders out of attacking him. But on October 14 a Mau Mau band did attack. Mrs. Leakey was strangled and her husband taken prisoner. After nearly a month of what must have been a ghastly captivity, the severely diabetic Leakey was found five miles from his home, buried alive upside down, his feet left protruding from the earth. When his body was found with the help of a turncoat Mau Mau woman diviner, it was obvious that Leakey had been tortured.

This appalling act was apparently ordered by a Kikuyu prophet who prophesied that the only way to drive the Europeans out of Kenya was to kill a European "elder" in the same way that the British were believed to have killed a famed Kikuyu named Waiyaki, who was a leader of a council of elders in 1892.[89] The prophet's version of history was a traditional one among the Kikuyu, but, needless to say, the British had always insisted that Waiyaki was not killed in this grisly manner. They admitted that Waiyaki died in their custody, but they claimed that he succumbed from the effects of a blow on the head received in a drunken imbroglio. A Mau Mau field marshal named "Kaleba" was later captured wearing Leakey's clothing.[90] He was convicted of the murder and hanged.

As the year wore on, the British Government grew increasingly impatient about the length and cost of the conflict. Late in 1954, Sir Michael Blundell, who was both the leader of the European elected representatives in Kenya's Legislative Council and a key member of the War Council, made an official visit to London, where Prime Minister Winston Churchill urged him to "come to terms with the Kikuyu." Blundell remembered that Churchill ". . . kept returning again and again to the need for negotiation; his arguments being that the tenacity of the hold of Mau Mau on the Kikuyu showed that they were not the primitive cowardly people which many imagined them to be, but people of considerable fibre, ability and steel, who could be brought to our side by just and wise treatment."[91] Churchill added that, of course, negotiations with the Kikuyu would have to proceed from a position of strength. Blundell tried to explain that there could be no position of strength as yet because British forces had not established complete military control. Official displeasure was expressed more directly when Blundell met His Royal Highness the Duke of Edinburgh, who chided him, saying, "Come on, can't you get a move on out there? The Queen and I want to come out and visit that house of ours," referring to the Sagana Lodge where the couple had stayed in 1947.[92]

By year's end, Erskine's headquarters believed that the Mau Mau rebellion could now be defeated. Reflecting this optimism, life in Nairobi, Mombasa, and Kenya's large towns had returned to a semblance of normality. Whites still carried guns and they were still wary, but the oppressive sense of constant danger had passed. For the settlers on isolated farms in the highlands, however, every day and every night was still an ordeal of fear and sleeplessness. What is more, poor harvests made economic survival precarious. After the new Secretary of State for the Colonies, Alan Lennox-Boyd, visited Kenya, he reported in a secret dispatch that he found the settlers despondent, and that many of them would sell their farms if they could.[93] Many were convinced their cause was lost. The settlers did not realize that the Mau Mau rebels were suffering from the cut-off of food and supplies from the reserves as well as from growing military pressure.

General Erskine decided to attack the forests in the first weeks of 1955, and the beleaguered Mau Mau rebels felt the full weight of British military might. The first operation, code-named "Hammer," was planned as a follow-up to Anvil. On January 6, Erskine ordered the nine full battalions assigned to Hammer to begin a sweep of the Aberdare Forest. Supplied by air, the equivalent of a full division of infantry was to move up through the moorlands into the bamboo forests, and then down into the black forest at lower elevations in search of what was estimated to be a Mau Mau force of fewer than 2,000 men. But despite their superiority in weapons, the British troops were still poorly prepared for forest fighting, while by now the Mau Mau were experts. The British were also hampered by unseasonal rains and cold so bitter that some unprotected pack horses actually died.[94]

The plan of Hammer was for the British troops to drive the fleeing Mau Mau into large ambushes that had been set up to intercept them. From the British perspective, the operation was not a success. With alarming frequency, the men in the ambush (called the "stopline") shot the British troops in the "sweepline."[95] When Hammer was terminated on February 11, the efforts of more than 10,000 British troops had accounted for only 99 Mau Mau killed, with another 62 captured. British casualty figures were not released. Later in February, a second operation, called "First Flute" after a winning racehorse, was begun in the Mt. Kenya area. The same forces were used, but instead of a vast sweep that resembled a hunting drive, British units were assigned a segment of forest where they remained until it was thought to be clear of Mau Mau. Again, the "bag," as it was called (using hunting terminology) disappointed the British. When First Flute ended two months later, only 277 of the estimated 3,000 Mau Mau in the area had been killed or captured.

Although their casualties had not been large, these two massive invasions of the forests created great hardship for the battle-weary rebels who were hungry, short of ammunition, and increasingly dispirited. Some units were reduced to fighting the British with poisoned arrows.[96] Even before these two forest "sweeps" took place, the leaders of several large Mau Mau forces once again began to consider surrender, and in early January they let it be known to the British that they might support a cease-fire so that a discussion of surrender with amnesty could take place. For several weeks, Mau Mau leaders met with British officials in a private home in a Nairobi suburb.[97] The security precautions taxed the ingenuity of the most experienced intelligence officers. As a result of the meetings, almost one thousand Mau Mau actually surrendered before their leaders changed their minds and decided to renew the fighting.[98]

When news leaked out that the government had allowed Mau Mau rebels to surrender with amnesty, white settlers were understandably outraged. Protest meetings were held in all the white farming areas where it was argued that it was impossible to believe that the government would deal with "people responsible for the most abominable crimes a perverted mind could conceive," as one settler put it.[99] Some settlers issued threats against any Mau Mau who did surrender, and one went so far as to fly over the forests dropping leaflets that threatened any Mau Mau rebel who did surrender.[100] What the settlers did not know, and could not easily be told, was that the amnesty offer was made in large part because General Erskine was seriously concerned that the many breakdowns in discipline among the Home Guard might portend a mass defection of these guardsmen with their newly issued weapons. Erskine was hoping to head off this potential "disaster," as he referred to it, by encouraging large-scale Mau Mau surrenders.[101]

There can be no doubt that many of the Home Guards had become an embarrassment to the government. Some sold their weapons to the Mau Mau, while others freely used their power to torture any opponent, whether a Mau Mau suspect or not, to rape their wives and daughters, and to appropriate their property.[102] By 1955, the loyalist Home Guard numbered 25,000, far more than the 6,000 or so Mau Mau who remained in the forest, and many had taken the law into their own hands in order to settle old grievances or enrich themselves. Erskine may have been justified in worrying that the Home Guards would cease to be a viable military force, but by this stage of the conflict there was such loathing between most Home Guards and the Mau Mau that there was little possibility of reconciliation. In the end, Erskine's amnesty offer accomplished little. The Home Guard, which was too important to be disarmed, continued to pursue its own interests, the Mau Mau remained in the forests, and the settlers continued to abuse Erskine for not ending the hostilities.

At the end of April, former American presidential candidate Adlai Stevenson passed through Kenya on his way home from doing business in South Africa. He made the standard tour of game parks, saw Governor Baring, and toured a Home Guard post overlooking the great ditch. Before he left, he declared that, "The problems here, while difficult in the extreme, will, I am sure from what I have seen and heard, yield to patience, moderation and restraint."[103]

By the time General Erskine's predetermined two-year tour of command in Kenya ended in April, 1955, his patience with settler criticism had been exhausted, and the government was equally happy to see him go. In May, he was replaced by General Sir Gerald Lathbury, a younger and far more diplomatic man. When "Bobbie" Erskine arrived in Kenya, the Mau Mau were killing about 100 people a month; now they averaged about 20 a month.[104] The settlers were hardly satisfied with this record, but when Erskine handed over command to Lathbury, the tide had clearly turned against the Mau Mau. Lathbury reviewed the situation he had inherited, and made valiant efforts to appease the settlers. It was estimated that fewer than 5,000 rebels remained in the forest, and Lathbury said he was convinced that the best way to conclude the insurrection was not by massive attacks like those of Hammer or First Flute. For one thing, London was displeased by the cost of the war. (It was costing the British an average of $28,000 to kill a single Mau Mau.) Now, fortunately, some enterprising police and army officers had proposed the use of Special Forces as an alternative. Security forces, especially the police and the Kenya Regiment, had sent patrols—often accompanied by African trackers and dogs—into the forest many times before, but now it was proposed to use former Mau Mau who had been captured and converted to the government side. It was hoped that these men, led by British Army intelligence or Kenya Police officers, could track down small Mau Mau units where big battalions could not.

Like Erskine before him, Lathbury approved of this plan to use what came to be known as "pseudo-gangs," but the new general still had big battalions at his disposal, and (yielding to what was apparently irresistible temptation) he decided to use them once again. On July 15, 1955, he sent four battalions (three British and one K.A.R.) back into the Aberdares. Heavy bombers, lighter Harvards, and British artillery once again saturated the forest, attempting to drive the Mau Mau toward the advancing troops. In terms of casualties, the operation was even less impressive than those mounted by Erskine. Most of the troops were new to forest combat and they managed to kill only a handful of Mau Mau. Far worse, the British lost several men to their own fire, including the battalion's commanding officer, Lieutenant-Colonel Rupert Brooke-Smith. This fiasco, known as Operation "Dante," marked the end of reliance on large-scale military attacks in the forest. Lathbury had learned his lesson. From this point on, the troops would patrol the periphery of the forest, and pseudo-gangs would go in after the Mau Mau.

The pseudo-gang program went forward under both police and army supervision. Some of these units were accompanied by Europeans and others were not. Some units did poorly, presumably because as former

Mau Mau who gave up the fight they were neither as tough nor as dedicated as the men who remained in the forest. But other pseudo-gangs did very well, and their presence not only led to Mau Mau casualties, it increased suspicion and divisiveness among the hunted men who were trying to carry on the fight. The pseudo-gang approach that served the government so well was an improbable war within a war. Led by white officers who blackened their skin and wore home-made Mau Mau wigs, small groups of "pseudos" attempted to defeat the forest-wise Mau Mau rebels on their own familiar ground. Because it was often necessary to kill silently, the pseudos had to rely on knives, and some units were equipped with cross-bows purchased from a company in far-away California.[105]

In addition to the pseudo-gang approach, the government promoted a series of "population sweeps." The term was meant literally. Under Home Guard supervision, the entire African population of a district was turned out with their pangas to hack into the forest, clearing the underbrush and killing any Mau Mau incautious enough to be found in the area. One such sweep involved 45,000 people, while another mustered no fewer than 70,000, mostly women of the Meru tribe, who enthusiastically cut to bits everything they saw, including 22 unfortunate men, 2 of whom were said to be Mau Mau generals.[106] The government reported that during the latter half of 1955, when the fighting was very nearly over, the two approaches together accounted for an average "bag" of 300 Mau Mau rebels killed each month.

In December 1955, General Lathbury decided that the Naivasha area had not been properly pacified; a large number of Mau Mau were thought to be operating out of the reeds and swamps that spread over some 400 square miles around Lake Naivasha. Thousands of British troops were given the task of rounding them up in what was aptly called Operation "Bullrush." The police were also involved, along with members of the Home Guard, as well as no fewer than 300 Mau Mau prisoners who were brought along to lead the way. For more than three miserable weeks, these men boated, waded, and sloshed their way through mosquito-infested swampland. When Bullrush ended after 24 days of unrelieved wretchedness for everyone concerned, only 24 Mau Mau rebels had been killed or captured. The operation was hardly a great success, but as 1955 came to an end, British intelligence estimated that no more than 1,500 Mau Mau rebels remained in the forests, and most of these men and women now spent more time looking for food than fighting. They no longer had the will or the ability to carry out major military operations.

When the Mau Mau first set up their military camps in the forest they built sturdy bamboo houses, some with running water piped in from nearby streams in hollowed out bamboo. They slept on mattresses with clean blankets and mosquito nets, ate well with European cutlery, had medical supplies including penicillin, and dressed warmly in European clothes (some even wore stolen military uniforms). Years later, in the beginning of 1956, the estimated 1,500 rebels who remained were half-starved, diseased, and often wounded. They slept in the open protected only by the clothing they had made out of animal skin. The cold forest was no place for bathing, and the Mau Mau were indescribably filthy, their hair plaited into spikes that jutted out in all directions so that it would be easier to kill the lice that plagued them. When captured, the Mau Mau rebels smelled so foully that Europeans were sickened; their white captors reported that the smell of soap regularly caused the Mau Mau to vomit.[107] To many of the British these men seemed scarcely human, but no one could deny that they were physically tough or that they knew the forest as well as anyone could.

Early in 1956 General Lathbury launched a few limited military operations in the forest. Code-named "Hannibal" and, remarkably, "Schlemozzle" (British slang for an argument or dispute), these operations had some success shattering one of the more formidable Mau Mau units still active there.[108] But by May there were no remaining targets large enough to justify large-scale military action. Accordingly, most of the British troops withdrew from Kenya, and the police took over responsibility for dealing with the remaining Mau Mau militants. One after another, the remaining Mau Mau units surrendered, were killed, or captured. Still, Mau Mau's most important forest commander, "Field Marshal" Dedan Kimathi, held out with a small band of followers. In September, Governor Baring wrote to Lennox-Boyd that "if we could only get Kimathi, it would be over."

In October, when a pseudo-gang wounded Kimathi and captured him, the government was exultant. Even though Kimathi had become increasingly unpredictable and brutal toward his own followers, and many rebels feared him, he still symbolized resistance for the Mau Mau. In recognition of Kimathi's importance, the government gave his captors 10,000 shillings to share, and planes flew over the forests and reserves, dropping a total of 100,000 leaflets with a photograph of Kimathi lying on a stretcher, his hands manacled. A caption read "Dedan Kimathi is captured." Another 20,000 of these leaflets were distributed in towns. Kimathi was eloquently defiant during his trial, and appealed his conviction and death sentence. The appeal was denied and Kimathi was hanged on February 18, 1957.

With Kimathi's capture, organized resistance in the forest ended. The remaining five hundred or so Mau Mau were no longer fighting for land or freedom; they were simply desperate fugitives without any purpose except survival. Some would attempt to escape to Ethiopia where they hoped to find a government willing to aid their cause, but most would remain in the forest until Kenya's independence in 1963.[109] Occasional acts of violence occurred as late as 1964, but Mau Mau was no longer more than a nuisance to the life of Kenya.[110]

Surprisingly, at no time during the rebellion, not even when the inevitability of defeat became obvious, did the Mau Mau make effective use of sabotage, potentially their most effective tactic. The rebels' failure to carry out widespread sabotage had nothing to do with their lack of understanding of these methods. Small bands regularly used their pangas to hamstring the settlers' cattle and other domestic animals; they also burned some wheat fields, cut down a few coffee trees, sometimes felled trees to block roads, and destroyed small bridges.[111] In 1953, Mau Mau raiders successfully blew up a military airplane at Nairobi's Eastleigh Airport by igniting its fuel tanks,[112] and about the same time, rebels obliterated a Home Guard Post by igniting an unexploded 35-lb R.A.F. bomb next to its complex of buildings, after dousing it with kerosene.[113] These acts were inventive, effective, and courageous, but so seldom attempted that they had no appreciable impact. Very few rebels had military training in the use of such tactics, but even so it is difficult to understand why such effective methods were used so rarely.

Kenya's lifeline was its railroad, and its great length could not easily have been guarded against marauders who could easily have torn up long stretches of track or destroyed switch-plates during the night. A few switch-plates were tampered with, but no part of the track was seriously damaged, and not one train was derailed.[114] Mombasa's harbor facilities and Nairobi's marshalling yards were also vulnerable to sabotage. A single kerosene fire-bomb could have done great damage, but apparently no such action was ever attempted. Similarly, a few fire-bombs could have caused great destruction to Kenya's power plants and oil storage facilities, and telephone wires could have been cut all over Kenya with virtually no risk. The Kikuyu were feared by other Africans for their knowledge of deadly poisons, and the rebels did sometimes try to poison streams used by security forces; yet there was apparently no systematic attempt to poison the water tanks that white farmers used for themselves and their livestock. The settlers knew that their huge wheat fields could easily have been burned during the dry season, and they were rightly fearful, but arson seldom took place.[115] The settlers' precious coffee trees, which could so easily have been cut down or ringed and left to die, with rare exceptions were also left untouched.

Of course, the Mau Mau were limited by having no reliable source of explosives. With dynamite, plastic explosives, and land mines, the rebels could have brought life in Nairobi and Mombasa to a standstill, destroyed much of Kenya's economy, and compelled the security forces to disperse themselves widely throughout the country. But Mau Mau's leaders had not arranged for allies who could provide them with explosives. The Indians and Arabs who could have smuggled them in by sea were not sympathetic to Mau Mau, nor were the Somali and other pastoral people who could have brought explosives into Kenya across its vast and indefensible Northern Frontier District. It is possible that the leaders of Mau Mau would have rejected the widespread use of explosives even if they had been available, fearing that such destruction would alienate too many of Kenya's Africans, and on some occasions they did decide against destroying electrical power plants rather than create hardship for their African supporters.[116] Guerrilla tactics might also have alienated other African communities by disrupting the economy, but it is equally plausible that a widespread program of sabotage would have made the rebellion seem successful and deserving of support. At the very least, the need for more men to guard the railroad and other vulnerable facilities would have reduced the number of troops available to contain the rebels in the forests unless the British sent more men. Rather than incur the great expenses that more troops would have entailed, the British Government—which as we have seen had offered settlement terms to the Mau Mau early in 1954—might have decided to end the conflict on terms more favorable to the Land and Freedom Army.

Mau Mau leaders clearly recognized the need to influence world opinion if their rebellion was to succeed, but they failed to do that either. The Soviet, Chinese, and Eastern European press criticized the Kenya Government, as did India, Egypt, and a few other countries; but all of these governments were so openly hostile to British colonialism that these criticisms could be brushed off. The rebellion needed the sympathy of the West, but the Kenya Government was so successful in portraying the Mau Mau rebels as inhuman savages that the Western press rarely gave favorable coverage to the men and women who fought in the rebellion, and, except for Canada, which for a time was sympathetic, no Western government supported their cause.

At the start of the Emergency, Canada's Prime Minister, Louis S. St. Laurent, embarrassed Britain and Kenya by declaring that the Mau Mau was a legitimate nationalist movement. However, government propaganda about Mau Mau atrocities eventually took its toll, and St. Laurent stopped far short of supporting the rebels.[117] Mau Mau leaders had hoped to convince world opinion that their rebellion was justified by sending letters to world leaders. Some letters were indeed sent, but if they were received they had no significant impact.[118] And with the exception of a few men like Peter Mbiu Koinange in London, the rebellion had no one to speak for it overseas. Since so few of Mau Mau's leaders were literate, it was not surprising that they would fail to mount an effective propaganda campaign outside of Kenya, but it is puzzling that they apparently never even considered publicizing their goals by holding Europeans as hostages until the British Government and international press agreed to hear their grievances. Similarly, they did not attempt to sway public opinion in Kenya or overseas by treating military prisoners well before releasing them. In the battle for world opinion, the Mau Mau lost at every turn.

On November 2, 1956, the last British troops—the King's Shropshire Light Infantry—left Kenya. Even though the State of Emergency would remain in effect until 1960, the active Mau Mau rebellion was over. The official government figure for the number of rebels killed by the security forces was 11,503,[119] and there can be little doubt that this figure is a substantial, and intentional, underestimate. Many wounded Mau Mau later died in the forest where their bodies were never found; hyenas, which often ate tin cans and flashlights, would completely consume a man's body, including his shoes, in a short time.[120] Others killed during interrogation were buried in unmarked graves and their deaths went unreported. But even accepting the government's figure, and allowing for a good many wounded who were unknown to security forces, the ratio of Mau Mau killed to those wounded was at least seven to one. The comparable ratio for much heavier fighting in Malaya was two to one.[121] Plainly the emphasis among all the security forces, including the British Army, was on killing the Mau Mau, not wounding or capturing them.[122]

The Mau Mau rebels killed 590 men of the security forces, 63 of whom were whites. About 200 white soldiers or policemen were wounded. They also killed 1,819 loyalists and wounded another thousand. In addition, 26 Indian civilians were killed. Mau Mau's original target had been the white farmers, and many people in Britain had been led to believe by sensational press reports that rebels had killed thousands of white Kenyans.[123] But during the entire Emergency, the total number of white civilians who died at the hands of Mau Mau rebels was 32. Over the same period of time, more white Kenyans were killed in traffic accidents in Nairobi alone than were killed by the Mau Mau rebels.[124]

4

"DEBASED CREATURES OF THE FOREST"

THE WARRIORS OF MAU MAU

Just as the Mau Mau rebellion had many forms and changed over time, so too the rebels came from various backgrounds and they also changed as the rebellion continued. Who they were and how they fought is a vital aspect of the story of Mau Mau. To be sure, more than 90 percent were Kikuyu or members of the neighboring Embu and Meru tribes, but many prominent rebels, including generals, came from other groups. Some had been committed to an armed confrontation with the government since 1947 or 1948, but most did not arm themselves until after the State of Emergency was declared, and some who later became Mau Mau heroes did not take an active part in the rebellion until many months later.[1] Some Mau Mau leaders played vital roles on its many committees but never took part in any violence. Hundreds of thousands did not fight but gave money, supplies, medicine, and weapons. The emphasis here will be on those Mau Mau who did the actual fighting, but they could not have fought without the support of many others.

White Kenya made no attempt to understand why the Mau Mau rebels fought, or what they were like as human beings. The Kikuyu had formerly been ridiculed, exploited, or ignored; but after the Emergency was declared, they were considered a deadly menace virtually overnight. Michael Blundell spoke for the whole white community when he called them "debased creatures of the forest." This dark image of the Mau Mau was so pervasive that it affected not only white Kenyans but the arriving British Army as well. One newly-arrived officer said what most other whites were thinking, when he associated the Mau Mau with "all that was foul and terrible in primitive savagery."[2] As far as most whites were concerned, the Mau Mau were filthy, long-haired "vermin" who mutilated cattle and dogs, and brutally murdered women and children. They were held to be contemptible, too, because instead of dramatic tribal war regalia or modern military uniforms they dressed in shabby and dirty European clothing, and instead of wielding modern weapons, they fought with ordinary agricultural tools, traditional swords, or home-made guns. Detestably, they renounced Christianity and practiced "obscene" and "primitive" rituals. No one would deny that they could be dangerous, but they were considered cowards who would never stand up to a white man—or a white woman, for that matter—in a fair fight. The image was distorted, of course, but few whites would ever learn what the men and women who fought for Mau Mau were actually like.

When the State of Emergency was declared most Kikuyu adults, including many who would later become Home Guards, had taken the Mau Mau oath. Many had been forced to take the oath and would do little to help the movement, but others aided the government by day and the Mau Mau by night. Directed by the War Council which had been formed in January, 1952, nearly a year before the Emergency was declared, these supporters of Mau Mau continued to live in Nairobi or the reserves, where they collected weapons and ammunition, clothing, food, and medicine.[3] Outwardly their lives had not changed. But these Kikuyu, whom the British called Mau Mau's "passive wing," were inwardly thrilled by their own clandestine activity, and shared vicariously in the great events that were sweeping over Kikuyuland. They knew that armed men were gathering in the forests, and that they needed supplies. Many people gave generously, often risking arrest, and then waited for news of great events.

The first armed rebels had entered the forests many months before
the Emergency was declared. Some were hard men who had killed for
Mau Mau before and were willing to do so again. A few leaders, like
Waruhiu Itote who called himself "General China," had gained combat
experience with the British Army in Burma during World War II, and
they were charged with the task of taking young men into the forest and
turning them into soldiers.[4] Soon after the declaration of a State of Emergency, these earliest rebels were joined by thousands of naive, even romantic men and women. Most of those who first went to the forest camps
were young men in their 20s, but they were accompanied by some elders
and prophets (who traditionally had played an essential part in Kikuyu
battles) and by women, perhaps a thousand of them in the last months
of 1952. Most, including prominent leaders like Stanley Mathenge and
General China, were illiterate. Throughout the rebellion, only three men
who fought in the forests had as much as a secondary school education.
The great majority spoke no English and knew very little about the world
outside their personal experience. They were tribal people, mostly Kikuyu, imbued with the traditional beliefs of their culture.

The Mau Mau began their fight for independence with a pathetic innocence about warfare. None of them had ever fought in a tribal battle,
and only a handful had been trained for combat in the British army.[5]
They naively believed that with their home-made guns and pangas they
could drive the whites out of Kenya. Few understood that it was not only
the hated white settlers whom they would have to fight, but the far-off
British Government which would send troops, airplanes, and tanks to
destroy them. They went to the forests with the exuberance of young
men the world over, thrilled by their new-found strength as warriors,
encouraged by young women, dazzled by dreams of glorious victories.
Those who had firearms believed that the weapons gave them immense
power and the courage to face their enemies. One young rebel who entered the Aberdare Forest armed with a stolen pistol said, "I felt strong.
With such a gun I could kill any *Mzungu* (white man) completely. No one
could treat me like a dog again."[6]

The new warriors did not leave their homes to the sound of martial
music, and children did not wave flags or throw flowers as they passed
by, but the rebels sang songs that spoke of the righteousness of their
cause and promised the destruction of their oppressors. They called
themselves warriors, *itungati*, and as they marched they experienced that
combination of excitement and foreboding familiar to young soldiers in
many lands. Once they received permission from the tribal elders to

enter the forests, they assembled in their forest camps. The young men dreamed of the exploits they would carry out as warriors, but they worried, too.[7] They knew that young Kikuyu women scorned men who did not fight for Mau Mau. Would these women now trill in honor of their heroism? Would they speak of their love and offer their bodies? Would fellow warriors compose songs recounting their deeds? Would their leaders reward them? Would their elders praise them and tell others of their bravery?

Like soldiers in other wars, the young men would become hardened soon enough, and the romantic innocence of these first months would be forgotten, but for now this gathering of warriors was exhilarating. As they came together they reassured themselves of their strength, their virtue, and their common cause—the fight for land and freedom. In the beginning, the kinsmen and neighbors who served as their leaders made little attempt to teach the young volunteers military tactics or to organize them into cohesive units. Instead, they sang patriotic songs and prayed to the Kikuyu god, Ngai, every night and morning, sometimes roaring their prayers like lions to show their fervor for battle. Except for a few who had visited the forest to collect honey, its wet darkness was as alien for the rebels as it would later become for the white men who would fight them. Although most had several blankets they had to accustom themselves to the cold, the night sounds of colobus monkeys, and to the singing of hundreds of birds that always began before dawn. During the day, the rebels had meetings, many meetings, and they ate well. In addition to the roasted beef or goat that were the favorite foods, they ate maize meal either baked in cakes or made into porridge, sweet potatoes and yams, roasted bananas and ears of corn, beans and—a particular favorite—small flavorful peas called *njugu*. In some areas, the rebels enjoyed fresh bread from bakeries in the reserves that had been commissioned to supply the Mau Mau soldiers.[8] And if the need arose, the rebels strolled back to their families in the reserves to visit their wives or girl friends, fetch a warm coat, take care of a business transaction, or supplement their larder.

It was all terribly unmilitary in the beginning and the Mau Mau leaders in Nairobi could do little to put matters on a more warlike footing. Before the Emergency was declared, the War Council had elected Stanley Mathenge as Chairman of the military movement, with General China in charge of the Mt. Kenya area, and Dedan Kimathi as Secretary. In the early months of the fighting the War Council, which saw itself as a civilian body, deferred to the leaders in the forests on military matters, and as time passed the military leaders became increasingly independent of the men in Nairobi.[9] Even during this initial period of organizational confusion, forest units made hostile forays. Between the declaration of a State of Emergency on October 20 and early spring of 1953, when Mau Mau forces began to consolidate in large camps deep in the forests, there were 10 attacks against whites and 2 others against Indians. It is not clear how many of these attacks, if any, were approved by the newly reorganized War Council, and how many were carried out independently by local leaders. It is possible, as the Kenya Police sometimes admitted, that some raids were not the work of Mau Mau at all but were carried out by gangsters; but that was a problem that would persist throughout the hostilities. With the single exception of an attack that took place in the European suburb of Karen in Nairobi (named after Karen Blixen), these raids were aimed at white settlers close to the Kikuyu homeland, rather than at those in the more distant Rift Valley or in the still more remote western white highlands. The fact that there were only 12 attacks over a period of five months would suggest that the Mau Mau leaders did not have a concerted plan to kill Kenya's whites or Indians, as the settlers believed.

With rare exceptions, these first attackers were armed only with pangas and swords. When confronted by gunfire—as on January 6, 1953, near Nyeri when two women fired at Mau Mau raiders, or on February 16 near Rumuruti to the north, when a woman alone at home with her daughter repelled several Mau Mau with a few gunshots—the inexperienced rebels fled rather than expose themselves to danger. This behavior reinforced the whites' conviction that the Mau Mau were craven cowards. The white Kenyans also believed that the Mau Mau were only capable of killing women and children, and it is true that the rebels sometimes did so. In addition to the attack against the Rucks' farm where young Michael was killed, several children were wounded or killed in two more of these early raids. On December 9, a well-to-do Indian shopkeeper near Thika was killed at home at 3 A.M. His wife and two children were injured, though not seriously, and the attackers left the survivors with these parting shouts: "We don't want you here. Don't come back. Return to India!"[10] In April, 1953, near Karatina, well-armed Mau Mau raiders wearing grass masks to disguise their faces attacked the home of an Italian sawmill foreman, who had arrived in Kenya with his family just 10 days earlier. He was not home but his wife, their 15-year-old daughter, and 10-year-old son were all killed.

Even so, white Kenyans were wrong in believing that Mau Mau raiders always killed women and children. In other attacks, women and children were spared. An Indian woman who worked on a British farm was strangled because she attempted to escape during a raid and raise an alarm, but her three children were not harmed. On February 16, 1953, a dozen or so raiders entered the house of a British woman in a posh Nairobi neighborhood. They cut the phone lines, but finding the man of the house away they did nothing more to his wife and children than slap the woman with the flat of a panga. Understandably, the government found no reason to celebrate the restraint that these raiders showed. For them it was terrible enough that attacks were taking place at all. But there was something more remarkable than restraint in the killing of women and children.

Raping the enemy's women has been a nearly universal concomitant of warfare, and Mau Mau did sometimes rape loyalist Kikuyu women and girls,[11] just as both black and white soldiers of the government security forces raped women whom they suspected of supporting the Mau Mau. Nevertheless, it went unremarked by the government or the press that despite ample opportunity no white or Indian woman was raped in these early raids. In fact, not one of the "debased creatures" of Mau Mau was accused of raping a white woman at any time during the entire period of the rebellion.

This sexual restraint was ignored by the white settlers and the government. The portrait of Mau Mau that they were presenting to the world press, and which many of them believed, was one of savages beyond the human pale. They described small "gangs" of "terrorists" who lived like animals in forests where they regularly engaged in shocking sexual orgies which the whites somehow imagined were taking place around North American Indian-style bonfires. They also let it be known that Mau Mau gangsters drove themselves into murderous frenzies by drinking alcohol, especially gin.[12] In reality, there were no sexual orgies in the forest camps and alcohol was strictly prohibited.

Early in 1953, at least 15,000 fledgling Mau Mau warriors were gathered in a few large forest camps to prepare for the serious business of fighting for land and freedom. Some of these camps held only a few hundred men, but others under charismatic leaders like Stanley Mathenge, Mbaria Kaniu, and Dedan Kimathi in the Aberdare Forest, and General China and General Tanganyika in the Mt. Kenya forests, gathered several thousand men. The largest of these camps, Kiriaini, which was meant to serve as a permanent base and headquarters in the Aberdares, sometimes held close to 5,000 people. Kimathi, who would later become the primary leader of the Mau Mau forest fighters, spent only one month in the British Army during World War II before he was discharged for drunkenness and attempting to intimidate other recruits,[13] but a few Mau Mau leaders including Stanley Mathenge and General China had combat experience with K.A.R. battalions during World War II, and many others had served in the British Army as non-combatants.[14] These leaders were faced with the daunting challenge of transforming thousands of young men from starry-eyed dreamers into soldiers who could defeat the British Army.

Unlike the earliest camps which were set up very close to the settled areas of the reserves, the large camps they organized were located deep in the forests. Some, like Kiriaini, were at such high elevations that they were inside the bamboo zone. The camps had store rooms for food and other supplies, hospitals, workshops for gun manufacture, kitchens, mess rooms, and housing for women, elders, soldiers, officers, and cooks. Kiriaini had three large kitchens with gabled roofs and (in a touch that would have amused the British if they had seen it) the officer's huts were built to resemble tents; in addition to providing sleeping quarters, each "tent" had a fireplace. There were food storage facilities and small vegetable gardens. The camp was ringed by sentries who challenged patrols and work parties as they returned to camp, and watched over groups of women as they gathered firewood and water. Each camp had a camouflaged escape path. No one danced around a bonfire, but mock camps were set up several miles away where fires were kept blazing to lead security forces away from the actual camps.

If Kikuyu warriors of a half-century earlier could have looked closely at Mau Mau camp life they would have been astonished. Traditional Kikuyu warriors fought together as members of age-graded regiments, men of the same age who had been ritually circumcised at the same time. Although they were greatly influenced by Kikuyu prophets who predicted the best times and places to fight, the most distinguished warriors among them formed a kind of officer corps that had considerable authority.[15] The Mau Mau leaders who established large camps in the forest imposed what was for the Kikuyu an entirely alien form of British military discipline. They were deadly serious. Orders had to be obeyed without question, and regulations were imposed to cover every aspect of camp life. Ranks were established, saluting was mandatory and the new warriors were required to obey their leaders or suffer the consequences, which could be death.

The men were bugled awake to the sound of "reveille" at 5:30 and fed a maize-meal porridge (officers had meat and tea as well); after breakfast, whistles summoned the warriors for morning prayers, followed by a "parade call" where men and women were assigned their duties for the day. Next, warriors actually performed calisthenics, marched, were taught to lay ambushes, use cover, clean and fire their weapons, and protect themselves during air raids.[16] After the evening meal the warriors knelt facing Mt. Kenya before being led in prayers that gave thanks for Ngai's blessings and asked for victory over the white enemy. As they prayed, they held their short Kikuyu swords high and twirled them so that they sparkled in the moonlight. After sentry duties were assigned, the men who were not on duty talked, sang, and smoked marijuana or native tobacco before falling asleep. Sometimes they sang until after midnight.

If the Mau Mau warriors had ever doubted that their new leaders meant business they quickly learned otherwise. These men not only conferred ranks on themselves—usually that of general—and on their subordinate officers who were "majors" or "captains," they also dressed to set themselves apart. Those who had one wore a British battle jacket, and all wore distinctive head wear. A few preferred berets or British military hats, but most affected white turbans that symbolized African independence from British missionary influence.[17] Not to neglect traditional Kikuyu culture, officers also carried elders' walking sticks. Equally important as a means of establishing authority, each leader wore a wristwatch and carried a holstered pistol on a gun belt. Some went much farther. When General Kurumu, a leader in the Mt. Kenya area, was killed during a raid, he was dressed in a British Army officer's khaki tunic on which had been sewn the buttons from several British regiments as well as the ribbons of the Distinguished Service Order and the Victoria Cross. His rank was shown by shoulder insignia from an R.A.F. uniform. He wore a British Army slouch hat bedecked with heron's feathers.[18]

One reason for the use of military titles was to strengthen military discipline. It was the privilege of leaders such as Mathenge, Kimathi, and General China, who were appointed to their commands by the Mau Mau War Council in Nairobi, to confer rank on others, although Mathenge, for reasons that are still unclear, refused to accept any title of rank for himself.[19] In the early months of the rebellion, there was little ceremony involved in conferring such rank. A leader like General China would simply call a meeting of his officers to witness the promotion of some deserving man to an officer's rank. Sometimes the new officer would receive an envelope containing a few shillings as "pay" or, more accurately as a promissory note of rewards to come, because each officer was promised a portion of the white settlers' land after Mau Mau victory. Later, rank, especially high rank, would be conferred with the utmost ceremony. The worthy officer would be handed a sword, spear, or club as symbols of warrior status and an elder's walking stick as a mark of high rank, and fulsome speeches about his virtues and courage would be made. Karari Njama recorded such a ceremony when "Field Marshal" Dedan Kimathi, leader of his newly declared "Kenya Parliament," became "Prime Minister," and a younger officer was raised to Kimathi's previous rank of field marshal. After directing the man (named Macaria Kimemia) to stand, Njama took his weapons away before pouring a horn of beer and gourd of sheep's fat over his head saying, "may this fat and honey soften your head and let it grow above other heads." Admittedly, wishing that someone's head would soften does not sound terribly military; but the idea was to exhort the newly-promoted man to superior wisdom.[20] After adding the words "May God bless, keep, and guide you"— strangely Christian-sounding in an anti-Christian Mau Mau military camp—Njama declared that the Kenya Parliament had promoted Kimemia to the rank of field marshal and had also "knighted" him "Sir Kimemia, Knight Commander of the East African Empire."[21]

The stated purpose of these puffed-up ranks and titles was to convince the outside world to recognize Mau Mau as a legitimate military force and offer it support.[22] The belief that the declaration of ranks and knighthoods would favorably impress the British or other western governments dramatizes the remarkable unsophistication of Mau Mau's forest leaders. General "Simba" (lion) had a nice ring to it, but "General Jimmy" did not sound military or menacing, and although the western press reported the activities of "General Kubukubu" and "Brigadier Nyamonduru," it is unlikely that either became a household word in Britain. It is also unlikely that the men who chose to call themselves "General Highclass," "Mwangi Cowboy" or "Major King Kong" made a wise decision if their intention was to impress westerners.[23] When it was reported that one Mau Mau leader was called "Lieutenant-General Montgomery," readers must have wondered when he had been demoted from his World War II rank of field marshal, and when it was learned that one of the major Mau Mau leaders was called "General China," and another "General Russia," the response was not respect but concern about communist influence.[24] And the decision of one Mau Mau leader to call himself "General Hitler" was, it seems safe to say, ill-advised as a means of gaining favorable international recognition.[25]

There was also a touch of posturing, even megalomania, in the quest by many Mau Mau leaders for ever more exalted ranks and titles. Mau Mau's most prominent leader was Dedan Kimathi, and none bestowed more titles or honors on himself. During his turbulent childhood, Kimathi was a brilliant student, but he was also combative and violent and he suffered from epileptic seizures. Shortly after KAU was founded, he became a militant member, and by 1950 he was a Mau Mau oath-administrator who carried a double-barreled shotgun and advocated the use of force in compelling people to take the oath. Shortly after the State of Emergency was declared he was arrested for murder, but despite being handcuffed he broke out of his prison cell and escaped. His many followers joined him in the Aberdare Forest, where his intelligence and oratorical skills made him a dominant leader. The British Government even appeared to recognize Kimathi's preeminence when, in 1955, Her Majesty's Stationery Office sent a package to Nyeri addressed to "The Prime Minister, Sir Dedan Kimathi." Police intercepted the package which contained a note regretting that the British Government publications Kimathi had ordered were out of stock. Kenya's white community was so enraged that the Stationery Office was forced to issue an apology to the Kenya Government.[26]

Kimathi not only knighted himself, then promoted himself to field marshal and prime minister, he made his girlfriend a colonel, the highest rank a woman was permitted to hold, declaring her "Knight Commander of the Gikuyu and Mumbi Empire," and, in all seriousness, "Mother of God." It was traditional among the Kikuyu, as it was in most Bantu societies, for leaders to increase their stature by praising themselves and being praised by others, but Kimathi's titles were too pretentious for many of his followers to stomach.

Despite their ludicrous ranks and titles, most Mau Mau officers were tough, capable men who were able to keep the respect of their soldiers. They did so, in part, by maintaining discipline. Anyone found guilty of disobeying an officer's order was flogged; in one camp the standard number of strokes was 18, and in addition the offender went without food or water for 12 or 24 hours while he lay in pain tied hand and foot.[27] Some offenses carried a sentence of death. Anyone who kept money sent from the reserves for his own use could be executed, as could anyone who killed without orders or gave information to the enemy. The accused was tried in front of the assembled warriors by officers, some of whom specialized as judges. When a consensus about a man's guilt was reached, he was sentenced. Alphonse Nganga, known as "Chief Justice Karanini," said after he surrendered early in 1955 that he had handed down over 100 death sentences, not to mention a large number of flog-gings.[28] There are several eyewitness accounts confirming the penalties for such crimes were carried out, either by an officer—who usually shot the guilty man with his pistol—or by a Mau Mau version of military police who typically strangled the offender with one of the 3-foot-long leather ropes that each warrior was required to carry as a garotte.[29]

Although military discipline, like many aspects of Mau Mau camp life, was obviously adapted from the leaders' knowledge of British military practice, other aspects would have been entirely foreign to a British sol-dier. He would probably have understood the requirement for compul-sory prayer easily enough, although the content of some—such as those that asked for friendship of animals—might have seemed strange. Actu-ally, these prayers were quite practical from the Mau Mau perspective. They wanted to stay on good terms with the animals (except for rhinos that were considered hopelessly implacable enemies, and porcupines that ate the ivory that the Mau Mau hoped to trade for weapons), because many of them gave warning of the approach of British forces. The British might also have understood the Mau Mau passion for singing before, during, and after their many compulsory meetings but they might not have realized that they were not singing traditional songs, nor were they singing for pleasure. Their songs were filled with references to lost land and to past and present heroes, especially Kenyatta and Koinange. There were also continual refrains about pain and suffering, about the need for education, and the quest for freedom after the "Europeans" were driven out of Kenya. There were also repeated references to the many wrongs that the whites of Kenya had inflicted on Africans.[30] Like the slogans of Soviet workers, these songs sound terribly stilted in English, but they were said to be emotionally moving in Kikuyu and clever as well. They must have been, because, tired as they were, men often sang them until late at night.[31] The last refrain to one such song is as evocative in English as it was in Kikuyu:

> Mother, whether you cry or not,
> I will only come back when our lands are returned;
> When I obtain our lands and African Freedom![32]

There is nothing peculiar about the men of a revolutionary army singing songs about the reasons for their rebellion, although the amount of time they spent doing so was certainly remarkable. Somewhat more peculiar was the common practice of ending these song fests by reading a verse from the Bible.[33] Despite their explicitly anti-Christian policy, many Mau Mau rebels apparently saw nothing paradoxical about this practice; it was widespread, and the Mau Mau leaders who later wrote about their experiences made no attempt to explain or justify it. Even Kimathi carried a tattered copy of the Old Testament, translated into Kikuyu, at all times, and he often read from it.[34]

The presence of women in the military camps would also have surprised the British who, at least in the twentieth century, typically went to war without women. In earlier times, of course, British armies, like many others, did have some women in their camps to cook, wash, and occasionally provide sexual favors. Many European armies have allowed women to live near their military bases as "camp followers," and some, like the French, have paid young women to follow their troops in mobile brothels. Although women traditionally had played no active part in Kikuyu warfare, the Mau Mau not only had women in their camps, they had many of them. It was estimated that there were 450 women in one camp alone.[35] Before the big camps were organized, women who joined smaller forest bands carried out the usual domestic chores, including knitting sweaters for the warriors. As the large camps consolidated, some women returned to the reserves to be with their families, but many remained. They continued to perform their traditional duties of cooking, collecting wood and water, and generally caring for men. But some women demanded a larger role in the fight for land and freedom. They joined the men in military training and accompanied them into combat. They were soon to prove that they were warriors, too, not just cooks and sexual playmates.

Although white Kenyans imagined sexual orgies taking place throughout the forest, in most bands there was a strictly enforced rule against any sexual contact between the warriors and the women of Mau Mau. This rule was traditional. The Kikuyu had tabooed sex during wartime because it was thought to weaken men and divert their thoughts from the serious business at hand. The rule was also imposed as an attempt to avoid conflict in a situation where men greatly outnumbered women. But this prohibition was meant for traditional warfare, when a raid might last a week or so—not for a protracted war. The rebels only obeyed the taboos as long as members of forest bands, women as well as men, could easily and safely find sexual partners in the reserves. When the Mau Mau forces moved so deeply into the forest that they could not have sexual relations in the reserves, sexual tension inevitably arose. Officers took advantage of their authority to reserve some women for their exclusive use, and soldiers paired off with women whenever they could. Some women were shared by many men, but sexual relations were always conducted in privacy.

When Karari Njama arrived at one of Kimathi's camps and was shown to his sleeping quarters by a captain, he was pleased to find a comfortable bed and a warm fire. Njama was one of the three men in the forests with a secondary school education, and he served as military secretary to both Stanley Mathenge and Dedan Kimathi. He was accustomed to being treated well, but was startled to find a handsome young woman in his quarters. The captain explained that the girl had been assigned to Njama, and that she would be responsible for all his domestic needs, including whatever sexual requirements he might have. In Kimathi's camp all officers, or "leaders" as they were sometimes called, were provided with a girl of their own, many of whom had more or less been dragooned into this role after they entered the forest carrying food. Njama was shocked and he declined the girl's sexual services. The next day he complained that the warriors could not afford to feed and defend so many women, that women would create conflict, and that when they became pregnant they would be unable to escape from an attack. What is more, infants could not be raised in the forest, and he worried that some of the girls who had been forced to serve Mau Mau against their will would escape to the government and tell them all they knew.[36] Although some leaders shared Njama's concerns, it seems that no one else was willing to live without women; neither were most of the warriors, many of whom eventually managed to have their wives or girlfriends join them.

The presence of older men and women in these camps was also foreign to the British military model. Although elders traditionally took no direct part in Kikuyu warfare, their presence legitimated the Mau Mau movement. They also did much to celebrate war and to aggrandize warriors through their remembrances of past battles. As young men listened, they told exciting stories about their own experiences in battles against the Maasai or the Kamba, and they seldom overlooked an opportunity to tell the young men how wonderful it was that they would soon have the opportunity to serve as warriors. Sometimes, their remarks could be cutting, as in these words of an elderly woman to a group of Mau Mau recruits:

I want you to know that in the past, the country belonged to the young men; for it was they that fought for it and defended it. I should like you to realize that we are getting old and that the land of our forefathers has been grabbed from us. If you wish to let it go and condemn your children to slavery, that is your affair.[37]

As time passed, Mau Mau military leaders took control of events and the influence of elders in the forest camps waned, but in the early months it is likely that they made more than a few speeches like this one.

Betraying their faith in western medicine, Mau Mau leaders placed great emphasis on developing effective medical resources. Although no qualified doctor was permanently attached to any forest group, once in a while an African doctor from Nairobi would visit the forest and operate on wounded men.[38] In addition, most units contained at least one person who had received some training as a medical assistant, and until the last year or so of the conflict, had adequate medical supplies. Most of the rebels appear to have been vaccinated against typhoid fever, and modern anti-malarial drugs were purchased in large quantities. Penicillin was in good supply, and thanks to penicillin most gunshot wounds healed remarkably well, even those that were probed with a dirty pocket knife to remove a bullet. However, there were no effective anesthetics available, so wounded men had to endure surgery as best they could.[39] Like the British Army, the Mau Mau treated most abdominal complaints with a chocolate-based laxative called Brooklax,[40] and like their British counterparts, Mau Mau soldiers learned to pretend to take such medication before discreetly throwing it away.[41] Some traditional remedies were also used. Perhaps the most remarkable of these was the practice of removing a bullet by having a woman straddle the wounded patient and urinate on the wound. The urine, which had to come from a woman, was said to "float" the bullet, facilitating its removal; it was also said to heal the wound faster than Western medicine could.[42]

Although the Mau Mau relied heavily on Western medical and military practices, they did not abandon their traditional beliefs in omens, charms, and prophecies. All of the major Mau Mau military leaders believed strongly in omens of various kinds, and some rigorously regulated their lives and those of their men by supernatural signs and symbols. Kimathi, for example, believed absolutely in the portents contained in "Napoleon's Book of Charms," and he spent hours each day pouring over his dog-eared copy of this little book. But most leaders, including Mathenge, Kimathi, and General China, placed their greatest faith in their resident prophet, called *Mundo Mugo*, or *ago*. Prophets had played an important role in traditional Kikuyu warfare due to their ability to receive the word

of the Kikuyu God, Ngai, during their dreams. Ngai passed on information about impending enemy attacks, the best times and places to strike
back, what taboos would be necessary, and what supernatural actions
could be undertaken to enfeeble or confuse the enemy.

The Mau Mau leaders relied on these prophets for most of the decisions they made, and despite the unpleasant fact that prophets were
often wrong in their predictions about where and when Mau Mau forces
should attack and by which route, those that were right often enough
became indispensable. Those who made false prophecies were often able
to claim that Ngai's words had been distorted by the thick bamboo forest,
and those who were right prudently concealed the fact that they had
secular sources of information about government forces which, shall we
say, enriched Ngai's words. False prophets risked death, but those who
succeeded were treated like minor deities, being fed and cared for by
others, having their feet bathed, their hair deloused, and all their other
worldly needs seen to.[43] One successful female prophet used the unforgettable English name of "Mama Fortune." Another who was thought to
have exceptional powers was an 18-year-old boy who each morning went
into a trance-like state while praying to Ngai on Mt. Kenya for one hour,
then slept the next hour, repeating this over and over, all day long, from
six in the morning until seven each night.[44]

Even small groups of Mau Mau usually included a prophet whose vi-
sions of the future and interpretations of Ngai's will were accepted without question.[45] Part of the reason why good prophets exercised such
great influence was that they were members of a respected profession.
To become a prophet a man had to be initiated, undergo extensive training, pay substantial fees, and, not least, demonstrate exceptional ability.
The term "prophet" greatly oversimplifies the role of a mundu mugo. In
addition to foretelling the future, these men and—less often—women
treated illness, defended clients against witchcraft and sorcery, and di-
vined the causes of illness and misfortune. Their prophecies were made
possible by their special relationship with god.[46]

Some Mau Mau said that their predictions were startlingly correct.
Camps were attacked when they said they would be, and a path that was
declared safe proved to be so, while one declared dangerous proved to
be just that. As the years of conflict wore on, prophets came more and
more to specialize in predicting where the greatest dangers would be
encountered. In retrospect, it is obvious that they did not foresee enough
of the dangers that eventually decimated Mau Mau ranks, but many who
survived recounted amazing forecasts that saved the lives of those who

believed in them and cost the lives of those who did not.[47] At other times they were well off-target, as when one of the most respected Mau Mau prophets declared that all fighting would end in 1954.[48]

When the magnitude of the problems faced by the fledgling generals is considered it is no wonder that they sought the guidance and reassurance of omens and prophecies. They had to impose harsh military discipline on men who were wholly unaccustomed to it, train them to fight the British Army, somehow find arms and ammunition for them, prevent the sexual deprivation of the warriors from erupting into conflict, and organize a regular food supply from the reserves, all with little assistance from leaders outside the forest. As individual leaders attempted to deal with these and many other problems it is also little wonder that rivalries and misunderstandings grew among them. Because the various war councils in Nairobi, Nyeri, Fort Hall, Nakuru and other towns could not easily communicate with the forest fighters, everyone saw the need for a means of coordinating the activities of individual generals and their men. In response, a council of leaders called "Committee No. 4" was soon established, with five members from the Mt. Kenya forces and five from the Aberdares. In June, 1953, the committee was able to pass a resolution not to kill women or children, and in November 1953, they decided that they would have to wage war against small splinter-groups of Mau Mau—the *komereras*, or outlaws—because they were terrorizing people in the reserves. However, after a promising start, the committee achieved little influence; some of the leaders were already so suspicious of one another that they refused to cooperate. Mathenge, for example, believed that Kimathi had tried to kill him, and still intended to do so. The rivalry became so divisive that the leaders were asked to take a "leader's oath," swearing among other things not to criticize other leaders or—revealingly—to kill one another.[49] All the major leaders took the oath, but their rivalries continued.

When Committee No. 4 was finally established it conducted its affairs on the traditional Kikuyu model of consensus. If there was disagreement, and there often was, the council had no means of enforcing its decisions.[50] As a result, each forest leader had to deal with the organizational problems of creating and maintaining a guerrilla army on his own. Seemingly endless meetings between leaders and warriors were held, often in huge huts that served as meeting halls, in an attempt to create a stable and efficient army. They promoted men to ever-higher ranks, actually distributed pay envelopes once in a while, and passed "legislation" when needed. By mid-1953 most Mau Mau forces made it unlawful for warriors to force women to remain with them in the forest against their will. Women were henceforth to be permitted to choose their sexual partners, and most radical of all, women could now be given ranks as high as colonel based on their abilities as warriors.[51]

As time passed, committees continued to meet, but for the most part the forest generals would always operate independently of one another. No individual, not even Dedan Kimathi who eventually assumed a *de facto* role as leader in the Aberdares, was ever able to become more than a "local" leader based on his reputation in a particular locality, and followed mostly by men from that same territory in Kikuyuland. Perhaps Kenyatta could have unified these isolated armies, but given the difficulty of communication within the forest areas and the strength of the ties that bound local men together, it is doubtful that even he could have managed it. And so, from the beginning of the war to its end, there was no central command. Battles were planned and fought by individual leaders without any overall direction. There were many similarities in weaponry, tactics, and goals among the various military units, but there were many differences too, and as time went on these differences became more pronounced.

Paradoxically, as the men and women of Mau Mau consolidated into large military camps in 1953, attacks against white settlers did not increase; they dwindled. To some extent that was due to opposition by those Kikuyu laborers and servants who remained on white farms and feared the loss of their jobs and even lives if their white employers were attacked.[52] But attacks against whites also grew less frequent because unlike the early days of the rebellion, when small bands of Mau Mau warriors planned their own raids, now "armies" were under the orders of leaders who had decided to attack loyalist Kikuyu rather than settlers.

There were several reasons for this course of action. For one thing, the settlers were no longer easy targets. They were armed, alert, and supported by police and army patrols. British soldiers recovering from wounds or illness were billeted with settler families, where they completed their convalescence armed with sub-machine guns. To reach the settlers' homes usually required hazardous travel over open land, many miles from the protection of the Mt. Kenya or Aberdare forests, and when the raiders retreated into the forests they were bombed and strafed. The Kikuyu Reserve, on the other hand, offered concealment among Mau Mau supporters, with supplies of food, and the welcome of women whose company many warriors were unable to do without. There was also less danger, because in the early months of the conflict, the loyalist

Home Guards, who were usually armed only with spears, were no match for the Mau Mau rebels. What is more, in the minds of most Mau Mau leaders the support that loyalists in the reserves gave to the government was an outrage that could not be allowed to go unpunished. The opposition of the Home Guards was a direct threat to the rebellion, because they could cut off supplies to the forests, and without their supplies the rebels could not survive. The cruelty and venality of the Home Guard was also unforgivable.[53]

The fighting in the Kikuyu reserves between Mau Mau warriors on the one hand, and Home Guards, police, and British military forces on the other, left visible evidence of death and destruction that was duly publicized in Kenya and throughout the world. White opinion pictured the Mau Mau as callous, brutal killers, and some of their well-publicized raids into the reserves gave support to this view. They routinely killed dogs and cats and left them hanging by the neck as warnings to those who opposed them, and their attacks against livestock left hamstrung and disembowelled animals alive and in pain for hours until they were found and put out of their misery. Human victims could be treated with comparable cruelty. Women who opposed Mau Mau were strangled and men had their eyes gouged out. Because the Mau Mau warriors had few guns and less ammunition, much of their fighting was done with pangas and swords. Victims, including women, were sometimes slashed so repeatedly that they were virtually unrecognizable. Some Mau Mau who survived the conflict later wrote about such attacks without apparent concern. Gucu Gikoyo wrote that during an attack against a government post in the reserves he found a Home Guardsman hiding under a bed moaning. Gikoyo dispassionately reported that he chopped the man "into bits."[54]

Mau Mau soldiers also saw nothing remarkable about burning their enemies alive. On one occasion, the formidable General Kago, an officer who repeatedly led his men into fire-fights with British troops, was able to capture a Home Guard post by wearing stolen police and Home Guard uniforms. Thirty Home Guardsmen were disarmed and locked in a house. As Kago's soldiers watched, the house was set on fire. All 30 men died. Although their screams could not have been easy to forget, a man who witnessed their death made no mention of their suffering nor acknowledged any sympathy on his part. All he wrote was that General Kago had said that anyone who opposed Mau Mau could expect no pity.[55]

Whether in response to white brutality or as an attempt to intimidate their enemies, some Mau Mau groups intentionally used brutality as an instrument of war. Henry Kahinga Wachanga, a man with a secondary school education who served as a military secretary for both Stanley Mathenge and Dedan Kimathi, was in a position to know what took place. Two decades after the fighting ended, Wachanga wrote that when Mrs. Gray Leakey was strangled and her husband was buried alive, it was a "tremendous and marvelous" thing that brought "much fame" to the Mau Mau.[56] He also reported that in order to instill fear in their enemies, the Mau Mau killed them in many "different and ingenious ways." After a battle, they might cut a man in half, or if a wounded white soldier was found, they might break both his legs and arms before leaving him to die slowly.

Wachanga also reported that prisoners were invariably executed, euphemistically referred to as taking them to "herd cows for Field Marshal Kimathi."[57] Even white prisoners, who might have been exchanged for Mau Mau detainees or used for other political purposes, were killed. Sometimes a white prisoner would be bound, put in an empty bee-hive at the top of a hill, and rolled into a river to drown. Others would be doused with kerosene and burned alive. Prisoners were also strangled or used for target practice. Wachanga remembers that captive British soldiers were made to kneel while Mau Mau some 30 yards distant tried to shoot them so that the bullet would enter the anus and exit through the mouth. He also recalled the practice of placing three prisoners in a row and attempting to kill all three with one bullet. Once, when the bullet killed the first and third prisoner but missed the man in between them, the fortunate soldier was released with a letter to his commanding officer describing the miracle that saved his life.[58] Whatever the means by which the prisoners were killed, their genitals were usually cut off and their bodies hacked into as many as 50 pieces which were then taken to the reserves and conspicuously displayed for the government security forces to find. The idea was to so terrify the men of the security forces that they would be unwilling to enter the forests, something that Wachanga believed actually happened.[59]

Although Mau Mau rebels often killed prisoners savagely and sadistically, in battle they did not ordinarily kill either indiscriminately or with excessive brutality.[60] Analyses were made of all the bodies of Mau Mau victims brought to hospitals for postmortems before June 1954. Very few of the victims, perhaps 2 or 3 percent of the total, were killed by burning. Approximately 5 percent of all reported victims were strangled, and most of these were reported to be traitors to the Mau Mau, who were singled out for this form of execution. Over 90 percent of the deaths were the result of either gunshot or panga wounds. Contrary to press reports that routinely reported that victims of Mau Mau had been hacked so savagely that their bodies were unrecognizable, less than one percent of those killed had been mutilated, and with a single exception, always after death had taken place. Most of the victims had been killed by about six blows to the head. (This pattern was so common that the British pathologist who examined the bodies concluded that the Mau Mau had been trained to kill in this way.)[61] About 10 percent of the victims were women.[62] Most Mau Mau units eventually enforced rules against killing women, although some warriors believed that women who betrayed Mau Mau should be killed, and continued to do so. All units enforced a regulation against killing children, and the rule was rarely violated.[63] Like all soldiers, Mau Mau warriors sometimes killed thoughtlessly, callously, or in a frenzy, but for the most part they followed the rules of war as they understood them.

Even during the passion of combat, orders not to kill women or not to have sexual relations with them were usually obeyed. When these orders were infringed, the offender could be killed. When warriors under General Kago's command attacked a Home Guard post they slashed eight Home Guardsmen to death before discovering that one Mau Mau warrior had abandoned the battle and was having sexual intercourse with a woman he found in a house. Such behavior was against Kago's orders because sex at the time of battle was believed to endanger everyone by polluting them. The man was immediately "chopped to bits" (as one of the executioners put it) but the woman was untouched because their commander's orders forbade the killing of women. Similarly, when raiders were ordered to spare a white settler's life, they did so. When, in 1953, a Mau Mau band raided the farm of a white settler named Vias, the raiders took money, a gun, and some food. They also burned farm buildings, but their leader decided to spare Vias's life and his allegedly "savage" men obeyed.[64]

Another remarkable episode took place in late December, 1954. While her husband was away, Mrs. Anne Carnelley was at home on her farm with two small sons. As soon as she saw a well-armed Mau Mau unit of about 50 men approaching, she grabbed her two boys, aged two-and-a-half and one-and-a-half, and ran for a nearby forest. When several Mau Mau soldiers easily overtook them, Mrs. Carnelley fired one wild shot from her pistol before it jammed. She was soon surrounded by angry Mau Mau who pointed their guns at her menacingly; one man, who seemed drunk, threatened her with a knife until he was ordered to stop by the unit's commander. She pleaded with this officer to spare her life and those of her children. Anne Carnelley and her husband had been born in Kenya and had lived there all their lives. She must have been astonished when instead of ordering his "bestial savages" to slash her and her children "to bits," the Mau Mau officer agreed to spare her and her boys if she would promise to leave Kenya on the first plane for Britain. Mrs. Carnelley agreed and carried her children away, while the disciplined Mau Mau ignored her as they looted the house before burning it.[65] The warriors who looted the house laughed among themselves about Mrs. Carnelley's fright, because they knew all along that neither she nor her children would be hurt.[66]

Yet, most white settlers and some British military men continued to dismiss the Mau Mau rebels as cowards, capable only of killing unarmed women and children. General Erskine wrote in a foreword to a handbook on the Mau Mau, distributed widely to British officers, "We must certainly not overrate our enemy. He is a rotten shot, poorly armed and he seldom stays to fight."[67] It is true that most Mau Mau warriors were rarely willing to attack the homes of armed settlers, that they often chose quite elderly victims for their attacks, and they sometimes fled from armed women. It is true that most Mau Mau units usually avoided firefights against the heavily armed British troops, or men of the Kenya Regiment. It also happened that some Mau Mau, even leaders like Field Marshal Kanji (also known as "Sir General Hika Hika") gave up when the fighting got "too hot."[68] But it is also true, as a few white Kenyans were willing to admit, that many Mau Mau rebels who fought in the forests were dedicated and brave.[69] Most of the rebel warriors had little fear of the Home Guard, the African police, or even some K.A.R. battalions.[70] The Mau Mau warriors sometimes routed such units even when they were led by white officers and non-commissioned officers.[71] Sometimes the warriors charged British machine guns with suicidal courage, and officers often exposed themselves to British fire to inspire their men.[72] During a battle against British troops, one of General Kago's young officers exposed himself to British fire so often that his uniform was riddled by bullet holes. Kago was so certain that the man had been wounded that he ordered him to undress to prove that he was unhurt.[73]

When Mau Mau soldiers fought with reckless courage, whites typically said that they must have been drugged.[74] It is true that most Mau Mau in the forests smoked marijuana, and many chewed *miraa*, an amphetamine-like drug,[75] while others used opium; but there is little direct evidence about the effects of these drugs on men in battle. General China wrote that although the majority of Mau Mau leaders disapproved of it, drug use was not prohibited "where men were already accustomed to it," because "we found that some men gave a much more reliable performance if they were not denied it prior to battle."[76] But General China added that drugs were not used as stimulants for combat. The implication is that drugs served to calm men before battle, not arouse them to behave recklessly.[77]

Much of what the whites interpreted as cowardice in the Mau Mau reluctance to face British troops was a result of their chronic shortage of ammunition. When Mau Mau units had enough bullets they fought such ferocious battles against British troops that the forest sometimes caught fire around them, and on more than one occasion large Mau Mau forces attacked British forces in daylight to prove their bravery.[78] Once they fought so fiercely that a unit from the Malaya-hardened Devonshire Regiment was forced to withdraw.[79] Although Mau Mau soldiers envied the seemingly endless supplies of ammunition that the British troops possessed, they were not impressed by British marksmanship. Most of them later said that if they had had comparable weapons and ammunition, they would have defeated the British troops.

Courage was not a male monopoly among the Mau Mau. Many women shared the same hardships and dangers that men did, and in some instances took even greater risks. Much of the burden of stealing weapons and ammunition fell to women who travelled to the reserves where they relied on their wiles, and sometimes the allure of their young bodies, to steal guns, then find a way to escape to the forest with them. Some women risked their lives again and again in this role. When they were caught, as they sometimes were, they resisted the terrible tortures of their captors so courageously that General China wrote that they were braver than men.[80] The *Times* reported with surprise the refusal of 60 women, who were captured carrying supplies to the forest, to reveal any information to their interrogators.[81] In another act of courage, some mothers also volunteered the services of their young children to run errands or to spy. Children as young as 8 took the Mau Mau oath before collecting information about the security forces under the guise of children's games, and passing it along to Mau Mau contacts. Some were killed by suspicious Home Guards, who taunted the distraught mothers, saying that the children had "found independence."[82]

Women took a variety of active roles in the rebellion. One served as a judge on a Mau Mau court, where she passed death sentences on offenders. There were even some women who, along with men, served as Mau Mau executioners.[83] One was known to have strangled a white woman to death.[84] Many also fought in combat, firing their weapons effectively, and sometimes leading men in battle. During one battle, Wamuyu Gakura put down her sten gun and yelled at the men around her to use their pangas rather than waste their ammunition. The men obeyed. In other battles, groups of women warriors burned villages, set up ambushes, and fought alongside men.[85] When uniforms were worn, women wore the same uniforms that men did, such as the long black coats of General Kago's troops, and the green head-bands of General Kabu's soldiers. And at least one Mau Mau unit was commanded by a woman.[86]

The men and women of Mau Mau fought bravely in hundreds of battles and raids, but as for most soldiers in most wars, weeks and sometimes even months passed without fighting at all. During these lulls in action, meetings took up more time than any other activity. There were meetings about unity and solidarity, meetings to attract more non-Kikuyu into the Mau Mau, meetings to draft letters to the Kenya Government, to British officers, or the international press, meetings to confer ranks and titles, to declare a National holiday after victory, to reallocate the white settlers' land, to codify Mau Mau laws, to try offenders, and always, to discuss plans that would bring victory to the Land and Freedom Army. It was an unusual day when there was not at least one meeting of some kind. One Mau Mau veteran recalled that "when we were not at a meeting, we were on our way to one."[87]

Although the search for unity and victory dominated Mau Mau meetings, day-to-day activity still centered on acquiring food, guns, and ammunition. Food supplies were relatively reliable until mid-1954, when "Anvil" destroyed the Mau Mau support network in Nairobi and British forces largely cordoned off the forests from the reserves. But guns and ammunition were always a problem. Some Home Guards and K.A.R. soldiers were willing to sell weapons and ammunition, and the women of Mau Mau were adept at stealing guns and bullets, but only a limited supply of armaments could be acquired in this way, and, as Home Guards became better armed and more efficient at infiltrating the Mau Mau, the risks became grave. The penalty for possession of a gun or even a single bullet was death. Brave women still dressed as Muslims and smuggled rifles into the forest under their robes, and others carried bullets hidden in cans of milk, imbedded in maize meal, or even inserted in their vaginas, but more and more were being arrested after they had been betrayed by loyalists in the reserves. Sometimes large supplies of weapons and ammunition were captured in raids on military or police posts, but increasingly these raids failed with a heavy loss of life and of weapons already possessed by the Mau Mau. New sources of supply were sought in the Northern Frontier District where Somali, Boran, or Rendille traders would sometimes sell firearms, but other times they turned against Mau Mau buyers. Caravans were also sent to Ethiopia where it was hoped that even if the Government of Haile Selassie would not openly support the Mau Mau, it would at least surreptitiously sell arms. These caravans apparently never reached their destination.[88]

In desperation, Mau Mau units set up improvised "factories" to manufacture weapons. Gun-stocks were carved from hard wood taken from the forest, many yards of water pipe were taken from settlers' irrigation systems for gun barrels, and inner tubes were supplied by Nairobi to release the hammer that would hopefully detonate the bullet. General China had a factory in which 20 men produced rifles, including, as their experience grew, repeating rifles with ingeniously designed magazines, firing mechanisms, and trigger assemblies.[89] Remarkably, many of these weapons worked, although many British soldiers owe their lives to the failure of these weapons to fire at point blank range.[90] The Mau Mau also manufactured arrows, and for a while they mass-produced a deadly poison; but after another of their interminable meetings it was decided not to use it out of fear that the British would retaliate with poison gas.[91] Despite their remarkable skill in manufacturing firearms, the Mau Mau were never able to produce gun powder, a failing that greatly restricted their access to ammunition and, more insidiously, convinced some among them that they still had much to learn from the whites.[92]

Mau Mau forest units were always concerned about security, and security measures became all-important as the Kenya Police Air Wing began to make greater use of light "spotter" planes to search out their camps, while K.A.R. units, sometimes with blood hounds, began to search the forest. Everything had to be camouflaged or hidden in caves. Fires could only be burned at night when their smoke could not be seen, and alert sentries were now essential to survival. Passwords, whistles, and calls became highly complex. Large camps were vulnerable to detection from the air and bombing raids, so smaller, better-hidden campsites had to be found, and the warriors had to be ready to move at the first alarm or the sound of approaching bombers. Although false alarms greatly outnumbered actual attacks, occasionally a British patrol would be seen by sentries, there would be a brief exchange of gunfire, and the Mau Mau would usually retire deeper into the forest because it was impossible to know if the troops were only a small patrol or the advance guard of several battalions. When large-scale "sweeps" were carried out, they did not result in enough dead Mau Mau to please the British command, but they did scatter rebel forces, destroy their camps and supply caches, and leave them with a growing sense of insecurity.[93]

As difficult as it was for the Mau Mau to fight against British troops with their abundance of modern weaponry, it was at least a familiar kind of combat for them. Air raids, on the other hand, were utterly foreign to them; many had never seen an airplane before, and called a bomber's open bomb-bay door its "navel." Even though the many tons of bombs dropped on the forest killed relatively few, they did kill some, and the bombing and strafing frightened nearly everyone. Sometimes light bombers would appear at low altitudes with little warning, while at other times flights of heavy bombers would make pass after pass at high altitude, dropping thousand-pound bombs more or less in the vicinity of a camp spotted by a reconnaissance plane. Now and then a single large bomb would kill a score of men, but more often they missed their mark or fell on a camp that the Mau Mau had hurriedly left when they heard the drone of approaching planes.[94]

Even when the bombs missed their target, the tremendous explosions terrified the Mau Mau, who ran for cover, pressing themselves into a hole or under a fallen tree, where they lay praying to their god as massive detonations shook the ground and left their ears ringing for hours. Like soldiers in most armies, some Mau Mau were so unnerved by bombing and shelling that they left the forest for good.[95] In addition to demoralizing Mau Mau units, these heavy bomb blasts drove animals into a frenzy, sending terrified elephants, rhino, and buffalo stampeding through the forest. Soon animals came to associate the sound of thunder with a bombing attack, and an approaching storm would terrify large and small animals alike. The Mau Mau quickly learned that the best cover from a bombing raid was at the foot of a large tree where they could find at least partial protection. Monkeys apparently came to the same conclusion, and as the British bombers droned overhead, men and monkeys huddled together at the foot of trees in a touching testimony to the kinship that terror can bring.[96]

Although the Mau Mau had to be alert each day for an attack on the ground or from the air, months might pass without one. They quickly adapted to the cold and rain of the forest, learning to sleep soundly on the coldest of nights, and if they noticed the rain at all, they welcomed it as a cleansing shower.[97] The only time that the weather bothered these veterans of forest living was during July, when the forest was enveloped by gray, cloying mists that entirely blotted out the sun. Some found the

gloom so depressing that they left the forests and returned to the reserves.[98] Others were depressed because they missed their parents, wives,
or children, and did not even know whether they were alive.[99] Most Mau
Mau were not depressed, not yet; until Operation Anvil and the process
of "villagization" cut off their supply lines, they usually had enough food
from the reserves, supplemented with their favorite food, wild honey.
Many units still rustled settlers' cattle and drove them rapidly back into
the forests, sometimes knotting the cows' tails so that the men could hold
on while the animals painfully pulled them up slippery mountain paths.[100]

At times, life in the forest camps could be enjoyable. Many of the
rebels managed to find companionship, affection, and even love. Warriors sang, prayed, talked about everything, smoked marijuana, and even
had an occasional drink of prohibited maize beer. They played cards,
checkers, *bau* (a complex African game that resembled both chess and
Parcheesi), wrestled and danced. Men also played outrageous practical
jokes on one another: one favorite involved tying a sleeping man's feet
together so that he would fall when he got up in the night to urinate.
Contrary to the stereotype held by Europeans, the men and women of
Mau Mau laughed and enjoyed life. Some of their officers led by their
ability to make their men collapse in laughter when it was necessary to
relieve tension.[101] Humor was essential for survival in the forest, and
many Mau Mau were remarkably funny, as the British later discovered
when they captured them.[102] They especially liked to joke about the close
escapes that most of them had experienced.[103] And when death came to
their comrades, they did not allow themselves to grieve very long. They
said, "It's nothing," and went on as before.[104]

Not all the rebels fought from forest camps. The rebellion also depended on the support of sympathizers in the reserves, and in Nairobi
and other towns. Until mid-1954, the Central Committee and its war
council still purchased weapons, organized food supplies, and recruited
new fighters for the forest armies. These new recruits were issued special
identification cards in order to prevent infiltration by government informers.[105] Meanwhile, men and women in the Kikuyu, Embu, and Meru
reserves continued to supply money, information, food, and weapons.
Many risked their lives as often as those who fought in the forest. In fact,
much of the actual fighting was done by men and women who lived in
the reserves, and in Nairobi or smaller towns. Units from the forests
often entered the reserves at night, and spent the day sleeping in the
houses of sympathizers or hiding in a secluded area, before carrying out
their raids and returning to camp. But others who had never entered the

forests were sometimes called into action by a local leader, usually with
the approval of higher Mau Mau authority. Sometimes they were ordered
to kill a Kikuyu traitor, at other times to raid a Home Guard or police
post for weapons. Mohamed Mathu, who in his words was one of these
"urban guerrillas," described several raids in which police were killed for
their weapons, while Home Guards in African neighborhoods in Nairobi
were killed because they were, as Mathu put it, "amusing and enriching"
themselves at the expense of women, old men, and children.[106]

Mathu and his fellow urban Mau Mau also attacked mosques in Nairobi because it was thought by some that Muslim Indians were using
"evil magic" to help the government. In one attack against Eastleigh
Mosque, eight Muslims were killed and many others were wounded.[107]
And it was urban Mau Mau, not rebels from the forests, who planned
and carried out the attack on Lukenya Prison that freed many Mau Mau
prisoners. When, after the Lukenya Prison attack, one of these urban
rebels was badly wounded and could not keep up with his retreating
unit, the risk of leaving him behind was too great, as he might possibly
reveal the names of the others while being tortured and interrogated by
government forces. Told that he would have to be killed, the wounded
man agreed and urged his comrades to escape. After a close friend shot
him in the head, the rebels stripped him of his watch, jacket, shoes, and
pants.[108] The Mau Mau did not often stand on sentiment.

Although Operation Anvil made it difficult for Mathu and others like
him to operate in Nairobi, occasional raids in and around the city continued throughout 1955. As late in the conflict as April of that year, a
small Mau Mau unit led by General Njeke killed two teen-aged white
boys who were pigeon-hunting near a Nairobi suburb, because they
thought that one of the boys had a gun. It turned out to be an air-rifle.
The frustrated gang was cornered in a ravine behind the Prince of Wales
School, where most of Kenya's young white men were educated. Twelve
of the men who surrendered were tried for murder.[109]

After Operation Anvil, the already greatly limited ability of the beleaguered Mau Mau rebels to cooperate was further restricted. Warriors in
the Mt. Kenya area were cut off from those in the Aberdares, whose
loyalties were split between Stanley Mathenge and Dedan Kimathi. Both
Mathenge and Kimathi created councils that each declared to be the
supreme ruling body in the forests. Kimathi's was called the Kenya Parliament; Mathenge's, predictably more traditionally named, was called
Kenya *Riigi* (meaning, unity; literally, a traditional door made of reeds
woven together). The division between the two forest leaders widened,

as did divisions within their camps. Disgruntled warriors who felt they were the victims of injustice sometimes left their leaders; others shot it out with them in disastrous confrontations.[110]

These disputes sometimes involved high-ranking leaders, as when Field Marshal Kimathi and some of his officers ordered a group of young women, who had just arrived in camp with food from the reserves, not to return home. General Kago disagreed, feeling that these women would provide greater service by carrying food to the camp than they would as sexual partners for Kimathi and his officers. Kago was arrested, tried, and sentenced to death for questioning Kimathi's will. As Kago was being fitted with a noose, men loyal to him killed two of the hangmen and slashed the rope. Three hundred armed men and women left the camp with General Kago, leaving Kimathi's forces depleted and dispirited.[111] Kago soon became perhaps the best combat leader in the forest.

In addition to confrontations like this one, there were recurring complaints that Kimathi and other officers were living in comparative luxury while ordinary soldiers were hungry, filthy, and forced to live without women. Some leaders joined their disaffected warriors in demanding that "educated" leaders like Kimathi and his secretary Njama cede power to the non-literate majority. They believed that "educated" Mau Mau leaders had been so influenced by Christianity and white civilization that they had rejected the religion and values of traditional Kikuyu culture, and could not be trusted to lead the fight for freedom. It is no surprise that these warriors looked to Stanley Mathenge, who like them was illiterate, as their champion.[112]

From the earliest days of the Emergency, small bands of men created problems by breaking away from larger Mau Mau groups to form independent units. These komereras, or outlaws, lived by their own devices in pursuit of their personal goals. By late 1954, as a result of the isolation of the forests from the reserves and the conflicts within Mau Mau ranks, growing numbers of men slipped out of Mau Mau camps to become komereras. Most of them formed small bands near the forest's edge, where they hoped to be able to obtain some food, and perhaps surrender in safety. In order to discredit the Mau Mau, Home Guards sometimes paid komereras to steal food from rebel sympathizers in the reserves.[113] Although some komerera bands included former leaders, most of these abandoned rank and privilege to live with their followers as equals, although, paradoxically, one of the renegade leaders who had been most vocal in opposition to Kimathi's abuse of rank continued to call himself "Lord" Gicambira.[114]

During this period of growing internal conflict, some leaders imposed still more shocking oathing ceremonies in order to insure the loyalty of their followers. Throughout the Emergency, the Kenya Government prepared press releases describing graphic details of oathing ceremonies that included bestiality, orgiastic group sexual melees, drinking the menstrual blood of prostitutes, and cannibalistic frenzies that involved killing traitors, drinking their blood, and eating their brains. According to one such press release, an oathing ceremony that allegedly took place near Naivasha in September in 1953 was said to require initiates to place a piece of meat in the anus of an old women, to prick human eyes with a thorn, bite a human brain, drink menstrual blood, eat the brain of a dead European, and drink the urine of a menstruating woman. Each act had to be repeated 7 times. Other ceremonies were said to involve such sexual acts as inserting a dead goat's penis in a prostitute's vagina, and licking it after each insertion, a man inserting his own penis in a prostitute's vagina, and forcing a dog to insert its penis in a prostitute after which each initiate licked the penis. Each of the acts had to be repeated 7 times, after which the candidates jumped over the woman 7 times, repeating that just as she was lying on the ground, so would he lie dead if he revealed the oath. One Mau Mau veteran recently described an oath he took which involved killing a person, drinking some of the victim's blood, then jumping back and forth over the body 7 times to demonstrate that "people were like ants" who could be killed without a second thought.[115]

These reports, which were intended to discredit Mau Mau in the eyes of the security forces and the world, were often exaggerated and sometimes entirely false. Prisoners were often tortured to reveal the details of their oaths, and some soon learned that only by providing lurid accounts of purported ceremonies could they satisfy their captors. Although most oathing ceremonies never even approximated the grisly bacchanalia that the Europeans found so plausible, some units did conduct ceremonies involving ritual cannibalism and sexual behavior that many Mau Mau themselves found appalling. Mohammed Mathu reported that during a raid in Kiambu against a white settler's home, a Kipsigis watchman was killed. The raiders filled a calabash with the man's blood and cut out his heart and liver for use in an oathing ceremony. The details of the ceremony so upset the relatively well-educated Mathu, who served as his unit's secretary, that he refused to record the incident in his notebook.[116]

Many of the tensions that were tearing the Mau Mau apart existed even before Anvil and the "villagization" program. When General China was captured early in 1954, the cease-fire he arranged as a prelude to amnesty and further negotiation was violently opposed by Kimathi and received only lukewarm support from Mathenge, although many of the Mt. Kenya leaders loyal to General China accepted it. Even the Kikuyu forest fighters were divided, and Mau Mau members from peoples like the Embu, Meru, Kamba, and Maasai or part-Maasai already fought separately under their own leaders.[117] Many of these peoples had sought amnesty earlier, and, after Anvil and "villagization" had cut their sources of supply, many of the non-Kikuyu Mau Mau melted away.

Soon after Michael Blundell returned from London in January of 1955, with Prime Minister Churchill's urgings to negotiate with the Kikuyu still ringing in his ears, a new round of peace negotiations began. Governor Baring promised amnesty for "crimes" committed prior to January 18, 1955, to any Mau Mau who surrendered. Leaflets containing his offer were dropped over the forest, and small planes with loudspeakers broadcast the news in Kikuyu. Field Marshal Kimathi immediately ordered his secretary Henry Kahinga Wachanga to write to Baring rejecting the offer. For Kimathi and many other Mau Mau, surrender was unthinkable, but an offer of amnesty by the government was a sign of weakness that should be exploited.

A few weeks later, Wachanga, who had by then become separated from Kimathi, decided to take matters into his own hands by sending Governor Baring and General Erskine a list of demands to be met before peace negotiations could begin. Among his eight points were the demands that all security forces be disarmed, British troops sent back to England, all Home Guards disarmed and placed in detention camps, and all Mau Mau detainees released. Ignoring these manifestly impossible terms, the British urged the Mau Mau to meet with them, and with Stanley Mathenge's approval, a delegation of middle-level Mau Mau officers (including Henry Kahinga Wachanga) had a series of tragi-comic meetings with the British.

The first session began with a prayer led by the Reverend Colderwood, but the Mau Mau, whose spokesman was the educated secretary Wachanga, objected to the mention of Jesus Christ. One of those who complained was a Mau Mau officer who called himself "General Jesus." The Mau Mau then offered a Kikuyu prayer before the insults and accusations began to fly. Both sides accused the other of bad faith, and each knew the charges were at least partly true. The Mau Mau insisted on land and political independence; the British wanted surrender. Tempers flared, and General Erskine's deputy, General Heyman, went so far as to unholster his pistol and threaten the delegates with it. Apologies followed and the two sides agreed to meet again. This time, Wachanga—the only Mau Mau representative with a secondary school education—decided in all seriousness to "oath" the government representatives. He had what he called the "the oath ingredients" boiled and placed in a bottle. He then asked the government to bring a black lamb to the next meeting and they agreed. While the lamb was being roasted, the "oath" was surreptitiously poured over it in the belief, as Wachanga put it, that "the government would eat the lamb and become Mau Mau."[118] Somehow, the government representatives were not converted and in the end the meetings accomplished nothing.

After the meetings, which lasted on and off for two weeks, the delegates returned to the forest where Kimathi promptly arrested them. He was furious that any negotiations had taken place without him, and would listen to no excuses that the delegates had tried to reach him but could not locate his camp. Among other things, Kimathi insisted that any future negotiations in his name must be led by Ralph Bunche.[119] After four days of tense captivity, the peace delegates overpowered their guards and escaped with the loss of one life. Henry Kahinga Wachanga later wrote, "this was truly the lowest point in our struggle."[120]

Some Mau Mau units would continue to fight hard, but from this point on, every month brought greater disunity with ever-smaller groups scattering through the forest in increasingly desperate attempts to find food and survive. The offensive spirit of Mau Mau was dead. Mau Mau rebels rarely even talked about attacking white settlers anymore; it was far too dangerous and unproductive. The reserves were dangerous too, not only because they were filled with government security forces, but because most of the Kikuyu there had turned against Mau Mau. They were now convinced that the government would win, and after years of giving more than they could afford to marauding Mau Mau bands who had increasingly taken what they wanted by force, the Kikuyu in the reserves simply wanted their suffering to end.

Women took the lead in turning the reserves against Mau Mau. Even very early in the Emergency, women sometimes killed raiders who stole their crops or flocks, and now they did so more often.[121] Wives, mothers, and sisters tried to convince visiting warriors to give up the struggle. One Mau Mau general surrendered when he heard his mother's voice over a loudspeaker imploring him to give up because the cause was lost.[122] But when efforts like these failed, as they usually did, women betrayed their men to the Home Guards in the belief that even captivity was preferable to a continuation of the combat.[123] The Mau Mau soldiers who were trapped in the forests of the Aberdares and Mt. Kenya were no longer fighting for freedom or land, they were fighting to stay alive. They were depressed, hungry, without ammunition, and harried from every direction, but most of them were still not yet ready to surrender.

The days early in the rebellion when confident Mau Mau leaders would send insulting or hilarious letters to the British were over. In July of 1953, Henry Kahinga Wachanga, who signed his name then as "Gen. Sec. H. W. Kahinga," wrote to Baring and Erskine with the news that the Mau Mau had begun to build a tin can factory so that they could can the flesh of the defeated whites. A touch macabre, perhaps, but it was meant as a joke. About the same time, General Kago decided that his unit of 500 men would spend the night within 200 yards of a British camp. The following morning, after his men had safely left, Kago sent a letter to the British commanding officer thanking him for his hospitality.[124]

As 1955 wore on, the surviving Mau Mau were truly forced to become "creatures of the forest," as Blundell had called them years before. They still possessed remarkable good humor, but their spirits were beginning to wear decidedly thin and animosities grew. Some of the conflict about loyalty to Kimathi versus Mathenge continued (even though the latter had not been seen for some time), but the major source of disagreement was food. As the Mau Mau grew hungrier, failure to share food could lead to serious disputes, and sometimes to violence.[125] Accusations that a man had unfairly taken an ounce of cooking fat, or a few kernels of corn, could have fatal consequences. More and more, men kept whatever food they had tucked away in woven satchels that they carried with them at all times, adding the smell of rotting meat to their own body odors. When there was food, it was cooked after dark over a fire that was ready for quick extinction. The fire was made by arranging logs like the spokes of a wheel—if more heat was needed the logs were pushed in toward the flames, and if the fire needed to be put out they were pulled away.

The search for food dominated Mau Mau life. Although some bands were very skilled in trapping animals, or shooting them noiselessly with arrows, or even fishing (fish were a tabooed food under normal circumstances), other groups often went three or four days without eating before they could find some honey or kill a large animal.[126] Few could settle down long enough to assure themselves a steady food supply either from the reserves or the forests, because in addition to major sweeps by British battalions, patrols by the police, the K.A.R. and the Kenya Regiment, often aided by tracker dogs, the British were now sending into the forest their deadliest weapons—former Mau Mau rebels from forest units who, after capture, had agreed to fight against their former comrades.

Called "pseudos" by the British, these men knew the forest, knew Mau Mau bird calls of identification, and knew how to kill with the modern weapons the British gave them. Most pseudos were willing to turn against other Mau Mau because of the divisions that were tearing the movement to pieces. Mau Mau captives who had been loyal to Mathenge were often willing to work for the British in tracking down Kimathi and his men. Pseudos posed a deadly danger because they dressed and acted like true Mau Mau, knew the passwords and recognition signals, and often gained the confidence of a unit before either killing its members or taking them captive.[127]

Mau Mau rebels often covered their tracks so well that even the "pseudos" could not follow them, and if they were taken by surprise, they ran from danger with such astonishing speed that pursuit was usually impossible. With the aid of spotter planes, British officers were able to determine that even though a fleeing group of Mau Mau had to run on slippery forest paths that were seldom level and always obstructed by thorns, nettles, or sharp bamboo leaves, some could cover the amazing distance of 45 miles in a day as they fled uphill deeper into the mountain forest.[128]

Although Mau Mau units seldom stood to fight in those days, even their most implacable enemies—the white officers of the Kenya Regiment and Kenya Police Special Branch—admitted that the Mau Mau had never ceased to be courageous.[129] These ragged, filthy, lice-ridden men and women were hungry and miserable, but there can be no doubt that those who remained in the forests in 1955 and 1956 were dedicated. They made their own clothes from animals skins, even found their own medicines in the plants and trees of the forest. Mau Mau women were as forest-wise and hardy as the men. Many shared their bodies with the men of their unit, sometimes including "pseudos" who infiltrated their camps. On one occasion the "pseudo" in question was a white Kenyan police officer who begged off (for fear that his black make-up would run and betray him) by claiming that he had a venereal disease, something the Mau Mau greatly feared.[130] The woman, who had previously questioned his virility when he showed no interest in her sexual advances, now turned away from him in horror.

But even in these desperate times a few Mau Mau units managed to live comfortably in well-concealed, ingeniously constructed camps near streams. One had escape paths through giant ferns and creepers that would allow the Mau Mau to drop 20 feet out of sight without injury, while their pursuers were left behind baffled. There was also a fire-pit surrounded by shallow scooped-out sleeping pits made to accommodate a man's body and filled with soft leaves. There were food storage pits, too, containing maize, forest spices and herbs, and fresh meat from cattle killed on a nearby white farm.[131] Sometimes the rebels had cigarettes, like Kenya-made King Stork or Crown Bird brands that were no longer considered evils of white civilization, and now and then maize beer might be brewed as well, even though drunkenness was still considered a crime. So seriously was this prohibition taken that on one occasion, when a pseudo team came upon some authentic Mau Mau who were drunk, the pseudo leader felt obliged to flog the offenders. Such punishment would have been expected if suspicious eyes were observing the pseudos, but it also appears that the pseudos were as offended as real Mau Mau would have been.[132]

The Mau Mau achieved impressive mastery over their forest environment, but in their increasingly desperate search for hope and security they placed even more faith in the supernatural.[133] The members of one unit were required to shake out their blankets every morning and evening and spit on them to remove "evil spirits." One of the men, who was educated and skeptical, objected that he had entered the forest "to fight for land and freedom against European oppressors, not to kill Africans and practice useless oaths and magic."[134] The Mau Mau prayed with increasing fervor, clutching soil in their left hand as they raised their swords with their right, and they made pilgrimages to various sacred trees where their prayers were expected to have still greater force. They saw omens in anything out of the ordinary—a falling star, a strange sound, an animal that behaved in an unusual way—and leaders and ordinary warriors alike typically changed their plans dramatically and suddenly if they believed that they had received a supernatural warning. One man recalled that as he was following a forest path, a civet cat twice crossed his path. Such boldness was rare for a civet cat, so when it returned a third time, the man concluded that it had been sent to warn him of danger. He took cover and almost immediately saw a large force of British troops, Sten guns at the ready, moving up the path he had been taking.[135] Some leaders, like Kimathi, believed that their dreams were literally true. When Kimathi dreamed that there was danger, he moved his camp, and when he dreamed that one of his men was a traitor, that unfortunate man was killed.[136] Stanley Mathenge believed in dreams and omens every bit as much as Kimathi did.[137] The Mau Mau had always relied on the supernatural, and now, in an atmosphere of perpetual insecurity, their reliance turned to desperation.

By 1956, except for a handful of Mau Mau who remained in the forest for years after the fighting stopped, the only choices for most forest warriors were surrender, capture, or death. By this time only the very dedicated were still fighting, so very few surrendered. Many died, the largest number at the hands of their former comrades, the pseudos. One pseudo killed 47 Mau Mau, and captured others.[138] Many pseudos captured more Mau Mau than they killed, but few Mau Mau gave up without a fight. Some were clearly in shock as pseudos bound their hands; others struggled, shouted, frothed at the mouth, and struck the ground in rage and frustration.[139]

A few of the more educated Mau Mau had always imagined that Ethiopia would provide them refuge and perhaps even embrace their cause. The two best educated men in the forest in 1956, Karari Njama and Henry Kahinga Wachanga, both General Secretaries, tried to lead groups of Mau Mau to Ethiopia when it became obvious that further resistance was hopeless. Neither got more than a few miles from the forest before being captured.

Dedan Kimathi eloquently defended the cause during his trial, but as the date of his scheduled execution drew closer, he found solace not in the righteousness of Mau Mau but in the Christian faith that he had never abandoned. At 1 A.M. on the morning he was hanged, Field Marshal Kimathi, the best-known leader of Mau Mau's armed rebellion, wrote his last letter, to Father Marino, a Roman Catholic priest. Touchingly, Kimathi wrote that he was worried about his wife, his aging mother, and his son's education. He wrote in English, "I am so busy and so happy preparing for heaven tomorrow 18th February, 1957." He closed with these words: "I remain dear father Yours loving, and Departing convert."[140]

The Kenya Government exulted at the end of Mau Mau, but events would demonstrate that for thousands of men and women the death of one man did not mean the end. Although the fighting had ended, Mau Mau resistance would continue.

5

"DARK AND DREADFUL DISTORTIONS OF THE HUMAN SPIRIT"

THE WHITE REACTION TO MAU MAU

Although the rebels committed some atrocious acts, white Kenya's reaction was equally vicious. After an initial explosion of white rage, the settler community carried out a calculated policy of brutality and murder that in various ways implicated the government of Kenya and the British Army. Appalled by Mau Mau oaths, the maiming of cattle, and the murder of loyalist Kikuyu, many whites were convinced that the Mau Mau movement was a dark, primitive threat to Christianity and civilization even before the killings of whites began. After the murders of Bowker, Meiklejohn, and the Rucks, white Kenyans and their government were united in the conviction that the Mau Mau were bestial savages, crazed by unspeakable oaths, void of all human restraint, and beyond the reach of decency or redemption. They believed that the Mau Mau would kill women, children, anyone, in sheer animal frenzy. There could be no understanding "animals" like these; there could be no mercy, there could be no forgiveness.

For white Kenyans, Mau Mau was the embodiment of an atavistic return to the savagery that they believed had pervaded all of Africa before European colonization. In their view, Europeans had put a veneer of "civilization" over African magic, cannibalism, murder, and sexual perversion, but now it was clear to them just how thin that veneer had been. For the whites to protect themselves, and to protect other Africans not yet infected by the "disease" of Mau Mau, as they thought of it, the movement would have to be crushed, and those who had joined it cleansed of their evil or killed. In words identical to those heard on the American frontier a century earlier, some whites insisted "the only good Kyuke is a dead Kyuke," and they called for the extermination of the entire Kikuyu people.[1] Most white Kenyans would not go that far, but they were determined to exterminate Mau Mau.

In October 1952, shortly after the Emergency had been declared, Sir Oliver Lyttleton, the Colonial Secretary, flew to Kenya to take stock of the situation. Lyttleton was far from sympathetic to the Mau Mau. He found their oath ceremonies nauseating, their violence disgusting, and their rebellion totally without provocation. Yet, when he met with the elected European members of Kenya's legislative council, he was shocked by their proposals. First, Michael Blundell urged him to declare carrying a panga a criminal offense to be punished by immediate flogging. Lyttleton did not see how he could deny Africans the right to carry a simple agricultural tool, and he observed that if the government did so, Africans would "only get something sharper." Another member urged him to permit the 470 Somali and Turkana members of the Kenya police then stationed in Nairobi to be "turned loose" against the Kikuyu with no holds barred, assuring the Colonial Secretary that those 470 "were quite capable of taking care of the million Kikuyu." Lyttleton ignored this idea.

The white legislators then turned to the need for swift police action. Lyttleton objected to proposals for overt vigilantism, although Blundell tried to assure the Colonial Secretary that they were not recommending that the government should "line up 50 people and shoot them." Lyttleton snapped at him, "You went a very long way to give that impression." Blundell meekly replied, "I'm very sorry, sir." He then tried to explain that if the police saw a suspicious gathering of Kikuyu, they should be allowed to open fire. Another elected member, Major Albert Keyser, the European's elected legislative "leader" before Blundell was elected to that post, strongly supported Blundell. Lyttleton's notes recorded the following exchange:

> LYTTLETON: Are you suggesting they should be shot down?
> KEYSER: Yes, sir. Quite definitely. Having lived for 32 years in this country, I am quite sure that action should be taken.
> LYTTLETON: That means that anybody you do not like anywhere, you will shoot them down. You cannot do that.
> KEYSER: Have you been able to maintain law and order by these other methods? I think we have failed dismally by those methods.
> LYTTLETON: That is a matter of opinion.
> KEYSER: It is a matter of history.[2]

Many settlers thought that their elected leaders, including Keyser and Blundell, were far too "soft" on Mau Mau. They had already begun to take the law into their own hands, and they demanded that the government take much harsher measures as well.

When Field-Marshal John Harding, the Commander-in-Chief of Britain's Middle-East Command, returned from a hurried trip to Kenya early in 1953, he wrote the following secret appraisal of the settlers:

> They are hotly resentful of the disturbance to their lives in the Colony, very critical of the government and clamoring for drastic action. By this they mean that executions and floggings should take place after the slightest formality of trial, or without trial altogether. The Africaner community, which is of considerable size, is loudest in its demands for such action. The most immediate anxiety of the Governor is that some of the settlers will take the law into their own hands, and indeed there have been cases already, fortunately hushed up, of their doing so.[3]

Baring had sent secret warnings to the Colonial Office, as early as November 1952, that he feared the settlers would "go out of control" and launch a "civil war" against "blacks."[4] When the settlers focused their fury on Jomo Kenyatta, the "evil mastermind" of Mau Mau, Baring was eager to appease them by prosecuting Kenyatta. Actually Baring's government had two choices. It could have simply detained Kenyatta, Kaggia, Kubai, and the others as had been done 30 years earlier with Harry Thuku, or it could bring them to trial. Trying them was a political risk. An acquittal would stir the Kikuyu as nothing else could do, and a con-

viction would be seen by all Africans as a frame-up. Nevertheless, the
Colonial Office insisted on conviction in a court of law, and even though
the settlers pressed for a simple detention order, Governor Baring chose
to oblige the Colonial Office, but wanted a conviction in court guaranteed.[5] Baring, whom Britons might ordinarily have relied upon to uphold
British standards of impartial justice, knew how to achieve the result he
desired. The trial would be rigged.[6]

After considerable discussion, the government decided that Kenyatta
and five members of KAU's executive committee would be charged with
"managing" a proscribed society, namely the Mau Mau. The major problem the government faced was finding a judge they could rely on to
convict Kenyatta. With everyone's concern focused on Kenyatta, no one
seemed to have realized that among the other five defendants were two
of the actual "managers" of the Mau Mau, Bildad Kaggia and Fred
Kubai. Kenyatta, regarded as the malevolent revolutionary, trained in
the Soviet Union and thought to be capable of manipulating the entire
Kikuyu people, was the only defendant who mattered. Governor Baring
apparently approached at least one senior judge with an offer to try
the case in return for an agreement that Kenyatta would be convicted.
The judge was reported to have turned him down,[7] but another, Ran-
sley Thacker, Q.C., former Attorney-General of Fiji, and for 12 years a
member of Kenya's Supreme Court, accepted the governor's mandate.
As a special magistrate, he would judge the case without a jury. Kenyans
approved of the appointment, saying that Judge Thacker could be relied on because he was, in the highest possible Kenyan accolade, "a
sound chap." They were right. Thacker, an aging bespectacled man
with an imposing pot belly, had agreed to provide a conviction; with
less than judicial discretion, he told confidantes before the trial that he
would convict Kenyatta so convincingly that no court of appeal could
possibly overturn his verdict.[8] But Thacker insisted on £20,000 gratuity
so that he could live comfortably in the United Kingdom, saying that
he would not be safe in Kenya from African reprisals. Thacker's request
for what was frankly a bribe did not go through the office of Kenya's
Attorney General. It went directly to Governor Baring, who, in a remarkably indiscreet act of self-incrimination, agreed to this extraordinary
payment.[9]

With Judge Thacker safely on the bench, it still remained for the government to decide where to hold the trial. On the grounds of security
(though whether from the Mau Mau or Western reporters might be disputed), it was decided to try Kenyatta and the others at a remote admin-

Jomo Kenyatta, a British-educated African, became a spokesman for Kenyan nationalist aspirations when he published *Facing Mount Kenya* in 1938. Kenyatta would later be the symbolic leader of Kenya's Africans throughout their struggle for independence. Although he was not the master strategist the British took him for, and actually disapproved the use of violence, he was jailed in 1952 as the "evil genius" behind the Mau Mau insurgency. Above, Kenyatta campaigns in Nairobi in 1962, six months before becoming Kenya's first President. (UPI/Bettman Newsphoto) Below, a 1959 photo shows Kenyatta while still in detention at Lodwar. To his left is a young visitor named Daniel arap Moi who would serve as Vice-President under Kenyatta, and later succeed him as President after Kenyatta's death in 1978. The other men are fellow prisoners, among them the principal organizers of Mau Mau, including Fred Kubai (*extreme left*) and Bildad Kaggia (*extreme right*). (Courtesy A. Hopf)

A State of Emergency was declared in Kenya on October 20, 1952, and the
Lancashire Fusiliers were flown from Egypt to Nairobi on board long-range
Royal Air Force transport planes. It was the longest airlift in British military
history. The Fusiliers (*above*) spent their first day parading through Nairobi to
encourage Kenya's whites and intimidate its Africans. (Topham) Below, Sir
Evelyn Baring (*second from left*), who led their fight against Mau Mau, with other
prominent white Kenyans: Sir Michael Blundell (*far right*), the political leader
of Kenya's white settlers: to Baring's right, Deputy Govenor Sir Frederick
Crawford, and to his left, General Sir George Erskine, commander of British
military forces during the Emergency. (Courtesy William Collins)

The Fusiliers (*left*), pictured here being inspected by Governor Baring, were soon joined by other British battalions, including veterans of fighting in Malaya and Korea. The British also sent naval forces, artillery, engineers, heavy RAF bombers, light-bombers, and even jet fighters to crush the rebellion. (Topham) The Kenya Regiment (*below*), made up of the sons of white settlers, was also mobilized, and the Kenya Police were greatly expanded. These men were as heavily armed as Army regulars. Several battalions of the King's African Rifles—African soldiers led by British and noncommis-sioned officers—were also rushed to Kenya from other British colonies. (Topham)

White Kenyans were outraged when Mau Mau "terrorists" brutally murdered settler Roger Ruck, as well as his wife Esme and their young son Michael (*pictured above left*) in early 1953. (Topham) A crowd of 1,500 settlers marched on Government House in Nairobi to demand the use of every means to crush the insurgency, and serious mob violence was narrowly averted. Most white settlers took to carrying guns at all times, and housewives received instruction in how to use them (*above right*). Several women did use their weapons to drive off Mau Mau attackers. (Popperfoto)

Most of the 20,000 or more men and women who fought for Mau Mau joined clandestine military units located in the dense mountain forests north of Nairobi (*above*). From their secret forest bases, Mau Mau raided settled areas throughout central Kenya, especially those of loyalist Kikuyi. Later, large British forces tried to engage the rebels in the forests or to bomb them out. Neither tactic had much success. (Topham) In 1955, after logistical problems had weakened the rebels, the British found that small units employing African trackers or former rebels (*below*) were most effective in dealing with Mau Mau forest units. (Popperfoto)

Although hampered by their constant lack of weapons and ammunition, the Mau Mau fought many pitched battles against the British and acquitted themselves well, achieving a striking number of successes. But eventually their own weaknesses and the strength of the opposing forces overcame them. More and more rebels reluctantly surrendered to British security forces (*above*). The rebels avoided Kenyan whites, whom they feared would kill them. (UPI/Bettman Newsphoto)

In order to destroy the rebel's sources of support, police and military forces regularly rounded up and interrogated suspects, frequently using violence, threats of death, and torture. Below, officers of the Kenya Regiment supervise a roundup of men and boys in a Nairobi shantytown. The upraised hands were mandatory even when a camera was not present. (UPI/Bettman Newsphotos)

Native women were known to be the backbone of the Mau Mau support and supply system, and they were subjected to the same forms of intimidation and brutality as men. Above, police and troops of the King's African Rifles use switches to whip Kikuyu women out of their homes for questioning. (Popperfoto) Although many suspected Mau Mau were released after interrogation, over 80,000 were "detained" in hastily constructed camps like the one pictured below at Langata, outside Nairobi. Detainees were kept on a starvation diet with substandard medical attention; they were routinely beaten for minor infractions, and sometimes they were beaten to death. (Popperfoto)

Rebel leader Dedan Kimathi, pictured here in handcuffs after being wounded and captured in an ambush, was Mau Mau's best known military commander and a symbol of implacable resistance. A remarkable orator and charismatic figure, Kimathi inspired tremendous personal loyalty. He was also capable of great brutality, maintaining discipline by means of the gun and the garrote. Like other Mau Mau leaders, he had a penchant for extravagant titles, styling himself Field Marshal Sir Dedan Kimathi, and assigning similar honors to those in his retinue. Above, his ceremonial leopard-skin cloak and cap are displayed for the camera. Kimathi always carried with him copies of the Bible and *Napoleon's Book of Charms*, which he consulted as an oracle to guide him in his strategy. After a trial during which Kimathi remained defiant, he was sentenced to death and hanged on February 19, 1957. He converted to Catholicism in his cell and died after receiving absolution. His death brought an end to organized Mau Mau resistance. (UPI/Bettman Archive)

istrative post called Kapenguria. The place was so obscure that when Governor Baring signed the trial orders, he placed it in the wrong province. Kapenguria was a dusty outpost of the British Empire some 30 miles north of Kitale, the nearest settler town. Aside from a few colonial administrators and some Pokot tribesmen, no one lived near the place.[10] It was inaccessible by railroad, had no water, hotel, telephones, or restaurant. It did have a corrugated iron-roofed school room in which the court could be convened. Road blocks were set up so that no one could even drive to Kapenguria without special permission of the police. It was the perfect place to frame Kenyatta, but one problem remained. According to Kenya law, Kenyatta should have been tried in Kiambu where he was arrested. To deal with this awkward legal technicality, Kenyatta was released from police custody in Kapenguria but before he could take a step he was arrested again. Now Kapenguria could legally be the venue for his trial.[11]

Those who were permitted to visit Kapenguria were amazed to see its school room ringed with barbed wire and surrounded by troops behind sandbagged barriers. Planes circled overhead, and a yellow armored car was parked menacingly at each of the building's four corners. Kapenguria was impregnable against Mau Mau attacks, but the press was another matter. The government had badly underrated international interest in the case. Kapenguria was truly remote and well-guarded, but for the sake of appearances Kenyatta and his fellow prisoners had to be allowed counsel, and in the wake of his lawyers came reporters. Since the outcome of the case had already been decided, it mattered not at all who defended Kenyatta. Still, his choice of counsel made matters worse for him. Kenyatta was defended by Britain's most famous—and notorious— trial lawyer, Dennis Lowell Pritt, Q.C. Pritt was in his mid-sixties, but no less combative or trenchant for his age. The problem was that Pritt was well-known in Britain as a communist sympathizer, exactly what Kenyatta was thought to be. To inflame the settlers even more, when Pritt arrived in Nairobi, several thousand Africans gathered at the airport to greet him.

If Kenyatta's case could possibly have been damaged further, Pritt managed to do so by surrounding himself with an entourage of radical lawyers from Kenya and overseas. The government refused entry to several of these men but allowed Pritt to enter the country with a Nigerian lawyer named Davies, and a lawyer from India named Lall who was, to the horror of white Kenyans, a close friend of Prime Minister Nehru whose Indian Government was thought to support the rebellion in

Kenya.[12] These men were joined by two talented young Kenyan lawyers, and the whole team traveled to Kitale, where to Pritt's dismay his colleagues were not allowed to stay with him in the Kitale Hotel—a modest hostelry, but reserved for whites only. Pritt's team of lawyers eventually found lodgings with sympathetic Africans (who were promptly subjected to repeated police raids). Injudicious to a fault, Magistrate Thacker set up quarters in the settler-run Kitale Club rather than the slightly more neutral Kitale Hotel.

Pritt had as much chance of acquitting Kenyatta in the forthcoming trial as he would have had defending Hitler. In fact, in an article which was widely read in Kenya, Kenyatta's former University of London classmate Elspeth Huxley called Kenya's future president a "small-scale African Hitler."[13] The trial itself went slowly in the hot little courtroom, as every utterance had to be translated back and forth from Kikuyu to English. A little excitement was provided when the defense challenged the court's interpreter on the grounds that he was taking extraordinary liberties with the witness's words. Reluctantly the court dismissed its interpreter, Dr. Louis Leakey—yet another former classmate of Kenyatta's, and hardly an impartial appointee. Still, Pritt did his best, and after the prosecution had presented its evidence, he put it to Judge Thacker that the case against Kenyatta was the most "childishly weak" ever made against any man in any important trial in the history of the British Empire.[14]

On January 24, 1953, Thacker adjourned the court to consider Pritt's arguments. Later that evening the Ruck family was murdered and all of white Kenya erupted in outrage. As usual, Thacker spent the weekend with settlers at the Kitale Club, where he heard them say such things as, "the only good Kyuke is a very, very dead Kyuke," and "no bloody wog is running me off my land." The judge could not have remained unaware that, on the following Monday, white settlers stormed Government House in Nairobi with a savagery that few lynch mobs could exceed. Directed by white Kenyans now in the uniform of the Kenya Police Reserve, about 2,000 white men and women walked two miles from downtown Nairobi to Government House. Most were wearing their Sunday best, women in dresses and hats, men in suits and ties, most with hats including a few white pith-helmets. Despite their attire they were not there to show respect, and many were armed. When they reached the seat of Kenya's government they demanded that Governor Baring come out to meet them. Prudently, he refused, and instead sent the available policemen, who happened to be African, to cordon off the increasingly belligerent crowd.

The mob of Kenya's "civilized" white citizens responded with howls of obscene protest, and, as the African policemen tried to hold them back by clasping their hands in a human chain, they showed once and for all what contempt they had for black policemen. Shouting, "take your nigger police away," white men and women lit cigarettes and pressed them against the hands and faces of the policemen until they gave way. After singing "God Save the Queen," which would, apparently, justify whatever action might follow, the enraged settlers attempted to break down the huge main doors to the building. Michael Blundell, who was in Government House at the time, managed to intimidate the Commissioner of Police into ordering his African policemen to withdraw, but even that provided only temporary respite because, during the resulting lull, the very dark-skinned Sultana of Zanzibar had naively walked out onto a balcony in Government House to see what was happening. According to Blundell, a "little woman dressed in brown" who was the respected owner of a Nairobi shop, screamed, "There, there, they've given the house over to the bloody niggers, the bloody bastards!"[15] Others were equally out of control as they shouted abuse at anyone connected with the government. The crowd did not open fire or lynch anyone, but it was a near thing.[16] Later that day, in clubs and meeting halls from Nairobi to Nakuru, white settlers talked about plans for killing all the Kikuyu in a single location to set an example, and at a public meeting in Nakuru, the settlers seriously proposed to kill 50,000 or so Kikuyu to set a better example.[17] Some even spoke about exterminating all Kikuyu—over a million people.[18] One man argued that an atomic bomb should be used for this purpose.[19] Another settler's wife later wrote that the proper solution would have been to select a Kikuyu village and kill every man in it.[20] This woman's knowledge of the Kikuyu seems questionable since they did not live in villages, but there can be no doubt that her enthusiasm for killing was authentic.

When Thacker reconvened the court, which as usual was crowded with settlers who brought picnic lunches (attended by African servants), it was hardly a surprise when he ruled that the prosecution had indeed established a case against Kenyatta and his co-defendants. It is not known whether he had read a Nairobi newspaper that openly warned him against acquitting Kenyatta, but there was no danger of acquittal. After hearing the evidence, Thacker had declared that, although ten defense witnesses had exonerated Kenyatta, he had been far more impressed by the one prosecution witness who had implicated him as the leader of Mau Mau. That was hardly a surprise: This witness, Rawson Macharia, had been bribed, as he later swore in court when he provided documents showing that the government had agreed to send him to England for university study, to keep him there with his family, and to guarantee him a government job on his return to Kenya.[21] When Macharia revealed late in 1958 that he and six other witnesses had been paid to lie in court, there were demands in Britain for a judicial inquiry. Governor Baring was unmoved. He not only refused to order an inquiry into Kenyatta's conviction, but ordered that Macharia be prosecuted for perjury. Macharia was duly convicted and sent to prison.[22]

When Judge Thacker finally convened the court for his judgment against Kenyatta in early April 1953, Rawson Macharia had been in England for 3 months. Pritt had left Kenya a month earlier, realizing by then that he could serve no further purpose in this obviously political trial. Addressing the court, Kenyatta said that neither he nor his co-defendants were guilty, and repeated that he stood for peace and did not condone the mutilation of human beings. None of this could prevent Mr. Thacker from summing up with the bewigged solemnity that was his right as the presiding magistrate. Judge Thacker began by bluntly telling Kenyatta that he did not believe him, and then, in a judgment that (allowing for translation into Kikuyu) took an astonishing seven hours to deliver, he went on to say, "I am satisfied that the mastermind behind the plan was yourself. I also believe that the methods to be employed were worked out by you. . . . You have successfully plunged many Africans back to a state which shows little humanity. You have persuaded them in secret to murder, burn and commit atrocities which will take many years to forget. . . . Your Mau Mau society has slaughtered without mercy defenseless men, women and children in hundreds. You let loose upon this land a flood of misery and unhappiness. You put the clock back many years. You have much to answer for, and for that you will be punished."[23] Accusing Kenyatta of exploiting the "primitive instincts" deep in the Kikuyu character to make them commit "evil atrocities," Thacker gave him the maximum sentence—seven years hard labor followed by an indefinite period of restriction to some far-away part of Kenya. The judge added that the sentence was too light. Kenyatta was sent to Lokitaung Prison in the extreme north of Kenya, where Makhan Singh, who had more to do with the origin of Mau Mau than Kenyatta did, had earlier been held. Kenyatta's co-defendants received the same sentence. Judge Thacker left the courtroom in an armored car and immediately flew to London.[24]

By the time the trial had ended, much had happened to further inflame white passions against the Mau Mau. Every day, as white Kenyans read the *East African Standard* and listened to the radio, they learned that there had been more attacks against loyal chiefs, more attacks on Mission schools and Home Guard posts in the Kikuyu reserve, and more of their neighbors' cattle and horses mutilated. The death toll of white victims grew, too. The numbers were not large but many were well-known and sometimes beloved members of the small white farming community, and some were among the first settlers in Kenya. One—73-year-old James MacDougall—was so badly crippled by arthritis that he could not even attempt to defend himself against the panga blows of his assailants. Others were young men who had come to Kenya after World War II, but they too were remembered and mourned, like Anthony Gibson, a former British Army officer who had been captured by Axis forces in North Africa during World War II and whose father was a Rear-Admiral. Sometimes the victims were such recent immigrants that they were virtually unknown, but the circumstances of their deaths saddened everyone. So it was a few days after Kenyatta's trial ended, when a young Italian mother and her two children were killed while the husband was away. One hundred Kikuyu who were employed at the mill neither helped the victims nor reported their deaths. A Kamba worker had to run 10 miles to give the alarm.[25] Since the Italian family had arrived in Kenya just 10 days earlier, it was obvious that the only reason for these murders was the color of the victims.

For many settlers the most horrifying aspect of these Mau Mau attacks was the active assistance of previously trusted Kikuyu servants. The trust they had placed in their servants had been violated and the vengeance they sought came from a deep sense of disillusionment and betrayal. Anything that could turn their own servants into killers was primitive and evil. Governor Sir Philip Mitchell, who had for so long denied that Mau Mau was a threat to Kenya's stability, spoke for most settlers when he wrote that Mau Mau derived from the "black and blood-stained forces of sorcery and magic, stirring in the hearts and minds of wicked men" who represented "dark and dreadful distortions of the human spirit."[26]

Equally dark and dreadful distortions of the human spirit were taking place throughout the white Kenyan community. Extremist settlers led by 78-year-old Colonel Ewart "Grogs" Grogan, one of Kenya's pioneers and most prominent citizens, formed a new political party—the Kenya Empire Party—dedicated to "Kiboko" (whip) justice and the abolition of constitutional rule. Two days after the murder of the Italian immigrant family, hundreds of assembled settlers cheered when Grogan told them that the time had come to rule Kenya with "iron discipline," beginning by confiscating all Kikuyu lands.[27]

Although the government stopped well short of confiscating all Kikuyu land, it did confiscate the land of many suspected families, and encouraged the settlers to take up arms against Mau Mau. Later on the same day that 2,000 whites tried to storm Government House in the wake of the Ruck family killings, Michael Blundell rushed to a meeting of the still-agitated white Kenyans, where he shouted this histrionic announcement: "I have just left Government House and I am glad to tell you that I now, at long last, bring you your shooting orders."[28] He went on to announce that the government had declared some "special areas" in which any African could be shot on sight, and other areas where they could be shot immediately after being challenged to halt. The settlers cheered. They knew that the solution was an iron fist, and many now believed that the government had given them a license to kill. Long before Kenyatta's trial ended, central Kenya had become a killing ground for enraged whites. In the past, when they spoke of "wiping out" the Kikuyu as a people, as they often did, they had been indulging themselves in the catharsis of hyperbole; but when they now said, as also frequently happened, "let's go blot some Mickeys," that is precisely what they did—they went hunting for Mau Mau.

Sometime very early in the Emergency, an unknown wit decided to refer to Mau Mau as "Mickey Mouse," presumably because of the double m's in both. Soon, almost all whites began to call a member of the Mau Mau a "Mickey," or a "mouse," and if there were several they would be referred to as "Mickeys" or "mice." It was a way of making Mau Mau rebels contemptible and vermin-like. Settlers who took it upon themselves to kill Mau Mau "vermin" were seldom very selective. One settler led several armed men from the Nandi tribe in an attack on an encampment of Kikuyu. The Kikuyu men were tied up and flogged and three of the women were raped. It is unlikely that this episode did much to discourage Mau Mau because the victims of this assault were loyalist Kikuyu who had gathered together as protection against Mau Mau attacks.[29]

Some settlers hired other Africans to do their killing for them. The practice of paying Wanderobo hunters 20 shillings for every presumed Mau Mau they killed became so open that it was reported in the United States press.[30] Other whites did their own "exterminating." Several professional hunters began to stalk Kikuyu just as they would some relatively dangerous game.[31] One hunter, who was not usually given to braggadocio, said that he had killed more than 100 Kikuyu whom he thought to be Mau Mau, although he admitted that his policy of "shooting first and asking questions later" made it difficult to be certain.[32] In July 1953, one of Michael Blundell's bodyguards, a former British Army Regimental Sergeant-Major named "Davo" Davidson, told the *Daily Express* that he had killed 33 Mau Mau. When the story appeared in London, Lyttleton fired off a curt note to Baring demanding to know by what authority "Mr." Davidson was shooting "Her Majesty's Subjects."[33] Later in 1953, a Boer who lived near Thomson's Falls told another reporter that the British military were too "chicken-hearted" to deal with the Mau Mau because they called "halt" before firing at a suspect. "We just take out our Sten guns and, vee-vee-vee, vee-vee-vee, we let the bloody vermin have it!" He added approvingly that a friend of his had killed 26 suspicious men on his farm in one night. Laughing, he said that the Mau Mau didn't "come around any more."[34]

Whites who served in the Kenya Police Reserve or the Kenya Regiment did not make the mistake of speaking to the press about killing Africans. In fact it would not have mattered if they had so long as they spoke only to the Kenya press, which was engaged in a tacit and successful conspiracy with the police and the Kenya Government not to reveal indiscriminate brutality on the part of the security forces.[35] The use of what white's called "the third degree" was so widespread that D. H. Rawcliffe, a settler himself, wrote in 1954 that "Every European in the security forces knew about these beatings, talked about them, and very often had ordered them or participated in them."[36] Some white soldiers and police officers also killed Africans whom they suspected of belonging to the Mau Mau rebellion. One security officer ordered 30 Kikuyu men taken from their houses, tied to trees, and shot; one man survived to tell the story.[37] A white police officer routinely selected 2 or 3 prisoners at random, drove them to their homes, then, as their families watched, shot them dead and drove away.[38] Another police officer was said by Africans to have shot hundreds of men whom he suspected of Mau Mau activities in the Lari area.[39] In the early months of Emergency, many policemen shot Africans on the flimsiest of pretexts; others offered no reason at all. They simply killed. All of this was "hushed up," as white Kenyans said.

It was not just the young men in the Kenya Police or the Kenya Regiment who tortured and killed indiscriminately; some of their fathers were determined to be as "tough" in the fight against Mau Mau as their sons were. A rough and ready Australian who was in Kenya throughout the Emergency, was horrified by his experiences with one of these men.

> I was staying with old Bill one weekend on his farm near T-Falls [Thomson's Falls] when we got a call that some Mickeys was attacking a farm nearby. Now Bill was at least 60 but he was up before I was, strapping on his pistol and grabbing both a shotgun and a great bloody elephant rifle. He tossed the rifle to me but I said "No thanks, cobber, I'll stick to my Colt .45." We was joined by two of Bill's mates in another Land Rover and just about dawn we seen two Africans crossing the road ahead. Bill fired a shot across their bow and they put their hands up. I tried to tell Bill that those lads, hardly more than boys they was, didn't look like Mickeys to me but he says, "They're Kyukes and that's enough for me." Well he roughs them up some but they say they don't know where the gang of Mickeys went to, so he gets some rope and ties one to the rear bumper of his Land Rover by his ankles. He drives off a little ways, not too fast you know, and the poor black bastard is trying to keep from plowing the road with his nose. The other cobbers are laughing and saying, "put it in high gear Bill" and such as that, but Bill gets out and says, "Last chance, Nugu (baboon), where's that gang?" The African boy keeps saying he's not Mau Mau, but Bill takes off like a bat out of hell. When he comes back, the nigger wasn't much more than pulp. He didn't have any face left at all. So Bill and his mates tie the other one to the bumper and ask him the same question. He's begging them to let him go but old Bill takes off again and after a while he comes back with another dead Mickey. They just left the two of them there in the road.
>
> We drove around after that but never did find the gang and by then there was police all over the place, so we went back to T-Falls for lunch. Bill ordered beers all around. I was feeling a little shaky but I drank my beer. The other blokes was laughing and feeling fine as near as I could tell. Bill says, "How do you think one of those Mickeys would've looked if I'd had him stuffed and mounted?" One of his mates says, "You mean when he still had a face or after?" Another one says, "Hell, he was better lookin' afterwards." They had a good laugh over that. I spent the war with Wingate in Burma and I met some rough cobbers but I never seen men as cold as Bill and his mates was.[40]

Foreign journalists, who were not part of the press conspiracy to cover up brutality, derisively termed such men "Kenya Cowboys." In fact, some of the newly-uniformed men of the Kenya Regiment and the Kenya Police Reserve readily admitted that they were "playing at Cowboys and Indians" as they tried to rescue fellow settlers who were besieged on their isolated farms.[41] There was some justification for this comparison with America's Western frontier, because many young settlers organized themselves into informal cavalry units and rode on horseback from farm to farm to relieve and encourage the embattled settlers.[42] Sometimes patrols like these arrived just in time to save beleaguered white farmers from Mau Mau attacks. In March of 1954, a Mau Mau force killed two elderly white settlers in their Fort Hall farmhouse before attacking the house of the Kenya-born farm manager. His wife grabbed their three-year-old son, while her husband ran firing from window to window to give the impression that there were several people in the house. The farm manager's wife joined in, firing her shotgun until a police patrol arrived.[43]

Another rescue took place in January 1954 in South Kinangop, where Mr. P. P. Grimwood and his wife held off a Mau Mau unit of between 60 and 100 men armed with Sten guns, rifles, shotguns and hand grenades. The Grimwoods were able to lock themselves in their farmhouse, turn off the lights and call the police before the Mau Mau attacked in the moonlight, shouting, blowing whistles and bugles, and firing flares from a Verey pistol. For about 30 minutes the Mau Mau attackers fired over 500 rounds at the Grimwoods; some climbed onto the roof to fire down into the house and drop grenades down the chimney. As Grimwood fired his rifle from window to window, several Mau Mau tried to force their way through the back door, but they withdrew after Grimwood killed two of them. In true "Western" tradition, just as the Grimwoods were down to their last cartridges, a 20-year-old Kenya Police Reserve officer named Robert Crouchey came to their rescue. Crouchey stopped several hundred yards from the gunfight to send his three African policemen toward the rear of the house on foot; then, headlights blazing, Crouchey drove his police Land Rover directly up the driveway toward the Grimwoods' embattled house. When he was only a few yards away from the Mau Mau attackers, he leaped out of the car and rolled away from it into the grass. As the Mau Mau fired at the onrushing vehicle, Crouchey got to one knee and fired his Sten gun. To his amazement, the entire Mau Mau force fled.[44]

Other settlers formed private vigilante groups. One group, preten-
tiously named "Dobie Force," was said to have killed many Africans before the military persuaded them to desist. Another group, formed under
the auspices of the United Kenya Protection Association, called itself a
"commando." Its 70-odd members, who lived some distance from the
troubled area around the Kikuyu Reserve, offered their services to the
government whenever they might be needed.[45] Other individuals built
gallows on their farms where they served both symbolic and practical
purposes. The government also constructed a portable gallows which was
trucked from town to town to intimidate Mau Mau sympathizers. In late
November 1952, when close to 3,000 Kikuyu squatters in the troubled
Nyeri area were rounded up for questioning, the men were taken to a
barbed wire enclosure built around a prominently displayed gallows.[46]

By the latter part of 1953, pressure from the Kenya Government and
the British Army was curtailing the violence of white civilians. But most
of the white officers in the expanded Kenya Police were settlers, and
they continued to take the law into their own hands. Sometimes they
were overcome by their anger. One officer who "lost control" was a trim,
wiry young man with a blond moustache who recalled taking three Mau
Mau suspects prisoner.

They were caught red-handed; absolutely no question about it. I
had half a dozen askaris [soldiers] in two long-wheel base Land
Rovers so we threw the Mickeys in and took them to the nearest
police station. When we arrived, there was no one in the station
except one askari, so while we were waiting for the sub-inspector
to come back I decided to question the Mickeys. They wouldn't say
a thing, of course, and one of them, a tall coal-black bastard, kept
grinning at me, real insolent. I slapped him hard but he kept right
on grinning at me, so I kicked him in the balls as hard as I could.
He went down in a heap but when he finally got on his feet he
grinned at me again and I snapped, I really did. I stuck my revolver
right in his grinning mouth and I said something, I don't remember
exactly what, and pulled the trigger. His brains went all over the
side of the police station. The other two Mickeys were standing
there looking blank. I said to them that if they didn't tell me where
to find the rest of their gang I'd kill them too. They didn't say a
word so I shot them both. One wasn't dead so I shot him in the ear.
When the sub-inspector drove up, I told him that the Mickeys tried

to escape. He didn't believe me but all he said was "bury them and see the wall is cleaned up."[47]

Brutality was not always a product of passion. Often it was a calculated part of what white Kenyans called "counter-terrorism." A young sergeant of the Kenya Regiment remembered what it was like to raid the homestead of suspected Mau Mau supporters early in the Emergency.

There'd be two or three of us Europeans in charge of 20 or so K.A.R. askaris. First we'd hound everyone out of their huts; not too gentle, you know, we'd knock 'em about some. When we got the lot sorted out, we'd question them, the women, kids, everybody. We didn't expect to get any useful information, really, we just wanted to make them fear us more than they feared the Mau Mau. If we thought that any family was supporting the Mau Mau we'd toss a grenade in their hut and watch it blow to bits. One time after we threw a grenade in a hut a young girl came running up crying, saying that her father was in the house. Seems he'd been sick and hadn't come out when we'd rounded up the others. My lieutenant just laughed at the girl and told her that her father wasn't feeling sick any more, he wasn't feeling anything. Then he yelled at the whole lot that anyone who supported the Mau Mau would get the same. But the funniest thing I saw was once when I picked out a Mau Mau suspect and said to an African corporal who fancied that he spoke English well, "Corporal I want to run this man in for questioning." He took the Mickey away for a few minutes before he came back and said, "Ready for questioning, Effendi!" I didn't know what he was talking about but I followed him and there was the Mickey groaning on the ground. Standing there at attention was an askari with his bayonet dripping blood. Before I could say anything, the corporal said, "The prisoner has been run in, Effendi. You can question him now." When I told the story to my lieutenant, he laughed and said, "Maybe that's how we should question all of them."[48]

Most of the brutality was committed, or ordered, by officers of the police. The Kenya Police had never been an elite force. Its low salaries meant that it could attract few educated Africans, and most whites who joined the police had no other alternatives. There were some good and decent white policemen in Kenya but the majority were rough and bigoted men who believed that brutal methods were necessary to control Africans.[49] Long before 1952 it was routine for the police to rough up Africans in public and to beat them unconscious when they were taken behind closed doors for questioning.[50] When the Emergency was declared, the ranks of the police were quickly almost doubled. In addition to recalling white reserve policemen, many Africans were recruited. The new African constables were not only illiterate, they were tribesmen from remote areas who were wholly naive about even the rudiments of Western culture or technology.[51] Training films, for example, baffled them because when the film ended they could not understand where the actors had gone. In addition to new African recruits and the recalled white police officers of the Kenya Police Reserve, new white policemen were recruited from Britain, Rhodesia, and South Africa. Many of these new police officers were misfits in their own countries, and almost all were totally untrained for police work.[52] They believed they were at war with the Mau Mau and in times of war legal niceties should not be allowed to prevent the police from killing as many of the enemy as possible.

The police were almost as heavily armed as the British infantry. They carried rifles, sub-machine guns, light machine guns, and grenades. Some were organized into what were called "General Service Units" that served as highly mobile military forces. By the end of 1953, there were nearly 12,000 police in Kenya, more than 1,000 of whom were white.[53] It did not take Africans, particularly Kikuyu, long to learn exactly what to expect from these new police. Like other African constables, they stopped men and women whenever they pleased and unless they were quickly offered a sizeable bribe, the unlucky victims would be beaten, robbed and sometimes raped.[54] When the askaris were drunk, which was often, they were particularly vicious. White police officers also took bribes or stole valuables now and then, and they routinely called African suspects "baboons." Sometimes everyone in a suspected village was forced to strip naked to humiliate them.[55] And for many suspects, there was "the third degree" and death.

With rare exceptions, police brutality continued to be hidden from the press, but early in 1953 a few Kenyans were so disturbed by what was happening that they wrote to friendly M.P.s in Britain. At the same time, Nairobi was filling up with journalists from many countries. Some wrote bitter articles contrasting African poverty with the enormous multicourse meals that whites ate (and often wasted), and all reported government press releases about Mau Mau atrocities.[56] But some were after bigger news, and a story about white atrocities could make headlines in

several countries, especially Britain, where they also attracted the attention of the opposition Labour Party. In 1955, one of these British Labour
Party M.P.s, Barbara Castle, visited Kenya to investigate widely-rumored
charges that, with government approval, white policemen tortured and
murdered innocent Kikuyu. She found evidence to support these accusations and wrote indignantly about an incident in which a Kikuyu man
named Kimau Kichina had been arrested for suspected theft. With the
assistance of a chief police inspector and a former district officer, two
white Kenya Police Reserve officers tortured Kimau for several days until
finally he died without admitting his guilt or any association with Mau
Mau. Castle was outraged by this episode of police brutality but even
more so by the complicity of the Kenya Government. She said that the
entire system of justice in Kenya had a "Nazi" attitude toward Africans,
a charge that quickly caught the attention of the British press who rushed
to interview the attractive, blond M.P. Even before she visited Kenya,
Castle minced no words. "In the heart of the British Empire there is a
police state where the rule of law has broken down, where the murders
and torture of Africans by Europeans goes unpunished and where authorities pledged to enforce justice regularly connive at its violation."[57]
Castle also pointed out in subsequent newspaper articles, as well as in
Parliament, that a report by former Kenya Police Commissioner, Colonel
Sir Arthur Young, that was harshly critical of police conduct had been
suppressed by the Kenya Government.

Young, a former Commissioner of Police in London, had come to
Kenya in April 1954 only to resign nine months later in protest against
police brutality.[58] He had been determined to establish a police force in
Kenya that would be as independent of the administration as the police
had long been in Britain's parliamentary democracy. But Baring would
have none of it. Kenya was not a democracy for Africans; it was more
nearly a dictatorship. The administration liked to be thought of as en-
lightened, but Baring and a majority of his ministers in the War Council
decided that a State of Emergency was no time to grant the police what
Baring called "a lone wolf status." The conflict between Young and Baring was dramatized when Young accused the Governor of interceding to
prevent the police from prosecuting a loyalist chief accused of killing
Mau Mau suspects in cold blood. Baring backed down, admitting that he
had been wrong, but Young resigned in disgust, writing a long letter that
he fervently hoped would be published. Its contents have never been
revealed, but Young let it be known to his friends that his charges implicated both Baring and Colonial Secretary Lennox-Boyd.[59]

White Kenyans predictably condemned and ridiculed Castle for her liberal views. Apologists insisted that the security forces were often framed by the Mau Mau who mutilated the bodies of their own dead in order to incriminate the security forces.[60] It was also widely believed that a few former police officers or detention camp guards who had been fired for misconduct spread lies as revenge. There was also resentment toward liberal soldiers who wrote to British newspapers with exaggerated tales about atrocities.[61] The reaction to Castle's charges in England was only slightly more favorable; yet not only were her accusations true, but conditions in Kenya were worse than she realized, and had been since the Emergency began.

When the police captured a Mau Mau suspect, it was perfectly legitimate for them to interrogate that man or woman in search of information such as sources of support in the reserves, planned operations, and the names of other Mau Mau. Sometimes these interrogations were limited to long question and answer sessions, in which the suspect usually refused to say anything of relevance, and the interrogators eventually gave up frustrated and exhausted.[62] More often, however, if a question was not answered to the interrogator's satisfaction, the suspect was beaten and kicked. If that did not lead to the desired confession, and it rarely did, more force was applied. Electric shock was widely used, and so was fire. Women were choked and held under water; gun barrels, beer bottles, and even knives were thrust into their vaginas.[63] Men had beer bottles thrust up their rectums, were dragged behind Land Rovers, whipped, burned, and bayoneted. Their fingers were chopped off, and sometimes their testicles were crushed with pliers. Two Special Branch officers of South African origin, Heine and Van Zyl, were said to have been especially vile torturers.[64] To have achieved such notoriety they must have been monstrous beyond imagining. Some police officers did not bother with more time-consuming forms of torture; they simply shot any suspect who refused to answer, then told the next suspect, who had been forced to watch the cold-blooded execution, to dig his own grave. When the grave was finished, the man was asked if he would now be willing to talk. Sometimes suspects were forced to watch while others were killed, often slowly, with knives instead of bullets.[65]

Whether a prisoner was killed by a gunshot, a knife, or by prolonged torture, the reason for the death was usually listed as "trying to escape" or "resisting arrest." Newspaper stories regularly and unquestioningly reported the deaths of Kikuyu suspects who were shot while attempting to escape the police.[66] Despite the cover-up, word of police brutality spread so widely in Kenya that both the *East African Standard*, Kenya's principal English-language newspaper, and *Baraza*, its European-owned Swahili-language counterpart, eventually printed allegations about brutality by the security forces. On April 17, 1953, the Government of Kenya felt obliged to answer these charges by saying that although some abuses were "inevitable" in emergency conditions, they had been few in number and committed by "junior leaders and the rank and file." Given the savagery of Mau Mau crimes, it concluded, "restraint was most difficult to exercise."[67] A week later in London, Oliver Lyttleton, Secretary of State for the Colonies, told the House of Commons that while he was concerned by the fact that 430 Africans had been shot "resisting arrest" or "trying to escape" during the first six months of the Emergency, he assured the House that he had no evidence of wrongdoing.[68] Lyttleton did not comment on information supplied to the Colonial Office that another 92 Kikuyu had been reported to have "died in custody."[69]

Sometimes, rather than placing prisoners under arrest and risking the possibility that a judge might mistakenly free them, men of the Kenya Regiment and the police beat them to death or shot them in cold blood. William Baldwin, an American adventurer who joined the Kenya Police Reserve in April 1954, remarked that the police would recruit anyone who was white. Baldwin wrote a book describing in detail eight separate incidents in which 17 Mau Mau prisoners were killed in custody by police, often by Baldwin himself, who said that he was proud to have helped rid Kenya of Mau Mau "baboons."[70] What stands out in the matter-of-fact story he tells is the utter callousness of Kenya Police officers as they killed suspects whom they regarded as less than human. Except for Baldwin's ingenuous willingness to admit his own murders, there is nothing unique about his report. Other police officers admitted killing prisoners whose hands were tied or handcuffed.[71] Some of these victims had their hands cut off for fingerprint identification. More often, hands were kept as ghastly trophies. Men had become so callous that, according to Baldwin and others, if a police office asked another officer for help saying, "give me a hand," he was likely to be given exactly that.[72]

There were many bars in Kenya where, during the Emergency, and even after it ended, off-duty police officers could be heard boasting about their kills; one laughingly recalled how a captive begged for his life just before being shot in the testicles.[73] Others spoke in sadistic detail about the pain they inflicted on men and women alike as they were tortured. The newspaper, *Baraza*, which was ordinarily sympathetic to the government, complained about this boasting in its April 11, 1953, edition. Some of the brutality was committed by regular police officers or recruits from England, but most of it was due to the anti-black hatred of police reservists from Kenya, and recruits from Rhodesia and South Africa.[74]

Only a few of these men were ever brought to trial. For example, Brian Hayward, a young assistant district officer, and several African constables under his command were found guilty of stringing up Mau Mau suspects by their necks, whipping the soles of their feet, and pushing burning cigarettes into their ears. Although the British judge found Hayward guilty, he told the courtroom that "it is easy to work oneself up into a state of pious horror over these offenses, but they must be considered against their background. All the accused were engaged in seeking out inhuman monsters and savages of the lowest order."[75] Hayward was fined £100 (the fine was paid by a lady settler) and sentenced to three months "hard labor" which he performed in a hotel doing clerical work for the administration. Governor Baring tried to prevent Hayward from returning to government service, and he was embarrassed when Hayward resumed his duties as soon as his three-month sentence had been served.[76] Hayward's brother and a senior police officer were fined £25 and £20 respectively for burning another prisoner (their fines, too, were paid by others).

In other incidents, a Danish-born police sergeant named Frantz Hvass was fined £50 for brutally flogging several prisoners; two other police officers were fined for beating an African to death, another for setting a dog on a prisoner, and two others for roasting a prisoner over a fire. When a private in the Kenya Regiment named Leslie Hughes was charged with torturing an 18-year-old girl, his defense was by then the standard one. If there was any abuse, something Hughes very much doubted, it was done by Africans after he had left the girl in their charge. But Hughes added an ingenious twist to his defense, claiming the girl had conspired with her African guards to be mutilated in order to discredit Hughes and the Kenya Regiment. Hughes was acquitted.[77]

In late December 1953, Sergeant-Major L. Ruben of the Kenya Regiment and R. G. Keates, a Kenya Police Reserve Officer, admitted to a court that askaris under their command had beaten to death Mr. E. G. Njeru, a Mau Mau suspect. The two men told the court that although they had ordered the prisoner to be beaten, they had not intended that he be killed. They were fined £100 and £50 respectively and allowed to return to their duties.[78] District Officers and senior policemen were also charged with condoning such crimes, and even being present while they took place. The list of charges went on, but so few offenders were brought to trial that Colonial Secretary Lyttleton was able successfully to argue in Parliament that such cases were isolated incidents that did not call for a general inquiry into police or army conduct.

Whites who opposed police brutality were sometimes treated almost as badly as Africans. Late in 1953 a baronet, Sir Henry Dalrymple-White, who was serving as a Home Guard District Officer, took a suspected Mau Mau prisoner to the local police station where the unfortunate man was promptly kicked in the face by a white police officer. Another white police officer said that he would have the man shot. Sir Henry was sufficiently upset that he reported these horrors to his superior. The two white police officers who were involved quickly heard of Sir Henry's report, and later that night they broke into his room and beat him so badly with a bottle that he was hospitalized for eight days. The officers admitted in court that they were guilty and apologized. One was fined £50, the other £30.[79] When a deadly attack against a baronet who was a government official went so lightly punished, it is not difficult to understand how more serious crimes against Africans could be treated with even less concern.

Visiting M.P.s, including some conservatives, expressed concern that police brutality had threatened public confidence. They meant African confidence, of course, not that of whites, who could hardly have been more approving.[80] But a few Kenya Police officers were so sickened by the sadism of some of their colleagues that they took the almost unthinkable, and dangerous, step of filing complaints against them.[81] One officer, David Drummond, a Kenyan who never shrank from killing Mau Mau in open combat, was disgusted by the conduct of a fellow police officer from Rhodesia who killed Mau Mau in cold blood because they were "bloody baboons" who were no longer, as he put it, "protected animals."[82] Before Drummond was forced to take any action, the man killed himself playing Russian roulette for money in a Nakuru bar. Men like this one stood up when white women entered a room, cherished white children, and went to church on Sunday. Their savagery was reserved for Africans.[83]

Barbara Castle accused the Government of Kenya of covering up and condoning police atrocities, and so they did. A few in government, like Baring's Deputy Governor, Sir Frederick Crawford, admitted that the police had been "excessively tough in a few cases," but attempted to excuse the offenders as untrained "local men" serving under extreme pressure. Many others in government wrote official denials that any wrongdoing had taken place. Some in government did their best to prevent abuses. The Criminal Investigation Division of the police, under D. G. McPherson, consistently tried to detect and charge offenders, and the Attorney-General of Kenya, John Whyatt, demanded disciplinary measures and prosecution for police officers who violated the law.[84] Yet those who openly opposed police savagery were powerless against the government, which consistently sought to remove men like Whyatt, who embarrassed them. Even Sir Michael Blundell, by no means the most conservative of the white settlers in government, joined in the government's efforts to have Whyatt replaced.[85]

Blundell's state of mind at the time is suggested by a trivial but telling incident. In what Blundell referred to as an "amusing experience," he recalled receiving a letter in "childish handwriting" from a 12-year-old boy in Dallas, Texas. The youngster, perhaps understandably caught up in the sensational newspaper coverage of Mau Mau atrocities, asked Sir Michael for a Kikuyu sword with blood on it. He addressed his letter to "Mike Blundell." What is remarkable about this exchange with Blundell is the Kenya Minister's response. "In due course," Blundell wrote, he sent the boy a sword with "the necessary blood on it."[86]

White settlers stood drinks for sadistic killers as well as honorable policemen. Most Kenyans were so enraged by the Mau Mau that they did not scruple much about how they were killed. The greatest beneficiaries of this blind-eye on brutality were the Home Guards. Most police and administrative officials who were charged with overseeing Home Guard conduct chose to ignore almost everything they did, as long as they did not collaborate with the Mau Mau. Using British weapons and backed by British authority, many Home Guards took whatever they wanted from families who supported the Mau Mau. Others threatened to denounce perfectly loyal Kikuyu unless they were given bribes. It was a threat that could not be taken lightly. Those who protested the theft, intimidation, and rape committed by these agents of the empire, or objected to their insufferable arrogance, were subjected to the same tortures used by the Kenya Police and then some. In addition to crushing a man's testicles, Home Guards often castrated male prisoners. Women were cut, beaten, and burned, and in addition they had their vaginas stuffed with stinging nettles, penetrated by snakes, or filled with boiling water.[87]

The government ignored repeated protests by Kikuyu and church groups about the Home Group rule of terror, until it became apparent that their excesses were driving loyalist Kikuyu into the ranks of the Mau Mau. When six Home Guards, including a chief, were finally brought to trial, the presiding Magistrate, A. L. Cram, bitterly denounced the system that allowed Home Guards to arrest anyone without cause, to torture them until a confession was made, then try the person before a native court solely on the basis of that confession.[88] Justice Cram also observed that the Kenya Police often proceeded in precisely the same manner. Cram said that the African court at Karatina had been run contrary to "elementary canons of justice," and that the Home Guard post at Ruth-agati, where the crimes took place, resembled the "stronghold of a rob-ber baron." Finding that atrocities took place in this post "every day," the judge held that the six men on trial were guilty of perverting justice and oppressing their fellow Kikuyu. It took the judge 20,000 words to express his indignation, and despite the fact that his judgment was never published in Kenya, the government soon after appointed a commission to investigate the administration of justice in African Native courts.[89] Cram convicted all six Home Guards and sentenced the chief, Muriu, to death for the murder of two prisoners.

Where the government's priorities lay was soon made abundantly clear. On April 5, 1955, Governor Baring informed the colonial secretary that he had commuted the sentence of the Home Guard Chief and had man-aged to have charges against Home Guards dropped in three other pend-ing cases. Baring explained his actions: "Had the investigations proceeded, the Kikuyu Guard would have collapsed and with their col-lapse the whole structure of our fighting against Mau Mau would have been undermined. Without them, troops would not have got informa-tion. Without them it would have been impossible to withdraw the Army from the Reserves such as Fort Hall which police and the Kikuyu Guard are now taking over. Without them we would have had no support among any members of the Kikuyu tribe." Evidence later made available indi-cated that 25 prima facie cases of murder by Home Guards were dropped.[90]

Although a few members of the colonial administration were accused and convicted of brutality against Africans, for the most part the admin-istration tried to protect the rights of Africans. The police, on the other hand, typically took their job to be the protection of settlers against Africans. Despite their supposed cooperation in the demanding business of colonial rule, there was a profound gulf between these two branches of government. Almost all administrative officers were the products of public schools and were graduates of either Oxford or Cambridge. They had been selected by the Colonial Office not only because they had a sense of public service but a "habit of authority." They demanded the authority to protect the interests of Africans—*their* Africans—against the interests of the settlers. It was entirely predictable, then, that when the Emergency came they often clashed with settlers, the police, and the British Army, all of whom they saw as interfering with their right to administer their fiefdoms as they saw fit.[91]

When the Emergency sent so many of Kenya's settlers into the ranks of the police, it dramatically tipped the scales toward the oppression of Africans, not their protection. The arrival of British Army troops increased the tensions between the police and the colonial administration. The police saw the newly arrived soldiers as "useless." Incapable of speaking Swahili or patrolling quietly in the forest, the soldiers were, in police eyes, to be kept out of combat lest they put police patrols in harm's way. The administration saw the army with its large battalions and senior commanders as a threat to their control over African affairs. By either view, the British Army was less than completely welcome. Baring's government was concerned, as this "secret and personal" letter from a member of Baring's Secretariat to the Colonial Office indicates: "I am a bit worried about the tie-up between GHQ and the Administration. The soldiers tend to work in a water-tight compartment and being an unimaginative lot, have difficulty understanding political stresses and implications (one senior officer who has been dealing with the Emergency for more than six months, asked the other day what a 'squatter' was)."[92]

History suggests that if the newly arrived British Army forces in Kenya had found themselves engaged in combat against a conventionally armed enemy, they would immediately have ignored, and perhaps scorned, the police and would have done their best to dominate the colonial administration. But faced by a guerrilla war in which sizeable enemy forces could only rarely be brought to battle, the army needed to cooperate with both the police and the administration. Only the police or the closely associated Kenya Regiment could provide intelligence service liaison along with knowledge of the country and its languages, and only the administration, through its network of district commissioners, district officers, native chiefs, and courts could effectively bring loyalist Kikuyu into the Home Guard forces.

It was a difficult role for any army to play, and it was to become particularly difficult for the British Army because they too were soon accused of committing brutality. The newly arrived army officers were quickly exposed to the settlers' hatred of Mau Mau and of the Kikuyu. Settlers targeted officers for elementary lessons about Kikuyu perfidy and Mau Mau beastliness, while private soldiers, who were often invited to spend leave time and convalescence from minor ills or wounds in settlers' homes, were given an indoctrination that was no less impassioned. Although relatively few officers were fervent colonialists, and some of the soldiers were outspoken Labour Party opponents of colonialism, few officers or soldiers knew anything about Kenya or the Mau Mau before their arrival in Nairobi. Most of these officers and men had left Britain with firm convictions about the racial superiority of whites (especially those from the British Isles), and their service overseas in places like Egypt, Cyprus, Palestine, and Malaya had only confirmed for them that "wogs" and "niggers" were a lower form of life. These attitudes were incorporated in a British Army Handbook which was distributed to all officers. Under a section discussing the handling of African trackers assigned to Army units, it read: "The African is simple, not very intelligent, but very willing if treated in the right way. Do not regard him as a slave or an equal. You will find that most Africans have an innate respect for the White Man."[93]

As soon as British troops arrived in Kenya, they either saw or were told about Mau Mau atrocities, and they were required to read copies of Mau Mau oaths printed in a pamphlet called *The Kenya Picture* that described horrifying oathing ceremonies which the government routinely referred to as "orgies." When the troops actually saw members of Mau Mau, either as prisoners or as corpses, it only increased their contempt—they were foul-smelling, their hair utterly unlike anything the British had ever seen before, their clothes ragged and hopelessly unmilitary, their weapons often homemade and laughable.[94]

The British officers who commanded the six K.A.R. battalions that were rushed to Kenya as soon as the Emergency was proclaimed were familiar with African soldiers, but they were just as certain of their racial superiority as were the officers who had just arrived in command of white troops. They commanded, after all, only because they were white. Whatever their racial sentiments, they had no sympathy for Mau Mau, and little for the Kikuyu. Most of the men they commanded were not sympathetic either. British Army units would eventually be suspected of brutality, but the K.A.R. were the first to be accused of atrocities. K.A.R. troops, like those of the Kenya Regiment, routinely burned the houses of Kikuyu who were thought to sympathize with the Mau Mau, and it was K.A.R. troops under the direct command of white officers who were said to have shot more than 90 prisoners in cold blood in what came to be known to the Mau Mau as the Kagahwe River massacre.[95] In another incident early in the conflict, it has been alleged that a white officer ordered his K.A.R. troops to shoot all prisoners, including women.[96]

Whether under orders by white officers or not, K.A.R. soldiers often treated wounded Mau Mau by casually shooting or bayoneting them, or throwing them on top of dead Mau Mau in the back of a truck before driving off on a long journey during which the wounded either died on their own or were helped to do so.[97]

Most of what the K.A.R. troops did went unnoticed by everyone except the Mau Mau, but much that the all-British battalions did came under scrutiny, and what they did often could not bear close attention. Units set up scoreboards showing their kills, and officers offered a bounty for each company's first kill, usually £5.[98] Kills had to be confirmed, of course, and carrying a dead body back for identification was definitely not pleasant duty, so hands were cut off and brought back as proof that a Mau Mau rebel—or someone, at least—had been killed. In principle, these hands could be used to identify the deceased Mau Mau through fingerprints, but since very few fingerprints of Mau Mau suspects existed in police files it was difficult to claim that the hands were cut off only as evidence.

While some British soldiers were cutting off hands and sometimes ears as trophies of war, British airmen in the Royal Air Force were decorating their aircraft with their own trophies. Instead of the "kill" decals that in previous wars showed downed enemy aircraft, their decals pictured an African holding a spear.[99] Other British soldiers were demonstrating their dislike for the Mau Mau in the streets of Nairobi. Some soldiers, usually after drinking, stopped Africans at random, beat them, and stole whatever valuables they possessed.[100] In the Kikuyu reserves, British soldiers sometimes fired indiscriminately, possibly doing more harm to loyal Kikuyu (and, sometimes themselves) than to the Mau Mau.[101] It is impossible to know how many innocent Africans were shot either by accident or design. It was reported that a company of "Buffs" who came to the rescue of a Home Guard post besieged by the Mau Mau at night mistakenly shot four loyalist women and children.[102]

Kikuyu sources also charged that British soldiers were guilty of rape, and it is likely that some of these charges were true.[103] Military authorities seldom found any evidence, which was hardly surprising given the widespread belief that all African women were promiscuous, and the fact that some Mau Mau women did seduce British soldiers in the hope of receiving a bullet or two in return.[104] K.A.R troops were often accused of rape and were sometimes convicted, but Home Guardsmen, who frequently were guilty, were rarely prosecuted.[105]

When General Erskine arrived in Kenya early in June 1953, he was so distressed by what he saw and heard about the conduct of his troops that he issued a message that was read to all British soldiers and given to all officers who subsequently arrived in Kenya. The general's message began by reminding the "security forces" about their discipline, honor, and integrity. Erskine assured them that he knew they faced a difficult task and did not want to tie their hands, nor should anyone fear him, he said, if a "mistake" were made "in good faith." But then he changed his tone, saying that he disapproved strongly of "beating up the inhabitants of this country just because they are the inhabitants." He went on to say that any "undiscipline" of this sort (something he disingenously said he "hoped" had not happened in the past) would do great harm to the reputation of the security forces, and make "settling" Mau Mau more difficult. He then ordered every officer in the police and army to "stamp at once on any conduct which he would be ashamed to see used against his own people." After issuing this vague but menacing order, he again appealed to his forces for their "loyal support" so that he could "stand up for" their honor with a clear conscience.[106]

Few Kenya Police Reserve or Kenya Regiment officers changed their conduct as a result of General Erskine's order or his plea for honor, but for the most part the British Army did respond, although reluctantly. "Kill" records were still kept at both company and battalion levels, but there no longer was open competition between companies and battalions for the largest number of kills. The practice of paying for "first kills" also stopped, and so did the taking of hands or ears. In fact, several British Army officers officially reported that they intervened when they observed police or K.A.R. units engaging in what they considered to be atrocities against Africans.[107] Other British Army officers who did not make any official report of their actions also prevented police atrocities, sometimes by the threat of force. One British Army captain who drove up with an army patrol while two white policemen were savagely flogging a handcuffed Kikuyu prisoner threatened to flog both of them if they did not stop. When the policemen told the Army officer to "bugger off," they found themselves surrounded by soldiers, disarmed, and arrested.[108] Police officers who had previously thought the army merely hopelessly inept now complained that they were meddlesome "nigger-lovers."[109]

After "Bobbie" Erskine's crackdown, the British regiments by and large were innocent of atrocities like those committed by the Home Guards, the Kenya Police Reserve, the Kenya Regiment, and some K.A.R. units. Perhaps that was so because, compared to the booby-traps of Palestine, the leeches of Malaya's jungles, and the heavy casualties of Korea, Kenya was a pleasant and relatively safe duty station for British troops. The Kikuyu in the reserves did nothing to provoke the animosity of the British; soldiers there did not have to concern themselves about anti-personnel mines, booby-traps, or ambushes, and when they relaxed in their camps they were safe. Except for the Mau Mau, who usually avoided direct clashes with British troops, most Kikuyu were not even openly hostile. Many women, in fact, were downright friendly, and the greatest danger many soldiers faced was venereal disease. Most regiments, like the 1st Gloucesters who had earlier lost 552 of their 622 men during desperate fighting in Korea, hated to see their tour of duty in Kenya come to an end.[110]

K.A.R. units were much slower to change their practices. Soon after Erskine's message was read to his troops, an incident was reported in which 2 Africans were alleged to have been murdered by 20 African soldiers of a K.A.R. battalion. Erskine was suspicious about the charges, and ordered further investigation, which led to a K.A.R. officer, 43-year-old Captain G. S. L. Griffiths, being charged with the murder of one of the victims. Griffiths was a regular army officer who owned a farm where several of his horses had been killed by Mau Mau. He issued orders to one of his white sergeants to the effect that "he could shoot at anyone he liked so long as they were black."[111] Griffiths also admitted to the Court that he kept a scoreboard in the officers' mess that recorded Mau Mau kills and captures. He offered a five-shilling bonus for every Mau Mau shot. Sergeant-Major William Lleyellyn testified that he saw Captain Griffiths fire at one of two prisoners until the bullets "practically poured out of the man's stomach." The sergeant added that as the captain fired, he shouted: "When the Mau Mau killed my horse, it screamed longer than you will scream."[112] The court-martial, which was inexplicably delayed for five months, attracted almost as much attention in Britain as it did in Kenya.[113] Although Griffiths insisted that the prisoners were trying to escape, he was convicted of shooting one of the victims to death. However, in a preposterous example of legal bungling, it turned out that the prosecution had charged Griffiths with killing one of the two prisoners but had proved him guilty of killing the other man. Griffiths was acquitted.

Thanks to angry public opinion in Britain and an angrier General Erskine in Nairobi, Griffiths was tried again on the next most severe charge—torturing prisoners. The prosecution alleged that Captain Griffiths ordered an African sergeant to cut off the ear of one prisoner and use a bayonet to mutilate the ear of another man. In the now standard defense, Griffiths acknowledged that the acts had taken place, but insisted that African soldiers had committed them without his orders or knowledge. He did admit that he had threatened to cut off the prisoners' ears and to castrate them, but insisted that he had no intention of actually *doing* such things. He did not explain how it happened that both men died in his custody. Griffiths was convicted, cashiered from the army, and sentenced to five years in prison.

The conviction of Captain Griffiths did not signal wholesale prosecutions of officers suspected of wrongdoing. For example, during Griffiths's court-martial, a lieutenant named Innes-Walker admitted that he had committed perjury before the court. Moreover, an African sergeant— the same one accused of cutting off prisoners' ears—testified that he had been with Innes-Walker while African prisoners were taken into the forest, told to "run for it," and then shot down. Lieutenant Innes-Walker was never put on trial. General Erskine also chose not to bring to trial a Kenya Regiment sergeant named Jeremy Allen, whom several African witnesses had implicated in the shooting of two Kikuyu prisoners. Peter Evans, an Irish lawyer, investigated this case, and found evidence to support the charge that Sergeant Allen was guilty of murder. Perhaps coincidentally, Evans soon after was deported from Kenya.[114]

White rage did not end when Mau Mau rebels were killed in action against security forces. The dead were typically treated with the utmost contempt. When Mau Mau were killed in the reserves, their bodies were lined up for public display. Sometimes they were photographed with their dead eyes staring into the lens of the camera. Afterwards the dead were often kicked, spat at, urinated on, and mutilated. When a prominent Mau Mau officer was killed, his body might be left on public display for days. White Kenya Police Reserve officers brought the body of General Nyoro back to the reserves and displayed it to the inhabitants. The police, who wanted to leave no doubt that his death was ignominious, kept his body on display for 48 hours as it swelled in the heat and dogs nibbled at it.[115] Sometimes badly wounded Mau Mau were displayed to the crowds of Kikuyu who were forced to look at the suffering rebels. After General Kago was wounded in one of the conflict's longest battles late in 1954, he was captured and taken to the reserve where he was placed on a pyre, soaked with gasoline, and burned to death as horrified Kikuyu farmers were forced to watch.[116]

With the exception of the British Army, which for the most part avoided misconduct after General Erskine's warning, Kenya's security forces continued their systematic use of torture and murder throughout the Emergency. Their actions had the enthusiastic approval of many in the white settler community as well as the tacit support of some government officials. Despite increasing criticism in Britain of Kenya's security forces, attempts to put the best possible face on events in Kenya persisted. The British public began to learn about possible wrongdoing on the part of its soldiers early in 1954 when the Devons' regimental magazine, which mentioned the practice of paying soldiers for first kills, came to the attention of a Labour M.P. who promptly asked about the practice in the House of Commons. The London *Daily Herald* publicized the issue under a front-page headline that asked, "Is your son a murderer?"[117] Embarrassed, the War Office convened a court of inquiry under Lieutenant-General Sir Kenneth McLean that quickly exonerated the British troops of brutality; but Parliament, led by the Labour Party opposition, decided to send its own delegation to Kenya. This delegation, composed of Conservatives as well as members of the Opposition, spent 18 days touring Kenya, after which it declared that it had neither seen nor heard of any cases of brutality by the army or police. This conclusion was not surprising, since neither soldiers nor policemen were likely to commit atrocities in front of the M.P.s, and members of the delegation spoke neither Swahili or Kikuyu, making it virtually impossible for a victim of brutality to complain to them except through an English-speaking interpreter.

Although the delegation could find no direct evidence, it found much to be displeased about in the attitudes of the white settlers, whom they criticized for condoning police malpractice and general disrespect for the law.[118] Soon after, the *Sunday Times* of London reported that a "vociferous minority" of the white settlers wanted to discard the principles of British justice.[119] With characteristic understatement the paper added that, "Perhaps—though not so explicitly avowed—some settlers want as near an approach to Lynch law as British public opinion will tolerate." That is exactly what many of them had wanted from the start. Many settlers were convinced that the only reason Mau Mau spread as it did was because the government had been too soft, and the security forces had to fight "with one hand tied behind their back."[120] They insisted that the government should have "taught the bastards a lesson" they could not forget.[121] To support those among the Security Forces who had done so and been charged with crimes as a result, they set up legal defense funds. They also threatened lenient officials, or accused them of being Communists. They planned marches on Nairobi to intimidate the government, and threatened any former Mau Mau who might surrender in hope of amnesty. They also intimidated the press. In January 1954, Norman Harris, a settler member of Kenya's Legislative Council, wrote to the *East African Standard* that the paper should not report legal cases brought against members of the security forces because it might affect the morale of the "fighting men."[122]

Although the settlers were criticized in Britain and detested by General Erskine, there were those in the Kenya Government who shared their views. Late in 1954, *The Times* of London reported that the Kenya Government had had the audacity to ask the British Government to consider imposing censorship on "provocative and mendacious matter" in the British Press which it argued might hamper the war effort against the Mau Mau.[123] It apparently seemed reasonable to the Government of Kenya that settler opinion should determine what news of the war in Kenya was fit to print in Britain.[124]

Conservative members of the British Government were not always averse to denying that Kenya's Security Forces had behaved brutally. After the Emergency ended, the former Colonial Secretary, Sir Oliver Lyttleton (by then Lord Chandos), followed the party line when he wrote that "One or two isolated incidents of atrocities by the British occurred in Kenya."[125] Denials of wrongdoing continued to appear in books sympathetic to the settlers and to the Security Forces, as well as in the Kenya Government's own report of its conduct. Soon, however, the Government of Kenya would be implicated in far more serious charges involving the treatment of thousands of helpless men and women held in detention camps. This time government attempts to deny the truth would fail, and those who would suffer the most as a result were the white settlers.

6

"A SHORT, SHARP SHOCK"

DETENTION AND REHABILITATION

Even before the State of Emergency was declared, Kenya's courts were crowded with persons charged with crimes relating to Mau Mau. Very soon after the Emergency, its courts were overwhelmed. Convictions were duly handed down, but they came slowly and only after magistrates, most of whom did not share the anti-Mau Mau hysteria that swept Kenya, had observed the due process of law. Prisons were soon crowded with men serving long sentences, and, on the average, one African was hanged every morning, after being offered Christian counsel and a sedative the night before. However, many "Mau Mau" cases were thrown out of court for lack of evidence, often because witnesses disappeared or refused to testify. The police and the settlers were furious. They were convinced that the Kikuyu who had been released were dangerous to Kenya's security, as were many others against whom the police could not bring charges. They insisted that something had to be done.

Governor Baring quickly issued a detention order that for all practical purposes allowed the government to put anyone it wished into a concentration camp for as long as it liked. Evidence of wrongdoing was not required. All that was necessary was the word of some more or less reliable person that a man, woman, or even a child had Mau Mau sympathies or had taken the oath.[1] There was ample precedent for the use of what the government called "detention camps." The British had made infamous use of them during the Boer War and were still using them in Malaya. The Government of Kenya was about to make detention camps infamous once again.

For the settlers and the government alike, the oath was the key to Mau Mau. They were convinced that the witchcraft embodied in the Mau Mau oath had transformed "decent," compliant Kikuyu, including their own trusted servants, into inhuman monsters. Before their very eyes the evil Mau Mau oath had turned "Sambos" into savages. How much white Kenyans feared and detested the oath can be seen in the fact that 222 of the first 1,015 Mau Mau who were hanged during the Emergency were found guilty of no crime except administering oaths.[2] Few white Kenyans questioned the idea that the Mau Mau oath was at the root of Kenya's problems, but before a plan for neutralizing its effects was put into action, the government consulted Harry Thuku, who was now vehemently anti-Mau Mau, as well as Dr. Leakey, and Kenya's most respected psychiatrist, Dr. J. C. Carothers.

Carothers, who had practiced medicine in Kenya for some 20 years before becoming the psychiatrist in charge of Mathari Mental Hospital outside of Nairobi, had some remarkably muddled ideas about the Kikuyu. He believed, among other things, that they were especially prone to violence because they lacked the "mental integration" to cope with anxiety, that their "forest psychology" made them so individualistic that they were isolated from group pressure, and that they lacked "general moral principles." He also believed, as did Leakey and Thuku, that the Mau Mau oaths were invented by someone with a knowledge of European witchcraft, and Jomo Kenyatta was the obvious candidate.[3]

The committee was convinced that anyone who took a Mau Mau oath became so deranged that he or she was literally diseased, or, as they sometimes put it, "infected" or "poisoned."[4] In a decision that pleased white Kenyans, the committee decided that these infected people would have to be "quarantined" in camps where they could not contaminate others, and where they might be rehabilitated. It was also decided that the only way to rehabilitate these "victims" was to force them to confess to having taken the oath. As Governor Baring put it, rehabilitation required full public renunciation and denunciation.[5]

The committee's conviction that confession would produce catharsis did not derive from Kikuyu culture, where confession played a less prominent role in curing the ill for the Kikuyu than it did for many other African societies.[6] The committee's faith in the curative powers of confession came instead from a blend of Christian theology and psychoanalytic theory. The committee believed that, by confessing, Mau Mau captives would enjoy emotional catharsis by repenting their sins. They would also learn that violating the Mau Mau would not kill them. Once they were relieved of the oath's disease—its terrible burden of guilt and fear—they could be reintroduced to Christianity and its civilizing moral principles.

The findings of this committee were enthusiastically accepted by both the government and the settlers. Kenya's program for rehabilitating the Mau Mau would follow their guidelines. Confession, which was often called "cleansing" after the Kikuyu practice of purifying those who had been ritually polluted, would remain the mandatory first step toward returning Mau Mau to normal Kikuyu life. After the Emergency ended, the white Kenyans' belief that Mau Mau was a disease that confession could cure would make reconciliation easier, but during the Emergency, it created a serious problem because most persons accused of taking the Mau Mau oath refused to confess.

For the settlers as well as the government, Mau Mau could not be considered a nationalistic political movement. It was not even rational. For them, Mau Mau was led by an evil and sophisticated man named Kenyatta whose ambitions were crassly political; the rank and file of the movement obeyed him largely—and in many cases entirely—because of the Mau Mau oath. The men and women who took the oath could not be expected to confess when they believed that confession would result in their death. The problem therefore was how to compel confessions in spite of this mortal fear. The answer for the Government of Kenya, and for the settlers, was to make those people suspected of Mau Mau sympathies more afraid of the whites than they were of the oaths they had taken. As John Nottingham, a former District Officer among the Kikuyu, put it, what the government believed Mau Mau sympathizers required was a "short, sharp shock" which meant, in plain terms, pain followed by the fear of more pain.[7]

The cleaning process began with an interrogation intended to "screen out" the innocent and send the guilty to detention camps. Sir Michael Blundell, who would later prove to be far more liberal than most settlers wished, wrote approvingly about a screening program that, according to the settler who directed it, was intended to make prisoners fear the British more than the oath or the Mau Mau themselves. They began, according to Blundell, by letting it be known that the atrocities committed in their screening camp were truly horrendous. These "rumors," as they were called, were buttressed by seemingly deadly threats. Armed white men would enter a camp in the night, seize an uncooperative prisoner and haul him away without a word of explanation. Soon afterward, inmates of the camp would hear screams and shouts from the forest nearby followed by a shot, then silence. It was said that the next morning would see a decidedly improved atmosphere in camp.[8] Blundell went on to say that, "of course," the prisoner had not been shot, but merely transferred to another screening camp.

Even when prisoners were transferred—and Blundell to the contrary, some were not—the next camp could be worse. Some screeners specialized in the use of electric shock; others preferred to burn suspects with cigarette butts, or slowly hang them until they were unconscious.[9] A screening camp near Nakuru was infamous for castrating recalcitrant prisoners. A loyalist Kikuyu who carried out the castration explained that the Mau Mau were evil and deserved castration, and added, as an aside, that he wanted to see if castrated men would grow fat like castrated cattle did.[10] The police and Home Guards had regularly used torture to compel suspected persons to reveal information. Now the same techniques would be used to force political detainees to confess that they had taken a Mau Mau oath. It would not matter that the confession was brought about by force; like exorcism, the confession would cleanse however it was brought about.[11]

It would also not matter, at least not to the government, that many of these screening teams were composed of white civilians who had no police powers. Mr. Justice Cram, a Kenya magistrate, accused one of these teams of "Gestapo Tactics," and ten days later the Court of Appeal for eastern Africa also expressed alarm over the violence employed by screening teams. The Vice President of the Court, Sir William Worley, asked what legal powers the screening teams had and under what au-

thority they acted. Concluding that they must operate under some sort
of governmental orders, Sir William accused the government of condoning unlawful violence and negating the rule of law. As visiting lawyer
Peter Evans observed, it was extraordinary for Kenya's highest judicial
authority to charge its government with Gestapo tactics.[12] It was perhaps
more extraordinary that the government managed to ignore these
charges.

Prisoners who had already been convicted of Mau Mau crimes were
excluded from rehabilitation. For them there would be no redemption,
only punishment. Many awaited execution in Nairobi's notorious Kamiti
prison. Others served long sentences of hard labor. Kenyatta and the five
men convicted with him were imprisoned in the most remote part of
Kenya, a place called Lokitaung, near Lake Rudolf on Kenya's northern
border with the Sudan. But it was not enough to imprison Kenyatta, the
government also set out to obliterate his past and his identity. It was
ordered that his home be turned into rubble. His land was given away,
and his car was stripped and left to rust. In prison, his beard was shaved
off, and his ring, walking stick and clothes were replaced by shackles and
prison garb. Watched by guards who spoke no Kikuyu or Swahili, it was
intended that Kenyatta would spend his remaining days breaking up
stones in heat that usually reached 120 degrees Fahrenheit in the shade.
Because of his ill health, he was later given lighter duties; but lonely, ill,
stripped of his past, and the target of several assassination attempts, Kenyatta would endure the Emergency in prison, while more than 80,000
Mau Mau suspects would be screened and "cleansed" in the new rehabilitation system, called the "pipeline."[13] Unrepentant Mau Mau would
be sent "down" the pipeline through camps of increasing severity until
they saw the error of their ways; then they would be sent back "up" the
pipeline toward full rehabilitation and eventual freedom.

The pipeline process began when a man or woman was taken into
custody by a Home Guardsman or police officer as a Mau Mau "suspect."
At this stage the prisoner did not know what the charges might be. Possession of a gun or a bullet carried a death sentence, and so did administering oaths. Simply taking food to forest fighters could bring a long
prison sentence. Even admitting to taking an oath could lead to prolonged torture as the police tried to force the prisoner to implicate others
who took the oath and to identify the oath administrator. When 40-year-
old Karigo Muchai, a member of Kiambu's Mau Mau district Committee,
was arrested for the first time near his home, Special Branch officers,
ably assisted by black policemen, beat him unconscious, then revived him

by throwing him into a deep pit filled with muddy water. For two weeks Muchai was kicked and punched, then beaten with rifle butts, clubs, and whips before being thrown into the water. He did not confess anything, and to his surprise, he was released.

Most detainees confessed nothing despite terrible and prolonged torture, but instead of being released as Muchai was, they were taken to a screening camp where their ordeal continued. Handcuffed, shackled, and locked in small cells without food or sanitary facilities for several days, they were "softened up" by more beating and whipping. One white police officer specialized in bending a prisoner's thumb so far back that it was dislocated. It was also common to lock these suspects in cells with men who had been wounded by gunshots. Their agony was terrible to witness, and the possibility of being shot next could hardly be discounted.[14] Other prisoners were locked up in cells with dead bodies, conveying a message that was anything but subtle.[15]

Screening took place in a variety of police and civilian-run centers which employed their own methods of persuasion, until 1954 when all detainees, including those rounded up in Operation Anvil, were screened at Langata, a former military base on the outskirts of Nairobi. After some preliminary roughing up by askaris armed with batons, whips, clubs, and rifle butts, new arrivals at most screening centers found themselves living in tents in large barbed-wire-enclosed compounds. There might be food, and free time to talk and play cards, checkers, and *bau* for a day or two before guards marched into the compound and stole everything of value. After a few days, the detainees were rounded up to face what the government referred to as "hooded men"—a motley assortment of Kikuyu who were willing to identify detainees as members of Mau Mau. Some were strongly anti-Mau Mau chiefs, headmen, or pillars of the church; some were government employees ("tie ties") who were afraid to refuse the government's request for help, and others were former small-time criminals who found betrayal a reliable source of income.[16]

Like Mafia informers, these men wore hoods equipped with eye holes. To damn a detainee as a member of the Mau Mau, all that was required was for one of these men to point to a prisoner and say, "I know you." There was no appeal. The accused was immediately set upon by guards who administered a thorough beating before a screening team took over with renewed determination to force a confession; one detainee who was identified in this way was beaten for hours before he was asked any questions at all.[17] Still, despite brutal interrogations, there were few confessions at this stage of the pipeline. The screening team usually had little reliable information to work with, but they nevertheless classified each detainee as "white" (innocent of Mau Mau involvement), "grey" (some Mau Mau activity), or "black" ("true" or "hard-core" Mau Mau). Whites were usually released, but greys and blacks were sent on to detention camps. Unfortunately the hooded men made mistakes, as when a psychotic who had lived on the streets of Nairobi was identified as a "black" Mau Mau and sent to a camp. They also sometimes implicated personal enemies.[18] The screeners made mistakes, too, but they chose to err on the safe side by detaining anyone who was even slightly suspicious. Sometimes when they thought that they had identified a Mau Mau leader they chose to pass their own sentence, since the courts could not be relied on to convict such men. Lions were more reliable. Some screening officers later boasted of taking prisoners into the Royal Nairobi Game Park, which adjoined Langata Camp, where they were released in the midst of a pride of lions.[19] If questions were asked, and at this early stage of the Emergency that was uncommon, the prisoner had obviously tried to escape.

Almost all of the administrative officers in the Kenya Government, like many of the white settlers, had attended public schools in Britain, and they modeled their ideal detention camp on that experience. They believed that detainees should learn to fear the camp commandant just as schoolboys feared their headmaster.[20] Like schoolboys, they should learn the value of hard work and discipline, of vigorous exercise in manly games, and of moral and spiritual cleanliness. The task of putting these ideals into action was given to Thomas G. Askwith, the African Affairs Officer in Nairobi.

Askwith was an unlikely choice for the job of designing a detention camp system to rehabilitate the "bestial savages" of Mau Mau. A former Olympic oarsman from Cambridge University, he was openly pro-African. With his own hands he had helped build a controversial multi-racial club in Nairobi in 1946. Furthermore, when C. M. G. Argwings-Kodhek, the first Kenyan to be called to the English Bar, returned to Nairobi in 1952 with his Irish wife, stirring a racist outcry, Askwith insisted that the couple stay with him. Askwith also believed that the Kikuyu had a legitimate grievance that could only be remedied by ending racism and giving them more land.[21]

When the government asked him to develop a "rehabilitation" plan for Mau Mau detainees, he flew to Malaya to study the methods employed there to deal with the Chinese and Malay rebellion. The British High Commissioner, General Sir Gerald Templer, warned Askwith that the only way to control the Mau Mau was by winning the "hearts and minds of the people,"[22] a motto that would be heard again in Vietnam. The program Askwith devised was a modification of the public school model. Mau Mau detainees would be rehabilitated by exemplary Christians who would serve as both "father confessors" and "school masters." He acknowledged that his plan amounted to a form of "brain-washing," a common term during these Korean war years, but he vehemently insisted that neither force nor duress was ever to be used.[23]

In 1953, Askwith wrote a primer for Africans stating that the cure for the disease of Mau Mau was the "medicine of rehabilitation"—work, education, religion, and recreation. He assured his readers that this was a system practiced "in all advanced prisons in Europe and America," and that it was having "excellent" results.[24] Sir Richard Woodly, a prominent settler, publicly disagreed with this approach. To enthusiastic applause at a Nairobi dinner, Woodly declared that what was needed was "slavery from dawn to dusk, on a ration sufficient to keep him alive and working but no more—powers to prison officials in charge to cut rations, and inflict corporal punishment of a severe nature for misdemeanor."[25] Woodly's harsh vision proved far closer to reality than Askwith's gentle plan.

There was little time for Askwith and the government to work out the details of this rehabilitation model. By the end of 1953, more than 16,000 Africans were in prisons or camps, and a year later their numbers exceeded 67,000. By 1955, Askwith would be in charge of 55 detention camps. Those to which the grey or black Mau Mau detainees were sent were far from the Kikuyu reserves. Several were in the hot semi-desert near the coast, others were far to the north, and one was on an island in Lake Victoria. Most of the camps had to be built from scratch, although some military bases closed since World War II were renovated. The government needed enormous amounts of barbed wire to enclose each camp, and had to build living quarters for the camp staff of African guards and European officers. The inmates themselves had to be provided with tents, aluminum huts, old wooden barracks as living quarters, and cells for solitary confinement. In the rush to complete these camps, sanitary facilities were sometimes overlooked, drinking water was scarce, and medical facilities were primitive. Since most camps were located in low-lying areas where diseases such as malaria, typhoid, and meningitis were endemic, the lack of medical care was particularly tragic.

The camps themselves were run by the Prison Department, but the rehabilitation process was the responsibility of Askwith's Ministry of African Affairs. Between the Ministry of African Affairs and the Prison Department, bureaucratic muddles assumed gargantuan dimensions. Sometimes ample supplies of food sat undelivered, while requisitions for essential medical supplies were never processed at all. Food and clothing were perpetual problems. Many detention camp commandants did as Woodly recommended, putting detainees on near-starvation rations of a single bowl of maize porridge every other day; other camps suffered periodic food shortages.[26] Nevertheless, when an American church organization offered to deliver large amounts of food and clothing to detainees and their children in the reserves, the offer was declined with the explanation that existing supplies were adequate. In reality, the government feared American missionary and governmental intervention.[27]

After a government medical officer inspected the detention camps and reported finding "swollen, discolored, bleeding gums" indicating "gross pyorrhea," someone in the Ministry of African Affairs recommended that all 48,000 detainees now in camps be given a toothbrush. K. M. Cowley, Secretary for African Affairs, rejected the idea as too costly, derisively asking whether the detainees would require different brands of toothbrushes, and concluding that it would be cheaper to give them all a "free issue of Rose's Lime Juice."[28] The administration faced more urgent problems than pyorrhea.

The government not only had to build camps, it had to find people to staff them. There were far too few qualified prison officials or medical personnel available in Kenya. There were not even enough Africans to serve as prison guards, and, in the rush to supply them, men were recruited from the Home Guards, many of them being proven killers. Guards were also recruited from many other tribes in Kenya, Tanganyika, and the Sudan; even military construction workers ("pioneers") in the Suez Canal Zone and elsewhere were conscripted as prison guards. White prison officers were recruited from Rhodesia and South Africa, as well as from Canada, Australia, and Britain. The government could not afford to be very selective about the qualifications or psychological stability of these men, so it was hardly surprising that many behaved brutally. Kenya hired one S. A. Wilkin from South Africa as a detention camp officer even though Wilkin had been discharged from the British South African Police Force in 1953 for assaulting a prisoner. In 1955, he was charged with intentionally shooting a Kikuyu, but the charges were later dropped. In 1964, one year after Kenya's independence, Wilkin was convicted of manslaughter when he killed an African who entered his house during the night.[29]

What took place in the camps conformed closely to Woodly's model. Several camp commandants were known to detainees as sadists. Wells at Manyani Camp was one,[30] Harris at MacKinnon Road Camp was another,[31] and Brooke at Saiyusi Island Camp was nicknamed "famine" because he seemed to enjoy cutting the detainees' rations.[32] It was not uncommon for prison officers to drink heavily before beating inmates until they were too exhausted to continue. The commandant at Hola, a diminutive man named Kraft, was notorious for drunkenness and cruelty. He would question a detainee while holding the man's ear away from his head. If the man refused to answer, the commandant would shoot him through the ear.[33] Kraft was often drunk and sometimes in the evening after a particularly heavy bout of drinking and smoking marijuana, he would enter the compound, fire his pistol, and order everyone out of their barracks. Then he would beat men at random until he was too tired to go on.[34]

African guards, called "warders," were sometimes equally brutal. A Maasai guard for whom the camp commandant was said to have paid five shillings for every prisoner he beat to death, was said by detainees to have enjoyed his work.[35] Others who forced detainees to spend hours in pits filled with viciously biting ants, or crushed their testicles, cut off their fingers, or whipped them until they were unconscious, were said to have enjoyed inflicting pain. Eliud Mutonyi, the former chairman of the Mau Mau central committee, saw two fellow detainees beaten to death by African guards at Mariira Works Camp. Long after it was obvious that the victims were dead, the guards continued to beat their lifeless bodies.[36]

To be fair, not all African guards or white prison officers were brutal. Some guards, particularly from the Luo and Kamba people, were sympathetic and kind; their gifts of food and medical supplies probably saved many lives. There were also white officers who would not allow anyone to be beaten, and most Mau Mau detainees mentioned a few whites who were consistently kind and sympathetic.[37] Under a Canadian Commandant named Belsen, detainees at Saiyusi Island Camp were not beaten, and they were well-fed.[38] Similarly, Kowop Camp in northern Samburu District was decently run by a Kenya Police Reserve officer who neither punished nor verbally abused any of the detainees, and they were saddened when he was shot to death by another white in a drunken brawl.[39]

But men like these were a minority. The camp system did not call for kindness. It mandated fear and pain—a "short, sharp shock"—and even good men were desensitized by a system of camp life that was founded on brutality. The regulations that the government established were meant to be tough. Regulations specified what acceptable food rations were and under what circumstances they could be reduced, when medical care should be provided, and how and when detainees could be made to work. Regulations also specified the circumstances and extent of permissible force to maintain order in the camps. Kenya prison regulations permitted prisoners to be flogged for virtually any imaginable offence, and so did detention camp rules, except that the commandant was limited to ordering 12 strokes. The force with which the blows were delivered was not specified. Twelve strokes was very painful punishment. Unfortunately, neither the Prison Department nor the Ministry of African Affairs insisted on close and independent oversight to assure that the intended toughness did not become institutional savagery. In the absence of close supervision the Camp Commandants ruled their camps as they saw fit, and most of them ruled through terror. Nyeri District Work Camp was one of the worst. It was known to detainees as "God help me!"[40]

Not only was there nothing in the rehabilitation system to prevent a reign of terror, it was clearly understood by camp personnel that they were expected to be "tough." The line between toughness and brutality was easily overstepped. With a very few exceptions, whenever a shipment of detainees arrived at a detention camp, the men had to run a gauntlet of African guards—always under the command of whites—who whipped and beat them with rifle butts and batons until they were inside the wire. On one such occasion at Saiyusi Island Camp, as the men were being beaten, the Camp Commandant who had succeeded the humane Belsen taunted them by telling them not to cry, because they were getting the "freedom" they wanted. Then as the men were being beaten inside the camp, he invited them into his "dance hall" where they "danced" under a rain of blows from the guards' batons.[41]

When the detainees entered a camp they were forced to walk through a 5-foot-deep, 20-foot-long pit of water and disinfectant. Before emerging they were told to dip their heads under the water. Those who were slow to obey were held under water by African guards. It is not recorded that any of these men drowned, but there can be no doubt that the effect on them was sheer terror.[42] Regulations called for the new detainees to surrender their valuables for safekeeping, but in many camps the guards pocketed almost everything.

In most camps, detainees were taught the virtues of discipline by being marched to work at dawn or even earlier, after nothing more than a cup of maize gruel for breakfast. While African guards watched, men broke up large rocks, cleared irrigation ditches, tilled fields, or simply dug great holes in the ground before being ordered to refill them and begin all over again. Now and then guards looked the other way if the detainees paused for a moment, but there was no guarantee that a detainee would survive such an indiscretion. Often, anyone who stopped work even for a moment was beaten to unconsciousness, before being tossed into a pit of water (kept ready for the purpose) to revive him. Like slaves in years past, men learned to speak as they worked with their heads lowered and their eyes averted. Those who attracted the guards' attention might be flogged or ordered to pull out every hair of their beard, a punishment that left men's faces painfully swollen for days.[43] Askwith's plan for rehabilitation without force existed only on paper. The public school model had been forgotten. In its place, Sir Richard Woodly's prescription for dawn-to-dusk slavery with a bare survival diet and severe punishment had been taken to heart.

In addition to being forced to work a 12-hour day, detainees were required to display a submissive attitude. It was not enough to call white men "Bwana" ("Sir"); they had to be called "effendi," a Turkish term for superiors that was used in some police units and K.A.R. battalions. African guards had to be respected, too, and to prove their authority, they sometimes imposed tests on the detainees, such as demanding that they repeat after the guards "Jomo Kenyatta is a dog," or "Dedan Kimathi and Stanley Mathenge are dung." The prisoners were beaten until they complied.[44] Some guards, like their Japanese and German counterparts in World War II, were occasionally friendly to the prisoners, but these displays had to be surreptitious because their superiors would not tolerate the breach of discipline. As a result, a guard who was friendly one day might beat a prisoner savagely for no apparent reason the next. The purpose of this senseless brutality was presumably to make the Mau Mau fear their captors. It did, but even more than fear it generated hatred and contempt.

Although a prisoner could be beaten for any reason on any day, the arrival of a "screening team" at a camp meant that torture was a certainty. Teams of five or six whites accompanied by African Home Guards and police travelled from camp to camp attempting to cleanse the inmates by compelling them to confess their involvement with Mau Mau. Once in a great while a screening team would ask questions without any violence at all, and now and then a screener would do nothing more than degrade a detainee by spitting in his mouth, but most detainees who were called out of their barbed-wire compound could expect the worst.[45] Usually a few questions were asked before the torture began, but sometimes the screeners began to beat, whip, burn, or apply electric shock before asking any questions at all. The torture was usually initiated by the Europeans. Sometimes they began as if in resignation, as a school master might do, saying, "this will hurt me more than it hurts you." Sometimes they worked methodically, holding a man's head under water in an oil drum until he was close to drowning, then starting over again.[46] More often they attacked the detainee in a frenzy, and when African screeners joined in, the room filled with the victim's screams and the screeners' grunts of physical exertion. Sometimes, the inmates who stood outside awaiting their turn could see dust billowing out of the interrogation room as several screeners beat and whipped a detainee on the room's dirt floor.[47]

The white screeners did not torture with the mechanical ingenuity of the Inquisition or the Gestapo, and they lacked the technical sophistication employed later by the police and military forces of many other nations, but what they missed in these regards they made up for in rage. They hated the Mau Mau in principle and they hated the sullen, obstinate refusal of the detainees to confess having taken an oath. Day after day they gave vent to their hatred with a frenzy of punches, kicks, and blows from clubs, whips, and rubber hoses. As they attacked a detainee— and it was much more an attack than a carefully planned program of torture—they cursed and screamed before exhaustion forced them to step aside and let African screeners carry on the assault.

Some detainees screamed in pain, but a surprising number refused to cry out at all, and those who waited their turn nearby often heard only the sound of the blows and the exertion of the men delivering them. Detainees were sometimes beaten until they were unconscious, or dead, without screaming or pleading for mercy. The screeners were maddened by this stoicism, which they saw as mute animal obstinacy rather than courage, and eventually the beatings that were to have cleansed the Mau Mau cleansed the screeners instead. A Kenya Police officer who led a screening team for several months said,

At first, they weren't human to me, they were black animals who had done inhuman things to women and children. I was bloody well going to beat the Mau Mau poison out of them. At the end of a day my hands would be bruised and arms would ache from smashing the black bastards. I hated them and sometimes I wanted to kill them. A few times I did, or we all did together. I never worked alone, it was always a whole lot together like a rugger scrum. I screened those bastards for four months, almost five, and only got a handful of confessions out of them. I'd been drinking too much for some time before I really tied on one at Manyani. The next morning I realized that they'd won. I hated myself for what I was doing more than I hated them. I finally had to admit that they were brave men who believed in what they were doing more than I believed in what I was doing. I resigned and got out of Kenya as quick as I could.[48]

It was more difficult to explain the deaths of detainees in camps than it was to account for the deaths of men who had not yet been taken into custody; men could be shot "attempting to escape," and few questions would be asked. But explaining that someone who "had tried to escape" from a detention camp had died of a fractured skull or internal injuries, while his facial features were no longer recognizable, was awkward, especially when the medical staff were at odds with the camp's officers. When certain doctors saw a detainee with broken bones or gangrenous buttocks, a complaint would be made and the responsible white police officer was disciplined.[49] But other medical personnel knew their place. When a hospital superintendent, R. T. Potter, at Manyani Camp saw Roy Morrell, a Special Branch Police officer, beating a prisoner between the legs with a rubber hose (he remembered that the hose was blue) while the man was being held by half a dozen African guards, he rushed out to protest. Morrell brusquely told Potter that he needed information from the detainee and that Potter should mind his own business. Potter did not report this incident nor several others that he later witnessed.[50] Perhaps he was wise to say nothing, because sometimes when medical personnel complained, it was they who were punished. When the senior nursing officer in Kenya's Medical Department criticized conditions at MacKinnon Road, the infuriated camp commandant put *her* in detention.[51]

One common way around the problem of accounting for beating deaths was to forge death certificates. The cause of death in these cases was usually recorded as typhoid fever, and the bodies were disposed of in a common grave before an inquisitive medical officer started to wonder why a typhoid victim should be covered with bruises, burns, and lacerations. Because some detainees actually succumbed to typhoid, and because sanitation was known to be poor, this excuse usually worked.[52] Just how many died in this way will never be certain, but 350 detainees were said to have died of disease in 1953 alone. But as detainees asserted, and some camp officials admitted, many of these had not died of disease but had been beaten to death.[53] Others died later of their injuries.

The most obstinate "black" or "hard-core" Mau Mau inmates were typically young men, but one of the bravest among them was middle-aged. Karigo Muchai, who had been released earlier after successfully resisting police torture, was 40 years old when he was arrested again in March of 1954. He had worked for Mau Mau for several years, most of the time as a member of the Kiambu District Committee, and although he had made several trips to the forest with armed men, he had done little fighting himself. Shortly after security forces beat his aged father to death, leaving his body in a field for the son to find, Muchai began his ordeal at the hands of those who ran the pipeline. He was beaten and whipped almost every day for two weeks before his interrogators relented; he also had his thumb dislocated and was made to stand in a feces-filled cell for several days without food or water. Later, along with 200 other men, he was beaten so savagely that he felt lucky to have survived; nine of the others did not.[54] At Athi River Camp, the combination of hunger, brutal labor, and torture forced 50 "hard-core" men to confess. Muchai, who was ill and twice as old as many of them, refused. To persuade him, he was tied to a rafter by his ankles and whipped until he lost consciousness. He awoke in the camp dispensary where he stayed for a month recuperating from the beating; six other men who were beaten in the same way died.

Later, at other camps, Muchai was made to run with a bucket of wet sand or feces on his head. Once, as he ran, a guard hit him so viciously on the shoulder with a rifle butt that surgery was required and he spent 18 days in the hospital. Eventually he was transferred to Hola where he was one of the men who were beaten in the "massacre" that killed eleven and crippled many others. Finally, in December of 1959, after Muchai had made certain that all capital charges against him had been dismissed, he agreed to admit that he had taken an oath. The next month, the State of Emergency was officially ended.[55]

Another detainee who refused to cooperate or be intimidated by beatings was an educated man who had never taken up arms for the Mau Mau. J. M. Kariuki, who was 24 when he was arrested in late 1953, had taken the Mau Mau oath of unity twice. But his only Mau Mau activity involved bribing African elders who worked at Kwa Nyangwethu to release prisoners from that infamous Nakuru screening camp. At the time Kariuki worked at Nakuru hotel and the stories of brutality at this camp, including castration (done with full knowledge of European officers), so horrified him that he spent a large amount of his own money to save people from screening. He was found out and detained until the Emergency ended seven years later. For seven years, he drove the administration to distraction in virtually all of the 14 camps where he was detained. Kariuki was an intelligent, witty man (he later became a minister in Kenyatta's government) who refused to tolerate brutality or injustice, and when he saw abuses in the camps, something which occurred with depressing regularity, he wrote letters of protest to officials in Kenya and Britain.

All letters written by detainees were required to undergo censorship by the camp commandant, who was not likely to want atrocities that took place under his command made known to Parliament. Kariuki avoided censorship by bribing guards with money he had hidden in camp. His letters, which were literate, temperate, and accurate, usually brought a visitation of Kenyan or British Government officials who sometimes actually insisted on reforms. Afterward, Kariuki would be flogged—quite legally under camp regulations—for violating censorship rules. After his first letter he was given 24 strokes. When he complained again about six men being beaten to death, he received 12 very hard strokes and 7 days of solitary confinement; this might have killed him if a sympathetic Protestant missionary had not brought him water. The indomitable Kariuki's letters continued, and so did the punishment. In all he was sentenced to nearly 200 strokes, and once was savagely beaten by five Europeans. On one occasion, commandant Marlow of Manyani Camp was so enraged by Kariuki's letter-writing campaign that he threatened to shoot him if he did not sign a statement promising to cease all letter writing and cooperate with the government. When Kariuki refused, Marlow drew his pistol and fired at his head, just missing him. A second shot was closer, and a third grazed Kariuki's upraised hand. Nevertheless, Kariuki continued to write letters, and he was finally released without confessing that he had taken an oath.[56]

Almost 8,000 women were detained during the emergency, nearly all of them in Kamiti Women's Detention Camp outside Nairobi. Some of these women were teenagers, some were pregnant. They were guarded by men as well as women and their treatment was appalling. The senior of two "rehabilitation" officers at Kamiti was a white Kenyan woman, Mrs. Warren Gash, who never entered the camp without a large dog and a baton, and boasted about how much the inmates feared her. Women were required to perform forced labor as heavy as that expected of men,

as they built roads and cleared away tree stumps and boulders, all the
while being watched and sometimes whipped by male guards. Periodi-
cally, the guards raped anyone they chose and venereal disease became
epidemic among the detainees.[57] When women gave birth in detention,
they seldom received medical attention. That they gave birth at all was
remarkable, since most were so malnourished from their diet of water
and beans that many suffered from pellagra. Before a medical investigation improved their diet, several women and many of their infants
died.[58] The women were also beaten, kicked, whipped, and sadistically
made to bare their buttocks and sit on a wire mesh that had been heated
red hot over a charcoal burner.[59]

Early in 1956, Eileen Fletcher, a 55-year-old Quaker who had worked
with the women in Kamiti for nine months, shocked the British public
when she spoke about conditions in the camp in a London newspaper
interview.[60] Among other things, she described small children left alone
in the camp while their mothers were working; detainees as young as
eleven who were sentenced to 16 days of solitary confinement for defiantly singing a Mau Mau song; sexual abuse; and forced labor that over-
taxed frail and underfed young women, some of whom were pregnant.
Fletcher's charges were soon taken up by Labour M.P.s in the House of
Commons, and the Colonial Secretary was forced to admit that an "error" had been made in sentencing children under the legal age of 14.
He did not mention that boys as young as 10 were also detained at
Manyani Camp.[61]

But John Hare, Colonial Office Minister of State, categorically denied
all the rest of Fletcher's allegations, and asked why she hadn't provided
her information to the appropriate officials. In response, Labour M.P.
Fenner Brockway, long an opponent of colonialism, read to the House
letter after letter and report after report that Fletcher had sent to the
responsible officials without result.[62] Some improvements in camp conditions followed, but even though the Emergency had faded away during
1956, 3,000 women still remained behind barbed wire at the end of the
year at Kamiti. An official government inquiry into conditions in all
detention camps took place at the end of 1956 after military operations
had ended. The inquiry found no evidence that detainees had been subjected to "rough" treatment.[63]

Although physical and psychological brutality were ever-present reali-
ties of camp life, some camps did attempt to achieve rehabilitation
through other means. Educational programs were begun, including instruction in English; recreation activities were made available for men

who had the energy to do more than sleep after work; and Christians of all sorts attempted to teach "moral values" and to convert the detainees. For a time, members of the Christian "Moral Rearmament" (MRA) movement seemed to be having success in converting numbers of "grey" detainees, but it soon became apparent to camp administrators that detainees who were pledging their devotion to Moral Rearmament were only looking for a way out.[64] Mau Mau continued to be their true devotion. Other camps attempted to use a Kikuyu *mundu mugo* to carry out mass cleansing ceremonies for detainees. Known as "Her Majesty's Witch Doctors" to most of the whites, these usually elderly men were a familiar sight in many camps early in the Emergency. Their success rate was not encouraging, no doubt because, as the detainees laughingly acknowledged, most of them were as yet undiscovered Mau Mau oath administrators.[65]

For several months beginning late in 1955, the administration of the Athi River Camp was actually handed over to the Moral Rearmament organization under the control of Colonel Allen Knight, a Kenyan farmer who somehow convinced the Prison Department that he could "cure them all in a fortnight." Colonel Knight did not lack for confidence. Despite the fact that the Moral Rearmament movement had been censured by the Church of England, he prepared a film of his accomplishment at Athi River Camp.[66] In a letter to Alan Lennox-Boyd late in 1955, he offered to show the film in the Colonial Secretary's office or in Parliament. He then told Lennox-Boyd, "I have had much contact with leaders from many parts of the Colonial empire recently, and there is no doubt that many are looking to Moral Rearmament as the uniting force which can answer the divisions of the world. I am confident your wise understanding can do much to bring this about."[67]

Knight's MRA team at Athi River eliminated physical violence against the detainees, but when few confessions materialized, rations were reduced as punishment for those who would not confess.[68] Questionable as this was for men who preached higher morality, their next plan was truly shocking—they brought prostitutes into the camp. The women paraded safely out of reach of the goggle-eyed detainees, making seductive conversation, while they graphically reminded the men of the pleasures they were missing in their state of enforced celibacy. As if that were not enough, the men were told that even at that moment, as they were lusting after the provocative prostitutes, men of the Home Guard were having sexual relations with the detainees' wives and daughters.[69] Apparently no one was convinced enough to confess as a result of the prostitutes' visit,

and how their expense was recorded by Moral Rearmament administrators is an intriguing question.

Soon after the episode, Askwith began an investigation into the MRA
and its methods. His investigators found that MRA staff had not been
successful in converting detainees, and moreover that their methods were
alarming. They were not referring to the reduced rations or prostitutes,
however. They were distressed because MRA staff, particularly Reverend
H. J. Church, had told the detainees that Mau Mau marked the failure
of *all* communities in Kenya to live up to moral standards, and what is
more, that the government by confiscating Kikuyu land had to bear responsibility for creating the conditions that led to Mau Mau. Askwith's
investigation concluded that "such a philosophy was not only puerile but
dangerous," and the MRA staff at Athi River Camp was replaced in March
of 1956.[70]

At least one other detention camp had a prostitute who served the
detainees well, a woman named Maya who had somehow become available to the men at Hola. Although she was said to be "very ugly," men
lined up all day for her favors, which cost anywhere from a United States
penny to seven cents. Maya was so busy that she lay on her back all day
with her right hand extended for payment. The men did not complain;
they thanked God for this woman's kindness to them.[71] Despite Maya's
untiring efforts, most of them remained sexually frustrated. Among the
lucky ones were those at Hola's "Open Camp," who worked in the fields
during the day, where they sometimes met local women from the Pokomo
people. Unfortunately, these women fled in terror at the sight of the
Mau Mau, who were confused and frustrated by their reaction (as they
were by the appearance of Pokomo men brandishing spears), until they
learned that someone—no doubt the camp guards—had told the Pokomo that the men of Mau Mau had twenty-foot penises that they kept
tied around their waists. The detainees took to bathing naked in the
Tana River so that the local women could appraise their true proportions, and sexual liaisons soon followed with such success that some detainees married Pokomo women when their detention ended.[72]

Although camp life was dominated by the daily round of work and the
fear of beatings or torture, detainees did what they could to make it
bearable. They were usually shouted awake at 5 A.M. and, before lining
up for their morning cup of gruel, Christians and non-Christians met
together facing Mount Kenya, their arms outstretched, palms up, as they
joined in prayerful song.[73] After cleaning their eating utensils, and carrying away their sanitary buckets, they were marched off to work, with

their hands on their heads. After the evening meal, and on Sundays when there usually was no work, they would listen to radios and sing, sometimes to the accompaniment of a battered guitar. Other men played cards or bau, while the few literate prisoners sometimes read books thought suitably uplifting by the camp commandant, or a newspaper smuggled in for a fat bribe.[74] Throughout the day a loudspeaker blared government propaganda about the inevitable defeat of the Mau Mau and the invincibility of British military forces.[75] The loudspeaker was usually muffled with a blanket.

Even before the detention camps were built, when rebels were held in jails, the men set up their own regulations, appointed their own police to report offenders, and convened courts to deal with these men. The regulations they established spread from prisons to detention camps, and remained remarkably similar in all camps throughout the entire period of detention. The prevention of conflict was the major concern, so arguing or fighting was forbidden, as were crowding into a food line, malingering on the job, insulting another detainee, lying, stealing, drinking alcohol, smoking marijuana, or committing sodomy. Other rules attempted to reduce conflict with the guards and camp administration. Mau Mau detainees were not permitted to have sexual relations with the wives of the guards, nor to be disrespectful to the guards themselves. Each barracks (usually called a "club") or compound had a central committee that appointed its own police and court members. Anyone found guilty of an offense would be reminded of his obligation to the others, made to apologize, and, if a severe offender, made to walk on his knees around the hard cement floor—a bruising, bloody and humiliating punishment. Others were sentenced to carry many heavy buckets of water from a distant tap for the use of the men in the compound.[76]

Detainees agreed that these measures, which were observed remarkably well, helped maintain their solidarity. There was much need of solidarity if the men were to make certain that everyone got his share of the meager rations, that the old, sick and weak were protected against over-work, and that no one felt alone against the ever-present threat of brutality. They warned one another of potential informers and rehearsed the false stories they would tell under torture (so that no one could be charged with a capital offense), and after one of them had been beaten, they nursed him as well as they could.[77] Even so, more than one man hanged himself rather than face more torture, including at least one man who knew nothing about Mau Mau.[78]

But despite their best efforts, relations among inmates were never wholly tranquil or altruistic. There were continuing tensions between the better educated and boastful men of Kiambu, who tended to get the best jobs from the camp administration, and other Kikuyu, Meru, and Embu, who felt that the men from Kiambu were cowards who had not done their share of the fighting.[79] And when the administration instituted a policy of mixing a few hard-core detainees who would not confess with substantial numbers of detainees who had, there were some episodes of violence.[80]

Many of the more than 80,000 people detained or imprisoned for their involvement with Mau Mau actually had little or nothing to do with the movement. A few of these were quickly released but others were obliged to collaborate in some way before they could go free. Some who were active in Mau Mau lacked conviction, and were willing to cooperate when they realized that collaboration would lead to release. Perhaps a few also succumbed to Her Majesty's witch doctors or to Moral Rearmament, but by far the most effective way to convince Mau Mau detainees to confess and return to their former lives was a simple, but seldom used technique that amounted to nothing more than expressions of kindness and concern. George Dennis, a Scot who achieved remarkable rapport with detainees, was able to elicit many confessions simply by his inherent decency. He regularly underwent "blood brotherhood" ceremonies with detainees in which both men cut their wrists, then placed them together, uttering promises of trust. Dennis was a kind man, and when it came to confessions, kindness easily won out over torture.[81]

Even "hard-core" detainees who were determined never to confess could recognize a decent man when they saw one. When H. D. Montgomery, a senior probation officer, went to hard-core compounds without an armed escort—as the rules prescribed—he was surrounded by menacing but curious men. To their disbelief, he told them that he wanted to be their friend. But when he proved his sincerity by visiting their families and returning with letters and photos, the ice was broken. Eventually Montgomery and these determined men were on friendly terms with one another, and some real trust was almost certainly involved, but the hard-core were just that; they did not give him any confessions.[82] Instead, they insisted that they were prisoners of war who deserved to be treated under the terms of the Geneva Convention. These demands usually resulted in more beatings, but they did not relent.

Many detainees who had not confessed were released on the intervention of some well-connected employer. By 1956, 10,000 Kikuyu men had been returned to the Rift Valley because white settlers insisted that they were better workers than the Luo or Kipsigis who had tried to replace them.[83] But even in late 1956, when it became obvious to even the most fanatic settler that Mau Mau was no longer a threat, the Kenya Government felt no great urgency in releasing detainees.[84] At that time there were still more than 20,000 persons in detention camps and another 8,000 in prisons. After 1956, thanks largely to growing pressure from Britain, camps began to be phased out, and detainees were sent back "up" the pipeline toward their homes. Increasingly, however, these last detainees were made ready for their return to "civilization" by capricious beatings and torture. Yet, by 1959, despite the terrible means employed to make them cooperate, 1,100 detainees still refused to confess to anything.

Despite the pressure from Britain to normalize the situation in Kenya by releasing detainees, some remained so adamant that the government decided the only solution was to send them into exile, to remain perhaps forever beyond the pale of Kenyan society. The chosen place was a town named Hola, next to an almost desert waste some 60 miles from the coast near the Tana River. A few Pokomo and Orma farmers scratched out a living along the banks of this often-flooded river that originated in the highlands where the Mau Mau had fought, but most of the area was uninhabited. The government's plan was to settle the detainees at Hola permanently, after they had built enough irrigation ditches to support themselves as farmers. Eventually, their families might be allowed to join them.[85]

The detention camp at Hola was unbearably hot, and plagued by clouds of mosquitos. When the exiles arrived, they suffered so much from the heat that mid-day work had to be cancelled. The heat and the mosquitos were only part of the problem. The decision to assemble all the remaining hard-core detainees at Hola was not without risk, and it soon became apparent that the unrepentant Mau Mau were not going to accept their exile with good grace. Some were willing to join what was known as the "open camp," in which men worked in the fields during the day and had some freedom after work; but even these retained their sympathies with other detainees who frequently refused to work and remained in the "closed camp."

For years the government had carried on ingenuous discussions about the amount of force they would permit camp officers and guards to use. The notion of "compelling force" was favorably contrasted with "overwhelming force," which the government termed unacceptable.[86] It was clear that if the detainees in the closed camp were ever going to support themselves—and submit to the authority of the government—they would have to work. After all, they were intended to live in Hola in permanent exile. Yet much of the time they refused to work, claiming to be prisoners of war for whom the Geneva Convention rules forbidding forced labor should apply. Thus they would have to be forced to work by "compelling" but not overwhelming force.

The Senior Superintendent of Prisons for the area was J. B. T. Cowan. As Officer-in-Charge of Mvea Detention Camp, Cowan indicated that he was not opposed to physical force when he invited District Officer John Nottingham to have a look at the camp, saying, "It's all just like a good clean rugger scrum."[87] Cowan had a reputation for success in bringing about rehabilitation. Now he devised a plan for forcing "hard-core" detainees to work, an act that would violate their oath. The plan called for a massive show of force. Hundreds of armed guards and white riot police vastly outnumbering the recalcitrant prisoners would assemble in full view of them. Then a small contingent of hard-core detainees, less than 20 in number, would be ordered to work outside on the agricultural program. If they refused to march to the work site, they would be "man-handled" or "frog-marched."[88] Once at the site they would be ordered to begin pulling weeds, a task which did not require tools that could be used as weapons. If the detainees still refused, two guards would seize each man's hands and force him to pull weeds, the idea being that once even enforced compliance had taken place, the men would believe they had violated their oath and begin to cooperate.[89]

In February 1959, responding to a report that the hard-core detainees were increasingly idle and insubordinate, the Commissioner of Prisons sent Cowan to discuss his plan with the officer-in-charge of the Hola Camp, G. M. Sullivan, and the District officer, Arnold Hopf. Cowan carefully explained his plan before leaving, convinced that Sullivan had understood it. But Sullivan, who was later characterized as "not a clear thinker," and "a bit thick," had not.[90] Sullivan advised the Commissioner of Prisons that he could think of no jobs that would not involve the use of tools and that he anticipated the possible need for "summary punishment," which meant the use of considerable force. The Commissioner of Police advised the Minister of Defense that Sullivan could not carry out the "Cowan Plan" without someone being hurt or killed, but since Sullivan would have over 100 guards to control only 15–20 detainees, he thought the risk was minor and authorized him to go ahead. So did Askwith who believed that the original Cowan plan would be implemented.[91]

In early March when the Cowan Plan was to be tried at Hola, Cowan himself was in Britain on leave, so Sullivan was left on his own to carry it out. A former Royal Navy Officer, Sullivan was an inexperienced Camp Commandant. His second in command was A. C. Coutts, a former British Army Regimental Sergeant Major, and equally new to the job. The government's decision to use Cowan's Plan on the hard-core detainees was misguided from the start, because these men *had* worked under government orders in the past. It was only occasionally that they went on strike in protest. Their current strike was in its ninth day. Forcing them to work, when they had already worked more or less freely, made no sense.

Nevertheless, on the morning of March 3, 1959, Sullivan assembled 111 African guards, 20 of whom were armed with rifles, the rest with batons. In crude Swahili he told them, "If they [the detainees] refuse or bring any trouble at all, you will try to strike knees and strike just a little. If you see they have stones or something bad in hands, you can use force completely." He gave the guards no orders about how the Mau Mau should be forced to work. Sullivan then ordered out of the camp not 15 to 20 detainees as Cowan's Plan called for, but 85 men.[92] Sullivan confronted the men and demanded to know if the Mau Mau were willing to work. He was startled when their leader, a man named Kiburi, said that they were. The detainees had seen the force assembled against them and feared fatalities if they did not cooperate; they planned to continue passive resistance later.[93]

Sullivan ordered all 85 detainees to march to work, and they did so without resistance, flanked by guards. Sullivan followed in a Land Rover, but left Coutts and his three other white officers behind at the camp. When the detainees reached their work place, Sullivan blew his whistle and the guards attacked the prisoners.[94] It is not clear whether the beating began because the Mau Mau refused to take farm tools from a waiting truck, as one witness reported, or whether it was entirely unprovoked as another witness insisted.[95] When the whistle sounded again and the beating ended, at least one man was dead and several others were seriously injured. According to a survivor, Sullivan again asked if the men were prepared to work and Kiburi again answered that they were.[96] Whatever was said, Sullivan's whistle sounded again and the beating resumed for about ten minutes. Sullivan later insisted that he had meant to stop the beating with his whistle, not to order it, but that the excited guards could not easily be stopped. Two reliable witnesses, a Ministry of Works engineer, A. J. Peters, and Ezekiel, his African assistant, watched this second beating from about 100 yards away. They reported that the guards and the Mau Mau had argued, and that the Mau Mau had squatted down before the guards attacked them. They added that the second beating continued for five to ten minutes, while Sullivan stood by. Once the beatings ended, Sullivan got into his Land Rover and drove to Hola Camp, ostensibly to locate a water wagon and to ask Coutts to take command of the operation.

While Sullivan was gone, a period of about 15 minutes, about 30 of the men actually worked; but some others began taunting the guards, who again attacked the men—many of whom lay down in self-defense—with batons, rifle butts, and boots for another ten minutes or so.[97] At camp, an Assistant District Officer asked Sullivan how the operation was going. Sullivan replied that there had been "the odd spot of trouble," but that everything was "satisfactory."[98]

When Sullivan's "test" of the Cowan Plan finally ended, eleven detainees were dead and another 20 had to be hospitalized with serious injuries. Sullivan decided to send the less badly injured men back to the compound, while he sent a message to Peters to bring a tank of water to the scene. When Peters arrived with the water truck he was told to park it near the dead bodies. For reasons that are still unclear Sullivan also called for massive reinforcements of security forces who arrived in helicopters and later by truck but found no sign of indiscipline, much less a prison break. Later in the day the Provincial Commissioner arrived and asked for an explanation of the deaths. In a stunningly inept lie, Sullivan told him that the detainees had died from drinking contaminated water. Peters immediately challenged Sullivan's lie and a water sample was taken for analysis. Sullivan then claimed that the detainees had confronted the guards using farm tools as weapons. Again, Peters contradicted Sullivan and told the disturbed administrative official what really happened.[99]

As soon as Governor Baring had been informed about the events at Hola, he sent three senior government officials to investigate. During their visit these officials did not bother to view the eleven dead bodies or the injured men in the hospital; nor did they speak to the guards or detainees. Sullivan lied to them about the use of batons and repeated his tale that they had died from drinking bad water. After a brief visit, the investigators returned to Nairobi, where they told the governor that the victims had probably died not from drinking polluted water but because they drank too much water in the heat. Although over the years Baring had heard endless allegations about atrocities in the camps, he willingly accepted this preposterous explanation and authorized a press release that attributed the deaths to the lethal water cart.[100] The press release did not mention the fact that an autopsy was underway. A week later, an inquest at Mombasa revealed the extent of the murderous violence that had been inflicted on the victims. Pathologist M. G. Rogoff found the cause of death in each case to be "shock and hemorrhage due to multiple bruising caused by violence." He also found that the men suffered a severe vitamin C deficiency.[101] Soon after, the Kenya Government changed the name of Hola to Galole. The reason for this action was to make people forget what had happened there. The name change was not successful.

The reaction in Britain was immediate and intense. Harold Macmillan's Conservative government was facing a general election in October of 1959 and the Labour Party saw Hola as a political scandal that might lead them to an election victory. As Barbara Castle said, at last they had the evidence of brutality they had been looking for.[102] Labour M.P.s called upon Colonial Secretary Lennox-Boyd to resign, and, embarrassingly, staunch conservatives joined in the outcry. During June and July of 1959 there were two major debates on Hola in the House of Commons. J. Enoch Powell, a leading Conservative M.P., called Hola an "administrative disaster," and demanded that those responsible, from the Governor down, be called to account. Prime Minister Macmillan later wrote that Hola was a "tragic incident" and that the government of Kenya had "badly muddled" matters, but he was determined not to sacrifice the careers of either Baring or Lennox-Boyd.[103] Although Lennox-Boyd offered his resignation, Macmillan refused it, and Baring was allowed to remain in office until the scheduled date of his retirement later in the year. Macmillan's government was further embarrassed when Cowan, whose plan had been at the root of the Hola killings, was awarded an M.B.E. on his retirement late in 1959.

To the outrage of the Liberal Opposition, and some within government, no one in Kenya was punished for any wrongdoing. Sullivan, who was found to have intentionally lied about events at Hola, and the Commissioner of Prisons were forced to retire, but they were allowed to receive their pensions. Coutts was exonerated. Meanwhile, Baring was in a terrible predicament. He not only had eleven deaths at Hola to explain, he also had evidence that senior officials in his government, including at least one minister, had ordered the use of violence in camps. Even after Hola, new cases of brutality were reported to him, including one that involved the intervention of a government officer who had ordered a prisoner whipped with a *kiboko* rather than the regulation cane, and given more than the permitted number of strokes.[104] If prosecution in this and earlier cases known to him were allowed to go ahead, the re-habilitation program—which he believed had been successful—would be called into question, and his entire administration could be discredited.

Baring's letters to his wife show clearly that he was angry about the brutality in detention camps, but it is difficult to say whether this was because the brutality disgusted him or was simply a political embarrass-ment. Whatever his feelings, he chose not to risk his administration's reputation in a quest for justice. Instead, he worked out another amnesty deal. The State of Emergency would be declared at an end, and in return there would be amnesty for all crimes committed by Mau Mau, whites, and loyalists.[105] Macmillan's Conservatives won in October, but Lennox-Boyd resigned soon after. Convinced by the events at Hola that the pace of change in Africa had to be speeded up, Macmillan made a decision that would change the course of Kenya's future. He replaced Alan Lennox-Boyd with Ian Macleod, a man who was profoundly offended by what had happened at Hola.

Macmillan also appointed an investigative committee of outsiders headed by R. D. Fairn, a British Prisons Commissioner. For the first time, charges of excessive force in detention camps would not be investigated by members of the administration. The Fairn Committee report did not mince words, saying the commissioner had seen and spoken with injured men in the camps, and had heard "impressive testimony from responsi-ble people on all sides that violence, not just corporal punishment, was often used in the past by the 'screening teams' to compel confessions." The committee demanded that this "shock treatment," as it was still called, must stop. It also confirmed that death certificates had routinely been falsified and that the detainees had not been fed the diet prescribed by regulations.[106] Fairn's committee further observed that the hard-core de-tainees were determined never to admit their guilt or to cooperate with the government. It suggested, quite seriously, that what was called for was a Kikuyu-speaking, Christian psychiatrist to work with the men. It even suggested that it would be useful to hire a Kikuyu comedian to coax them out of their grim defiance.[107] However whimsical these suggestions now appear, the committed clearly understood that the use of force was not the royal road to rehabilitation.

Many people in and out of government in Kenya knew that excessive force was common in detention camps. The settlers knew this too, and most approved.[108] Some in the Colonial Office were also aware of the problem, but did nothing to order a reduction in the violence.[109] Except for an occasional police official like Commissioner Young, his C.I.D.

(Criminal Investigation Department) counterpart McPherson, and some army officers including General Erskine, few even complained. One who did was Victor C. Shuter, an officer in Her Majesty's Prison Service. From late 1955 throughout 1956, Shuter served at Mayani, where 20,000 detainees were guarded by 58 white officers and 3,500 African guards; later he served at two smaller camps in the Fort Hall District. In January 1959, Shuter swore an affidavit to the effect that brutality was commonplace in these camps. He testified that entire groups of prisoners were routinely punished for the offenses of a single man, that the heavily armed riot squad was used to intimidate detainees, and that white officers beat prisoners regularly with whips and sand-filled rubber hoses. He also swore that he had seen European officers beat men behind closed doors, that some detainees had been seriously injured, and that the injured men had been hidden when the camps were inspected.

An investigation headed by A. P. Jack, a Kenya Government Public Prosecutor, took testimony from many of the men Shuter had accused of wrongdoing. Predictably enough, they denied Shuter's accusations, saying they had never seen a whip in camp, and had never beaten a prisoner or seen anyone else do so. But when Jack called upon camp medical officers, a nurse, and some detainees (all of whom had cooperated with the administration), the charges were confirmed. Furthermore, Brigadier H. F. H. Durant, former commandant at Manyani, admitted that many of his officers may have "ill-treated" detainees.[110] Nevertheless, Jack concluded that brutality was not common, and was typically caused by a few "bad" officers who had been dismissed. Jack declared that he was a good judge of men; the officers impressed him as reliable, "decent" people who would neither ill-treat prisoners nor lie. On the other hand, Jack reported allegations of impropriety against Shuter himself as if they were demonstrably true; and when he learned that Shuter had lied about being a former British Army officer (he had actually been a sergeant with a good military record), and had probably also misrepresented his educational background and home address, he dismissed Shuter's charges.

Jack's report whitewashing the camps was published in Kenya in April 1959, one month after Hola. It was an embarrassment to many in government, but its refusal to find fault with the conduct of camp officers was approved by most white Kenyans. As a woman settler who was not an extremist put it, "Some of the lads in the camps may have been a bit rough, I suppose, but I really think the Mau Mau deserved it, don't you? Anyway the rough stuff was almost always done by *askaris* who got out of control because they hated the Mau Mau."[111] A former police officer who served on a screening team took a harsher but typical view: "The Mickeys were hard men and only hard methods would work with them. It was a war to save white civilization in Kenya and in war people get killed."[112]

Some of the brutal violence that took place in the camps was the work of sadistic individuals who, for whatever reason, took pleasure in savaging helpless prisoners, but detention camp brutality cannot be dismissed simply as the regrettable consequence of the government's decision to recruit prison officers and guards without adequate information. The whole system of detention and rehabilitation was founded in violence. The "short, sharp shock" theory led otherwise decent men to use any means of coercing confessions, or at least to look the other way while other men did so. By institutionalizing violence, officials of the Kenya Government assured their own infamy. They also assured the failure of their efforts to "rehabilitate" the Mau Mau.

It is tragic that the dishonor of public officials as well as the suffering and death of their victims resulted from two false beliefs, namely that only confession could rehabilitate, and that only violence could bring about confession. Some prisoners confessed because they were beaten or tortured, but many more, including the hard-core prisoners who had taken the most active part in Mau Mau, refused to confess no matter how terribly they were abused. Torture only hardened their will to resist. Brutality was the wrong tactic and the Mau Mau oath was the wrong target. It is true, as many Kenyan whites insisted, that some of the oaths were invented by sophisticated men who wished to control their more credulous, "ignorant" followers, as Fred Kubai called them.[113] It is also true that many of the men and women who took the oath, particularly in the early stages of the Emergency, believed that it did have the power to kill them. But many others never feared the oath itself, only the retribution of Mau Mau enforcement squads.[114] Even those who had originally believed in the power of an oath to kill soon became disillusioned when they saw thousands of men and women violate their oath by cooperating with the government, either as Home Guards or as members of screening teams. When others who confessed in detention did not die, all doubt was removed.

Most of the detainees who refused to cooperate did so because they felt a commitment to nationalism, to their goals of land and freedom, and to one another as victims of British oppression. In varying degrees, they also thought of themselves as heroes and warriors; brave men and women were expected to resist. As time went on, they defied their white jailers as much through hatred as anything else. It is impossible to say exactly how large a role these motivations played in the refusal to confess. However, fear of the oath they had taken rarely had anything to do with it.

In the wake of the Fairn Committee revelations about conditions at Hola, plans to exile hard-core Mau Mau were forgotten; in an about-face that made a mockery of their entire rehabilitation program, the Government of Kenya immediately declared that all the unconfessed prisoners at Hola were free to go home. When some of the hard-core detainees refused to cooperate even to this extent, they were quite literally implored to leave. Finally, these most unrepentant detainees were carried to waiting government vehicles and driven to their homes. Some of these men not only refused to utter a single word to their former captors, they had to be carried to their own doorstep.[115]

7

"BLACK MAN'S COUNTRY"

THE PATH TO INDEPENDENCE

As 1959 began, most white Kenyans felt reasonably secure about their future. In January, Colonial Secretary Alan Lennox-Boyd presided over a conference attended by the Governors of Britain's three East African colonies, where it was decided that independence would probably not come to Kenya before 1975.[1] In April, a month after Hola had made headlines, Lennox-Boyd told Parliament, "I am unable to envisage a time when it will be possible for any British Government to surrender their ultimate responsibilities for the destiny and well-being of Kenya."[2] Soon after, Governor Baring toured the settler areas, where he told gratified white farmers that Kenya would become a "fortress colony," containing a British Army base, because an East African military presence was strategically essential for Britain's defense. He assured them that independence, if it came to Kenya at all, was far in the future.[3] Some

extremely conservative Kenyans, led by former R.A.F. Group-Captain
L. R. "Puck" Briggs and A. T. Culwick, still demanded white supremacy,
including racial segregation, but most settlers reluctantly supported Michael Blundell's efforts to achieve a multi-racial form of government.
They were certain that the Government would continue to be controlled
by Kenya's white community.

Kenya's new British-imposed constitution allowed for some African
representation on Kenya's Legislative Council. Even politically moderate
settlers were anything but enthralled by the African politicians who took
advantage of their newly-granted right. Tom Mboya, an outspoken and
radical young Luo, became the prime target for the settlers' displeasure.
The British Government shared their concern. In 1956, Mboya began a
13-month tour of the United States and Britain, where he spoke against
the white supremacist views that had been popularized by Robert Ruark's
best-selling novel, *Something of Value*. Mboya made important friends
among American Democrats and labor leaders and Britain's Labour
Party. The Colonial Office asked the United States to deny Mboya a visa,
and, when that failed, they monitored his speeches closely. While he was
in London, they hoped to convince him to become more moderate, and
discussed arresting him if he did not.[4] When Mboya returned to Kenya
in 1957 to take his seat in the Legislative Council, he proved that he had
not become a moderate by insisting that Africans had earned the right
to rule themselves. After Mboya spoke out against Governor Baring's
cherished Mau Mau rehabilitation program, the irate governor unsuc-
cessfully tried to restrict Mboya's right to hold public meetings. With a
sense of indignation that few settlers could exceed, Baring, a Roman
Catholic, told his wife that his government must fight Mboya, because,
in addition to his threatening alliance with the British Labour Party, the
young politician was "a lapsed RC with the morals of a monkey."[5]

Although Nationalist African politicians were an annoyance, most settlers were profoundly relieved that the Mau Mau violence had ended.
True, white Kenyans had been alarmed in 1958 when a non-violent group
calling for land and freedom arose in Kiambu, but the government
quickly cracked down on these protesters with the same ruthlessness used
against the Mau Mau.[6] Showing unquestioning faith in the success of the
rehabilitation process, white farmers readily accepted "cleansed" Mau
Mau detainees as farm laborers or family servants.[7] As 1959 ended, Kenya
was returning to normal, the economy was reasonably good, and the
future looked promising. Most settlers believed that their farms in the
Kenya highlands had been promised to them by the British Government

"in perpetuity."[8] It is unlikely that any of them were aware that when Harold Macmillan served in the Foreign Office in 1942, he had quickly seen that the Kikuyu would have to be allowed to settle in the "white highlands" after the settlers had been bought out.[9]

As the end of 1959 approached, Kenya's white settlers were remarkably insensitive to the effect that world events might have on "fortress Kenya." For one thing, although Macmillan's government was in torment over Hola, few in Kenya were unduly disturbed by it. What happened at Hola might have been unfortunate, but it had happened to "hard-core" Mau Mau and no tears were shed. Kenya's white community should not have ignored Hola, and there had been earlier warning signs they should have noticed. For example, when the Gold Coast achieved independence as Ghana under Kwame Nkrumah in 1957, Kenyans were not alarmed. They pointed out that there were virtually no Britons in Ghana, while Kenya was a "kith and kin" colony whose large white population would never be abandoned to "black rule" by the home country. A year earlier, settlers predictably did have violent views about the debacle at Suez, where the United States and the Soviet Union forced the 1956 British and French invasion of Egypt to be withdrawn in ignominy, but even then few realized that Britain's growing international weakness would affect them so directly and so soon.[10]

Most of Kenya's whites breathed a sigh of relief when Harold Macmillan's Conservative Party won the general election in October of 1959. The Labour Party, they feared, would not have protected their interests. Instead of celebrating the conservative victory, the settlers should have rushed to the battlements of "fortress Kenya," because Macmillan was determined to bring independence to Britain's African colonies as quickly as possible. Macmillan had learned from France's bloody struggle in Algeria that there could be no military solution to the rising tide of nationalism in Africa. By the end of 1959, 12,000 Frenchmen had died in that war, along with nearly 150,000 Algerians.[11] Macmillan understood that if whites were to retain power in Africa, the British Government would have to be willing to kill large numbers of Africans, and he was determined to avoid bloodshed. He also understood that Britain no longer had the strength to hold its African possessions by force, even if it had had the will to do so.[12]

Clear evidence of Macmillan's determination to decolonize Africa came early in January 1960, when he toured the continent. He was not only the first prime minister ever to visit Africa, he stayed for six weeks. In Ghana he declared, "we [British] share the strong tide of feeling among

Africans that this is their time of destiny."[13] In another major speech on January 19, 1960, he said that the rise of nationalism in Africa was a fact that British policy would have to acknowledge.[14] A few days later in South Africa, Macmillan referred pointedly to the "wind of change" in Africa. For the settlers in Kenya, that wind was about to strike with gale force.

To carry out his plans for the decolonization of Africa, Macmillan appointed Ian Macleod as his new Secretary of State for the Colonies. At 46 the youngest minister in the cabinet, Macleod had shown little interest in colonial affairs, and in fact had never set foot in any of Britain's colonies.[15] But Macleod had been so disturbed by the murders at Hola that he was emotionally as well as intellectually prepared to carry out Macmillan's charge. He too was convinced that delay would lead to terrible bloodshed. He also believed that independence was morally right. Macleod's wealthy predecessor, Alan Lennox-Boyd, lived in a large and elegant London house where he entertained colonial political leaders in lavish style. Macleod lived in a modest apartment with his wife, who still suffered the after-effects of a serious case of polio. The Macleods could not afford a servant, so Mrs. Macleod had to cook for the many guests her husband was obliged to entertain. Because the government did not reimburse its colonial secretaries for these expenses, Macleod had to cash in his insurance policy to pay for the cost.[16] It is unlikely that Macleod's African guests failed to notice the difference between his standard of living and that enjoyed by his predecessor, nor that enjoyed by many of the settlers in Kenya.

Macleod made Kenya his first priority. Before taking action he tried to win the support of moderate Europeans in Kenya. Although the new Colonial Secretary had never seen the country, his younger brother, Rhoddy, had been one of the men who had helped Michael Blundell organize the moderate New Kenya Party. Rhoddy Macleod had served in East Africa during World War II, and returned there in 1946 to become a "soldier settler." Conservative settlers were convinced that Rhoddy would persuade his older brother to support them, but instead he supported Macleod's policy. This decision was not based solely on fraternal loyalty; Rhoddy Macleod was one of the few Kenyans who was not convinced that Jomo Kenyatta had been the leader of the Mau Mau, nor did he regard all the rebels as monsters.[17]

Except for his brother, Macleod found little support among Kenya's white moderates. The situation was altogether different in Britain, where economic weakness rendered the largely unprofitable African colonies a painful burden; furthermore, it was becoming increasingly difficult to resist pressure from the new Kennedy administration in Washington to decolonize. Led by Belgium, which would soon abandon the Congo, opposition to colonialism was growing in Europe as well, and even Britain's Conservative Party had lost most of its zeal for imperialism. Led by M.P.s who owned property in Kenya, there was still a small but outspoken settler lobby in Parliament, but many Conservatives were fed up with the settlers' demands. Michael Blundell reported that during a dinner in the House of Commons a young Conservative M.P. colorfully voiced what Blundell referred to as the "prevailing mood" when he said, "What do I care about the f...king settlers, let them bloody well look after themselves."[18]

By early January, Macleod was ready to act. He invited both white and African delegations from Kenya to a conference at Lancaster House, an ostentatious London mansion. Macleod planned each move with the skill of a chess master. He did not discuss his plan for Kenya with anyone, not even his own men in the Colonial Office. Instead, he let all sides talk themselves out, occasionally making good use of world events—such as Belgium's decision to grant independence to the Congo on July 1, 1960—to convince white delegates that Britain had to speed up its own time-table for African independence. After five tumultuous weeks of debate and compromise, Macleod made his plan known—Kenya would become a parliamentary democracy based on universal franchise. Kenya's white delegates were stunned. Kenya's African delegation (ably advised by Dr. Thurgood Marshall) scaled back their demands, Michael Blundell's New Kenya Group accepted the inevitable, and an agreement was struck. Macleod's plan would immediately enfranchise more than one million Africans; soon after, there would be universal suffrage. But no date for independence was set.

Shocking as the events at Lancaster House were to Blundell, he left the conference firmly believing that the British Government did not intend to grant Kenya its independence for at least ten years—enough time, he thought, to prepare the country's 60,000 whites and six million Africans for African rule.[19] By this time, Blundell's efforts to lead Kenya toward a multi-racial government had turned so many settlers against him that he felt the pressure keenly. When Lennox-Boyd was Secretary for the Colonies, he illustrated Blundell's state of mind with this example: "There's a story in the Muthaiga Club that he [Blundell] went up to someone who he said was glaring at him, and said that he thought it very wrong that politics should be allowed to follow him even into the club. The chap replied that indeed he was glaring at him, but only because he had pinched his table."[20] After Lancaster House there would be no mistake about settler hostility. When Blundell returned to Kenya, Africans at Nairobi's airport cheered him, but a settler symbolically threw 30 pieces of silver at him, and many of his friends now refused to speak to him.[21]

When Briggs returned from Lancaster House, he said, "I regard the outcome of this conference as the death blow to the European Community in Kenya. It is a very sad thought that all those who stuck out seven hard years of Mau Mau did so apparently for no purpose."[22] "Grogs" Grogan characteristically used more colorful language: "Our African co-citizens ... have already achieved tacit recognition by a minister of the crown that the religion of Mau Mau, its Messiah and his apostles, constitutes the very soul of Kenya African Nationalism."[23] Cavendish-Bentinck resigned from the Legislative Council in protest, and other settlers joined in a chorus of indignation and foreboding, but their leader, "Puck" Briggs, changed his mind about the "death blow." Ten days later he declared, "the war was not lost on the beaches of Dunkirk, nor was the battle for Kenya lost at Lancaster House."[24] Briggs may not have surrendered, but Britain had.

Macleod had rejected demands by Kenya's African delegation at Lancaster House for Kenyatta's immediate release. He knew that Kenyatta would soon have to be freed and that the British Government would have to deal with him, but he was playing for time so that Kenya could be readied for African self-government. As Macleod waited, the bloodshed that he feared would spread over Africa began. Early in 1960, violence broke out in newly independent West Cameroon, while the intertribal warfare that had disturbed the Belgian Congo for months flared up more violently than ever. In March, as the fighting grew worse, Dr. Verwoerd, the South African Prime Minister, warned of impending chaos, and invited whites from all over Africa to immigrate to South Africa.[25] Two weeks later, at a place called Sharpeville, South African police fired into a crowd of African protestors, killing 67 and wounding close to 200. On July 1, 1960, independence day for the Congo, Belgian King Baudouin's sword was snatched away by an African, setting the tone for what followed. The Congolese Army mutinied against its Belgian officers, white civilians were attacked, and civil war followed. Within days, 13,500 white Belgians fled with nothing but the clothes on their backs. At least 2,000 went to Kenya, where the settlers showed them sympathy and hospitality but crowds of Africans were hostile. When a trainload of Belgian refugees arrived in Nairobi on July 14, 1,000 Africans shouted "freedom now," "leave now," and "the same thing will happen to the Europeans here."[26] That same day, Kenya's settlers called for the government to create a European Defense Force, and the Mayor of Eldoret reported that white farmers were stockpiling food, water, and weapons at easily defended strong points. On July 25, Tom Mboya met U.S. President John F. Kennedy in New York. He told the President that "I can definitely say that Kenya is ready for independence."[27] The next day, Britain airlifted a battalion of British troops to Nairobi, to be followed soon after by the aircraft carrier, *H.M.S. Bulwark*, carrying 600 Royal Marines.

As African politicians quarrelled publicly about whether the Mau Mau should be called a "glorious" and "heroic" national movement, Mau Mau violence once again broke out, this time in the Meru reserve and the adjoining forests on the eastern slopes of Mt. Kenya. British troops were needed to control the uprising and restore confidence.[28] Many settlers had been thinking about leaving Africa ever since the results of the Lancaster House Conference became known, and now they panicked. As "for sale" signs sprang up across the highlands, property values fell, stock prices dropped by more than 50 percent, and capital poured out of the country.[29] A British peer, Lord Lambston, captured the settler's mood when he said in reference to Macmillan's "wind of change" policy, "we have upset a delicate balance and, for the sake of a phrase, confounded a continent."[30]

In an attempt to restore European confidence and save Kenya's endangered economy, Macleod permitted the new governor, Sir Patrick Renison, to issue a statement that the government would not release Jomo Kenyatta. Renison was a long-time colonial servant but he knew virtually nothing about Kenya, or Africa for that matter. All he knew about the Mau Mau was what his advisors told him, and what he read in a 1960 Kenya Government report written by Frank Corfield.[31] Corfield, who also knew little about Kenya, relied exclusively on government and loyalist sources in producing a document that declared the Mau Mau to be "wholly evil," and identified Kenyatta as its leader. Belief in Kenyatta's guilt also persisted in Britain. Even as late as 1962, after Kenyatta had been released, former Colonial Secretary Sir Oliver Lyttleton wrote, "Only the most prejudiced can now claim that the trial was other than fair and impartial."[32] In his statement on Kenyatta, Renison insisted on referring to him as a "leader to darkness and death," and when Macleod objected to this phrase, Renison threatened to resign. Rather than risk worsening the crisis of confidence in Kenya, Macleod authorized Renison's statement. Speaking over the radio, the solemn governor assured his listeners that Kenyatta would remain under restriction.

Although Renison's words helped to reduce the fears of some settlers, more conservative Kenyans like those in Brigg's white supremacist Kenya United Party continued to predict disaster if African rule were actually to come about. They and their sympathisers insisted that if it had not been for the Europeans, Kenya's prospective African leaders would still be—as Brigg's colleague, A. T. Culwick put it—"racing through the bush, spear in hand, dressed as the Heavenly Tailor turned them out."[33] Culwick added that the answer for Kenya was not more freedom—which would only lead to a repetition of the rape, murder, and looting that had ravaged the Congo—but greater white control like that practiced in South Africa, where, he insisted, black Africans were happy.

Extremists like Culwick believed that if their demands for an apartheid-like separation of the races in Kenya were rejected, the Europeans would leave and all essential services would cease to exist. What else, Culwick asked, could anyone expect when the "African States" were incapable of manufacturing "a bicycle, let alone an atomic bomb." In addition to the demise of civilization, the settlers predicted wholesale violence. And in fact, many settlers prepared to defend themselves at what they called "selected strong points."[34] Not all the settlers were as alarmist (or as racist) as Culwick, who soon emigrated to South Africa; but there was widespread anger and fear in August 1960, when Macleod refused to advise the Queen to intervene on behalf of a former Kenya Police Reserve Officer named Peter Poole who had been found guilty of murdering an African in 1959. There were rumors that armed whites would storm the prison and free Poole, but in that same August, as a crowd of 300 whites waited expectantly outside Nairobi Prison, Poole became the first white man in the history of Kenya to be hanged for murdering an African. Many of the whites were armed but there was no violence. Later there was despondent drinking, and a renewed realization that Kenya was no longer "white man's country."

Demands that Kenyatta be released grew when, in February 1961, an election was held based on the new constitution forged at Lancaster House. There were two main parties, KANU (Kenya African National Union) and KADU (Kenya African Democratic Union). Many of the prominent African leaders of KANU, which was the Kikuyu-Luo coalition party, campaigned on the pledge that they would not accept office unless Kenyatta were released. Luo Leaders like Tom Mboya and Oginga

Odinga understood the symbolic value that Kenyatta could have in uniting KANU, and they had little doubt they would be able to control Kenyatta, whom they believed to be elderly, alcoholic, feeble, and out of touch with current events. The European population of Kenya watched the election with their bags packed. Kenya's six million Africans watched too, as the drama over Kenyatta's freedom was played out. KANU, which had demanded confiscation of European property, nationalization of all industry, and closing down foreign investment, won over the more moderate KADU by 16 seats to 9. The pressure to release Kenyatta intensified and so did the settlers' fears.

In response, the government slowly began allowing selected politicians and journalists to visit Kenyatta. He was clearly not as robust as he had been before his prison term, but he had stopped his heavy drinking and his mind was sharp. A Russian-speaking doctor who attended him was amazed to discover that he still remembered the Russian he had learned three decades before.[35] Michael Blundell, who a few months earlier had said, "I don't find it in my heart to have anything to do with him,"[36] now paid Kenyatta a visit. When Blundell met Kenyatta for the first time he found him to be one of the ablest and most intelligent Africans he had met, but he was fearful that Kenyatta's only concern lay with Kenya's Africans. Blundell urged Kenyatta to repair fences with the Europeans who mistrusted him, reminding the "Mzee" (the respected elder) that Kenya would need to keep its white population.[37] Some favorable reports about Kenyatta began to appear in the press, but settler opinion remained firmly opposed to his release.

The idea of releasing Kenyatta had first arisen in 1953, when General Erskine had realized that the only solution to the Mau Mau crisis was political, and that Kenyatta would have to be part of it. Kenya's most influential living settler, the venerable Ewart "Grogs" Grogan (who as a young man became legendary by walking all the way from the Cape to Cairo, and who as a new settler had "guided" the Zionist delegation on its ill-fated tour of Kenya) agreed that only Kenyatta had the power to end the violence. Grogan asked his friend Sir Charles Markham, a member of Kenya's Legislative Council, to sound out the views of his colleagues about releasing Kenyatta. Markham reported back that there was no sympathy for Grogan's "crazy idea." Grogan said, "Pity. It might have saved many many lives, but we shall see one day whether I was right."[38] Most settlers not only rejected the idea of Kenyatta's release, they would have preferred to see him dead, and there were those in government who agreed. Although the aging Kenyatta had been relieved of his sentence of hard labor when it became clear that he could not survive it in the great heat, he was nevertheless made to sleep on a stone floor that was covered only by a thin rush mat, his medical care had been indifferent at best, and little was done to protect him against assassination attempts, which occurred more than once.[39] When Edward Windley, then Chief Native Commissioner for Kenya, visited Kenyatta in prison in 1955, he expressed the disappointment of many in Government when he found the old man "disgustingly well."[40]

When Lieutenant Colonel P. de Robeck, the District Officer responsible for Lokitaung Prison, handed over his duties to J. R. M. Tennent on July 5, 1956, he wrote, "Kenyatta himself will not last long. He has a very high heart rate and will snuff out at any time. He is not allowed to do any hard work or even put his head lower than his heart." De Robeck went on to instruct the new District Officer that "when he dies," the following signal should be sent "immediately": "Kenyatta died (time and date) heart failure request outside medical officer for post mortem soonest." He added, "there is a ready typed signal in the left draw (sic) of the office desk. The object of the above is to guard [against] future machinations of politicians and agitators (sic) that Kenyatta done (sic) to death by the wicked British Administration."[41]

Not everyone wanted Kenyatta dead. One of his jailers at Lokitaung, former District Commissioner L. E. Whitehouse, came to know him well, and later said that in many ways Kenyatta was a great man, adding that he doubted Kenya "will ever see as great a man again."[42] Kenya's Special Branch also wanted Kenyatta alive, but not because they thought him a great man. Late in 1958, Special Branch officers approached Governor Baring with an appeal for Kenyatta's release. Like Grogan, these police intelligence officers were convinced that Kenya's politics would be in turmoil as long as Kenyatta remained a martyr in prison. There is some evidence to suggest that Special Branch knew from the outset that Kenyatta was not the architect of Mau Mau, but a purely pragmatic, even moderate African nationalist who could be relied on to steer a safe course if he were free to return to politics.[43] Some officers in the Special Branch intimated that they had helped to see that Kenyatta was convicted because his imprisonment would make him an irresistible symbol for Africans; after his release he could be relied on as a "safe" leader from the British point of view.[44] Whatever the truth of this alleged conspiracy to make Kenyatta into Britain's man, Governor Baring firmly rejected the Special Branch request for his release. Baring believed that Kenyatta could never be set free.[45]

So Kenyatta remained in custody, but in April 1959 he was moved to an administrative and police post at Lodwar, 90 miles closer to Nairobi. Lodwar was even hotter than Lokitaung—nights were seldom cooler than 90 degrees Fahrenheit—but Kenyatta was pleased that his latest wife, Mama Ngina, was allowed to join him. One of his first visitors was a relatively unknown non-Kikuyu named Daniel arap Moi, a former school teacher who had recently been elected to the Legislative Council. Kenyatta preached moderation, telling Moi that salvation for Kenya lay in the unity of all its peoples, including the settlers. His favorite term, which would later become Kenya's official motto, was *Harambee*, a Swahili word meaning "let's all pull together." Before Moi travelled to London and the United States to further the cause of Kenya's independence, he urged the government to release Kenyatta. While Moi was in Atlanta, he was refused service in a restaurant because of his race, an affront that he did not forget.[46] Nineteen years later, Moi would succeed Kenyatta as President of Kenya.

In April 1961, Kenyatta was flown to a cooler location at Maralal, and it was there that Blundell and the press met with him. Four months later, he was allowed to return to his rebuilt house in Kiambu. After a week of confinement behind barbed wire, all restrictions were lifted and a huge crowd gathered outside Kenyatta's house. On the day of Kenyatta's release, 50 uniformed members of the Kenya Land and Freedom Army paraded near the Norfolk Hotel in Nairobi before the police shooed them away. Fearing more trouble, hundreds of police were on guard outside Kenyatta's house, but the crowd only danced and sang, jubilantly calling for *Uhuru*, the Swahili word for freedom. While dozens of reporters watched, Kenyatta walked among the ecstatic thousands, wearing a pair of cheap plastic sandals that had been painted with the word "Uhuru."

In many ways, white Kenya was the same in 1961 as it had been in 1952 when Kenyatta was arrested. Whites in Nairobi still insisted that waiters serve them barefooted, and addressed them as "boy" in imperious tones. They were still rude to African and Indian shop clerks, refused to stay in Indian-owned hotels, and did not say "please" or "thank you" to their servants. They still refused to pick up hitch-hiking Africans (to their disgust, visiting Americans regularly did so), preferring to drive by, showering them with clouds of red dust. On weekends, they still had their golf, tennis, croquet, and horseback riding, and on Saturday nights even small hotels in the highlands had dances that lasted all night. They still spoke freely about the stupidity of the Africans, and they railed against politicians in Britain who believed that the natives were capable of self-government. The color bar was a little less obvious, but the Kitale Hotel, which had refused accommodation to African and Indian lawyers during Kenyatta's trial, was still a "white" hotel.[47]

But there were changes, too. There were "For Sale" signs on farms and businesses, and settlers worried about their safety if, as some expected, squatters tried to return to the highlands or tribal warfare broke out. Some settlers reported that their cars had been stoned by Africans, and white policemen warned white motorists not to stop to offer assistance if they happened to hit an African pedestrian or bicyclist; they were advised that, to avoid being beaten by an angry crowd, they should keep driving to a police station and report the accident there. Most settlers said bitterly that they wanted nothing more than to leave Kenya, but others admitted that life in Britain could never compare to the life they had enjoyed in Africa.[48] White Kenyans waited expectantly for the aftermath of Tanganyika's (now Tanzania) independence, which was granted on December 9, 1961. When there was no violence, they were relieved, but, as they said, Tanzania was not Kenya. They entertained themselves with stories about the incompetence of Tanzania's new government officials. In one particularly popular story, a new African District officer was said to have used the wooden furniture in his government-provided house for firewood.[49]

In 1961 Jomo Kenyatta was probably nearly 70 years old, and he had been isolated from the rough and tumble of Kenya politics for almost a decade. Although he stopped drinking and seemed to gain strength each day, he had to struggle to regain his political touch within KANU as it fought against KADU. Many white Kenyans, including Michael Blundell, were already supporting KADU, which was pledged to protect the interests of Kenya's smaller ethnic groups—including the whites—by setting up strong regional governments that could not be controlled by a Kikuyu-dominated central government in Nairobi. Although it was not known at the time, the British Government was also secretly supporting KADU.[50] Kenyatta not only wanted to win white political support, he wanted whites to stay in Kenya, and most of them had serious thoughts about leaving. A poll taken a few months after the Lancaster House Conference indicated that 75 percent of the white settlers said they would leave Kenya as soon as it was feasible. While white Kenyans considered their options, their fears of Kenya's collapse under an African government quickly affected the economy. It was estimated that, after January 1960, capital flowed out of Kenya at a rate of £1 million per month, while virtually no new capital came in.[51] And in 1961, more than 6,000 Europeans made good on their threat by leaving the country.

It was obvious that if very many more whites left Kenya the economy could collapse. It was not simply that white-grown farm produce accounted for most of Kenya's income; the whites were Kenya's principal consumers. Many foreign companies that had located in Kenya to serve the needs of the white population were already suffering severely from a loss of sales. To make matters worse, the economy was also hard hit by the weather. In 1961 Kenya suffered from the most severe drought in its history; crops failed and there was no grass for cattle. Dead livestock could be seen lying by the hundreds along many roadsides. When at last the drought broke, the heaviest rains in Kenya's history fell, washing out roads and bridges and destroying farmlands. Several parts of the country suffered the effects of serious famine.

As soon as he was released, Kenyatta attempted to reassure the white Kenyans that they were welcome to remain and that a KANU-led government would not confiscate their property. Schools and government services would remain excellent, he promised, and inter-tribal war, which many settlers were sure was coming, would be prevented. Kenyatta said all the right things, but white Kenyans still felt betrayed by the British Government, and few cherished the prospect of having as their new head of government "the leader to darkness and death." Whether the settlers liked it or not, in October 1961 Kenyatta accepted the presidency of KANU.

With memories of the Congo still horrifyingly fresh, the settlers' fears of tribal war were heightened when the Maasai and Kamba fought several bloody battles, and the Kipsigis of Western Kenya (who had contributed 15,000 men to the security forces during the Emergency) swore that their "tribal land" would always remain their land. They warned that a KANU-sponsored central government would have to fight if it thought otherwise. Some 8,000 Luo supporters of KANU who worked on European-owned tea estates in Kipsigis territory were threatened with violence if they did not leave, and the Kipsigis began to make arrows by the thousands. In retaliation, the Kikuyu began to stockpile arrows, spears, and poison, and on several occasions war alarms led to the mobilization of "thousands of excited warriors."[52] Smaller-scale inter-tribal cattle raids occurred in many parts of Kenya, sometimes with severe loss of life. Backed by British troops, the government was able to prevent the outbreak of large-scale violence, but most of the settlers had no confidence that a newly independent "African" Government could prevent war among its tribal peoples.

Against this background of fear, Kenyatta continued his efforts to calm the settlers. He began by ruthlessly dissociating himself from the Mau Mau. He had not gotten along with Bildad Kaggia or Fred Kubai in Lokitaung Prison, and his sympathies now were clearly with the same Kiambu elite that had supported him in KAU before his arrest, not the Nairobi leaders of Mau Mau who had threatened him with death. But it was not the Mau Mau who remained in the forests that worried Kenyatta most, it was the former "hard-core" Mau Mau detainees who had joined together in a new organization called the Land and Freedom Army (usually known as the LFA). The members of this tightly organized and well-armed society had taken oaths pledging to fight if Kenya's new government betrayed their cause of land and freedom.[53] Along with other veterans of Mau Mau like Kaggia and Kubai who had joined KANU, they wanted aid for their widows and orphans, education for their children, reparations for their confiscated property, and, most of all, free land. The opportunity to buy land previously owned by white settlers did not satisfy them; they had not fought and suffered for the right to pay for land that they believed already belonged to them.

The LFA began oathing members in 1960, but the organization had been infiltrated by police who soon arrested 74 people, half of whom were former "hard-core" detainees. Despite intense police surveillance, the movement grew as more former detainees took its oath. It spread widely through the Rift Valley, as well as through the western highlands all the way to Kitale.[54] The settlers and the Kenya Government were thoroughly alarmed. A few of the LFA leaders took military titles, such as "Colonel Nasser," and there were some attacks against whites and Indians, just as there were clashes with armed Africans from tribes that supported KADU and saw the LFA as an arm of KANU. However, LFA oaths were primarily non-violent, and the titles the leaders took were governmental, such as "District Commissioner," "Mayor," and "Governor." Their membership was being readied to assume responsibility for governing all of Kenya. When an LFA leader, Kihika Mungai, was arrested in October 1962, he said that the movement's goal was to drive the whites out and for the "LFA Government" to rule an independent Kenya.[55]

Not everyone in Kenya was convinced that the LFA was simply a continuation of Mau Mau. Some Africans, including members of the LFA and Tom Mboya, alleged that Briggs and other white supremist settlers had paid former detainees to create LFA in order to delay independence by alarming the British Government.[56] Other Africans, including politicians in KANU, believed that the LFA was financed by "reds," either in China or in the Soviet Union.[57] Both KADU and KANU denounced the LFA, and by the end of 1962 more than 3,000 of its members had confessed to police that they had taken an LFA oath.[58] Kenyatta and others in KANU were fearful that members of the LFA, most of whom were former squatters in white highlands, would try to claim white-owned land by force,[59] but nevertheless he rejected the growing demands of the Mau Mau veterans in the LFA, saying again and again that people must not take oaths and that "nothing is free." The former Mau Mau rebels were told that they, like everyone else in Kenya, would have to work for anything they wanted, and would have to pay for any European land that became available. KANU's slogan, emblazoned everywhere in Kenya, was "Uhuru na Kasi"—freedom and work. Meanwhile, Kenyatta ordered the Mau Mau remaining in the forests to "surrender," in his words, and hundreds did so. As often as possible, he arranged to be filmed by newsreel cameras as he spoke out against Mau Mau.

In the fall of 1962, much of the world fixed its attention on the confrontation between the United States and the Soviet Union over Cuban missiles, and on the border war between China and India. Kenyatta condemned Chinese aggression, reiterating that KANU stood for peace; but he was soon involved in his own crisis as the demands of the Mau Mau veterans grew more strident. He quarreled openly with Kaggia and, as speech followed speech, Kenyatta increased his criticism of Mau Mau until he finally uttered these scathing words: "We are determined to have independence in peace, and we shall not allow hooligans to rule Kenya. We must have no hatred towards one another. Mau Mau was a disease which had been eradicated, and must never be remembered again."[60] In April 1963, he wrote an article for *The East African Standard* which concluded with these words: "I myself suffered for long. But I promise you I am not bitter. I ask those of you who still have hatred in your hearts to cast it aside. We cannot build a happy and progressive nation as long as men harbour ill-feelings about the past."[61] Soon Kenyatta's followers were repeating another slogan—"forgive and forget." But in spite of Kenyatta's efforts, the white exodus continued. Another 6,000 whites left Kenya in 1962, and 4,700 more Europeans left Kenya in 1963 than entered it. Many others remained only because they could not sell their land.[62]

As the electoral contest between KADU and KANU approached in mid-1963, Kenya's transition to independence was once again threatened by the continuing violence between the para-military "youth wings" of the two parties. Truck-loads of young men, dressed in their party's colors and carrying clubs and knives, intimidated voters and clashed with one another. Their taunts and "V-for-victory signs"—in this case, "U for Uhuru"—upset many whites who felt, as Kenyatta did, that they had taken the law into their own hands. Kenyatta denounced KANU's own youth wing, but massive police intervention was still necessary to prevent them from jeopardizing the election. Despite everything, the election took place on schedule and KANU won a clear victory. Kenyatta was invited by Governor Renison's successor, Sir Malcolm MacDonald, to form a government, and on June 1 he became Kenya's first Prime Minister.

On August 12, 1963, Kenyatta was offered his greatest opportunity and challenge by the white community. For the first time, he was invited to speak to an all-white settler meeting in Nakuru. Three hundred white settlers filled every seat in the hall. They knew that Kenya's Independence Day was set for December 12, but they still did not know Kenyatta. As Kenyatta entered the room there was a smattering of polite applause, then silence as he stood at the podium surrounded by microphones, newsreel cameras, and reporters. If Kenyatta could reassure this audience he might yet save Kenya's economy, but if he failed the damage could be incalculable. He wore a dark double-breasted suit, a white shirt and tie, and the beaded Luo cap that symbolized Kikuyu-Luo solidarity within KANU. If he was nervous he did not show it. Speaking clearly and confidently, he delivered perhaps his greatest speech. According to Sir Charles Markham and others who were present, the speech did more than anything else to convince the settlers that they could still have a future in Kenya.[63]

Assuring his audience that what he was about to say was not meant just to please them but was the policy of his government, Kenyatta said, "There is no society of angels, whether it is white, brown or black. We are all human beings, and as such we are bound to make mistakes. If I have done a wrong to you, it is for you to forgive me; and if you have done something wrong to me, it is for me to forgive you.... You have something to forget just as I have." Then he went to the heart of the settlers' concern: "This has been worrying many of you, but let me tell you Jomo Kenyatta has no intention of retaliating or looking backwards. We are going to forget the past and look forward to the future. I have suffered imprisonment and detention, but that is gone and I am not going to remember it.... Many of you are as Kenyan as myself.... Let us join hands and work for the benefit of Kenya, not for the benefit of one particular community. We want you to stay and farm well in this country: that is the policy of this government.... We can all work together harmoniously to make this country great, and to show other countries in the world that different racial groups can live and work together."[64] Before Kenyatta finished, the crowd was laughing heartily at his jokes and interrupting him with cheers and shouts of "Harambee." When he left the dais, the white settlers gave him a long and loud standing ovation. The Nakuru settlers soon spread the word that the Mzee might be trustworthy after all. But other whites continued to stand in line for British passports.[65]

As Governor MacDonald watched with growing respect, Kenyatta rose to the demands of his office by becoming dramatically more energetic, decisive, and masterful. Behind the scenes of government, he dominated cabinet meetings, and when his ministers relaxed with alcoholic drinks, Kenyatta drank Coca Cola.[66] In public, he dominated crowds even when he scolded them about the need to work hard, or told them that he would allow no "blacklists" of whites or loyalists to be dealt with after independence. He also showed his decisiveness in dealing with crises. In October, while Kenyatta was in London for a conference, KADU proposed a plan for partitioning Kenya so that minority populations, including whites, could have self-rule. Kenyatta quickly killed the plan, reminding all Kenyans that he was the Prime Minister and he would rule. But he showed restraint and compassion, too, refusing to authorize unlimited military action against Somali rebels in the north of Kenya saying, "I do not believe in destroying life unless it is very necessary,"[67] and eulogizing John F. Kennedy for his civil rights achievements.

Kenyatta still had to deal with the threat posed by Mau Mau. Although he promised amnesty to non-violent LFA prisoners, he continued to demand that remaining armed Mau Mau rebels surrender. In one memorable performance, he appeared before newsreel cameramen and reporters with an utterly bewildered (but thoroughly bathed and sanitized) newly-surrendered Mau Mau "Field Marshal" whom Kenyatta triumphantly said wanted only to live in Kenya as an ordinary citizen "under an African flag." When asked by a reporter what would happen to the weapons of the field marshal and his men, Kenyatta said grandly that the weapons would be surrendered "to me," then, catching himself, he said, "to the government."[68] At the same time that he was urging Mau Mau soldiers to surrender, Kenyatta visited a resettlement program in the Aberdares that offered land to 2,500 Africans. Among the first to accept new land was Dedan Kimathi's widow, who was photographed shaking Kenyatta's hand as she took possession of a 14-acre plot of land.[69] She wore an old, worn overcoat and a modest headcloth, but she would soon prove that she was not a humble, grateful widow.

Kenyatta referred to December 12, 1963—Kenya's Independence Day, and the day he himself became its first President—as the "happiest day of my life" and the "greatest day in Kenya's history." Britain was represented by the Queen's husband, the Duke of Edinburgh, who wore the white dress uniform of an Admiral of the Fleet. The Duke arrived at the stadium just in time to see a Scots Guards bandsman collapse, but he retained his affability even as spear-wielding Turkana and Samburu dancers, whose tribes had been killing each other only weeks before, rushed the royal box in a series of mock attacks.[70] After the Duke had handed over to him the instruments of independence, Kenyatta stepped to the rostrum, where he put aside his prepared address in English, and spoke extemporaneously in Swahili. The crowd roared its approval and celebrations began. As Kenyatta and Governor MacDonald were being draped in colobus monkey and leopardskin cloaks, tribal dancers, drummers, and massed bands entered the stadium and thousands of people came out of the stands to join in the dancing. A reporter saw two little white girls, aged about six and eight, wandering "hand-in-hand through the crowd in wide-eyed wonder."[71]

Kenyatta joined in the African-style dancing at "Uhuru" stadium, and later enjoyed European-style dancing for dignitaries at State House (formerly Government House). He was warm in his greeting to Stewart Udall, the American Secretary of the Interior who represented the United States. During a long evening of fireworks, food, and drink, Kenya's new President reminisced with special guests (including his former lawyer, D. N. Pritt) and his English wife Edna, and their son Peter who was then 20 years old and a student at Cambridge. Edna had been loyal to Kenyatta throughout their long separation and he seemed genuinely fond of her, but it did not escape notice that having an English wife was no longer a political liability for him. At midnight on December 11, the Union Jack was lowered, and under the glare of a searchlight, Kenya's flag was raised. For a moment, the flag refused to unfurl and the Duke of Edinburgh whispered to Kenyatta, "Do you want to change your mind?" In his moment of triumph, Kenyatta only smiled.

Former Governor Sir Evelyn Baring decided not to attend the independence ceremony out of respect for the loyalists who died as a result

222 ► MAU MAU

of Mau Mau. If Kenyatta resented the rebuff he did not show it. Two years later, in October of 1965, Baring made his first trip back to Kenya since independence, and a meeting was arranged between him and Kenyatta. Baring, who had never before spoken to Kenyatta, was nervous when he met the man he still believed had brought the horrors of Mau Mau to Kenya, but he attempted to make conversation by saying that he had sat at the same desk Kenyatta was seated behind when he signed his detention order. Kenyatta answered, "I know. If I had been in your shoes at the time I would have done exactly the same." After relieved laughter by everyone in the room, Kenyatta showed Baring around the redecorated State House, posed with him for photographs, and invited him to stay at State House whenever he was in Kenya.[72]

About the same time, Dr. Louis Leakey made his sensational fossil discoveries that seemed to show that mankind evolved in East Africa. Malcolm MacDonald, then Governor-General of Kenya, asked him if he had told Kenyatta about his findings. Leakey said that he would like to meet Kenya's President but feared that Kenyatta would refuse because of their adversarial roles in the infamously rigged Kapenguria trial that had sent Kenyatta to prison. MacDonald assured him that Kenyatta was too "noble a character" for that, and arranged a meeting. When the two men met, Leakey was visibly uneasy, but Kenyatta greeted him warmly, and displayed a lively interest in his research; the two men wound up speaking Kikuyu and laughing. MacDonald said that he had never attended a "more interesting, scholarly, and cordial lunch party."[73] The "mastermind of Mau Mau," as Baring and Leakey had called him, had proved to be a master of magnanimity. But before he could become the master of Kenya he would once again have to deal with Mau Mau.

Kenyatta had reassured the settlers and loyalists by his public rejection of Mau Mau, but there were still some 90,000 former Mau Mau detainees and soldiers in Kenya. Some of these men and women agreed with the protagonist of Godfrey Wachira's novel, *Ordeal in the Forest*, that Mau Mau had proven to be a "misbegotten and worthless dream,"[74] but others were determined to see that their sacrifices had not been in vain. These veterans joined together in the LFA and other secret organizations with names like "Freedom Soldiers," "Weeping Kamau" (the Kikuyu equivalent of "weeping Smith"), and even "Soldiers of Kenyatta," that agitated for land and a role in Kenya's new African government. What is more, the election of 1963 that had put Kenyatta in office had brought some former detainees into positions of power and influence. Among them were Bildad Kaggia, Fred Kubai, Josiah Kariuki, Paul Ngei, and Achieng Oneko, the Mau Mau leaders who had been detained with Kenyatta.[75]

With Kenya's independence assured, but its future in doubt, Kenyatta took a calculated risk. In an about-face that shocked the white community, he pardoned the Mau Mau prisoners still in custody—including Kariuki Chotara who had tried to kill him when both men were prisoners in Lokitaung Prison—and he offered amnesty to any rebels "still hiding in the forests."[76] Several hundred rebels had never left the forests, and during the last few years others had joined them, especially in the region around Mt. Kenya. In December 1963, more than 1,000 men along with their wives and children were living in large, comfortable forest camps where the police left them strictly alone unless they raided the reserves. Initially, there was no response to Kenyatta's amnesty offer, but a few days before the scheduled independence celebrations on December 12, emissaries from the various forest groups came to Nairobi to discuss terms. They had hoped to negotiate directly with Kenyatta, whom they wanted to treat as an equal, but he sent his friend Peter Koinange to talk with the rebels. They demanded free land, reparations, the expulsion of all loyalists and Indians from government jobs, and Mau Mau absorption into Kenya's armed forces, among other things. Kenyatta finally satisfied them by promising them land, a welfare program, and a public tribute after independence.[77] In response to their demands to be treated as equals, he also agreed to let them fly the same flags in their camps that flew on Kenyatta's official automobiles, and he ordered the Kenya Police to salute the Mau Mau officers.[78]

The first of the Mau Mau from the forests began to surrender on Independence Day, at Nairobi's Uhuru Stadium. Kenya's new president appealed to the crowd of 40,000 people to respect the rebels, saying that they had been "fighting for Kenya's independence" and "no matter what they did during the Emergency, that is finished now."[79] Although she had accepted 14 acres from Kenyatta only a month earlier—and despite the fact that her husband had spent his years in the forest with another woman—Dedan Kimathi's widow made a speech declaring that all the land confiscated from Mau Mau fighters by the government should be returned.[80] The slogan of the day was "Uhuru na Kenyatta" (Freedom and Kenyatta), but she led the crowd in chorusing, "Uhuru na Mau Mau." It is unlikely that Kenyatta was pleased. But trucks brought some of the surrendered Mau Mau to the stadium, where several of their leaders joined Kenyatta on the speaker's platform. As they handed Kenyatta their weapons, the crowd cheered. Kenyatta dutifully admired their home-made guns, but told them to use their pangas "for cultivation and other peaceful tasks."[81]

For over a week, crowds continued to gather at Nyeri's Ruringu Stadium to welcome the returning forest rebels who arrived in large numbers. More than 800 surrendered on the third day after the independence ceremony, followed by another 300 the following day. The government admitted that they could not tell how many of these young men were true Mau Mau rebels and how many had simply claimed to be Mau Mau in order to qualify for the government's promised benefits.[82] For a week, the government slaughtered oxen to feed the thousands of surrendered Mau Mau, but when "the oxen ran out," as the rebels put it, and no other benefits were forthcoming, many of them promptly returned to their forest camps, where some of them showed their contempt for the new government by raiding the reserves where they stole food, raped and abducted women, and beat men who interfered.[83] By now thoroughly angered, Kenyatta declared that the amnesty offer would end on January 15, 1964, and after that date anyone who administered or took an oath or possessed firearms would face a prison term of seven years, the same maximum sentence he had served.[84] Despite these threats by the government, most of the Mau Mau protestors in the forests refused to surrender unless they were given guarantees of land and positions in the government, including those then held by former loyalists.

There were to be no jobs, and, when the government made some land available, many Mau Mau veterans found it unsuitable, and began to seize better land by force.[85] The government also offered loans for the purchase of land, but the Mau Mau veterans rejected the offer when they learned that they would have to repay the loans. More men returned to the forests, while others established themselves in Nairobi, where they lived by extorting money—called "fees," "fines," and "subscriptions"— from African residents.[86] Kenyatta was angry and frustrated, but with much of Kenya distressed that independence had not brought them any advantages, and with the Somalis in northeastern Kenya fighting Kenyan troops for their own independence, for a while he chose restraint. However, in late April successive police operations were mounted against the forest rebels, and by the end of May it was thought that only 200 remained at large.[87] Kenyatta later toured the troubled areas himself, warning people against the oath-taking and violence. The best known of these Mau Mau leaders, Field Marshal Mwariama, agreed to accept loans for land and to repay them, but General Baimuingi refused, saying that if the land were not free, he wanted "a six by three foot" plot of land.[88] Kenyatta angrily called the forest fighters "vagabonds" and scorned their refusal to live like ordinary Kenyans.[89] But despite Kenyatta's efforts and increased police pressure, Mau Mau robberies and intimidation continued throughout 1964. When Kenyatta's second amnesty offer, in January 1965, went unheeded, the police launched a major operation in which all of the major Mau Mau leaders still in the forest, including General Baimuingi, were killed.[90] Although a few Mau Mau bands remained in the forests, their last serious challenge to Kenyatta's authority had been crushed.

Some who knew Kenyatta insisted that he disliked pomp and ceremony, but after Independence Day Kenyatta was always called "His Excellency, the President, Mzee Jomo Kenyatta," and even before independence Kenyatta made certain that everyone in Kenya would show respect.[91] In November 1963, while he was still Prime Minister, legislation was passed making it a crime to show disrespect to his person. A week before Independence, Nairobi's main street, Delamere Avenue, was renamed Kenyatta Avenue, and the centrally located statue of Lord Delamere was pulled down to be replaced by a bronze of Kenyatta. After independence, it was required that Kenyatta's photograph be displayed in every shop window, and his face was imprinted on Kenya's new currency. He never went anywhere without an entourage that would embarrass European royalty, and whenever he entered his Rolls Royce (or Mercedes, Lincoln Continental, or one of the other new cars given to him by foreign admirers), Kenyatta was surrounded by a phalanx of police and personal bodyguards, and followed closely by his own film crew. Ironically, the Lincoln Continental convertible given him by American businessmen was the same model car in which President Kennedy had been assassinated.

While Kenyatta was adopting the trappings of royalty, diplomatic missions from all over the world, including the People's Republic of China, hurried to Nairobi, followed by their business representatives. Before 1964 ended there would be 1,900 Americans in Kenya, and 21 American companies would be represented in Nairobi by regional offices.[92] This international attention was welcomed, but the new government still faced grave problems. In addition to the Mau Mau challenges to his government, Kenyatta was forced to declare a State of Emergency in Kenya's Northern Frontier District in an attempt to deal with the raids of disaffected Somalis against police posts and traders. And in January 1964, the main Nakuru-based battalion of the Kenya Army mutinied. Inspired by a successful military coup in Zanzibar a week earlier, the army protested the continued presence of white officers, as well as slow promotion, low pay, and insufficient prestige in newly-independent Kenya.

Kenyatta dealt swiftly with this military challenge to his civilian government. Although some Kenyans had noticed that British troops had remained in their bases after independence, the government had avoided calling attention to their continuing presence in Kenya. Now, Kenyatta asked these British soldiers for help, and they quickly put down the mutiny by, among other things, firing bazookas into the Kenya Army barracks. Black Kenyans were profoundly embarrassed by newspaper photographs showing British troops herding Kenyan Army mutineers with their hands on their heads.[93] But the realization that Kenya had been threatened by a military coup was even more shocking.[94] There were calls for British troops to leave Kenya, but the government quickly made it known that they would remain for "training" purposes. Their weapons would give Kenyatta's government the power to defeat any future military coup. But Kenyatta did not rule by repression alone. He immediately instituted reforms to improve conditions in the military, and at the same time infiltrated all military units with intelligence personnel, who were instructed to alert the government at the first sign of dissension.[95]

While Kenyatta attempted to cope with these crises, he continued to show concern for the welfare of Kenya's whites. He appointed a settler, Bruce Mackenzie, to the key post of Minister of Agriculture, and he appointed as Kenya's first Chief Justice the same judge who had dismissed his appeal, and had sent him to prison for more than nine years. He even retained Ian Henderson as an officer in the Kenya Police. Yet General China, whom Henderson had interrogated, was not given a commission in the Kenya Army; instead, he was forced to enlist as a private, and to endure the humiliation of taking basic training under the command of British officers. After sustained pressure from Kenyatta's ministers, Henderson was deported in August 1964.

When 1964 began, 45,000 whites remained in Kenya. By the end of the year there were 40,000. Half of those who left were whites who, thanks to a British Government-financed plan to buy them out, had been replaced by 19,000 Africans by year's end. In the Afrikaner farming area near Eldoret, 400 of the 530 white farmers left Kenya.[96] Yet Kenyatta's efforts to reassure the white population were successful enough that, by 1965, those whites who remained thought of Kenyatta as a trusted statesman. The tide of immigration turned as well, and, for the first time since 1960, more whites entered Kenya in 1965 than left it.[97]

While Kenyatta's new government struggled to come to terms with the Mau Mau challenge, as well as the Somali rebellion, an army mutiny, and a jittery white community, Kikuyu loyalists were complaining that the government was not doing enough for them.[98] Most loyalists had been relatively well-to-do before the Emergency and many had been wealthy, but the Emergency allowed almost all of them to prosper as never before. For one thing, during the Emergency the government created a "Loyalty Certificate" that exempted its holder from paying school fees and allowed him to serve on important government committees such as those that reallocated and consolidated land. It also permitted the loyalists to plant profitable cash crops such as coffee, and obtain valuable licenses permitting them to operate trading stalls in markets. Most valuable of all, perhaps, was the government's agreement that no holder of a Loyalty Certificate could be prosecuted for any action against a non-loyalist.[99] This immunity allowed many loyalists to steal land, extort money, and have their farms worked by those who had no Loyalty Certificate and were fearful of being accused of Mau Mau sympathies.

Loyalists also benefitted when the government chose to consolidate land (from 1953–56) in the Kikuyu reserve.[100] Although these plans were ostensibly intended to ease the burden of landless Kikuyu, it was the wealthy loyalists who controlled the land committees and thereby profited most.[101] The government hoped that by giving greater wealth and power to the loyalists, they would continue to serve as a conservative segment of Kikuyu society that would act as a buffer against renewed subversion.[102] The loyalists accepted these advantages, and looked forward to more once the settlers consolidated their power after Mau Mau. They not only expected their children to be educated at government expense, they were confident that they would continue to monopolize government jobs, and they had been assured that their Mau Mau enemies would never be allowed to return.[103] To their surprise and horror, the British Government ended settler rule, and the rebels did return. One settler wrote to the *East African Standard* that this "betrayal" of the loyalists was so unfair that "it makes one ashamed to be British."[104]

Although some of Kenyatta's closest friends and associates were Kikuyu loyalists, he was the president of all Kenyans and he could not favor the loyalists as openly as the white government of Kenya had done. However, when he had no other choice, Kenyatta supported the loyalists against Mau Mau groups, as when the loyalists and Mau Mau veterans contested for control of KANU. The loyalists had money, education, support by the churches, and most important, the backing of government officials. In politically critical Murang'a District, the loyalists' most visible and important representative was Dr. J. G. Kiano, who had earned a Ph.D. from the University of California at Berkeley, and was the first Kenyan to hold a doctorate. Kiano was opposed by Bildad Kaggia, James Beauttuh, and other prominent Mau Mau leaders.

Most of the population supported the former Mau Mau leaders, and in August 1964 Kaggia was elected Chairman of the Murang'a KANU party while other Mau Mau leaders won important offices, and then used their offices to campaign for free land and other benefits for Mau Mau veterans. Soon after, Kenyatta openly attacked Kaggia and his policy, and, with government support, Kiano's loyalists organized a coup to remove the Mau Mau group from office. Kaggia and the other Mau Mau were publicly accused of being Communists, and, with the help of the suddenly resurrected paramilitary KANU Youth Wing, Mau Mau leaders were captured and tortured until they confessed having taken an oath to kill loyalists. Some of the leaders were murdered.[105] Mau Mau veterans would never again seriously challenge for political power. Pathetically, a number of former Mau Mau leaders tried to sue for their rights in Kenya's courts. They did not find relief.

Mau Mau veterans were not alone in seeking power. At the time of Independence, there were 180,000 Indians in Kenya. They had wealth and were willing to use it to achieve political influence, but most Africans were antagonistic toward Indians, whom they accused of economic exploitation and racial discrimination.[106] Their hopes for representation in the new government rested on the fact that most of them had openly sided with the Kenya Government during Mau Mau.[107] In fact, thousands of Indians volunteered for military duty during the Emergency, and at least one all-Indian combat unit saw action in the forests.[108] Unfortunately for Indian aspirations, this unit performed so badly under fire that it was not used in combat again.[109]

The Indian alliance with Kenya's whites against Mau Mau obscured a long history of common cause between Indians and African nationalists. Even during the Emergency some Indians risked their lives to help the rebels, while others like Makhan Singh and Pio de Gama Pinto played important roles in launching the movement.[110] For his efforts, Singh spent eleven and a half years in detention, longer than any African nationalist. Another Indian, A. H. Patel, endeared himself to Kenyatta by caring for his daughter Margaret and illegally sending him food and clothing while he was in prison.[111] But most Africans, including many in government, remembered the racial slights they suffered at the hands of Indians, the economic power of Indian merchants who dominated the retail trades, and the stranglehold that Indians had on the lower ranks of the civil service, where their officiousness became legendary. African hostility sometimes boiled over into looting and arson,[112] but the Indian community was too divided to mount an effective political protest. The Hindu majority, sometimes aligned with Sikhs and Goans, had been seriously at odds with the Muslims since 1947, when the partition of India reverberated throughout Kenya and large-scale killing was only barely averted by the police.[113] After independence, Kenyatta would keep all but a few Indians at arm's length.

By the end of 1964, Kenyatta and his government were confronted by foreign involvement. Even before memories of Mau Mau had cooled, the "Cold War" came to Kenya. Although Kenyatta, along with most of his associates in KANU, including Tom Mboya, were thoroughly committed to Western-style capitalism, Oginga Odinga, Kenyatta's friend and a key Luo figure in KANU, maintained many close associations with Communist countries. Odinga travelled extensively in Eastern Europe, the Soviet Union, and China. In Beijing, he told a mass rally that Mau Mau "was a glorious and heroic struggle of our people," a theme he repeated when he returned to Kenya.[114] He also accepted large sums of money from the Soviet Union and China—perhaps as much as a million dollars—to spend as he wished. Other Kenyan M.P.s were contacted by Soviet or Chinese representatives, and many Kenyan students, most of them Luo, went to Communist countries to study and receive military training.[115] Kenya's Special Branch, with the enthusiastic assistance of British and American intelligence, warned Kenyatta about the threat of a Communist *coup d'état.*

Early in 1965, the government took action. Pio de Gama Pinto, a former Mau Mau supporter and now Odinga's chief adviser and liaison man with Communist embassies in Kenya, was murdered. Shortly after, Kenyan troops surrounded Odinga's office building, his office was searched, and several dozen crates of weapons, including grenades and machine guns, were confiscated.[116] At the same time a Chinese pamphlet that was circulating in East Africa, calling for the overthrow of Kenyatta's government, was banned, and Chou En-Lai, then in Tanzania, was denied entry to Kenya. When Kenyan students returned from the Soviet Union complaining of racial prejudice, their criticisms were widely publicized by the Kenya press. In April 1965, a Soviet freighter that was loaded with

tanks and heavy weapons docked in Mombasa, and two days later a Soviet military mission of 17 men checked into an expensive Nairobi hotel.
Kenyatta refused the arms, sent the Russians away, and subjected the
Soviet Ambassador to a tongue-lashing. Furious with Odinga, Kenyatta
stopped wearing his beaded Luo cap.

Tom Mboya, the other major Luo leader, also turned against Odinga
and became a principal ally of Kenyatta. Despite the fact that Mboya was
not Kikuyu, many saw him as Kenyatta's heir-apparent. When Mboya was
later assassinated in 1969, so many Luo blamed the Kiambu elite that
supported Kenyatta that the president traveled to the Luo homeland in
an attempt to calm the waters. But young Luo supporters of Odinga
heckled Kenyatta as he tried to speak. Kenyatta turned on Odinga, who
was seated nearby, and snapped, "We are going to crush you into the
floor!"[117] As Kenyatta's motorcade attempted to leave, his car was stoned.
His bodyguards fired into the crowd with automatic weapons, and the
loss of life was heavy. Odinga was banned from public life, and the
Kikuyu, encouraged by Kenyatta, began to take oaths pledging their devotion to Kenyatta and the constitution; but the specter of Kikuyu oath-
taking so increased tensions throughout Kenya that the government had
to end the practice.[118]

Despite an abortive military coup in 1971 (again put down by British
troops), and constant rumors about Kenyatta's health, Kenya continued
to attract tourists and foreign investment. Although the country became
renowned in Africa for political stability and prosperity, it was hardly a
picture-book democracy. Kenyatta's family and close associates became
enormously wealthy through the open practice of nepotism, favoritism,
and bribery.[119] No one did business in Kenya without approval from
Kenyatta, or his relatives, or from one of his intimates, who became
known as the "Royal Family." Governor-General Malcolm MacDonald,
who rarely criticized Kenyatta, nevertheless wrote, "One of Kenyatta's
most serious errors is his tacit assent to the acquisitiveness of some of
his Ministers and civil servants. Soon after attaining power they began
to buy (sometimes with money gained by dubious means) large houses,
farms, motor cars and other possessions. This development not only
tainted his administration with a reputation for corruption, but also produced a wide economic division between governors and governed, the
former becoming rich 'Haves' whilst many of the others remained poor
'Have-nots'."[120]

Everyone knew about the corruption, but few in Kenya dared to joke
about the "Royal Family," much less to speak openly against them. One

who did speak out was J.M. Kariuki, the former Mau Mau detainee whose letters about detention-camp conditions led a succession of camp commanders to order him beaten. After the Emergency, Kariuki grew close to Kenyatta, serving as his private secretary before he fell out with the Mzee over the "Royal Family's" continued enrichment while the plight of the poor grew steadily worse. Kariuki was a dandy, an inveterate gambler and a womanizer, but he was also wealthy, and a powerful M.P. He was on his way toward developing a mass following of his own when, in November 1975, he was abducted outside the Hilton Hotel in Nairobi by senior police officers. Soon after, he was found murdered. The press protested, students rioted, accusations were made in parliament about Kenyatta's role in the murder, and the Kikuyu were split into factions.

Kenyatta attempted to quiet the uprising by appointing a blue-ribbon investigative committee, but when their report accused the police of the murder, and suggested that high government officials may have been involved, Kenyatta tabled the report and cracked down forcibly against anyone who continued to speak out. Opposition within Kenya was silenced, but someone with inside knowledge leaked details of the sordid affair to a British reporter. A three-part series in the *Sunday Times* of London described the murder in detail, implicating not only senior police officers but persons very close to Kenyatta, and revealed the extent of the government's cover-up. The story also described the vast land and business holdings of members of the "Royal Family," including Kenyatta himself, his relatives and friends in Kiambu, and his youngest wife, Mama Ngina. The article took particular note of the widespread bribery and graft that had increased the "Royal Family's" wealth. It also accused them of profiteering in illegal ivory-poaching, and denuding Kenya's forests to make charcoal for sale to various Gulf states of the Arab world. The great wealth of Kenya's governing elite was contrasted to the poverty of Kenya's majority. According to the newspaper, the system survived by eliminating anyone who threatened the reign of the ruling elite.[121]

Despite highly-charged debates in Parliament, Kenyatta survived this crisis, although it was his most troubled time in office. Thanks to a coffee boom, the economy was thriving, and many Kenyans were better off than they had been before. Everyone understood that, in order for anyone to do big business in Kenya, it was necessary to ply the "Royal Family" with proposals, promises, and guaranteed profits. Ordinary Kenyans resented the wealth of this governing elite, but in Kenya's vibrant economy, most also improved their standard of living, and even the poor usually maintained hope for better times.[122] For all its corruption and inequity,

Kenyatta's government had provided health care, education, and transportation. At times Kenyatta had been ruthless, but, for the most part, he protected free speech and avoided the worst of police terrorism. Even though he had become increasingly autocratic, Kenyatta continued to have the respect of most Kenyans, and many held him in complete awe. When he died in August 1978, the nation was distraught. Tributes arrived from around the world, and the Mzee was eulogized, not as the creator of Mau Mau who led his people to "darkness and death," but as the Father of Kenya, a statesman to be revered.

Kenyatta was succeeded by his Vice-President, Daniel arap Moi, an experienced politician from a small Kalenjin people, the Tugen. Moi had been loyal to the Mzee, but he was not the ruling elite's choice for the Presidency. Moi managed to survive several Byzantine attempts to change Kenya's Constitution so that he would not be in line to succeed Kenyatta, and he took office.[123] The new President adroitly consolidated his power until 1982, when non-commissioned officers (largely Luo) of the Kenya Air Force rebelled, seizing a radio station, Nairobi's post office, the international airport, and other key facilities in Nairobi. The coup leaders used the radio to explain that they were taking over the government because "rampant corruption and nepotism have made life almost intolerable in our society. The economy is in a shambles, and the people cannot afford food, housing, or transport."[124] After fierce fighting, Kenya Army troops put down the rebellion, this time without British help. The government reported that 159 people had been killed, but unofficial estimates ran from 600 to 2,000. The coup attempt was followed by extensive looting of Indian shops and sexual assaults against Indian women, as African hostility toward Indians once again seemed ready to explode.

Many members of Kenya's elite attempted to flee the country believing that the coup would succeed, but Moi's government survived, and the economy continued to grow thanks in large part to Kenya's continuing appeal to tourists. Every year between 1972 and 1982, 350,000 tourists visited Kenya, most of them from West Germany and Britain, and, in 1987, the number rose to 614,000.[125] At least as important as economic growth to the stability of Moi's government was the removal from power of Charles Njonjo, a powerful Kikuyu politician, who was thought by many in Parliament—and probably by Moi himself—to be guilty of conspiring with other governments to overthrow Moi. With Njonjo's faction out of power, Moi easily won re-election in 1983, and again in 1988.

Over the years, Kenya's population has undergone profound changes. When the Emergency ended in 1960, there were 60,000 Europeans and approximately 6 million Africans in Kenya. In 1988, there were probably only 40,000 whites in Kenya, 9,000 of them Americans. Less than 5,000 whites had Kenya citizenship. Kenya's population has been increasing by almost 4 percent per year, one of the world's highest growth rates. While the birthrate rose dramatically, the death rate fell for children and adults alike. The population by 1990 may well be approaching 24 million; Nairobi is already a city of more than 1 million people.[126]

The Kenya elite live luxuriously in the same neighborhoods that were once reserved for whites. They drive expensive cars, vacation in Europe, send their children to private schools, and have their needs taken care of by servants. Their life-styles resemble those of the wealthy whites who used to live in the same large houses, except that they hire more guards, have embedded more broken glass on top of the walls that surround their estates, and spend more money on electronic security systems. There are many more desperately poor people in Nairobi today than ever before, and they often burglarize and sometimes kill the wealthy "Black Europeans" (or "Benzi," as they are often called, after the Mercedes-Benz cars they often drive). There are even more poor people in rural areas, many of whom remain landless. Only about 25 percent of Kenya's land is arable, and the fertile land that was once not plentiful enough for six million people must now support four times that number. But the vast "white highlands," that were once a symbol of injustice and dispossession, are now almost entirely in African hands. Wealthy Africans are the new targets of discontent.

In 1974, Mau Mau veteran Mohamed Mathu wrote, "The vast majority of Africans remain very poor. Are the masses of people simply to become the slaves of a handful of Black men?"[127] Kenya has achieved remarkable political stability and economic growth, but its prosperity has not been shared by all its citizens, and among those who have benefitted relatively little are the veterans of Mau Mau. Even before Independence, former rebels demanded free land but Kenyatta was compelled to refuse. He was trying to forge a nation, and any decision that favored the Kikuyu would have weakened his credibility as the president of all Kenyans. What is more, the negotiations between Nairobi and London in search of a land settlement policy had resulted in an agreement that the British Government would provide the money for loans necessary to buy out the white settlers, but these loans would have to be repaid.[128] Most Mau Mau veterans had no resources that would make loan payments possible. They also insisted that paying for "their" land was wrong. As many pointed out, they had not been paid for their service during the rebel-

lion, and although some detainees received token payment for their labor, it was not nearly enough to enable them to buy land. Eventually
almost all of the smaller farms in the highlands would be sold to Africans, but no preference was given to former Mau Mau.[129]

Some veterans made the more modest demand that the land and stock
confiscated from them during the Emergency be returned. In 1964, President Kenyatta promised that the land confiscated from more than 3,500
Mau Mau rebels would be returned. But when nothing had happened by
1969, the government explained that records about confiscated land were
not readily available.[130] Most of the lost property was never returned.
When Bildad Kaggia, Oginda Odinga, and others pressed the Mau Mau
cause by arguing that they had fought for Kenya's freedom, the Kenyatta
government invariably responded by saying, "we all fought for Uhuru."
National unity was vital for the new government and the Mau Mau veterans were a political embarrassment.

General China became one of Kenyatta's staunchest defenders, speaking out harshly against the resurgence of Mau Mau oath-taking and
intimidation after independence; but when he published the story of his
own involvement with Mau Mau in 1967, he concluded with what he
called "A note on the treatment of Former Forest Fighters." He observed
that Loyalists "in high places" feared revenge if former rebels achieved
power. He added that those who sat in places of authority because of the
blood and sweat of those who fought "look down on the fighters as
fools."[131] General China then took aim at those politicians who said that
"we all fought for Uhuru," pointing out that there were "different degrees of fighting," and that in other countries those who served in the
armed forces received "pensions, loans, education, medals, and honors."
He went on to say that Mau Mau veterans deserved free grants of land,
and said their widows should be aided and their children educated. Those
who lost land or property should be compensated, and those who were
disabled should receive government aid. He also called upon the government to issue an award to the veterans, and to locate and mark the graves
of those who had been killed. General China closed his remarks by saying
that, although he was not dissatisfied with "our African Government,"
he was obliged to remind it that "those who sacrificed everything cannot
be expected to receive nothing in return, or to be made the laughing
stock of other, more successful men."[132] He warned that it would "probably not be wise" to assume that the Mau Mau veterans "will tolerate
their present position indefinitely."[133]

General China's threatening comments had no effect. Except for token gestures in which the widows of Stanley Mathenge and Dedan Kimathi were given plots of land, there was to be no free land for Mau Mau veterans, and there were no government programs to aid widows or orphans, or disabled rebels.[134] Despite repeated requests, not until 1970 was anything done for orphaned children of more than 11,000 Mau Mau killed in the fighting. In that year Kenyatta made much of his government's generosity in selecting 160 orphans of the Emergency to be cared for and educated by the National Youth Service (of which General China was an officer). However, only a small minority of these people—who were by then hardly children, being between the ages of 16 and 22— came from the Kikuyu, Meru, or Embu. The majority came from other tribes that had not supported the Mau Mau rebellion.[135]

Few Mau Mau veterans had enough education to compete for desirable jobs in business or government, but when they petitioned Kenyatta's Government to restore to them the jobs they had lost because of their activities during the rebellion, they were once again rebuffed. Those jobs had been filled by other Kenyans, and it would have been politically unwise to remove them in favor of Mau Mau veterans, almost all of whom were Kikuyu. There were no medals or statues either, and the graves of the dead were not marked. In reality, nothing that General China asked the government to do was done. What is more, General China was wrong about the possible Mau Mau resurgence. The veterans did tolerate their lot indefinitely.[136]

Kenyan novelists wrote bitter stories about the disillusionment of these men and women.[137] And when Mau Mau veterans began to write accounts of their experiences during the Mau Mau rebellion, they often included sardonic descriptions of their lives after independence. Henry Kahinga Wachanga wrote about one man, Wanjohi Mung'au, who was imprisoned by the colonial government for nearly 10 years. After independence he attempted to organize Mau Mau veterans into cooperatives that would try to force the Europeans off their land. Kenyatta's Government put him in jail for another 7 years. More typical were the lives of Domenic Gatu, who had been detained for 8 years, and his wife Wanjiru, who had fought in the forest. In 1975, Domenic and Wanjiru lived together with their children and his mother and father in a "lean-to shanty" behind an Indian crematorium in Nairobi. There was only room for a single bed, and a small sleeping platform for the children. They survived by selling *irio*, a traditional Kikuyu dish of maize, beans, peas, green vegetables, and potatoes. Wachanga wrote that Gatu wondered why he still suffered so much, when some of his countrymen were so wealthy and enjoyed the benefits of independence that he and his wife helped to bring about.[138]

Solomon Memia, another veteran living in the Nairobi slums, under-scored Gatu's words: "I regret to state that those of us who fought for freedom were never given a chance to participate in the present govern-ment. The majority of ex-freedom fighters are among those who live here in these shanties, because they have nowhere else to go. We weren't given jobs because it was alleged we were uneducated. The young who were in school during the freedom struggle are the ones who have the say in our government, and they are not concerned with our affairs."[139]

During the Moi presidency that began in 1978, some veterans began to receive favorable attention from the government, apparently because President Moi felt the need to counter the entrenched privileges of the Kikuyu elite with a grassroots Kikuyu power base of his own.[140] And signs of Moi's professed sympathy for Mau Mau continue to appear. In March 1988, Nairobi's largest newspaper, *The Standard* (formerly *The Eastern African Standard*), carried a story celebrating Moi's reelection. The story revealed that, in 1955, Moi was so sympathetic to the cause that for two dangerous weeks he sheltered and fed a group of Mau Mau soldiers before giving them 500 shillings and showing them the safest route to their destination.[141] It is highly unlikely that this information would have been printed without President Moi's approval.

While President Moi has been in office, a few veterans have been elected to Parliament, and a few more have been appointed to mid-level government positions. Some others, including the late Kariuki Chotara (the man who attempted to kill Kenyatta in prison), achieved prominence in local politics. But the great majority of men and women who fought for land and freedom during the rebellion still do not have land of their own, and they are still poor.[142] Meanwhile, the plight of landless veterans continues to attract attention in Kenya. In August 1988, the *Daily Nation*, a prominent newspaper, carried a feature story about a veteran whose Mau Mau name was Ruku Kanini. Ruku was wounded while fighting in the Aberdare Forest and spent many years in detention, where he was beaten so severely that he still suffers from a spinal injury. The paper emphasized that Ruku still owns no land, and survives only because peo-ple who appreciate his contribution to Kenya's independence, give him food and clothing, and allow him to grow some crops on their land.[143] There are many aging men in Kenya like Ruku Kanini.

In Kenya today, the most visible remembrance of the men and women who fought and died during the Mau Mau rebellion is a street in down-town Nairobi named after Dedan Kimathi. Nairobi's main street is still named after Kenyatta. There is also a street called "Mama Ngina," and another called "Harambee."

8

"THEIR FIERCE SELF-INTEREST"

MAU MAU IN PERSPECTIVE

The rebellion of the Land and Freedom Army did not achieve its goals. When the fighting ended in 1956, white settlers still owned their farms in the highlands, and white Colonial administrators still ruled Kenya. The leaders of Mau Mau had hoped that their rebellion would become an irresistible force for freedom spreading throughout Kenya. Not only did it not unite the African peoples of Kenya, it even failed to unite the Kikuyu. Instead, it led Kenya's largest tribe into a bitter and bloody civil war. By 1956, most of Kenya's Africans had repudiated Mau Mau. The rebellion was over, its goals unmet, its legacy uncertain.

Nevertheless, even though the leaders of Mau Mau did not realize it, their rebellion inadvertently brought about one vitally important change in Kenya. Before the rebellion, Kenya's white settlers were determined to achieve a form of self-rule that would assure their continuing control. Once the Mau Mau rebels forced the settlers to call for British military support, the political dominion of whites in Kenya was over.[1] It was obvious to everyone except the least intelligent and most intransigent settlers that Kenya's future would be decided by Britain. The British Government poured enormous resources into Kenya to defeat Mau Mau, but by 1954 the cost of intervention had become such a heavy burden that if the rebellion had not ended when it did, Britain would have had difficulty continuing its military commitment in Kenya much longer. In fact, by 1956 British economic and military power had declined so much that Britain had to accept the humiliation of an American-imposed retreat from its invasion of the Suez Canal Zone. At the same time, Britain's African Colonies had become serious economic liabilities, and as European and American pressure to decolonize intensified, they became a political embarrassment as well. It was obvious that Britain could no longer afford the cost of holding Kenya by military might.

Yet only a few whites in Kenya seem to have understood that the end of colonialism in Africa was approaching, and only a few began to work toward the goal of economic reform buttressed by some form of a multiracial government. If the white settlers had seized this opportunity to enhance economic and social justice, they might yet have assured a place for themselves as full partners in Kenya's future. But most would have nothing to do with reforms or African participation in government. They insisted on their economic privileges, their political power, and their racial superiority. In the fullness of their victory over Mau Mau, they overestimated their strength, and they badly misread the course of world events. "Their fierce self-interest," as Churchill had noted 50 years earlier, would bring about their final ruin.

The settlers' ruthless pursuit of their interests during the rebellion not only embittered the supporters of Mau Mau, it helped to radicalize educated young Africans as well. The white Kenyans' implacable refusal to share Kenya's future with the country's African population turned even many loyalist Africans against them just as it weakened their support in Britain. Only a few years after the fighting had ended, world developments having little to do with Kenya itself would persuade Harold Macmillan to grant independence to Britain's East African territories. But one critical event did involve Kenya, and it was a direct result of the settlers' excessive use of force against the Mau Mau. That event was the massacre at Hola. For many in Britain, Hola symbolized white Kenya's lawlessness. But for Macmillan and Macleod, Hola was more than a symbol; it was a bloody reminder that white minority government could only continue in Kenya by the use of deadly force. The unlimited use of force by the white settlers and the colonial administration had given them victory over the Mau Mau rebellion, but in the end it lost them Kenya. They had only themselves to blame.

In fairness, the white settlers cannot be held responsible for everything that led to Mau Mau. The gulf between prosperous land-owning Kikuyu and their poor, landless tenants existed before the whites arrived, and the settlers were not responsible for the disease and famine that had depopulated the highlands before they arrived. Nonetheless, the Government of Kenya had appropriated vast tracts of African land and urged whites to settle on it. When the settlers demanded more power and extended privileges, the colonial administration chose to accommodate them instead of protecting the interests of Kenya's Africans. Even when administrative officials attempted to assist Africans with various medical, livestock, and agricultural programs, their paternalistic arrogance in forcing these measures upon reluctant and uncomprehending tribal people alienated the very people they intended to help. So did governmental favoritism of chiefs and other wealthy supporters of the administration. What is more, colonial administrators allowed African grievances to reach a flashpoint by ignoring the needs of the rapidly growing numbers of urban poor, and by refusing to permit emerging African leaders to play a meaningful part in Kenya's political life.

Whatever the failings of the colonial administration, accountability for the genesis of Mau Mau nonetheless falls primarily on the settlers. Although the white community in Kenya had varied interests that, to take one example, sometimes brought cattle ranchers into conflict with farmers, in general they were united in exploiting African labor for the lowest possible wages, and united too in denying Africans the opportunity to compete with them as farmers or stockmen. They also shared the belief that Africans were inferior, childlike beings who should be denied social equality, not to mention self-government. As a result of the settlers' racism and their demands for profit, they consistently ignored the welfare of Africans who grew poorer and more aggrieved whether they lived in reserves, labored on European lands, or gathered in the towns and cities searching for work.[2] When African protest movements arose, the settlers demanded that the government smash them. The settlers professed to understand Africans and insisted that they were bringing the benefits of British civilization to them, but these claims were sanctimonious. What they understood was their own narrow self-interest; what they gave to

Kenya's African populations was continuing social inferiority and economic exploitation. Most significant of all in accounting for the origin
of Mau Mau, the white community made it absolutely clear to Kenya's
Africans that the future would bring no fundamental change.

The attitudes and practices of Kenya's whites were neither pathologi-
cal nor an aberration brought about by conditions unique to Kenya, as
some have argued.[3] They had deep roots in British culture and history.
For one thing, British society was founded on the belief that some men
were much more equal than others. The well-known bit of doggerel, "God
bless the squire and his relations, and keep us in our proper stations,"
may have been partly derisive, but class distinctions were not merely
remembrances of the nineteenth century for Kenya's whites—indeed,
these distinctions gave legitimacy to white rule in Kenya.[4] Even though
the Labour Party had some success in challenging the authority of Britain's ruling class, few Britons in the 1950s disputed the idea that white
people were superior to Africans. They were not unique. That black
people were inferior to those of other races was taken for granted in
much of Europe, Latin America, China, and Japan, as well as in the
United States, which professed the equality of all yet maintained a color
bar similar to the one in Kenya. It hardly needs saying that this belief is
still widely-shared in many parts of the world.

White Kenyans' antipathy for Kenya's Africans was not only based on
ideas of racial superiority, it was also a product of fear. Kenya's whites
feared black Africans as much as white Americans in the antebellum
South feared their slaves when they began to grow in number. Even
though whites outnumbered blacks in the South, these Americans established a virtual police state for self-protection.[5] In Kenya, 40,000 whites
were surrounded by perhaps 6 million Africans whom white Kenyans
believed were only a few years removed from bestial savagery. In such
circumstances, it is not surprising that the white settlers failed to tran-
scend their own racism as well as that of much of the developed world
by working for a multi-racial society in Kenya. Yet the fact remains that
the degrading racial policies they institutionalized went well beyond
measures necessary for self-protection.

There can be no doubt that the settlers' racist attitudes and practices
contributed to the outbreak of Mau Mau, but so did the settlers' uncom-
promising determination to rule Africans. Like many other Europeans
who colonized Africa, Kenya's white settlers were convinced that it was
not their superior weapons but their "superior civilization" that gave
them an indisputable right to rule. Bolstered by their deep-seated belief

in the principle that a small elite class could rightfully dominate a majority, white Kenyans from modest middle-class backgrounds eagerly joined settlers from Britain's "ruling class" in governing Kenya's Africans. Supported by the ruling-class ideology of the colonial administrators, white dominion became so deeply ingrained in the culture of Kenya's whites that even the kindest and most thoughtful of them were held in its thrall. White Kenyans understood that they could survive only as long as their economic symbiosis with Africans continued, but they chose to ensure that continuity, not by compromise or even understanding, but simply by the use of force. There were few voices of protest. Theirs was a society that left little room for dissent, and when the violence of Mau Mau struck, there was virtually no dissent at all. White Kenya was a society of masters—of "bwanas" and "memsahibs"—and, like masters throughout history who were threatened by rebellion, they closed ranks and responded ferociously.

When Mau Mau intimidation, arson, and violence first began, the settlers urged Draconian measures. When violence continued despite the government's declaration of a State of Emergency, the settlers took the destruction of the Mau Mau menace—and also took the law—into their own hands. Not all white men and women demanded the deaths of the "Kyukes," not all white Kenyans shot suspicious Kikuyu first and asked questions later, and not all whites in the Kenya Regiment or the Kenya Police Reserve tortured or murdered Mau Mau suspects. But many white Kenyans did all of these things, and those few who privately deplored what their friends and neighbors did rarely spoke out against them. Even the most liberal became entrapped in the convulsion of rage and revenge that engulfed the white community. The vicious reaction that swept through white Kenya grew in intensity as one example of brutality by whites was followed by another. White mothers whose children were cared for by Kikuyu women called for the execution of the inhabitants of entire Kikuyu "villages." Men who as children had played with young Kikuyu, and who later employed Kikuyu as servants and laborers, now thought of them as animals to be hunted, or vermin to be exterminated, while otherwise quite respectable white settlers became torturers and murderers.

The severity of the white reaction was heightened by the earliest Mau Mau killings. The first white victims, women as well as men, were chopped and slashed to death with pangas and swords. Their mutilated bodies were terrible to see or even hear about. When six-year-old Michael Ruck was killed by a flurry of panga blows, most settlers were convinced that

the Mau Mau rebels were inhuman savages. Their rage was also intensified by a profound fear that African savagery, if not repressed, would
engulf them all. The settlers were convinced that Africans were "primi-
tives" whose "savage" impulses had been unleashed by the Mau Mau
oaths. At best, they said, Africans were not fully human, and the Mau
Mau rebels were clearly not the best of Africans. The feelings of a 31-
year-old settler who had been born in Kenya were widely shared: "I was
raised with Africans, you know. Kyukes mostly. I thought I knew what
they were like but when the Mau Mau terrorism began I realized I didn't
know them at all. They weren't like us. They weren't even like animals—
animals are understandable. They're natural. The Mau Mau were ...
what's the word? Perverted, I guess. It was the oath, you see. Once they
took it, life didn't mean anything to them. If we couldn't drive the (Mau
Mau) poison out of them by getting them to confess, all we could do was
kill them."[6] Settlers like this one killed Mau Mau suspects in an attempt
to save all that was dear to them, and to destroy all that they did not
understand. Most of them killed because they believed they had no other
choice.

The settlers loved Kenya's beauty, its excitement, its comfortable and
privileged way of life. As they saw it, Africans had done nothing to "develop" Kenya, and as a result they deserved their roles as servants and
laborers for white men and women who had brought "civilization" to
them. The Mau Mau rebellion was not only a direct threat to the lives of
these white Kenyans, it was an affront to their sense of the natural order
of things. If the challenge to white supremacy had come from a respected
"fighting" people like the Somali or Massai, these settlers would still have
insisted that the rebellion be crushed. But an uprising by "warriors"
might at least have been understandable. Warlike peoples were expected
to fight, and while they would have had to be killed, it would have been
with some regret.[7] The Kikuyu-led Mau Mau were thought of as cowards
with no military tradition who had long been the subservient employees
of whites. Many settlers thought of them as little more than slaves, and
for people like these to repudiate white civilization and challenge white
rule was galling.

For many settlers, Mau Mau was a modern-day equivalent of a slave
uprising, and like white slave masters throughout history, they exacted
terrible vengeance. White Kenyans had always feared the disastrous potential of a violent uprising by some or all of Kenya's millions of Africans, but they usually masked their underlying fear with exaggerated
assurances that Africans were loyal, docile, and—most comforting of all—

cowardly. They reassured themselves that their African servants and farm workers, would not—could not—have the temerity to harm white people. When this carefully crafted illusion of trust and security was shattered, the settlers felt betrayed and violated. As slave holders had done for centuries, they fought back for their pride, power, and privilege, as well as for their lives. And like the slave owners of history, their reaction was more violent than the actions of the Mau Mau rebels, and far more cruel. It must be remembered that, whenever African slaves rebelled in the New World, they were not only killed in large numbers, they were tortured and mutilated to demonstrate the futility of insurrection.[8]

C. L. R. James, who taught Kenyatta about political history in London, wrote that "The cruelties of property and privilege are always more ferocious than the revenges of poverty and oppression."[9] Kenya's experience confirmed James' formulation. The whites were not content simply to kill the rebels, they insisted on teaching them an unforgettable lesson. The white Kenyans killed in the passion of the moment, as did the rebels, but unlike the Mau Mau, the whites routinely killed in cold blood, and they methodically tortured helpless captives. Many settlers believed that in order to teach Africans that whites would always be supreme, many more than 11,000 Kikuyu should have been killed. Three years before the Mau Mau rebellion erupted, tribal people on the island nation of Madagascar off Africa's east coast rose against French rule. While the world press paid virtually no attention, the French Army, aided by enraged French colonists, put down the rebellion with the same brutality that they would soon display in Algeria. When the French torture-chambers closed and the killing stopped, somewhere between 50,000 and 120,000 Malagasy were dead.[10] When news of the French slaughter reached Kenya, many settlers approved.[11]

The settlers often attempted to justify their brutality by referring to the rebels as "niggers," "baboons," "vermin," and the like. White ruthlessness certainly was inflamed by racist bigotry, but their cruelty had as much to do with "property and privilege" as racism. Although human savagery has often been motivated by racial hatred, many of history's most ghastly atrocities have had nothing to do with race. Racial hatred played a part in the white reaction to Mau Mau just as it did in the actions of many Mau Mau rebels, but the rebellion was fundamentally about power, not race, as the killing between the Kikuyu loyalists and the rebels demonstrated.

Whites were determined never to relinquish power, and many white men and women who considered themselves to be decent, fair-minded, and law-abiding used any means, however indecent, unfair, and unlawful, to defeat the Mau Mau, without thinking any less of themselves. They knew that the acts they carried out or condoned were unlawful, and they conspired with one another to conceal what they did, but few admitted that their actions were morally wrong, and when they were accused of wrongdoing they were quick to justify themselves. It is tempting to think of the cruelty of their reaction to Mau Mau as a temporary outburst of hysteria, but, after the rebellion came to an end in 1956, few white Kenyans voiced any remorse. Even after the killings at Hola in 1959, very few expressed regret about what had happened there or elsewhere during the Emergency. Instead, they continued to insist that the Mau Mau had been a scourge so terrible that anything that had been done to destroy it was morally justified.

Even after 1956, when the Mau Mau rebellion had suffered military defeat and it was clear that Britain would require that some form of multi-racial government be established in Kenya, most settlers still showed little sympathy or concern for the interests of Africans, including those who worked on their own farms. They continued to neglect Africans' needs, degrade them by the same words and deeds that had so offended them before the rebellion began, and opposed attempts to improve race relations. When a liberal settler offered his highlands farm to the government as an inter-racial boarding school, his offer was rejected by the Minister of Education on the grounds that "no community" in Kenya would accept the idea.[12] He meant, of course, no *white* community. Frustrated by this kind of intransigence, Governor Baring wrote to the Colonial Office about the settlers, saying that "There is a block of die-hards who cannot and will not be reconciled. Their fear and hatred of the African cannot be removed by any reasonable argument."[13]

Baring neglected to say that there were those in the colonial administration who also feared and hated Africans. These men had behaved brutally and had covered up the brutality of others in government. Other high-ranking officials believed that they were serving the interests of Britain or Kenya by ordering or condoning actions that were both callous and unlawful. Governor Baring himself was deeply implicated. Although Baring took both his Roman Catholicism and his personal honor very seriously, he was nevertheless directly involved in rigging the trial of Kenyatta and five other defendants, and he helped to cover up the murderous brutality of the screening teams. His policy of enforced labor was punitive and cruel, and, as a result of his support for so-called villagization, many Kikuyu, particularly elderly persons and children, died of disease and malnutrition. By intervening to dismiss murder charges against Home Guardsmen in an attempt to bolster the morale of the loyalists, he made it abundantly clear that defeating the Mau Mau was more important than either principle or law. Yet in one of colonialism's many contradictions, Baring also worked devotedly to bring economic reform and multi-racial government to Kenya.[14] Like other colonial officials in other lands, he had done his duty by crushing the rebellion, but now that the fighting had ended his duty called for him to lead Kenya toward lasting peace and prosperity.

Baring was not the only high official who sacrificed principles to defeat Mau Mau. Other members of the government cynically supported policies that were unlawful and indecent, then lied to cover their tracks.[15] What is more, there were men in the Colonial Office in London who knew that the Government of Kenya was condoning criminal violence in its fight against the Mau Mau. Two successive Colonial Secretaries expressed concern over the excessive violence of Kenya's settlers, and even demanded that Baring explain allegations of brutality; but both Oliver Lyttleton and Alan Lennox-Boyd defended the actions of Kenya's colonial administration in Parliament, and they did not demand impartial investigations of alleged misconduct. They may not have liked what was happening in Kenya, but they chose not to have it exposed.[16]

It would be unfair not to acknowledge that there were white men and women in Kenya who displayed admirable qualities throughout the rebellion. Some colonial officials never wavered in protecting the rights of Africans, even though they had to oppose their superiors, the police, and the settlers to do so. Until Baring had him replaced, Attorney-General John H. Whyatt unfailingly insisted that all security forces act within the law,[17] and some judges upheld the law despite pressures and threats. There were officers in prisons and detention camps who were fair and compassionate, and some settlers opposed the indiscriminate use of brutality against Mau Mau suspects; a few even took the risk of doing so openly.[18] There were also men in the Kenya Police and Kenya Regiment who openly deplored the brutality of their fellow Kenyans, and showed truly remarkable courage and devotion as they repeatedly led small patrols into the forests. Some of these men were killed, and others were killed in return, but they did so in open combat, took prisoners when they could, and refused to allow the use of torture.[19]

A great many settlers, women as well as men, showed great courage and fortitude in defending their homes and families. They fought for the country they loved and they fought bravely. But the fact remains that many whites in Kenya did commit atrocious acts and many others approved. What is more, they believed that what they did was not only necessary but right. Many who have fought in other brutal wars later developed self-doubts and feelings of guilt, and some repudiated their actions. If white Kenyans felt any guilt, it did not compel them to make public disavowals of what they did. Like the Americans who settled the West, these white settlers were tough, self-reliant people, and like those same Americans, they were ruthless in pursuit of their interests. In earlier times, such ruthlessness might have insured their continued survival and dominance, but the wind of political change that swept through Africa as the 1950s came to a close was far too strong.

The pressures that drove so many whites to lawlessness also imposed terrible stresses on the Kikuyu, and to a lesser extent on other Africans, especially the Embu and Meru. The Ordeal of the Mau Mau was not confined to the forest-based combat units or the detention camps; it was felt throughout the cities, towns, and reserves. Except for chiefs, well-educated people, and devout Christians, for whom there was no choice, almost every individual Kikuyu had to decide whether to join the emerging rebellion by taking the Mau Mau oath, or remain loyal to the government. It was not an easy choice.[20] In the beginning, there was an exhilarating emotional appeal to the rebellion, but there was fear too: fear of the government, fear of the whites' power, and fear of the unknown. Soon there was even greater fear of the oath-administrators who began to force people to swear allegiance to Mau Mau. Many who refused, or who later gave evidence to the police, were killed. Friends, families, and clans were soon divided as the commitments of rebels and loyalists hardened and led to more and more killing.

Once a State of Emergency was declared, life became even more perilous. In addition to the danger from armed rebels or the loyalist Home Guards, all Kikuyu were now suspect in the eyes of armed white settlers, police, and soldiers. A man could be shot on sight, a woman raped, a house burned, all without apparent reason or warning. If a man or woman were picked up as a suspect, the danger was so terrible that many prisoners were too frightened to speak. Some would be released, but many would be tortured, some killed, and others sent to prisons or detention camps. Everyone, even those who remained uncommitted to either side, lived in perpetual fear of sounds in the night. No one, not even children, could be sure that they would not be attacked by rebels, Home Guards, the Kenya Police, or armed white settlers because someone regarded them as an enemy, or mistook them for one. For these

Africans, the fear of sudden death became an inescapable part of daily life.

The threat of sudden violence was only one of the ever-present horrors of life. Many worried about loved ones in the forests or in detention camps. While they waited for news of their sons or fathers or sisters, they were forced to build roads, dig ditches, construct new villages, and endure the spread of hunger and disease. Some loyalists suffered almost as much as Mau Mau sympathizers. Many were killed or wounded, saw their houses burned, their crops destroyed, and their livestock stolen.

The Kikuyu suffered most during Mau Mau, but they were not the only people in Kenya who were tormented by the rebellion. Kenyans in some remote parts of the country were little affected by Mau Mau, but other people like the Maasai, Luhya, Luo, and Kamba were torn by divided loyalties. Still others, such as the Kipsigis and Nandi, chose to cast their lot primarily with the government. These peoples, along with the Kamba, provided most of the men who served in the expanded Kenya Police and as detention camp guards. Animosities between peoples who supported the government during the Emergency and those who did not endured for many years after Independence, as they did in families and clans. In some respects, Kenya's Indian community was the least divided. Many Indians were sympathetic to the idea of African independence, but they knew that the leaders of Mau Mau, like many other Kenyans, were so hostile to them that their only choice was to support the government. Their greatest concern was whether their loyalty to a government that treated them as second-class citizens would be appreciated.[21] It was not, and their place in the life of Kenya is still uncertain.

For most Kenyans, including those who actually benefitted through new employment or government aid, Mau Mau was a period of uncertainty and anxiety. For those most intimately involved with the conflict, the rebellion brought years of suffering. How the millions of people who were affected by the rebellion reacted to its pressures was as varied as the people themselves, but those Africans who had the closest connection to the ordeal reacted just as the whites did—with extremes of cruelty and courage. Many loyalists were corrupt, cruel, and cowardly, but so were some people who supported the Mau Mau, and some loyalists were as brave and steadfast to their cause as any of the rebels.[22] It is impossible to do more than speculate about the motives of the vast numbers of people who were caught up in the horror of Mau Mau, but one thing seems obvious. Kenya's Africans were every bit as concerned about furthering their interests as the settlers were; but unlike the settlers, who knew where their interests lay, the interests of the majority of Africans could shift as rapidly as the fortunes of war. For most of them, principles like freedom and social justice were often secondary to economic survival, and to survive they continually had to assess the relative strengths of the Mau Mau rebels and the security forces. Many calculatingly changed loyalties more than once as they watched the balance of power oscillate. Many whites accused Africans of being opportunistic, and they were right. Most Africans knew full well that their lives depended on their ability to avoid being caught in the crossfire. They experienced the truth of the African proverb that when elephants fight, it is the grass that gets trampled.

Those who held power in colonial Kenya—the whites, the Indians, and the African elite—were the natural enemies of Mau Mau.[23] Some wealthy and powerful Kikuyu, like the Koinange family, supported the rebellion, as did a few wealthy Indians, but they were exceptions. Mau Mau was primarily a rebellion by the poor and powerless. Unless most of the educated, wealthy, Christian government loyalists joined Mau Mau—something equivalent to Tsar Nicholas and the Russian nobility joining the Communist revolution—conflict between the poor and powerful was inevitable. As it happened, the earliest victims of Mau Mau violence were wealthy Kikuyu chiefs and headmen who opposed the movement.

The conduct of the men and women who fought for Mau Mau included acts of conspicuous courage and military skill, senseless savagery and cowardice, and self-serving exploitation of others. These extraordinary differences reflect a similar diversity in the commitment of individuals to the causes of "land and freedom." Some who took the oath made no more than a pretense of supporting Mau Mau, because they believed that the rebels might win and because it was dangerous to oppose them. They also hoped for rewards if and when the rebels won. It is likely that the majority of those who actually fought for Mau Mau did so because their friends, relatives, or spouses did, and their commitment was more to these people than to the cause itself.[24] Many marginally-committed Mau Mau gave up when it became clear that the rebellion could not succeed, and although some of the rebels who fought to the end did so because they knew that capture would mean death, many who were captured were profoundly committed to the goals of Mau Mau, and were therefore able to resist "rehabilitation" despite extreme duress.

Whatever one may choose to conclude about the tactics and strategies of Mau Mau's leaders, the actual fighting was done by ordinary men and women. Some of these rebels fought with undeniable brutality. They mutilated animals, raped African women, killed innocent children and pregnant mothers, strangled old women, gouged the eyes out of living victims, and burned people alive. What is more, some of their oathing ceremonies were so ghastly that many participants were appalled. None of these facts should be glossed over. But many other rebels, almost certainly the majority, did not participate in the more extreme oath ceremonies, nor did they kill women and children or commit other brutal acts against their enemies.

It must be kept in mind that most of the rebels had little if any knowledge of European ideas about the kinds of violence that should be permissible in warfare. In traditional Kikuyu battles, older women, men, and boys were always killed; only young women and girls were spared to be taken away as captives.[25] With this conception of combat as their cultural heritage, it is remarkable that the majority of Mau Mau rebels showed as much restraint as they did. On the whole, they followed the rules of combat as their leaders defined them. With the military odds so hopelessly against them, many fought bravely by any standard, and when they were tortured in prisons and detention camps, their steadfast resistance was truly heroic.

All of Kenya's peoples who were touched by Mau Mau showed courage, all made sacrifices and all suffered. Yet no faction, neither the rebels, nor the loyalists, nor the whites, should be glorified. They all behaved in ways that are as horrifying now as they were then, and they all fought for their own interests. The whites and the African loyalists fought to retain their privilege and power under British colonialism. The rebels of Mau Mau fought to improve their own lives, but their rebellion was also intended to end colonial rule and to benefit Africans throughout Kenya. If political freedom, economic opportunity, and social justice are laudable goals, then the rebels were laudable in ways that those who fought to defend the colonial regime were not.

Ironically, most of the men and women who actively supported the movement gained nothing from it, while even before the Emergency ended, the Kikuyu loyalists and other tribes that opposed Mau Mau improved their land-holdings and many acquired new acreage. It is true that the lands of the white settlers were eventually sold to Africans, but only a handful of Mau Mau veterans had the money to afford this new property. In fact, most of those who had owned land before the rebellion began had their land and livestock confiscated, never to be returned. With a very few exceptions, former Mau Mau rebels were also not able to find jobs in government or in business. Loyalists retained the government jobs they held before the rebellion began, and when new positions became available, they were filled by the educated children of loyalists, not by uneducated rebels.[26] Indians still dominated retail business, and former Mau Mau were not even allowed to serve in the army or police. Instead, virtually all of the Africans in the K.A.R. and the Kenya Police were retained by Kenyatta's government. These were the same men who had killed and tortured Mau Mau suspects. A rebellion by poor Africans forced Britain to withdraw from Kenya, but the land they had hoped to share and the government they had hoped to lead was taken over by wealthy and educated Africans who had either not fought at all, or had fought against the rebellion. There was no revolution in Kenya as a result of Mau Mau, only the replacement of elite white rulers by another elite, this time black.

In Kenya today, Mau Mau is a fading memory, little taught in schools, seldom discussed by intellectuals, uncelebrated by monuments, holidays, or songs. Yet no one can be certain what Mau Mau's legacy may eventually prove to be. It may continue to recede into Kenya's past as a regrettable prelude to the nation's independence. But remembrances of the rebellion are very much alive for some Kenyans, and like many other historical events, Mau Mau may take on greater symbolic significance as time passes. That may already be happening: In 1987, a group of Kenyan exiles assembled in London on the thirtieth anniversary of Dedan Kimathi's execution to announce the formation of a movement dedicated to the overthrow of Kenya's Government. Calling themselves "Ukenya"— Movement for Unity and Democracy in Kenya—the leaders of the movement evoked the memory of Kimathi's strength in demanding that the Kenya Government end political detention, equalize wealth, restore democracy and, once again, return the "lost" lands to the people. In August 1988, Jomo Kenyatta's nephew, Andrew Kibathi Muigai, was sent to jail for six years for belonging to Ukenya's underground organization in Kenya.

NOTES

CHAPTER 1 ▶ "THERE WILL BE A GENERAL RISING"

1. This prophet, named Muru wa Kibiru, had many clients who travelled to and from the coast, and it is likely that he was well informed about the plans and activities of Arabs and Europeans (Muriuki 1975:137); for a longer version of this prophecy see Kenyatta (1956:40–41) and Leakey (1977:1151). Kenyatta spells his name Mogo wa Kebiro.
2. Miller (1971). British fears were not completely baseless. Some French imperialists were so convinced that they could turn the Nile off like a garden hose that they considered financing an expedition to the Nile's headwaters (Lewis 1987:48).
3. Hindlip (1905:48).
4. Muriuki (1975).
5. Muriuki (1975:155). A highly positive, even romantic, view of Hall's relations with the Kikuyu is offered by Mungeam (1966).
6. More land was "alienated" from pastoral tribes, such as the Maasai, Nandi,

and Kipsigis, than from the Kikuyu or their neighbors, the Kamba (Sorrenson 1968), but the loss of pastoral land was not as catastrophic as the loss of farmlands.

7. Meinertzhagen (1983).
8. Meinertzhagen (1983:67).
9. Muriuki (1975).
10. Muriuki (1975:165). Official reports about African casualties as a result of military operations routinely reduced the number of deaths to more acceptable figures.
11. Meinertzhagen (1983:41).
12. Brantley (1981).
13. Farrant (1981); see also Trzebinski (1986).
14. Sorrenson (1968:35).
15. Ibid., pp. 66–67.
16. Meinertzhagen (1957:31).
17. CO 2/835, Cd. 2099, Eliot to Lansdowne, 9 April 1904.
18. Koff and Haworth (1979:14).
19. Churchill (1908:25).
20. Miller (1971).
21. Miller (1984).
22. Cranworth (1912).
23. Churchill (1908:42).
24. Sorrenson (1968:232).
25. Lovell (1987).
26. Sorrenson (1968:103).
27. Miller (1984:12).
28. Cranworth (1912:14).
29. Kennedy (1987).
30. Perham (1956).
31. Kennedy (1987). Although there was plague, malaria, meningitis, and polio, among other diseases, in the highlands, relatively few whites were affected.
32. The prefix "ki" means "language" in Swahili and many other Bantu languages.
33. Huxley (1959).
34. Furedi (1976:163).
35. Kenya Government, "Evidence and Report of the Native Labour Commission 1912–1913," p. 108.
36. Mungeam (1966:194).
37. Gicaru (1958).
38. Miller (1974).
39. Leakey (1937:45).
40. Leys (1973).
41. Koff and Haworth (1979).

42. Frost (1978:108).
43. Furedi (1978:183).
44. Miller (1971:402).
45. Foran (1962).
46. Fox (1984).
47. Miller (1984).
48. Brett (1973).
49. Seidenberg (1983).
50. Ibid.
51. Brockway (1955:175).
52. Furedi (1974:493).
53. Brett (1973); Swainson (1980:24).
54. Waciuma (1969:52).
55. Leigh (1954:16).
56. Huxley (1935: Vol. I, 221).
57. Abuor (1972:345–47).
58. Stoneham (1955).
59. Kennedy (1987:164).
60. Gicaru (1958).
61. Pickering (1957).
62. Stigand (1913).
63. Brockway (1955:144).
64. This expression was common in 1962, and so was the approval of most whites who heard it.
65. Cranworth (1912).
66. Rosberg and Nottingham (1966:131).
67. Carey-Jones (1966:66).
68. Blundell (1964:81).
69. Brett (1973).
70. Farson (1950). The managerial successes of the formidable "Pussy" Trench were particularly renowned.
71. Majdalany (1960).
72. Although the color bar was relaxed even before Kenya's Independence in 1963, and never fully existed in Kericho and Kisumu (Frost 1978:173), many whites in Nairobi today retain their 1950s life style. Most restaurants and hotels were owned by Indians, who chose not to serve Africans for fear of offending their European guests (Brockway 1955:116).
73. Leo (1984:171).
74. Cox (1965); Abuor (1972); Frost (1978).
75. Frost (1978).
76. Ibid., p. 47.
77. KNA DC/NKU/2/4/2: "Nakuru Annual Reports."
78. Stoneham (1955).

79. Evans (1956).
80. Stoneham (1955:103).
81. Cameron (1961).
82. Frost (1978:176).
83. Frost (1978:188).
84. Mitchell (1952).
85. *Sunday Times*, October 19, 1952.
86. Meinertzhagen (1957:152–53).
87. Miller (1971); Meinertzhagen (1957).

CHAPTER 2 ▶ "SOMETHING CALLED MAU MAU"

1. KNA Lab 9/1751, "African Housing." General, 1946–51, T. G. Askwith's report on overcrowding in Pumwani, 30 July 1946." See also, Throup (1985).
2. Throup (1987). This book, *Economic and Social Origins of Mau Mau*, provides a valuable analysis of factors that contributed to Mau Mau.
3. Gicaru (1958:145).
4. For this and other episodes in Kenyatta's life, see Murray-Brown (1972); Delf (1961).
5. Evans (1956:3). For similar examples see Frost (1978).
6. KNA secretariat 1/12/8. "Labour unrest: Intelligence Reports, Central Province, 1947," C. Penfold to P. Wyn. Harris, 9 October 1947.
7. Kamunchuluh (1975).
8. Throup (1987).
9. Gicaru (1958).
10. Barnett and Njama (1966).
11. Kanogo (1977).
12. Murray-Brown (1972:104).
13. Frost (1978:62). A much earlier District Commissioner at Nyeri had forced Kikuyu laborers to build a golf course for the European community, which at that time numbered five (Trzenbinski 1986).
14. Throup (1987:67).
15. Tignor (1976:45). See also Muriuki (1974) and Mungeam (1966).
16. Muriuki (1974:168–69).
17. A. Kibao, *Standard*, Aug. 13, 1988.
18. Tignor (1976:54).
19. Throup (1987).
20. In addition to the AIM, Roman Catholic missions (many of them Italian) and Scottish Presbyterians also arrived in Kikuyu territory early in the century.
21. Kenyatta (1965).
22. Kikuyu men and women, like those of several other East African societies

that practice female circumcision, assured me in 1961–62 that circumcised women continue to be orgasmic.
23. Sandgren (1982).
24. Kenya Government records leave no doubt that police and administrative officials were concerned. For example, KNA/MAA/1/7, "Unrest in Central Province;" DC/NKU/1/5/6 "Mau Mau activities reported to have affected the administration, 1945–1950"; MAA 8/102 "Intelligence and security; Press Cuttings 1948–50"; MAA 8/106, "Intelligence and security: Mumenyereri, 1947–50"; MAA 8/68, "Intelligence: Chief Waruhui, 1948–1952;" DC/NYK/3/15/6 "The Fear of Mau Mau."
25. Corfield (1960).
26. Throup (1987:227).
27. Corfield (1960:109).
28. Kennedy (1987).
29. Thuku (1970).
30. Barnett and Njama (1966:36).
31. *Daily Worker*, January 21, 1930.
32. Kinyatti (1977); Beauttah (1983).
33. Leakey (1952:88).
34. Foran (1962).
35. Corfield (1960:39).
36. Rosberg and Nottingham (1966:52).
37. Koff and Haworth (1979:39).
38. Ibid.
39. Beauttah was an Anglicized version of his Kikuyu name, Mbutu. The ambitious Beauttah was under the impression that his new name would be easier for Europeans to pronounce (Spencer 1983).
40. Murray-Brown (1972:167); Kenyatta (1968).
41. C. L. R. James, interview, Los Angeles, California, November 1979.
42. Kenyatta (1968:38).
43. Delf (1961:95).
44. They had carved this quite realistic spear from a wooden plank.
45. Murray-Brown (1972:196).
46. C. L. R. James, interview, November 1979. James was concerned because Kenyatta thought only about Kenya, not Africa or the world. This single-mindedness may have been one of Kenyatta's strengths.
47. Barnett and Njama (1966:175). James Mwarama, interview, August 1961.
48. Murray-Brown (1972:223).
49. Polygyny was a perfectly acceptable practice for most Kikuyu, including some who professed to be Christian.
50. Spencer (1983).
51. Lapping (1985).
52. Farson (1950).

53. Brockway (1955).
54. Evans (1956).
55. Rosberg and Nottingham (1966); Spencer (1985).
56. Blundell (1964).
57. Rosberg and Nottingham (1966).
58. T. G. Askwith, Rh Mss. Afr. S 1770, "Memoirs of Kenya, 1936–61." Michael Blundell (1964) admitted that political leaders in Kenya knew virtually nothing about African nationalist aspirations.
59. Throup (1987:229).
60. Abrahams (1960).
61. Ibid.; Brockway (1955).
62. Barnett and Njama (1966).
63. Berman (1976:165).
64. Rawcliffe (1954:18). In 1952, the European leader, Michael Blundell, was seriously concerned that so much European-owned land remained wholly undeveloped (1964:88).
65. How much Singh and his Communist ideology influenced the men who developed Mau Mau is still not known, but it is clear that his commitment to militant labor tactics was influential. See Singh (1969).
66. Kaggia (1975).
67. *East African Standard*, April 22, 1939.
68. Farson (1950).
69. Spencer (1977:220–21); see also Spencer (1985).
70. Leakey (1954).
71. Blundell (1964).
72. On February 6, 1984, *Standard* (formerly the *East African Standard*) carried a headline story alleging that recently declassified British Colonial Office Records revealed that a prominent Kenya politician had warned the government against Mau Mau in 1950. A Zairean newspaper created a tempest when it reported that the politician had been Tom Mboya. In reality, as Fred Kubai pointed out (*Standard*, Feb. 20, 1984), the politician was the government loyalist Tom Mbotela, not Tom Mboya.
73. Spencer (1977).
74. *East African Standard*, May 19, 1950.
75. Throup (1985).
76. *End of Empire—Kenya*. A BBC Film Production, 1987. It may be an exaggeration to say that Kenyatta "knew nothing," but he clearly was not privy to the plans of the men of the Central Committee.
77. Huxley (1985:199).
78. Lapping (1985:420); *End of Empire—Kenya*, 1987.
79. Koff and Haworth (1979).
80. Itote (1979:167).
81. Kariuki (1964:51). Eventually, many members of the movement came to re-

fer to it as Mau Mau, and it is this name by which it is most commonly known today in Kenya.

82. CO 822/422. In partial defense of Lyttleton, another threatening militant uprising in Kenya a few years earlier, Dini Ya Musambwa, did have a religious basis; Lyttleton and others in the British Government assumed that Mau Mau was more of the same.

83. Spencer (1977).

84. Kabiro (1973).

85. Kaggia (1975).

86. Kabiro (1973:25).

87. Leakey (1977:1210).

88. Muriithi and Ndoria (1971:5).

89. Lyttleton (1962:394).

90. Kaggia (1975:110).

91. Rosberg and Nottingham (1966:272–73).

92. *Times* (London), August 23, 1952.

93. Murray-Brown (1972:248–49).

94. *East African Standard*, August 26, 1952.

95. Spencer (1977:222).

96. Ibid., p. 216; personal correspondence, August 1988.

CHAPTER 3 ► ''A STATE OF EMERGENCY''

1. Wachanga (1975).

2. Kinyatti (1977:298).

3. For a review of Mau Mau songs, see Ogot (1977).

4. Douglas-Home (1978:231).

5. Clough (1977).

6. Rosberg and Nottingham (1966:280).

7. Blundell (1964). For a Mau Mau perspective, see Wachanga (1975).

8. Colonial Office Report on the Colony and Protectorate of Kenya for the year 1952. London: Her Majesty's Stationery Office, 1953.

9. Ibid., p. 1.

10. Majdalany (1962).

11. Leigh (1954).

12. Wachanga (1975); Itote (1967:43).

13. Muchai (1973:27); Wachanga (1975:74).

14. Abuor (1972). The market was named for the African soldiers who had served in Burma during World War II.

15. Wachanga (1975:18).

16. *Illustrated London News*, February 7, 1953.

17. Clayton (1976:5).

18. Majdalany (1962).

19. CO 822/461.
20. CO 822/448.
21. Throup (1987).
22. Leigh (1954). Governor Baring seriously proposed that the settlers replace their lost Kikuyu laborers not with other Africans, but with East Germans! The settlers rejected Baring's idea in no uncertain terms (CO 822/696).
23. CO 822/781.
24. The settlers had little respect for the Kenya Police whose officers were disparaged for their lower-class social origins. After Naivasha, the settlers were particularly strident.
25. Leigh (1954:17). For details of the Naivasha raid see Wachanga (1975:57).
26. Rosberg and Nottingham (1966); Sorrenson (1967:101).
27. Ibid.
28. Evans (1956:170).
29. Sorrenson (1967:100). See also Muchai (1973:23) and Wachanga (1975:60), both of whom blame white security forces for much of the slaughter. It should be noted here that, as will become apparent in the following chapter, both women and children risked their lives in active support of the Mau Mau rebellion. Also, traditional Kikuyu tribal warfare, which may have been the model for Lari in the absence of direct Mau Mau leadership, always included the killing of women and boys. Nevertheless, Mau Mau leaders were furious to be blamed for a massacre that they believed was largely the work of security forces.
30. Anonymous (1954:11).
31. Wachanga (1975); Barnett and Njama (1966).
32. *Time*, April 13, 1953, p. 38.
33. CO 822/448.
34. Ng'ang'a (1977).
35. Wachanga (1975:118).
36. KCA, January 24, 1954, p. 13453.
37. Maina (1977:48); Gikoyo (1979).
38. Maina (1977:61).
39. *Times* (London), May 27, 1954.
40. Clayton (1976).
41. CO 822/693.
42. Clayton (1976:11).
43. Erskine to Lady Erskine, October 9, 1953.
44. Blundell (1964).
45. Douglas-Home (1978:304–305).
46. Blaxland (1967:81).
47. Ibid., p. 85.
48. Blaxland (1967); Clayton (1976).
49. Itote (1979:118); Gikoyo (1979:57).

50. Clayton (1976:24); Blundell (1966).
51. CO 822/478.
52. CO 822/701.
53. CO 822/489. Bunche, then a professor at Howard University, went to Africa in 1936 on a two-year fellowship. One of his students at Howard was a Kikuyu who arranged a welcome for him in Kenya at which time he was given this Kikuyu name. Bunche had no other connection with the Kikuyu, especially not as a descendant of Kikuyu slaves, as the Colonial Office should have known (Haskins 1974).
54. Majdalany (1962:188).
55. Howard (1968).
56. *Times* (London), December 28, 1953.
57. *Times* (London), November 28, 1953.
58. CO 822/696.
59. KNA, *Kenya Calling*, No. 46, July 3, 1954.
60. KNA, *Kenya Calling*, No. 22, January 9, 1954.
61. CO 822/781.
62. *Times* (London), February 24, 1954.
63. Lapping (1985:427).
64. *Times* (London), February 24, 1954.
65. *Sheffield Telegraph*, November 24, 1955.
66. *Times*, October 2, 1953.
67. KNA, *Kenya Calling*, No. 34, April 10, 1954.
68. *Time*, April 19, 1954, p. 29.
69. Mathu (1974:27).
70. *Times* (London), May 7, 1954.
71. Mboyo (1963).
72. Barnett and Njama (1966:57).
73. Likimani (1985:60 ff); Waciuma (1969:113).
74. Blundell (1969:170).
75. Barnett and Njama (1966:436–39). Wanjugu Mbutu, interviewed in the film, *End of Empire* (1987). Women were targeted for much of this propaganda in the belief that they had grown weary of Mau Mau.
76. Interview, Njeroge Karari, December 1961. The same song is described in Barnett and Njama (1966).
77. Gikoyo (1979:126).
78. *Time*, March 8, 1954, p. 38.
79. Gikoyo (1979).
80. *Kenya Calling*, No. 65, November 13, 1954.
81. CO 822/701.
82. KNA MB/5/2.
83. The so-called "Swynnerton Plan" to improve the efficiency of African agriculture and provide as many as 600,000 new farms, benefitted the Kikuyu

loyalists primarily, but the Kamba profitted as well (see Leo 1984). The United States contributed £1,388,300, much of which went to the Kamba (*Kenya Calling*, No. 95, June 10, 1955).

84. KNA, *Kenya Calling*, No. 59, October 2, 1954. Of 7,515 Asians called for service to that date, 6,412 had complied.
85. KNA, *Kenya Calling*, No. 51, August 6, 1954.
86. Ibid., No. 30, July 30, 1954.
87. Ibid., No. 59, October 2, 1954.
88. Ibid., No. 67, November 27, 1954.
89. Wachanga (1975:18–44).
90. *East African Standard*, October 25, 1954.
91. Blundell (1964:184).
92. Ibid., p. 181.
93. CO 822/451.
94. Blaxland (1963).
95. Baldwin (1957:194).
96. Gikoyo (1979).
97. Blundell (1964).
98. KNA, *Kenya Calling*, No. 94, June, 1955.
99. Pickering (1957:213).
100. Blundell (1964).
101. Clayton (1976:28).
102. Gordon (1986); Ogot (1972).
103. KNA, *Kenya Calling*, No. 88, April 30, 1955.
104. Blaxland (1963:287).
105. KNA, MB/3/3 August 2, 1955.
106. Holman (1964:186); Kitson (1960:204).
107. Henderson (1958:75).
108. Maina (1977:119).
109. Wachanga (1975).
110. Holman (1964).
111. Gikoyo (1967:84); Barnett and Njama (1966).
112. Itote (1967:119).
113. Wachanga (1975:80).
114. See Whittier, in Wachanga (1975).
115. Blundell (1964).
116. Wachanga (1975).
117. Blundell (1964:112).
118. Barnett and Njama (1966); Wachanga (1975).
119. Leakey, Vol. 3 (1977:1068).
120. Buijtenhuijs (1971:223).
121. Holman (1960).
122. Clayton (1976).

123. Blaxland (1967:84). WO 236/21.
124. Lapping (1985).

CHAPTER 4 ► "DEBASED CREATURES OF THE FOREST"

1. For example, Paul Mahehu, a decorated British Army combat veteran of World War II, became one of Mau Mau's most audacious leaders, but he did not take the oath or become actively involved until two months after the Emergency was declared (Itote 1967:109). Others who became prominent rebels joined even later than this.
2. Kitson (1960:2).
3. Itote (1967:43). After the Emergency the membership of the War Council changed (Odinga 1967:115). The War Council had representatives from each of the three Kikuyu districts (Kiambu, Murang'a, and Nyeri) as well as Embu and Meru.
4. Ibid., p. 47.
5. For example, see Gikoyo (1979), Itote (1967) and Wachanga (1975). Most senior Mau Mau leaders knew that the rebels lacked the weapons to defeat the British Army.
6. Interview with J. Wanjau, August 1961.
7. Wamweya (1971:57).
8. Itote (1967).
9. Wachanga (1975:24).
10. *Times* (London), December 11, 1952.
11. KNA, *Kenya Calling*, No. 9, October 10, 1953.
12. This misleading stereotype was given particular prominence in Ruark's best-selling novel, *Something of Value*, and in the motion picture based on the book.
13. Maina (1977:128).
14. Ibid.; Itote (1967).
15. Muriuki (1974); Fadiman (1981).
16. Itote (1967); Muriithi and Ndoria (1971).
17. Barnett and Njama (1966:17).
18. Stoneham (1955:123).
19. Some believed that Mathenge would only accept rank from Kenyatta himself (Wachanga 1975).
20. To be "hard-headed" was to be childish, impulsive, and stubborn, hence the use of "softening" as an idiom.
21. Barnett and Njama (1966:451).
22. Ibid., p. 425.
23. Gikoyo (1979:192); see also CO 822/781 and KNA DC/MUR/3/13/3.
24. Itote (1967).
25. General Hitler was wounded and captured early in 1954, CO 822/781.

26. *East African Standard*, June 6, 1955.
27. Gikoyo (1979); Interview, J. Mwangi, July 1962.
28. KNA, *Kenya Calling*, No. 76, January 29, 1955.
29. Barnett and Njama (1966); Wachanga (1975:36).
30. Ogot (1977).
31. Barnett and Njama (1966).
32. H. Kunyanja, interview, July 1962. Barnett and Njama (1966:182) report the same song.
33. Wachanga (1975:88).
34. Henderson (1958:124).
35. Barnett and Njama (1966:243).
36. Ibid., pp. 242–43.
37. Gikoyo (1979:37).
38. Itote (1979:101–5).
39. Muriithi and Ndoria (1971:37–38).
40. Wilkinson (1954:307).
41. J. Wanjau, interview, August 1961.
42. Wamweya (1971:148).
43. Barnett and Njama (1966); Henderson (1958).
44. Gikoyo (1979:193); M. Kihara, interview, July 1961.
45. Gikoyo (1979:187); M. Kihara, interview, July 1961.
46. Leakey (1977).
47. Kitson (1960); Barnett and Njama (1966).
48. Gikoyo (1979:192).
49. Barnett and Njama (1966:191).
50. Ibid., p. 304.
51. S. Kigo, interview, July 1962; Barnett and Njama (1966:226–27).
52. Itote (1957).
53. C. Nyamarutu, interview, August 1961. Early in 1953, attacks in the reserves were prohibited because they brought retribution down on Mau Mau sympathizers. Leaders who violated this prohibition were flogged or hung by their wrists from a tree limb (Muchai 1973).
54. Gikoyo (1979:77); Wachanga (1975).
55. Ibid., pp. 136–37.
56. Wachanga (1975:43).
57. Ibid., xxi.
58. Ibid., p. 44.
59. Ibid., pp. 44, 65.
60. Wilkinson (1954).
61. Ibid., p. 310.
62. Ibid.
63. Gikoyo (1979:118); Itote (1967:132).
64. Wachanga (1975:83–84).

65. *Times* (London), December 29, 1954.
66. Anonymous interview, Nairobi, August 1961.
67. KNA DC/NKU/6/1, "A handbook on 'Anti Mau Mau Operations' issued by the general Headquarters East Africa, with a foreword written by George Erskine, The General Commander-in-Chief of East Africa," 27 November, 1954.
68. Maina (1977:120).
69. Holman (1964). It should be acknowledged that many Home Guards were extremely brave as well (e.g., KNA, *Kenya Calling*, No. 33, April 3, 1954). The combat record of Home Guards, however, lies beyond the scope of this work.
70. Sometimes units of the K.A.R. intentionally fired high when they were in combat against the Mau Mau (Itote 1967:90). M. Kihara, interview, December, 1961.
71. Kitson (1960:43).
72. Maina (1977:39).
73. Gikoyo (1979:116).
74. See Thomas (1956), Ruark (1955).
75. Kennedy (1986).
76. Itote (1967:282).
77. One Mau Mau veteran reported that marijuana made men behave recklessly (Wamweya 1971:59), but another denied this assertion, claiming that it merely relaxed men who were accustomed to using it (M. Kihara, interview, December 1961).
78. Wachanga (1975:64); Muriithi and Ndoria (1971:52).
79. Blaxland (1963:284).
80. Itote (1967:105).
81. Saturday, May 30, 1953.
82. Kanogo (1987:147).
83. Ibid., p. 148.
84. KNA, *Kenya Calling*, No. 58, September 25, 1954.
85. Itote (1979). After initial opposition to women as warriors, Itote (General China) became a staunch advocate.
86. KNA, *Kenya Calling*, No. 64, November 6, 1954.
87. Wachanga (1975:xvii).
88. Itote (1967).
89. Ibid., pp. 101–3.
90. Barnett and Ndoria (1966:404); Anonymous interview, December 1961.
91. Itote (1967:108).
92. Barnett and Njama (1966:432).
93. Ibid., p. 426.
94. Itote (1979: 116–18), Muriithi and Ndoria (1971:43, 59, 66).
95. Barnett and Njama (1966:408–9).

96. Henderson (1958:103).

97. Ibid., p. 105.

98. Ibid., p. 64.

99. Muriithi and Ndoria (1971:61).

100. Henderson (1961:157).

101. Gikoyo (1979:166).

102. Kitson (1960); Holman (1964).

103. Wamweya (1971:159).

104. Ibid., p. 167.

105. Mathu (1974:19).

106. Ibid., p. 56.

107. Ibid., pp. 28–29. Paradoxically, after Mathu was captured he converted to Islam.

108. Ibid., p. 51.

109. KNA, *Kenya Calling*, No. 93, June 4, 1955.

110. Itote (1979:136); Gikoyo (1979:100).

111. Gikoyo (1979:110–11).

112. Barnett and Njama (1966:397–98).

113. Itote (1967:141).

114. Barnett and Njama (1966:407).

115. CO 822/800. *End of Empire* (1987).

116. Mathu (1974:43).

117. Itote (1967); Wamweya (1971).

118. Wachanga (1975:126).

119. Ibid. This request for Dr. Bunche's services should be compared with the British Government's suspicion of Bunche as a "part-Kikuyu;" see Chapter 3.

120. Wachanga (1975:123).

121. CO 822/696; KNA, *Kenya Calling*, July 18, 1955.

122. KNA, *Kenya Calling*, No. 111, October 3, 1955.

123. Barnett and Njama (1966:436).

124. Maina (1977:36).

125. Kitson (1960:179).

126. Barnett and Njama (1966:365, 390, 397).

127. Henderson (1958), Holman (1964), Kitson (1960).

128. Holman (1964:135).

129. Kitson (1960:176).

130. Holman (1964:68).

131. Ibid., pp. 82–83.

132. Kitson (1960:78).

133. Barnett and Njama (1966:490).

134. Mathu (1974:43).

135. Muriithi and Ndoria (1971:95–96).

136. Henderson (1958:197).
137. Barnett and Njama (1966:216).
138. Henderson (1958:153).
139. Ibid., p. 149.
140. Original handwritten copy, displayed in the Kenya National Archives, Nairobi.

CHAPTER 5 ► "DARK AND DREADFUL DISTORTIONS OF THE HUMAN SPIRIT"

1. Gicaru (1958).
2. CO 822/460.
3. CO 822/774.
4. CO 822/450.
5. Douglas-Home (1978). Sir Charles Markham, interviewed in the film, *End of Empire* (1987).
6. Lapping (1985); also Sir Charles Markham, interviewed in the film, *End of Empire* (1987).
7. Fitz de Souza, interviewed in the film, *End of Empire* (1987).
8. Ibid.
9. Lapping (1985); Douglas-Home (1978:247). A.R. Kapila, interviewed in the film, *End of Empire* (1987).
10. The Pokot were usually referred to by contemporary writers as the Suk.
11. Kenyatta (1968:128).
12. Although Nehru was critical of the Kenya Government for its social and economic policies, and for its mistreatment of the Kikuyu, there is no evidence that India provided any material support to Mau Mau.
13. Murray-Brown (1972:264).
14. Ibid.
15. Sir Michael Blundell, interviewed in the film, *End of Empire* (1987).
16. Blundell (1964:125–28).
17. Ibid., p. 137.
18. Murray-Brown (1972:264); Gicaru (1958).
19. Anonymous interview, Nakuru, Kenya, April 1961.
20. Leigh (1955).
21. Murray-Brown (1972); Lapping (1985:415); Douglas-Home (1978:246).
22. Kenyatta (1968:85). In a secret communication, Baring informed Lyttleton that "every possible effort has been made to offer them [the witnesses] rewards." Letter of November 24, 1952, CO 822/450.
23. *Times* (London), April 9, 1953, p. 6.
24. Koff and Haworth (1979).
25. *Times* (London), April 27, 1953.
26. Mitchell (1954:260).

27. *Times* (London), April 30, 1953.

28. Evans (1956:90).

29. Rawcliffe (1954:67).

30. *Time,* January 17, 1953.

31. Majdalany (1960).

32. Anonymous interview, Makindu, Kenya, August 1962.

33. CO 822/495.

34. Friedenberg (1953:12).

35. Rawcliffe (1954).

36. Ibid., p. 68.

37. Muchai (1973:24).

38. Ibid., p. 30.

39. Ibid., p. 28.

40. Anonymous interview, Kitale, Kenya, January 1962.

41. Cameron (1961); Anonymous interviews, Limuru, Kenya, August, 1961.

42. *Times* (London), February 14, 1953.

43. Ibid., March 17, 1954. In August 1954, a 10-year-old girl behaved with such calm and courage under a similar attack that the government awarded her a medal for bravery. (KNA, *Kenya Calling*, No. 92, May 28, 1955).

44. *Times* (London), January 15, 1954. Later, Crouchey was attacked on his farm by two of the Mau Mau, and, although wounded, managed to drive the men off. (KNA, *Kenya Calling*, No. 100, July 25, 1955).

45. *Times* (London), January 26, 1953.

46. Ibid., November 26, 1952.

47. Anonymous interview, Nairobi, Kenya, July 1962.

48. Anonymous interview, Nairobi, Kenya, December 1961.

49. Frost (1978:166).

50. Gicaru (1958).

51. Foran (1962).

52. Clayton (1976:18); Foran (1962:207).

53. Foran (1962).

54. Kabiro (1973:60).

55. Itote (1979:52).

56. Friedenberg (1953).

57. *Tribune*, September 30, 1955.

58. Abuor (1972).

59. Douglas-Home (1978:255).

60. CO 822/799; CO 822/499.

61. Majdalany (1960:226–27).

62. Kitson (1960).

63. Kabiro (1973).

64. Clayton (1976:45).

65. Baldwin (1957:174–75).

66. It is ironic that as these atrocities were taking place, Britain's Prime Minister, Sir Winston Churchill, was expressing his compassionate concern that the more than 6,000 cattle confiscated in 1953 from Mau Mau sympathizers were being properly cared for. Baring assured him that they were being taken care of (CO 822/701).

67. *Times* (London), April 18, 1953.

68. Evans (1956:81).

69. CO 822/485.

70. Baldwin (1957).

71. Anonymous interview, Machakos, Kenya, September 1961.

72. Baldwin (1957:143).

73. Anonymous interview, Machakos, Kenya, September 1961.

74. Majdalany (1960:226–27).

75. *Time*, November 7, 1953. See also CO 822/697.

76. CO 822/499. Hayward was excused by many in Kenya because his first experience of Mau Mau had been the "Lari massacre," but Governor Twining of Tanganyika, where Hayward's brutality took place, was not forgiving. White settlers were abusing him for prosecuting Hayward, a decision he said he could not avoid once the case "came to official notice" (CO 822/499).

77. Evans (1956:270–71); Clayton (1976:44).

78. CO 822/471.

79. Ibid., p. 272.

80. Clayton (1976:45).

81. Ibid., p. 45.

82. Holman (1964:119).

83. Anonymous interview, Nakuru, Kenya, April 1961.

84. Clayton (1976:43).

85. Ibid., p. 45.

86. Blundell (1964:149).

87. Kabiro (1973:46–47); Wamweya (1971:74–75); Ng'ang'a (1977:367).

88. Clayton (1976:46).

89. Abuor (1972:260).

90. CO 822/799. See also Clayton (1976:58). Although the government spoke of the "Kikuyu Guard" in official documents, virtually everyone in Kenya called them the "Home Guard."

91. Berman (1976).

92. CO 822/697.

93. KNA DC/NKU/6/1 "A Handbook on Anti-Mau Mau Operations, 27 November, 1954, General Headquarters, East Africa, Nairobi."

94. Blaxland (1967:71).

95. Wachanga (1975).

96. Itote (1967:91).

97. Muriithi (1971).
98. Blaxland (1967); Evans (1956).
99. Clayton (1976).
100. Okello (1967); Anonymous interview, Nairobi, Kenya, December 1961.
101. Clayton (1976). The number of British troops killed or wounded by mis-handling their own weapons or by firing at unseen targets in the forests has not been revealed, but all evidence suggests that the number was very large. It is possible that more British officers and soldiers were shot by their own gunfire than by the Mau Mau (Blaxland 1963, 1967).
102. Blaxland (1967:74). Despite the fact that Blaxland was a former major in this regiment, he is quite critical of their efficiency in Kenya.
103. Abuor (1972:258).
104. *East African Standard*, November 10, 1955.
105. Evans (1956:276); Barnett and Njama (1966:128).
106. Clayton (1976:38–39).
107. Blaxland (1967:84).
108. Anonymous interview, Nyeri, Kenya, August 1977.
109. Anonymous interview, Malindi, Kenya, August 1977.
110. Blaxland (1963:290).
111. Evans (1956:262).
112. *Time*, December 7, 1953.
113. *Daily Mirror*, December 1, 1953.
114. Evans (1956:218ff). Evans, who was an outspoken anti-colonialist whom the British believed to be a Communist, was ostensibly deported for an immigration violation.
115. Baldwin (1958:228).
116. Gikoyo (1979:143–44).
117. Blaxland (1963:281).
118. Evans (1956:269).
119. *Sunday Times*, April 11, 1954.
120. Pickering (1957:177–78).
121. Rawcliffe (1954:66).
122. Evans (1956:266).
123. *Times* (London), October 24, 1954.
124. Evans (1956:266).
125. Lyttleton (1962).

CHAPTER 6 ▶ "A SHORT, SHARP SHOCK"

1. *Times* (London), February 12, 1953.
2. Clayton (1976:54).
3. Carothers (1955).
4. Rosberg and Nottingham (1966:337).

5. CO 822/799.
6. Edgerton (1974); Leakey (1977).
7. Koff and Haworth (1979).
8. Blundell (1964:198–99).
9. Koff and Haworth (1979). In 1954, The District Commissioner of Nakuru District admitted that some screeners were so brutal that they had to be dismissed (KNA DC/NKU/4/2/2), "Annual Reports Nakuru District, 1949–1962."
10. Kariuki (1964:163).
11. John Nottingham, interviewed in the film, *End of Empire* (1987).
12. Evans (1956:275).
13. There were 81,920 Mau Mau suspects in 176 camps at the end of 1954 (*Further Documents, etc.* [Cmnd. 816], 1959). It is possible that as many as 90,000 people were detained over the duration of the Emergency.
14. Muchai (1973).
15. Cameron (1955:31).
16. Kariuki (1964).
17. Gikoyo (1979:204).
18. Kariuki (1964:89).
19. Ibid., p. 158. J. Karanja, interview in Tigoni, Kenya, July 1972.
20. Rosberg and Nottingham (1966:338).
21. Askwith, Rh. Mss. Am. S1770—*Memoirs Kenya*, 1936–61; Frost (1978:211); Abuor (1972:309).
22. Askwith, Rh. Mss. Am. S1770—*Memoirs Kenya*, 1936–61, p. 49.
23. Ibid., pp. 54–55.
24. Askwith (1953:78).
25. *East African Standard*, April 23, 1953.
26. Muchai (1973:40).
27. KNA, ARC (MAA) 2/5/222/II, "Detainees in Detention Camps," 1955–56.
28. KNA, ARC (MAA) 2/5/222/I, "Detainees in Detention Camps," 1954–55.
29. Abuor (1972:367).
30. Kariuki (1964:117).
31. Itote (1979:123).
32. Mathu (1974:79).
33. Wachanga (1975:148).
34. Mathu (1974:45). Arnold Hopf, District officer at Hola, confirmed that Kraft was considered unstable by members of the administration; interview, Ortum, Kenya, February 1962.
35. Wachanga (1975:140).
36. Mutonyi (1979:30).
37. Kariuki (1964).
38. Wachanga (1975:143).
39. Kariuki (1964:76).

40. Wachanga (1975:144–45).

41. Ibid., p. 142.

42. Jack (1959).

43. Gikoyo (1975).

44. Kariuki (1964:87).

45. Muriithi (1971); Wachanga (1975:138).

46. S. Kioko, interview, Makindu, Kenya, August 1962.

47. Gikoyo (1979:218).

48. Anonymous interview, Cheltenham, England, July 1972.

49. Jack (1959:36).

50. Ibid., p. 191.

51. Clayton (1976:55).

52. CO 822/801.

53. S. Kioko, interview, Ngelani Utui, Machakos District, Kenya, April 1961.

54. Muchai (1973:51).

55. Another man, two years older than Muchai, had very similar experiences, except that he was blinded in one eye by "the treatment," and lost the use of his left arm as a result of the beating at Hola. Ibid.

56. Kariuki (1964).

57. Wachanga (1975:162).

58. Presley (1984:61); M. Wambogo, interview, Limuru, Kenya, August 1961.

59. Likimani (1985:159).

60. *London Tribune*, May 25, 1956.

61. CO 822/794.

62. Abuor (1971:271).

63. *Report on the General Administration of Prisons and Detention Camps in Kenya*, 1956.

64. G. Dennis, interview, Nairobi, August 9, 1961.

65. Kabiro (1973:44).

66. H. D. Montgomery, interview, Nairobi, August 8, 1961; CO 822/794.

67. CO 822/799.

68. One detainee who did convert was David Mathu (1974:71).

69. Kariuki (1964:159); Wachanga (1975:160).

70. CO 822/795.

71. Wachanga (1975:155–56).

72. Ibid., p. 151.

73. Kariuki (1964:144–45).

74. Ibid., p. 75, 94; Muriithi (1971:113).

75. Wachanga (1975:159–60).

76. Kariuki (1964); Gikoyo (1979:215–16); Muchai (1973:43–46); Wachanga (1975:159–60).

77. Gikoyo (1979:226).

78. Ibid., p. 22.

79. Mathu (1974:83).

80. Rosberg and Nottingham (1966:343).

81. Dennis, interview, Nairobi, August 9, 1961. See also Holman (1964), Henderson (1958).

82. H. D. Montgomery, op. cit.

83. KNA ARC (MAA) 2/5/222(I) "Detainees in Detention Camps, 1954–1955," and, KNA DC/NKU/1/7 "The Government's View of Mau Mau."

84. Rosberg and Nottingham (1966).

85. Governor Baring hoped that one day it would be possible to allow their wives to join them in exile, CO 822/799.

86. Rosberg and Nottingham (1966:341).

87. Koff and Haworth (1979:30).

88. Terence Cavaghan, former district officer, interviewed in the film, *End of Empire* (1987).

89. Rosberg and Nottingham (1966:344).

90. A. Hopf said that while Sullivan was "thick," he was a pleasant and congenial man who did not have a reputation for cruelty; interview, Ortum, Kenya, January 1962.

91. *Further Documents Relating to ... Hola Camp* (1959).

92. Ibid., pp. 26–27.

93. Muchai (1973:79).

94. Kariuki (1964:153); see also the account of Eliud Mutonyi in Koff and Haworth (1979:33).

95. Muchai (1973:30).

96. Ibid.

97. Kariuki (1964:153).

98. *Further Documents Relating to ... Hola Camp* (1959:47).

99. *Further Documents Relating to ... Hola Camp* (1959).

100. Kenya Government Press Office Handout No. 142, March 4, 1959.

101. Ibid., p. 46. See also Douglas-Home (1978:289–90), and *"The Gaudie Inquest Findings"* (1959).

102. Interviewed in the film, *End of Empire* (1987).

103. Macmillan (1971).

104. Douglas-Home (1978:296).

105. Ibid., pp. 294–99.

106. Fairn Report (1959:11).

107. Ibid., pp. 10–11. In fact, comedians were used in some camps but without apparent success, H. D. Montgomery, op. cit.

108. Cameron (1955).

109. Will Mathieson, Head, East African Desk 1955–58, Colonial Office, interviewed in the film, *End of Empire* (1987).

110. *Jack Report* (1959:186).

111. Anonymous interview, Nakuru, July 1961.

112. Anonymous interview, Machakos, April 1961.
113. Fred Kubai, interviewed in the film, *End of Empire* (1987).
114. Ibid.
115. G. Dennis, op. cit.

CHAPTER 7 ▸ "BLACK MAN'S COUNTRY"

1. Fisher (1982:230).
2. Meredith (1984:111).
3. Douglas-Home (1978:282).
4. CO 822/799.
5. Douglas-Home (1978:279).
6. Ng'ang'a (1977:376); KNA DC/NKU/2/4/2, "Insecurity felt by farmers due to 'Mau Mau' society and its activities, 1949–1962."
7. Koff and Haworth (1979); Rosberg and Nottingham (1966:347).
8. Maurice Randall, interviewed in the film, *End of Empire* (1987).
9. CO 967/57/46709, 1942.
10. Blundell (1964).
11. Bogonko (1980).
12. Macmillan (1970; 1972).
13. *East African Standard*, January 11, 1960.
14. Fisher (1982:233).
15. Fisher (1973).
16. Ibid., p. 142.
17. Lapping (1985:436).
18. Blundell (1964:266).
19. Ibid., p. 277.
20. CO 822/823.
21. Blundell (1964); Fisher (1973). The man who threw the coins, Major L. B. L. "Jim" Hughes, was taken to task by another settler, who wrote to the *East African Standard* urging him to "grow up" (March 5, 1960).
22. *East African Standard*, February 22, 1960.
23. Ibid., February 8, 1960.
24. Ibid., March 4, 1960. Governor Baring was so unimpressed by Briggs that in a letter to Lennox-Boyd, he referred to him as "stupid"—CO 822/799.
25. *East African Standard*, March 11, 1960.
26. Ibid., July 5, 1960.
27. Ibid., July 26, 1960.
28. Kamunchuluh (1975:211).
29. Maughan-Brown (1985).
30. *East African Standard*, August 5, 1960.
31. Corfield (1960).
32. Lyttleton (1962:401).

33. Culwick (1963:86).
34. Ibid., p. 101.
35. Cox (1965:23).
36. *East African Standard*, September 7, 1960.
37. Blundell (1964:296).
38. Farrant (1981:255). Baring discussed the idea, but learned that Grogan had no specific plans. Moreover, according to the governor, Blundell was "totally opposed" to the idea (CO 822/496).
39. Murray-Brown (1972).
40. Douglas-Home (1978:287).
41. KNA DC/LOK/2/3, "Makhan Singh's Detention: Mau Mau Detainees, 1952–59."
42. Huxley (1987:201).
43. KNA MAA 8/8, "Intelligence reports—confidential, 1946–47."
44. Throup (1985). An anonymous Kenya Special Branch officer, in Machakos, September 1961, reported that the police had, indeed, bribed witnesses to convict Kenyatta, and, that some officers agreed that his resulting celebrity made him an ideal, but still moderate, leader for Kenya.
45. Douglas-Home (1978:287).
46. *Standard*, March 26, 1988.
47. Although the Kitale Hotel professed to have no color bar, in 1961 and 1962 I saw African guests turned away on the pretext that the hotel was fully booked when in fact it was half empty.
48. Leo (1984).
49. I heard this same story in such widely scattered locales as Southern Tanzania and Eastern Uganda.
50. MacDonald (1972:248).
51. *Economist*, Vol. 197, 1960, pp. 593–94.
52. KNA DC/NKU/2/4/2 "Insecurity felt by farmers due to 'Mau Mau' society and its activities, 1949–1962."
53. Kanogo (1987:165).
54. *East African Standard*, November 5, 1962.
55. Ibid., October 23, 1962.
56. Ibid., October 17, 1962.
57. Ibid., October 19, 1962.
58. Ibid., December 18, 1962.
59. Wasserman (1976); Kanogo (1987).
60. Quoted in Buijtenhuijs (1971:49).
61. *East African Standard*, April 24, 1963.
62. Attwood (1967:263).
63. Interviewed in the film, *End of Empire* (1987); MacDonald (1972:256).
64. *East African Standard*, April 13, 1963.
65. Ibid., November 1, 1963.

66. MacDonald (1972).

67. *East African Standard*, November 29, 1963.

68. *End of Empire* (1987).

69. *East African Standard*, November 22, 1963.

70. Ibid., December 13, 1963.

71. Ibid.

72. Douglas-Home (1978:311–12).

73. MacDonald (1972:263–64).

74. Wachira (1968).

75. Cox (1965:50).

76. Ibid., p. 63.

77. Ibid., p. 63.

78. Kamunchuluh (1975:213).

79. *Reporter*, December 21, 1963, p. 15.

80. *East African Standard*, November 22, 1963.

81. Cox (1965).

82. *East African Standard*, December 20, 1963.

83. *Reporter*, January 17, 1964.

84. Ibid.

85. Ibid.

86. Cox (1965:58–59).

87. *Reporter*, June 5, 1964.

88. Kamunchuluh (1975:213).

89. Kenyatta (1965:10).

90. Cox (1965:59).

91. Murray-Brown (1972).

92. Attwood (1967).

93. *East African Standard*, January 27, 1964.

94. Cox (1965).

95. Miller (1984:35).

96. Attwood (1967:176–77).

97. Ibid., p. 263.

98. Ng'ang'a (1977).

99. Ibid., p. 366.

100. Sorrenson (1967).

101. Leo (1984).

102. Ibid.; Throup (1988).

103. Ng'ang'a (1977:374).

104. March 4, 1960.

105. Ng'ang'a (1977).

106. Frost (1978); Gikoyo (1967:10); Itote (1967:34).

107. Seidenberg (1983).

108. *Times* (London), July 28, 1953.

109. Itote (1979:121); Majdalany (1963).
110. Seidenberg (1983:118).
111. Ibid.
112. Cox (1965:160).
113. Seidenberg (1983).
114. *East African Standard*, August 17, 1960.
115. Cox (1965:177).
116. Attwood (1967:246).
117. Miller (1984:46).
118. Murray-Brown (1972:317). In addition to detaining Odinga, Kenyatta banned his political party, the socialist Kenya People's Union.
119. Hazelwood (1979:196).
120. MacDonald (1972:279).
121. *Sunday Times*, August 12, 17, 23, 1975.
122. Miller (1984).
123. Karimi and Ochieng (1980).
124. Miller (1984:94).
125. *African Business*, September 1987, p. 55.
126. See Miller (1984).
127. Mathu (1974:87).
128. Kanogo (1907:163).
129. Ibid. p. 174.
130. Ochieng (1985:157).
131. Sorrenson (1967); Buijtenhuijs (1971:119).
132. Itote (1967:270).
133. Ibid., p. 272.
134. Ibid.
135. Buijtenhuijs (1971:125).
136. Ibid., p. 128.
137. Some veterans filed suit in Kenya's high court, but they did not receive any relief.
138. Kibera (1970); Ngugi (1967).
139. Wachanga (1975:175–76).
140. Gordon (1986:247).
141. *Standard*, March 26, 1988.
142. Hazelwood (1979:197–99).
143. *Daily Nation*, August 10, 1988.

CHAPTER 8 ► "THEIR FIERCE SELF-INTEREST"

1. See Gordon (1977); Mazrui (1987); Leo (1984).
2. Throup (1987).
3. Frost (1978).

4. I was reminded of this saying by Evans (1956).

5. Williamson (1984).

6. Anonymous interview, Kibwezi, Kenya, August 1962.

7. Anonymous interview, Machakos, Kenya, September 1961.

8. Genovese (1979); Williamson (1984).

9. James (1963:88–89).

10. Stratton (1964).

11. During anonymous interviews with white settlers in Machakos, Limuru, and Tigoni, during 1961 and 1962, it was frequently remarked that the Mau Mau rebels should have been dealt with as severely as the French did in Madagascar.

12. KNA ARC (MAA) 2/51/222/II, 29 January, 1955, "Detainees in Detention Camps, 1955–56."

13. CO 822/799.

14. Douglas-Home (1978).

15. R. H. Windley, Minister of African Affairs, was notoriously harsh towards Africans.

16. Lennox-Boyd was particularly skillful in such matters. For example, he succeeded in preventing Arthur Young's potentially explosive letter of resignation as Kenya's Commissioner of Police from being made public (Douglas-Home 1978:255). For a discussion of Lyttleton, see Goldsworthy (1971).

17. Whyatt's high principles and his brusque manner made him the bane of Baring's existence, as the Governor acknowledged by nicknaming him "stinker" (Douglas-Home 1978:304). Another who refused to compromise was District Officer John Nottingham, who later spoke out against white brutality (*End of Empire*, 1987).

18. Rawcliffe (1954).

19. Holman (1964).

20. Kabiro (1973).

21. Seidenberg (1983).

22. KNA MAA/7/235, "Kikuyu Guard Discipline;" KNA MAA/7/244, "Kikuyu Guard Congratulatory Letters."

23. The Arab community also had power in Kenya's coastal region, but it was little involved in Mau Mau.

24. Anonymous interviews, Pumwani, Nairobi, August 1961.

25. Leakey, Vol. 3, (1977:1068).

26. Charles Njonjo, the son of a Kikuyu loyalist, became Kenyatta's Attorney-General, a position of great power in post-independence Kenya.

BIBLIOGRAPHY

Abuor, C. O. *White Highlands No More*. Nairobi: Pan African Researchers, 1972.

Askwith, T. G. *Kenya's Progress*. 2d ed. Nairobi: East African Literature Bureau/ Eagle Press, 1958.

Attwood, W. *The Reds and the Blacks: A Personal Adventure*. New York: Harper and Row, 1967.

Baldwin, W. W. *Mau Mau Manhunt: The Adventures of the Only American Who Fought the Terrorists in Kenya*. New York: E. P. Dutton, 1957.

Barnett, D. L. "Mau Mau: The Structural Integration and Disintegration of Aberdare Guerrilla Forces." Ph.D dissertation, UCLA, 1963/64.

Barnett, D. L., and Karari Njama. *Mau Mau from Within: Autobiograph and Analysis on Kenya's Peasant Revolt*. New York: Monthly Review Press, 1966.

Berman, B. J. Bureaucracy and incumbent violence: Colonial Administration and the Origins of the 'Mau Mau' Emergency in Kenya. *British Journal of Political Science*, 6:143–75, 1976.

Blaxland, G. *The Farewell Years: The Final Historical Records of the Buffs, 1948–1967.* Canterbury: The Queen's Own Buff's Office, 1967.

———. *The Regiments Depart: A History of the British Army, 1945–1970.* London: William Kimber, 1963.

Blundell, Sir M. *So Rough a Wind: Kenya Memoirs.* London: Weidenfeld & Nicholson, 1964.

Boyes, J. *John Boyes, King of the Wa-Kikuyu: A True Story of Travel and Adventure in Africa.* London: Methuen, 1911.

Brantley, C. *The Giriama and Colonial Resistance in Kenya, 1800–1920.* Berkeley: University of California Press, 1981.

Brett, E. A. *Colonialism and Underdevelopment in East Africa: The Politics of Economic Change, 1919–1939.* London: Heinemann, 1973.

Bridgeman, J. M. *The Revolt of the Hereros.* Berkeley: University of California Press, 1981.

Brockway, F. *African Journeys.* London: Gollancz, 1955.

Buijtenhuijs, R. *Le Mouvement "Mau Mau."* The Hague: Mouton, 1971a.

———. *Mau Mau Twenty Years After.* The Hague: Mouton, 1971.

Cameron, J. *The African Revolution.* London: Thames and Hudson, 1961.

Cameron, R. W. *Equator Farm.* London: W. Heinemann, 1955.

Carey-Jones, N. S. *The Anatomy of Uhuru: An Essay on Kenya's Independence.* Manchester: Manchester University Press, 1966.

Carothers, J. C. *The Psychology of Mau Mau.* Nairobi: Government Printer, 1955.

Churchill, W. S. *My African Journey.* London: The Holland Press, 1908.

Clayton, A. *Counter-Insurgency in Kenya, 1952–1960.* Nairobi: Transafrica, 1975.

Clough, M. S. *Chiefs and Politicians: Local Politics and Social Change in Kiambu, Kenya 1918–1936.* Ph.D. Dissertation, Stanford University, 1977.

Corfield, I. D. *Historical Survey of the Origins and Growth of Mau Mau.* (CMND 1030). London: HMSO, 1960.

Cornish, M. *An Introduction to Violence.* London: Cassell, 1960.

Cox, J. R. *Kenyatta's Country.* London: Hutchinson, 1965.

Cranworth, L. *A Colony in the Making, or Sport and Profit in British East Africa.* London: Macmillan, 1912.

Davidson, B. *The People's Cause: A History of Guerillas in Africa.* London: Longman, 1981.

DeSouza, R. Interviewed in *End of Empire: Kenya* (BBC Film), 1987.

Delf, G. *Jomo Kenyatta: Towards Truth about "The Light of Kenya."* Garden City, New York: Doubleday, 1961.

Dinesen, I. *Out of Africa.* New York: Random House, 1938.

Douglas-Home, C. *Evelyn Baring.* London: Collins, 1978.

Evans, P. *Law and Disorder, or Scenes of Life in Kenya.* London: Secker & Warburg, 1956.

Fadiman, J. A. *An Oral History of Tribal Warfare: The Meru of Mt. Kenya.* Athens, Ohio: Ohio University Press, 1982.

Farson, N. *Last Chance in Africa*. London: V. Gollancz, 1953.

Farrant, L. *The Legendary Grogan: The Only Man to Trek from Cape to Cairo, Kenya's Controversial Pioneer*. London: Hamish Hamilton, 1981.

First, R. *The Barrel of a Gun: Political Power in Africa and the Coup d'Etat*. London: Allen Lane, 1970.

Foran, W. R. *The Kenya Police, 1887–1960*. London: R. Hale, 1962.

Fox, J. *White Mischief: The Murder of Lord Erroll*. New York: Vintage, 1984.

Friedenberg, D. "The Mau Mau Terror." *New Republic,* October 19, 1953, pp. 10–13.

Frost, R. *Race against Time: Human Relations and Politics in Kenya Before Independence*. London: Rex Collings, 1978.

Furedi, F. "The Social Composition of the Mau Mau Movement in the White Highlands." *Journal of Peasant Studies,* Vol. 1, No. 4 (July 1974), pp. 486–505.

Furley, O. W. "The Historigraphy of Mau Mau." In *Hadith 4: Politics and Nationalism in Colonial Kenya,* pp. 105–33. Edited by B. A Ogot. Nairobi: East African Publishing House, 1972.

Gatheru, M. *Child of Two Worlds*. New York: Vintage Books, 1965.

Gicaru, M. *Land of Sunshine: Scenes of Life in Kenya Before Mau Mau*. Foreword by Trevor Huddleston. London: Lawrence & Wishart, 1958.

Goldsworthy, D. *Tom Mboya: The Man Kenya Wanted to Forget*. London: Heinemann, 1982.

Gordon, D. F. *Decolonization and the State in Kenya*. Boulder: Westview Press, 1986.

Haskins, J. *Ralph Bunche: A Most Reluctant Hero*. New York: Hawthorn Books, 1974.

Hazelwood, A. *The Economy of Kenya: The Kenyatta Era*. London: Oxford University Press, 1979.

Henderson, I., and P. Goodhart. *The Hunt for Kimathi*. Hamish Hamilton, 1958. (Published in the United States as *Man Hunt in Kenya*. Garden City, New York: Doubleday, 1958.)

Hindlip, L. *British East Africa: Past, Present, and Future*. London: T. Fisher Unwin, 1905.

Hobley, C. W. *Kenya: From Chartered Company to Crown Colony*. London: H. F. & G. Witherby, 1929.

Holman, D. *Bwana Drum*. London: W. K. Allen, 1964.

Howard, P. *The Black Watch*. London: Hamish Hamilton, 1968.

Huxley, E. J. *A Thing to Love*. London: Chatto and Windus, 1954.

———. *The Flame Trees of Thika: Memories of an African Childhood*. New York: William Morrow, 1959.

———. *Out in the Midday Sun: My Kenya*. New York: Viking, 1987.

———. *White Man's Country: Lord Delamere and the Making of Kenya*. 2 Vols. London: Macmillan. 1935.

Iliffe, J. *A Modern History of Tanganyika*. Cambridge: Cambridge University Press, 1979.

Ingham, K. *A History of East Africa*. London: Longmans, 1962.

Itote, W. *"Mau Mau" General*. Nairobi: East African Publishing House, 1967.

Jack, A. P. Kenya Colony and Protectorate, *Administrative Enquiry into Allegations of Ill-Treatment and Irregular Practices Against Detainees at Manyani Detention Camp and Fort Hall District Works Camp*, April, 1959.

James, C. L. R. *The Black Jacobins: Toussaint L'Ouverture and the San Domingo Revolution*. Second Edition. New York: Random House, 1963.

Kabiro, N. *The Man in the Middle: The Story of Ngugi Kabiro*. Taped and edited by Don Barnett (Life Histories From the Revolution. Kenya, Mau-Mau #2). Richmond, B.C., Canada: LSM Information Center, 1973.

Kaggia, B. M. *Roots of Freedom*. Nairobi: East African Publishing House, 1975.

Kamunchuluh, J. T. S. "The Meru Participation in Mau Mau." *Kenya Historical Review*, 3:193–216, 1975.

Kanogo, T. *Squatters and the Roots of Mau Mau, 1905–63*. London: James Currey, 1987.

Karimi, J., and P. Ochieng. *The Kenyatta Succession*. Nairobi: Transafrica, 1980.

Kariuki, J. M. *Mau Mau Detainee: The Account by a Kenya African of his Experience in Detention Camps*, 1953–1960. Foreword by Margery Perham. London: Oxford University Press, 1963.

Keller, E. J. "A Twentieth Century Model: The Mau Mau Transformation from Social Banditry to Social Rebellion." *Kenya Historical Review,* 1:189–206, 1973.

Kennedy, D. *Islands of White: Settler Society and Culture in Kenya and Southern Rhodesia*, 1890–1939. Durham: Duke University Press, 1987.

Kennedy, J. G. *The Flower of Paradise: The Institutionalized Use of the Drug Qat in North Yemen*. Dordrecht: Reidel, 1987.

Kenyatta, J. *Facing Mt. Kenya: The Tribal Life of the Gikuyu*. 2d ed. Introduction by B. Malinowski. New York: Vintage, 1962.

———. *Suffering Without Bitterness: The Founding of the Kenya Nation*. Nairobi: East African Publishing House, 1968.

Kibera, S. *Voices in the Dark*. Nairobi: East African Publishing House, 1970.

Kinyatti, M. *Kenya's Freedom Struggle: The Dedan Kimathi Papers*. London: Zed Books, 1987.

Kitson, F. *Gangs and Counter-Gangs*. London: Barrie and Rockliffe, 1960.

Koff, D., and A. Haworth. *Black Man's Land*. Public Broadcasting Service, April 3–5, 1979.

Kushner, G. "An African Revitalisation Movement: Mau Mau." *Anthropos*, 60:763–802, 1965.

Lander, C. *My Kenya Acres: A Woman Farms in Mau Mau Country*. London: Harrap, 1957.

Lapping, B. *End of Empire*. New York: St. Martin's Press, 1985.

Leakey, L. S. B. *Defeating Mau Mau*. London: Methuen, 1954.

———. *Mau Mau and the Kikuyu*. London: Methuen, 1953.

———. *White African*. London: Hodder and Stoughton, 1937.

Leigh, I. *In the Shadow of the Mau Mau*. London: W. H. Allen, 1955.

Leo, C. *Land and Class in Kenya*. Toronto: University of Toronto Press, 1984.

Lewis, D. L. *The Race to Fashoda: European Colonization and African Resistance in the Scramble for Africa*. New York: Weidenfeld & Nicholson, 1987.

Leys, C. *Underdevelopment in Kenya: The Political Economy of Neo-Colonialism*. Berkeley: University of California Press, 1975.

Leys, N. M. *A Last Chance in Kenya*. London: Hogarth, 1931.

———. *Kenya*. 4th ed. London: Cass, 1973.

Likimani, M. *Passbook Number F.47927: Women and Mau Mau in Kenya*. London: Macmillan, 1985.

Lonsdale, J. M., and D. A. Low. "Introduction: Towards the New Order, 1945–1963." *In* D. A. Low and A. Smith (eds.), *History of East Africa*. Vol. 3. Oxford: Oxford University Press, 1976, pp. 1–63.

Lord, J. *Duty, Honor, Empire: The Life and Times of Colonel Richard Meinertzhagen*. New York: Random House, 1970.

Lovell, M. S. *Straight on till morning: The Biography of Beryl Markham*. New York: St. Martin's Press, 1987.

Lyttleton, O. *The Memoirs of Lord Chandos*. London: Bodley Head, 1962.

MacDonald, M. *Titans and Others*. London: Collins, 1972.

Macmillan, H. *Riding the Storm*, 1956–1959. London: Macmillan, 1970.

———. *Pointing the Way*, 1959–1961. London: Macmillan, 1972.

Maina, P. *Six Mau Mau Generals*. Nairobi: Gazelle Books, 1977.

Majdalany, F. *State of Emergency: The Full Story of Mau Mau*. Boston: Houghton Mifflin, 1963.

Markham, C. Interviewed in *End of Empire: Kenya* (BBC Film), 1987.

Mathu, M. *The Urban Guerrilla: The Story of Mohamed Mathu*. Story recorded and edited by Don Barnett. (Life Histories From the Revolution: Kenya, Mau-Mau #3). Richmond, B.C., Canada: LSM Information Center, 1974.

Matson, A. T. *The Nandi Campaign Against the British*, 1895–1906. Nairobi: Transafrica, 1974.

Maughan-Brown, D. *Land, Freedom, and Fiction: History and Ideology in Kenya*. London: Zed Books, 1985.

Maxwell, A., and F. Morris. "Brutality in Kenya." *Contemporary Issues*, 10:1–9, 1959.

Mazrui, A. "Ideology, Theory, and Revolution: Lessons From the Mau Mau of Kenya." *Monthly Review*, 39:20–30, 1987.

Mboya, T. *Freedom and After*. London: Andre Deutsch, 1963.

Meredith, M. *The First Dance of Freedom: Black Africa in the Postwar Era*. London: Hamish Hamilton, 1984.

Miller, C. *The Lunatic Express: An Entertainment in Imperialism*. New York: Macmillan, 1971.

———. *Battle for the Bundu: The First World War in East Africa*. New York: Macmillan, 1974.

Miller, N. M. *Kenya: The Quest for Prosperity.* Boulder: Westview Press, 1984.

Mitchell, Sir P. *African Afterthoughts.* London: Hutchinson, 1954.

Muchai, K. *The Hardcore: The Story of Karigo Muchai.* Story recorded and edited by Don Barnett. (Life Histories from the Revolution. Kenya: Mau-Mau #1). Richmond, B.C., Canada: LSM Information Center, 1973.

Mungeam, G. H. *British Rule in Kenya, 1895–1912: The Establishment of Administration in the East Africa Protectorate.* Oxford: Oxford University Press, 1966.

Muriithi, J. K. with P. N. Ndoria. *War in the Forest: An Autobiography of a Mau Mau Leader.* Nairobi: East African Publishing House, 1971.

Muriuki, G. *A History of the Kikuyu.* Nairobi: Oxford University Press, 1974.

Murray-Brown, J. *Kenyatta.* London: G. Allen, 1972.

Ng'ang'a, D. M. Mau Mau, loyalists and politics in Murang'a, 1952–1970. *Kenya Historical Review,* 5:365–84, 1977.

Ngugi, J. *A Grain of Wheat.* London: Heinemann, 1967.

Njonjo, A. L. "The Africanization of the "White Highlands:" A Study in the Agrarian Class Struggles in Kenya, 1950–1974." Ph.D. Dissertation, Princeton University, 1978.

Ochieng', W. R. *A History of Kenya.* London: Macmillan, 1985.

Ogot, B. A. Politics, Culture, and Music in Central Kenya: A Study of Mau Mau Hymns, 1951–1956. *Kenya Historical Review,* 5:275–86, 1977.

Okello, J. *Revolution in Zanzibar.* Nairobi: East African Publishing House, 1967.

Okumu, W. *Lumumba's Congo: Roots of Conflict.* New York: Oblensky, 1963.

Paget, J. *Counter-Insurgency Campaigning.* London: Faber & Faber, 1967.

Pavlis, P. A. "The Maasai and the Mau-Mau Movement: Avenues for Future Research." *Kenya Historical Review,* 5:253–73, 1977.

Perham, M. *Lugard: The Years of Adventure.* London: Collins, 1956.

Peterson, S. "Neglecting the Poor: State Policy Toward the Smallholder in Kenya." In S. K. Commins, M. F. Lofchie, and R. Payne (eds.), *Africa's Agrarian Crisis: The Roots of Famine.* Boulder, Colorado: Lynne Rienner, 1986.

Pickering, E. *When the Windows Were Opened: Life on a Kenya Farm.* London: Geoffrey Bles, 1957.

Presley, C. A. "Kikuyu Women in the 'Mau Mau' Rebellion." In G. Y. Okihiro, ed., *Resistance: Studies in African, Caribbean, and Afro-American History.* Amherst: University of Massachusetts Press, 1986.

———. "The Mau Mau Rebellion, Kikuyu Women, and Social Change." Paper presented at the African Studies Association Meeting, Denver, October 1987.

Ranger, T. *Peasant Consciousness and Guerilla War in Zimbabwe.* London: James Currey, 1985.

Raven, S. S. *The Feathers of Death.* London: Anthony Blond, 1959.

Rawcliffe, D. H. *The Struggle for Kenya.* London: Victor Gollancz, 1954.

Reid, V. S. *The Leopard.* New York: Viking, 1958.

Rosberg, C. G. and J. Nottingham. *The Myth of "Mau Mau": Nationalism in Kenya.* New York: Hoover-Praeger, 1966.

Rosenstiel, A. "An Anthropological Approach to the Mau Mau Problem." *Political Science Quarterly*. Vol. 68 (Sept. 1953).

Ruark, R. *Something of Value*. New York: Doubleday, 1955.

Ruthenberg, H. *African Agricultural Development Policy in Kenya, 1962–65*. Berlin: Springer-Verlag, 1966.

Seidenberg, D. A. *Uhuru and the Kenya Indians: The Role of a Minority Community in Kenya Politics, 1939–1963*. Delhi: Vikas, 1983.

Shapiro, H. *White Violence and Black Response: From Reconstruction to Montgomery*. Amherst: University of Massachusetts Press, 1988.

Singh, M. *History of Kenya's Trade Union Movement to 1952*. Nairobi: East African Publishing House, 1969.

Slater, M. *The Trial of Jomo Kenyatta*. London: Secker and Warburg, 1955.

Sorrenson, M. P. K. *Land Reform in the Kikuyu Country: A Study in Government Policy*. London: Oxford University Press, 1967.

———. *Origins of European Settlement in Kenya*. London: Oxford University Press, 1968.

Spencer, J. "Kenyatta's Kenya." *Africa Report*, May, pp. 6–14, 1966.

———. *The Kenya African Union*. London: KPI, 1985.

———. "The Kikuyu Central Association and the Genesis of Kenya African Union." *Kenya Historical Review*, 2:67–79, 1977.

———. *James Beauttah: Freedom Fighter*. Nairobi: Stellascope, 1983.

Stichter, S. *Migrant Laborers*. Cambridge: Cambridge University Press, 1985.

Stoneham, C. T. *Mau Mau*. London: Museum Press, 1953.

———. *Out of Barbarism*. London: Museum Press, 1955.

Stratton, A. *The Great Red Island*. New York: Charles Scribner's Sons, 1964.

Thomas, W. B. *The Touch of Pitch*. London: Allen Wingate, 1956.

Throup, D. W. "The Origins of Mau Mau." *African Affairs*, 84:399–433, 1985.

———. *Economic and Social Origins of Mau Mau, 1945–1953*. London: James Currey, 1988.

Thuku, H. (with Kenneth King). *Harry Thuku: An Autobiography*. London: Oxford University Press, 1970.

Trzenbinski, E. *The Kenya Pioneers*. New York: W. W. Norton, 1986.

Venys, L. *A History of the Mau Mau Movement*. Prague: Charles University, 1970.

Wachanga, H. K. *The Swords of Kirinyaga: The Fight for Land and Freedom*. (Edited by R. Whittier). Nairobi: East African Publishing House, 1975.

Wachira, G. *Ordeal in the Forest*. Hairobi: East African Publishing House, 1968.

Waciuma, C. *Daughter of Mumbi*. Nairobi: East African Publishing House, 1969.

Wainright, R. Interviewed in *End of Empire: Kenya* (BBC Film), 1987.

Wamweya, J. *Freedom Fighter*. (Translated from the Kikuyu by Ciira Cerere). Nairobi: East African Publishing House, 1971.

Wasserman, G. "Continuity and Counter-Insurgency: The Role of Land Reform in Decolonizing Kenya, 1962–1970." *Canadian Journal of African Affairs*, 7:133–48, 1973.

————. "European Settlers and Kenya Colony: Thoughts on a Conflicted Affair." *African Studies Review*, 17:425–34, 1974.

————. *Politics of Decolonization: Kenya Europeans and the Land Use*, 1960–1965. Cambridge: Cambridge University Press, 1976.

Wepman, D. *Jomo Kenyatta*. New York: Chelsea House, 1985.

Wilkinson, J. The Mau Mau Movement: Some General and Medical Aspects. *East African Medical Journal*, 31:295–314, 1954.

Wills, C. *Who killed Kenya?* London: D. Dobson, 1953.

Williamson, J. *The Crucible of Race: Black-White Relations in the American South Since Emancipation*. New York: Oxford University Press, 1984.

British Government Publications

Documents Relating to the Deaths of Mau Mau Detainees at Hola Camp in Kenya, H.M.S.O., London, 1959. Presented to Parliament by the Secretary of State for the Colonies by Command of Her Majesty, June 1, 1959 (comd. 778, known as *The Gaudie Inquest Findings*).

Public Record Office, London:
Series C.O. 822 East Africa Original Correspondence.
Series C.O. 967 Private Office Papers.
Series C.O. 968 Defence Original Correspondence.
Series C.O. 276 East African Command, 1936–54.

Kenya Government Publications

Kenya Colony and Protectorate, Evidence and Report of the Native Labour Commission, 1912–1913.

Kenya Colony and Protectorate, 1956, Report on the General Administration of Prisons and Detention Camps in Kenya. Government Printer, Nairobi.

Kenya Colony and Protectorate, 1953–1959, Treatment of Offenders, Annual Report. Government Printer, Nairobi.

Report of the Committee on Emergency Detention Camps. Special Supplement to the Kenya Gazette of September 1, 1959 (R.D. Fairn, Chairman). August 1959.

INDEX